IS THE PEOPLE'S ACTION PARTY HERE TO STAY?

Analysing the Resilience of the
One-Party Dominant State in Singapore

Other Related Titles from World Scientific

Can Singapore Fall?: Making the Future for Singapore
by Siong Guan Lim
ISBN: 978-981-3238-07-7
ISBN: 978-981-3238-62-6 (pbk)

Understanding Singapore Politics
by Bilveer Singh
ISBN: 978-981-3209-22-0
ISBN: 978-981-3209-23-7 (pbk)

Critical Issues in Asset Building in Singapore's Development
edited by S. Vasoo and Bilveer Singh
ISBN: 978-981-3239-75-3

Insights on Singapore's Politics and Governance from Leading Thinkers:
From the Institute of Policy Studies' Singapore Perspectives
by Institute of Policy Studies, Singapore
ISBN: 978-981-120-484-5
ISBN: 978-981-120-502-6 (pbk)

Insights on Singapore's Economy and Society from Leading Thinkers:
From the Institute of Policy Studies' Singapore Perspectives
by Institute of Policy Studies, Singapore
ISBN: 978-981-120-487-6
ISBN: 978-981-120-503-3 (pbk)

Tall Order: The Goh Chok Tong Story (Volume 1)
by Shing Huei Peh
ISBN: 978-981-3276-04-8
ISBN: 978-981-3276-13-0 (pbk)

My Journey in Politics: Practical Lessons in Leadership
by Peng Kee Ho
ISBN: 978-981-3143-87-6
ISBN: 978-981-3143-88-3 (pbk)

Battle for Hearts and Minds: New Media and Elections in Singapore
edited by Tarn How Tan, Arun Mahizhnan and Peng Hwa Ang
ISBN: 978-981-4713-61-0
ISBN: 978-981-4730-00-6 (pbk)

Civil Society and the State in Singapore
edited by Carol Soon and Gillian Koh
ISBN: 978-1-78634-246-1

Public Trust in Singapore
edited by David Chan
ISBN: 978-981-3279-63-6

BILVEER SINGH

National University of Singapore, Singapore

IS THE PEOPLE'S ACTION PARTY HERE TO STAY?

Analysing the Resilience of the
One-Party Dominant State in Singapore

World Scientific

NEW JERSEY · LONDON · SINGAPORE · BEIJING · SHANGHAI · HONG KONG · TAIPEI · CHENNAI · TOKYO

Published by

World Scientific Publishing Co. Pte. Ltd.
5 Toh Tuck Link, Singapore 596224
USA office: 27 Warren Street, Suite 401-402, Hackensack, NJ 07601
UK office: 57 Shelton Street, Covent Garden, London WC2H 9HE

National Library Board, Singapore Cataloguing in Publication Data
Name: Singh, Bilveer, 1956–
Title: Is the People's Action Party here to stay? : analysing the resilience of the one-party
    dominant state in Singapore / Bilveer Singh.
Description: Singapore : World Scientific, [2019] | Includes bibliographical references and index.
Identifier(s): OCN 1081358489 | ISBN 978-981-12-0145-5 (paperback) |
    ISBN 978-981-12-0009-0 (hardcover)
Subject(s): LCSH: People's Action Party (Singapore) | Political parties--Singapore. |
    One-party systems--Singapore. | Dominant-party systems--Singapore.
Classification: DDC 324.25957--dc23

British Library Cataloguing-in-Publication Data
A catalogue record for this book is available from the British Library.

For any available supplementary material, please visit
https://www.worldscientific.com/worldscibooks/10.1142/11271#t=suppl

Desk Editor: Jiang Yulin

Typeset by Stallion Press
Email: enquiries@stallionpress.com

To

Gurdial Kaur, Jasminder Singh,
Prabhinder Singh, Malwina Kaur,
Karanveer Singh and Jasmine Kaur

ABOUT THE AUTHOR

Bilveer Singh is a Singapore citizen, an associate professor at the Department of Political Science, National University of Singapore. He is concurrently an Adjunct Senior Fellow at the Centre of Excellence for National Security, S. Rajaratnam School of International Studies, Nanyang Technological University and the President, Political Science Association, Singapore. He received his MA and PhD in International Relations from the Australian National University. He has been lecturing on issues relating to Singapore's politics and foreign policy for more than 35 years. He researches and publishes on Comparative Politics and International Relations and some of his works include: *Understanding Singapore Politics*, Singapore: World Scientific, 2017; *Quest for Political Power: Communist Subversion and Militancy in Singapore*, Singapore: Marshall Cavendish, 2015; *Politics and Governance in Singapore: An Introduction, Second Edition*, Singapore: McGraw-Hill Education Asia, 2012; *Politics and Governance in Singapore: An Introduction*, Singapore: McGraw-Hill Education, 2007; *The Vulnerability of Small States Revisited: A Study of Singapore's Post-Cold War Foreign Policy*, Yogjakarta, Indonesia: Gadjah Mada University Press, 1999; and *Whither PAP's Dominance: An Analysis of Singapore's 1991 General Elections*, Petaling Jaya, Malaysia: Pelanduk Publications, 1992.

CONTENTS

1MDB	1Malaysia Development Berhad
AGC	Attorney-General's Chambers
AHPETC	Aljunied-Hougang-Punggol East Town Council
AHTC	Aljunied-Hougang Town Council
AMANAH	*Parti Amanah Negara* (National Trust Party)
ANC	African National Congress
ASEAN	Association of Southeast Asian Nations
ATMs	Automatic Teller Machines
BERSATU	*Parti Pribumi Bersatu Malaysia* (Malaysian United Indigenous Party)
Bersih	*Gabungan Pilihanraya Bersih dan Adil* (Coalition for Clean and Fair Elections)
BN	*Barisan Nasional* (National Front)
CAGED	Citizen Action Group on Enforced Disappearance
CDAC	Chinese Development Assistance Council
CEC	Central Executive Committee
CHAS	Community Health Assist Scheme
COS	Committee of Supply
CPF	Central Provident Fund
CPP	Cambodian People's Party
CSF	Centre for Strategic Futures
DAP	Democratic Action Party
DNA	Deoxyribonucleic Acid
DP	Democratic Party
DPM	Deputy Prime Minister

DPP	Democratic Progressive Party
EP	Elected President
ESM	Emeritus Senior Minister
FELDA	Federal Land Development Authority
FMSIS	FM Solutions and Integrated Services
FMSS	FM Solutions & Services
G-20	Group of 20 Summit
GIC	Government Investment Corporation
GLC	Government-Linked Company
GOLKAR	*Golong Karya* (Functional Groups)
GPS	*Gabungan Parti Sarawak* (Coalition of Sarawak Political Parties)
GRC	Group Representation Constituency
GST	Goods and Services Tax
HDB	Housing and Development Board
HIV	Human Immunodeficiency Viruses
HSA	Health Sciences Authority
ICJ	International Court of Justice
IHiS	Integrated Health Information Systems
ILS	Instrument Landing System
IP	Internet Protocol
ISA	Internal Security Act
ISIS	Islamic State of Iraq and Syria
JMCIM	Joint Ministerial Committee for Iskandar Malaysia

KPMG	Klynveld Peat Marwick Goerdeler
KPRP	Kampuchean People's Revolutionary Party
LDP	Liberal Democratic Party
LF	Labour Front
LKY	Lee Kuan Yew
LP	Labour Party
Mapai	*Mifleget Poalei Eretz Yisrael* (Workers' Party of the Land of Israel)
MCA	Malaysian Chinese Association
MIC	Malaysian Indian Congress
MND	Ministry of National Development
MOE	Ministry of Education
MOH	Ministry of Health
MOUs	Memorandums of Understanding
MP	Member of Parliament
MRT	Mass Rapid Transit
NCMP	Non-Constituency Member of Parliament
NGO	Non-Governmental Organisation
NIRC	Net Investment Return Contribution
NMP	Nominated Member of Parliament
NOTAM	Notice to Airmen
NSP	National Solidarity Party
NTUC	National Trades Union Congress
PA	People's Association

PAP	People's Action Party
PAS	*Parti Islam Se-Malaysia* (Malaysian Islamic Party)
PDIP	*Partai Demokrasi Indonesia Perjuangan* (Indonesian Democratic Party of Struggle)
PGP	Pioneer Generation Package
PH	*Pakatan Harapan* (Alliance of Hope)
PKMS	*Pertubuhan Kebangsaan Melayu Singapura* (Singapore Malay National Organisation)
PKR	*Parti Keadilan Rakyat* (People's Justice Party)
PMETs	Professionals, Managers, Executives and Technicians
PP	Progressive Party
PPP	People's Power Party
PRPTC	Pasir Ris-Punggol Town Council
PRs	Permanent Residents
PSP	Progress Singapore Party
PVP	People's Voice Party
PwC	PricewaterhouseCoopers
RP	Reform Party
SA	Singapore Alliance
SAF	Singapore Armed Forces
SARS	Severe Acute Respiratory Syndrome
SDA	Singapore Democratic Alliance
SDP	Singapore Democratic Party
SFP	Singapore First Party

SG50	Singapore 50 Years
SINDA	Singapore Indian Development Association
SJP	Singapore Justice Party
SMC	Single Member Constituency
SMEs	Small and Medium-Sized Enterprises
SPA	Singapore People's Alliance
SPO	Scenario Planning Office
SPP	Singapore People's Party
SSG	Secur Solutions Group
STUC	Singapore Trades Union Congress
SWF	Sovereign Wealth Fund
UMNO	United Malays National Organisation
UPKO	*Pertubuhan Pasokmomogun Kadazandusun Murut Bersatu* (United *Pasokmomogun Kadazandusun Murut* Organisation)
UPP	United People's Party (UPP)
URA	Urban Redevelopment Authority
Warisan	*Parti Warisan Sabah* (Sabah Heritage Party)
WIS	Workfare Income Supplement
WP	Workers' Party

ACKNOWLEDGEMENTS

I wish to thank the many people who assisted me in completing this study. First and foremost, my heartfelt thanks goes to the generation of students in the Department of Political Science, National University of Singapore, who patiently sat through the courses that I taught on Singapore politics, especially the modules on *Government and Politics of Singapore*, and *We the Citizens — Understanding Singapore's Politics*. These students' patience, engagement and understanding have made me a better teacher and I have learnt much from them. These experiences showed me how much these students were interested in Singapore politics and how concerned they were about Singapore's future, especially the fear that if anything wrong were to happen the consequences would be dire for all. In this regard, a consistent theme that emerged in almost all my discourses with the students, in and out of the class, was the critical importance of political leadership as the guiding factor in Singapore's success.

Second, I am very grateful to my friends and mentors in the National University of Singapore and Nanyang Technological University who have always encouraged me to pen down my thoughts on Singapore politics, partly due to the dearth of writings on Singapore politics. I am eternally indebted to them.

Third, I will always remain indebted to the publisher, World Scientific Publishing Company for dedicating themselves to publishing works on Singapore. This is highly commendable as there are not too many publishers prepared to do this in and outside Singapore. In this regard, my thanks to all in the World Scientific Publishing team and especially Mr Jiang Yulin, Editor, Social Sciences Editorial Team.

Finally, I am most grateful for all the blessings and support I received from my family members. They have always been my primary source of inspiration and strength. The love and affection of my wife, Gurdial Kaur, my sons, Jasminder Singh and Prabhinder Singh, my daughter-in-law, Malwina Kaur, and my adorable grandchildren, Karanveer Singh and Jasmine Kaur.

I, however, take full responsibility for the views put forward and for any errors that may occur in the book.

Bilveer Singh
July 2019

Words of warning from Singapore's modern Founding Father

"There will come a time when eventually the public will say, look, let's try the other side, either because the PAP has declined in quality or the opposition has put up a team which is equal to the PAP and they say, let's try the other side. That day will come…No system lasts forever, that's for sure. In the next 10 years to 20 years, I don't think it'll happen. Beyond that, I cannot tell. Will we always be able to get the most dedicated and the most capable, with integrity to devote their lives to this? I hope so, but forever, I don't know."

Lee Kuan Yew, 2011. Cited in Han Fook Kwang, Zuraidah Ibrahim, Chua Mui Hoong, Lydia Lim, Ignatius Low, Rachel Lin and Robin Chan, *Lee Kuan Yew: Hard Truths to Keep Singapore Going* (Singapore: Straits Times Press, 2011), pp. 68–69.

What others also said…

"The PAP has become one of the most successful political parties in history. But even as we acknowledge its exceptional success it is necessary to be mindful of another powerful lesson from history: In the modern era, no party has succeeded in staying in power continuously for more than seven decades."

K. Shanmugam. Cited in Zakir Hussain, "Educate students about politics — PAP must convince young voters about virtues of current system", *The Straits Times*, 17 December 2009.

"But no system lasts forever, as even MM [Lee Kuan Yew] himself acknowledges in his latest book called *Hard Truths to Keep Singapore Going*. So, we do not assume that the PAP will remain dominant indefinitely."

Speech by Prime Minister Lee Hsien Loong at Kent Ridge Ministerial Forum 2011, 5 April 2011 at the University Cultural Centre, National University of Singapore.

"Our equilibrium as a small country may well be a single party system. The party can be PAP today, but another party in the future — so long it is the most capable at that time."

Ong Ye Kung, Minister for Education (Higher Education and Skills). Cited in Martha Soezean, "Ong Ye Kung: Singapore's one-party system, a result of free and fair election", *The Online Citizen*, 24 January 2017.

The People's Action Party (PAP) is, historically speaking, one of the most successful political parties in the non-communist world. The first PAP government, led by Prime Minister Lee Kuan Yew, was sworn in on 3 June by the *Yang di-Pertuan Negara* (Head of State), William Goode, along with his cabinet. It is hence, worth expounding on the title of the book, *Is the People's Action Party Here to Stay?*. In a way, this is a micro but a crucial version of a question raised by Lim Siong Guan in his book titled, *Can Singapore Fall?* Lim's concern was about "survivability and sustainability of Singapore".[1] In a similar vein, this book is about the staying power and durability of the PAP, all the more when there are many narratives that argue that "the PAP is Singapore and Singapore is the PAP". A commonsense answer to the question — "is the PAP here to stay?" — is a simple no. Theoretically speaking, everything is transitory and nothing survives permanently, be it a political system and what more, a political party remaining in power till perpetuity. Probably, a more significant question and issue would be — what is one really talking about when the question "is the PAP here to stay?" is asked. Is it, how long will the current political structure and status remain, and survive? Or, is it how the present political system will evolve and change, and whether the PAP will still be in power for many years to come and if so, in what format, formula and political architecture?

Dominant political parties do not evaporate into thin air. They have a unique staying power and also have the capacity to adapt, reinvent and reinvigorate themselves into a new form and substance, as is evident in Japan, India and Indonesia. Also, when dominant political parties lose their dominance, they are also adept in coalition politics and coalition building, and this is also a possibility that should not be discounted, as it has happened in India, Japan and Indonesia. To that extent, the question raised is not a direct or a simple one and hence, the need to delve deeper into the subject matter more analytically and over the longer time span and horizon. Still, as the quotes in the preceding section of the book make clear, even senior political figures from the ruling PAP such as Lee Kuan Yew, have argued and signaled that the ruling party faces the danger of losing its dominance and even power in the future.

---

1. Lim Siong Guan, *Can Singapore Fall? Making the Future for Singapore* (Singapore: World Scientific, 2018).

The latest senior political figure to join the chorus about the future of the PAP is none other than Heng Swee Keat, currently the deputy prime minister and the prime minister-in-waiting. While in Switzerland to attend the 49th St. Gallen Symposium in May 2019, he was interviewed by the Swiss newspaper, *Neue Zürcher Zeitung*. In response to the question about Singapore's politics and future, Heng said, "If my party does not deliver what it promises, it's out. But my concern cannot be the survival of the party. My concern must be the survival and success of Singapore. If we do not do a good job and the Singaporeans think it is time to change the situation, then we will fall out and a more competent party will come; and we hope that it will advance Singapore."[2]

This makes studying and raising the question of how long the PAP will remain in power all the more relevant and significant as it is nearing the timeline of seven decades when similar entrenched political parties had lost political power. Hence, if the PAP falls, why and what can cause it? And if it survives, why and what is so exceptional about this one-party dominant system? Is it due to the party's abilities and skills, or could it be the electorate endorsing it notwithstanding the PAP's many shortcomings and in particular, the electorate's perception that the alternative to the PAP, namely, the opposition political parties are simply not up to the mark to form Singapore's government in place of the PAP?

The current 'crisis' facing the Workers' Party (WP) is instructive in this regard. When the WP first won a Group Representation Constituency (GRC) in May 2011, it was considered a watershed political development in Singapore's electoral politics. All being equal, national voters would have expected the WP to make the running of the Aljunied town council exemplary, with benefits for the voters of the GRC expanding and costs decreasing, at least compared to the PAP's wards. Instead, since 2012, the WP has been embroiled in a crisis of its own making over allegations of serious financial lapses that could end up with three of the

---

2. See Anna Maria Romero, "Heng Swee Keat: If my party does not deliver what it promises, it's out", *The Independent*, 20 May 2019, theindependent.sg/heng-swee-keat-if-my-party-does-not-deliver-what-it-promises-its-out/; also see, "Singapore's biggest challenge is to build 'a sense of unity' amid 'tremendous changes': DPM Heng", *Channel NewsAsia*, 20 May 2019, https://www.channelnewsasia.com/news/singapore/singapore-heng-swee-keat-st-gallen-switzerland-biggest-challenge-11547090

WP's leaders, namely, Low Thia Khiang, Sylvia Lim and Pritam Singh losing their parliamentary seats, dealing a serious blow to opposition politics in Singapore and in turn, reaffirming the entrenchment of the one-party dominant state under the PAP. The more opposition parties in Singapore are exposed for their weaknesses and shortcomings as well as discredited, in a simple zero-sum calculus, the more the PAP is strengthened and embedded in the political architecture and psyche of the Singaporean voters.

In addition to discussing the future of the PAP and the Opposition in Singapore, this study is also relevant in the light of Prime Minister Lee Hsien Loong's challenge for Singapore researchers and scholars to think out of the box, and place issues of national importance on the debating table. On 24 August 2018, he said:

> It is important for academics in our universities and think-tanks to study and debate issues that are of importance to Singapore and write about them and publish about them and get them published. There will be a diversity of views — that is the value of discussion and any academic worth his salt will have ideas how things can be done better, or at least try it out differently. We should encourage such debate, and conduct it in a constructive spirit. It will help us to understand issues better, come up with better solutions, see things in a fresh perspective, and move our debate, our policies and the outcomes forward.[3]

It is in this spirit that the study is also partially undertaken, raising the all-important question of how strong and resilient the PAP really is in Singapore's politics.

The discussion of the issue is also equally interesting, when in 1992, S. Rajaratnam, the former foreign minister, senior minister and deputy prime minister of Singapore was asked to write a Foreword to a book on the future of the PAP, and where he responded by making two points. First, he admitted that forecasting political future was a risky business. Second and which he thought was more significant, was to ask an even more important question: "What should therefore worry us at the moment is not the durability of the PAP but the durability of a

---

3. Prime Minister Lee Hsien Loong, transcript of speech at the launch of "Critical Issues in Asset Building in Singapore's Development", delivered on 24 August 2018 at the National University of Singapore.

credible Opposition during the Twenty-First century."[4] He even posited a counter-question: "Whither the Opposition after A.D. 2000?"[5] For the elder statesman and member of the foundational leadership of the Republic, if these questions can be adequately answered, these will also assist us in answering, mediating and navigating the question, "is the PAP here to stay?".

At the same time, the rise of democracies and democratisation is a global political reality. Yet, the prevalence and persistence of the one-party dominant state is undeniable, especially in Asia and Africa. While some studies exist, these are few and far in between, and tend to be general rather than focused on individual case studies. At a time when democratisation is viewed as a global norm and for some, a panacea for 'human development and progress', and a stumbling block to authoritarianism, the persistence of one-party dominant states has raised concerns about the manner in which such political systems tend to have a negative impact on the general health of democratisation. The resilience of such political systems is seen as retarding the well-being of society, including issues relating to political transparency and accountability, the system of checks and balances, and even the potential for abuse of power, with the political Leviathan trampling on both legitimate and illegitimate political opposition. Such single party dominant states are said to fail to represent all views, interests and perceptions in a society, what more, for societies that are diverse and stricken with racial, religious, geographical and economic fault lines. Most dangerously, the license to dictatorship is said to be counter-productive with many net losses for the society and state, with the main beneficiary being the political elites associated with the dominant party. Political and economic corruption, nepotism and cronyism are often the major consequences of such political systems. These negative consequences have led to the general antipathy and opposition to the continued existence of one-party dominant systems

---

4. S. Rajaratnam, "Foreword", in Bilveer Singh, *Whither PAP's Dominance?: An Analysis of Singapore's 1991 General Elections* (Petaling Jaya, Malaysia: Pelanduk Publications, 1992).

5. Ibid.

anywhere in the world regardless of the justifications that are often used to rationalise their existence.

Yet, in systems where such political parties exist, the *de rigueur* rationale is often the net benefits and gains the state and its people are said to accrue. This often includes much-needed political stability and certainty, economic development and social peace that is usually sacrificed in multi-ethnic and multi-racial societies. Often, considerations of stability and security trump over all other considerations in a society. The prioritisation of these goals and objectives, what more, with the legitimate support and endorsement of the electorate, is said to prevail over the various objections that are usually raised by many analysts, often in the West and some even in so-called matured democracies in the non-Western world. But is this really true?

By any count, using the minimal or maximal definition, Singapore's political system qualifies as a one-party dominant state. In fact, due to the latitudinal longevity and dominance of the ruling party, the PAP, since 1959, Singapore is a one-party 'predominant state'. Why is this so and what does it mean for Singapore politics and its future are discussed in this study. In contemporary politics, Singapore has since May 2018 become the last of the one-party dominant states in Southeast Asia — the last of the Mohicans — as far as such a political system is concerned.

Singapore as a one-party dominant state

Even though the ruling PAP has been in power since June 1959, the number of academic works and writings on various aspects of one-party dominance in Singapore is very small. It is as if this type of system is a natural state of affairs, something that has been socialised with vigour and promoted by the ruling elites whenever the opportunity avails itself. Still, if history is any lesson, such regimes may linger on for decades but eventually will collapse for a host of reasons, as has happened in Japan, India, Indonesia and the latest to fall, in Malaysia. Some of the key works on one-party dominance in Singapore include Shee Poon Kim, *The People's Action Party of Singapore, 1954–1970: A Study of Survivalism of a Single-Dominant Party* (1971), Chan Heng Chee, *The Dynamics of One Party Dominance: The PAP at the Grass-roots* (1976), Bilveer Singh, *Whither PAP's Dominance?:*

An Analysis of Singapore's 1991 General Elections (1992), and Lan Hu, *One Party Dominance Survival: The Case of Singapore and Taiwan* (2011). There are also a number of articles, including N. Ganesan's "Singapore: Entrenching a City-State's Dominant Party System" (1998).[6] Yet, at the same time, there have been a number of occasions when key policy makers have warned against accepting this as something permanent and not to assume that the PAP will be in power in perpetuity. Warnings of these nature have come from Minister K. Shanmugam, the late Minister Mentor Lee Kuan Yew and Minister Ong Ye Kung.

Singapore — the last one-party dominant state in Southeast Asia

To highlight the significance of the one-party predominant state in Singapore, this takes on a larger dimension when it is located within the regional political dynamics. Since the 1950s, non-communist Southeast Asia had its fair share of one-party dominant states in the region. This began with the Alliance Party, made up of UMNO (United Malays National Organisation), MCA (Malayan and later, Malaysian Chinese Association) and MIC (Malayan and later, Malaysian Indian Congress) coming to power in Malaya in 1957. Two years later, the PAP came to power in Singapore. Following the abortive coup in Indonesia in 1965, for all intents and purposes, GOLKAR (*Golong Karya*) was the dominant party in the largest Southeast Asian state. GOLKAR's dominance was terminated in May 1998, when a 'people's power' revolution brought down the Suharto leadership and his political apparatus centred around GOLKAR. Since then, GOLKAR has played second fiddle to other political parties in Indonesia with political coalitions centering around the PDIP (*Partai Demokrasi Indonesia Perjuangan*) and the Democratic Party ruling Indonesia. This left two of Indonesia's neighbours, Malaysia and Singapore, to continue practising a political system and tradition

---

6. Shee Poon Kim, *The People's Action Party of Singapore, 1954–1970: A Study of Survivalism of a Single-Dominant Party* (PhD Dissertation, Indiana University, 1971); Chan Heng Chee, *The Dynamics of One Party Dominance: The PAP at the Grass-roots* (Singapore: Singapore University Press, 1976); Lan Hu, *One Party Dominance Survival: The Case of Singapore and Taiwan* (PhD Dissertation, Ohio State University, 2011); N. Ganesan, "Singapore: Entrenching a City-State's Dominant Party System", *Southeast Asian Affairs, 1998* (Singapore: Institute of Southeast Asian Studies, 1998), pp. 229–243.

that qualified as a one-party dominant state even though both were very different in the manner the system operated in the two states.

In the case of Malaysia and Malaya before that, the political system that operated was what Arend Lijphart termed as 'consociational democracy'.[7] This involved racial or communal-based political parties entering into a formal pact with a senior political partner that continued to rule Malaya and then Malaysia. In 1957, the Malays, Chinese and Indians were organised in three political parties, namely, UMNO, MCA and MIC respectively and they successfully contested the 1957 and 1963 general elections. However, following the bloody racial riots that followed the 1969 General Elections, a broader coalition was established through the *Barisan Nasional* (BN) or National Front, and this broad-based electoral alliance ruled Malaysia for the next 40 years or so. However, the political formula came under challenge in the 2008 and 2013 general elections with the BN losing its two-third majority and even surrendering its electoral majority in the 2013 General Elections.

The 14th Malaysian General Elections, however, marked a paradigm shift. The May 2018 General Elections proved to be the turning point as the one-party (coalition) dominant state came to an end. The incumbent prime minister, Najib Tun Razak, was mired in corruption allegations, with worsening living conditions for the general public, especially following the introduction of the Goods and Services Tax (GST) in 2015. In the 2018 General Elections, an electoral coalition called *Pakatan Harapan* (PH) or Alliance of Hope, led by the former and the longest-serving prime minister in Malaysia, Mahathir Mohamad (formerly leader of the BN government from 1981 to 2003) won the elections, putting an end to the continued rule of BN, thereby ceasing Malaysia's status as a one-party dominant state. With the same political forces and elites having ruled Malaya and Malaysia, mainly through the senior partner of UMNO, a one-party dominant state operated

---

7. Arend Lijphart, *The Politics of Accommodation: Pluralism and Democracy in the Netherlands* (Berkeley, CA: University of California Press, 1968); Arend Lijphart, *Democracy in Plural Societies: A Comparative Exploration* (New Haven, CT: Yale University Press, 1977); Arend Lijphart, *Democracies: Patterns of Majoritarian and Consensus Government in Twenty-One Democracies* (New Haven, CT: Yale University Press, 1984); Arend Lijphart, *Patterns of Democracy: Government Forms and Performance in Thirty-Six Countries* (New Haven, CT: Yale University Press, 1999 and 2012).

in Malaysia from 1957 to 2018, for a total of 61 years, with the state entering into unchartered waters after the defeat of the BN.

What this electoral outcome in Malaysia meant was that since 9 May 2018, Singapore is the last one-party dominant state in Southeast Asia today. While it is true that Hun Sen's political party has been in power in Cambodia for a long time, its circumstances are, however, different. Hun Sen's Cambodian People's Party (CPP) was originally known as the Kampuchean People's Revolutionary Party (KPRP) and was the sole political party in the country from 1979 to 1991 in a communist state. With Cambodia officially abandoning the Marxist-Leninist system, the KPRP changed its name to the CPP and has continued to rule the country to this day even though a weak multi-party system exists. In communist Vietnam and Laos, single-parties rule the two states and hence, do not qualify as one-party dominant states as the term is only reserved for multi-party political systems in the non-communist world.

In view of these circumstances and developments, the continued resilience of Singapore as a one-party dominant state is worth studying, including discussing the question as to how long such a political system can last? Is the question, not whether but when such a system will collapse, relevant as far as Singapore is concerned? Or will Singapore prove to be an exception and prolong the one-party dominant state and system as has been argued by some analysts.

23 January 2017 will go down as an important date in Singapore's political history, especially as far as discussions on the issue of People's Action Party's (PAP) political dominance is concerned. The year would have marked 52 years of Singapore's independence since separating from Malaysia in 1965 and 58 years of PAP's dominance of Singapore's politics since the party romped to victory in the 1959 General Elections. While there exists many debates and views about democratisation, the need for checks and balances, and the need for political pluralism in Singapore, yet, on 23 January 2017, a leading member of the PAP's fourth-generation leadership, Ong Ye Kung or OYK for short, argued that Singapore would continue to be ruled by a one-party dominant state. When the statement was made, Ong was concurrently the minister of education (higher education and skills) and the second minister for defence. He also holds a number of other strategic political appointments including being a Member, Board of Directors, Monetary Authority of Singapore; Chairman, Advisory Council on Community Relations in Defence; Chairman, Chinese Community Liaison Group, tasked to strengthen relations between the government and the Singapore Chinese community; and being one of the Organising Secretaries in the last Central Executive Committee of the ruling PAP and its Assistant Treasurer in the current CEC, the apex body of the ruling party. He is also being touted as one of the most important politicians of the PAP's fourth generation in the coming years.

During the panel discussion on the possibility of Singapore having a two- or multi-party system at the Institute of Policy Studies' annual conference on Singapore Perspectives on 23 January 2017,[1] OYK argued that "a one-party system may give Singapore its best shot at success because it is a small country that needs to stay nimble and move fast in a changing global environment."[2] He held the view that this "need not be the PAP but whichever party that is most capable."[3] In OYK's words, "our equilibrium as a small country may well be a single party system. The

---

1. For speeches of both Ong Ye Kung and Ho Kwon Ping, see *Insights on Singapore's Politics and Governance from Leading Thinkers* (Singapore: World Scientific, 2019), pp. 175–187.

2. Charissa Yong, "One-party rule 'may be way for Singapore to succeed': Ong Ye Kung", *The Straits Times*, 24 January 2017.

3. Ibid.

party can be PAP today, but another party in the future — so long it is the most capable at that time."[4]

He further explained that "for multi-party to form, there must be at least two sufficiently different paths for Singapore to take and political views that are different for different parties to uphold."[5] In short, there should be deep socio-political cleavages in society.[6] However, in his view, "Singapore is not big enough geographically to have separate towns to evolve different views on national issues."[7] In fact, he argued that "a single-party system in the case of Singapore is not a prescription but an outcome of choice resulting from elections."[8] He pointed out that "the state of Massachusetts in the United States has been dominated by the Democrats for a long period", adding that "smallness and concentration often do go together."[9]

While arguing that "a country's success is always idiosyncratic and can never be replicated wholesale by another", nevertheless, "the formula for success is based on different political processes and ours happens to be a one-party system."[10] He also warned about simply following norms elsewhere as there were consequences for adopting a multi-party system. He observed that:

> Should the political landscape here evolve into one with more than one dominant
> political party, it could mean a lot more "jostling on the ground" as unions and

---

4. Charissa Yong, "One-party rule 'may be way for Singapore to succeed': Ong Ye Kung"; Martino Tan, "Minister Ong Ye Kung asked at IPS conference: 'What if S'pore becomes a 2 or multi-party system?'", *Mothership*, 23 January 2017; Martha Soezean, "Ong Ye Kung: Singapore's one-party system, a result of free and fair election", *The Online Citizen*, 24 January 2017.

5. Charissa Yong, "One-party rule 'may be way for Singapore to succeed': Ong Ye Kung".

6. "Why are people whacking Ong Ye Kung?", *Thoughtsofrealsingaporeans*, 25 January 2017.

7. Charissa Yong, "One-party rule 'may be way for Singapore to succeed': Ong Ye Kung".

8. Tan Weizhen, "Multi-party political system in which parties align along sinister lines could ruin S'pore: Ye Kung", *Today*, 24 January 2017; Martha Soezean, "Ong Ye Kung: Singapore's one-party system, a result of free and fair election".

9. Tan Weizhen, "Multi-party political system in which parties align along sinister lines could ruin S'pore: Ye Kung"; Martha Soezean, "Ong Ye Kung: Singapore's one-party system, a result of free and fair election".

10. Charissa Yong, "One-party rule 'may be way for Singapore to succeed': Ong Ye Kung".

various associations and even the media become split as parties seek support...
And should political parties align themselves along "sinister" lines, such as by
race, language or religion, this "toxic mix" could leave the country broken...".[11]

In his view, "even as political parties represent diverse views, that very same
essence can take a nasty twist, sowing discord and dividing societies."[12] OYK cited
his personal example of 'jostling' on the ground with rising clamour for political
diversity in the country:

> After GE2011, when the Workers' Party won Aljunied, I found myself becoming
> the opposition party in the GRC. Then, there are groups which will invite me
> as guest-of-honour for their functions, and others that will invite the Workers'
> Party MP. Most will invite both, and both will turn up. I got the feeling the guests
> enjoyed watching the jostling.[13]

He also noted that "one major long-term risk is that a multi-party system could
slow down decision-making and nimbleness while navigating an ever-changing
world and environment."[14] He wondered: "Imagine, if we have a multi-party system
back in 1965, will we have come so far so quickly?"[15] OYK also noted that a multi-
party system could have deleterious impact on the country's civil service. This is
because "the civil service would be the most tested among institutions under a
multi-party system, as it has to be neutral and serve whichever party forms the
Government."[16] Using the example of the United States, OYK pointed out: "You
can work on one set of policies for five years, then someone new comes along
and says, let's redo everything, or undo everything. It can be frustrating and very
demoralising."[17] He mentioned as examples that "the Affordable Care Act in the US

---

11. Tan Weizhen, "Multi-party political system in which parties align along sinister lines
could ruin S'pore: Ye Kung".

12. Ibid.

13. Martino Tan, "Minister Ong Ye Kung asked at IPS conference: 'What if S'pore becomes
a 2 or multi-party system?'".

14. Charissa Yong, "One-party rule 'may be way for Singapore to succeed': Ong Ye Kung".

15. Tan Weizhen, "Multi-party political system in which parties align along sinister lines
could ruin S'pore: Ye Kung".

16. Ibid.

17. Ibid.

has been repealed", and the US withdrawal from the Trans-Pacific Partnership after President Donald Trump took power.[18]

He concluded by saying that "If the people of a country wish for a multi-party system, it will be so."[19] However, "the job of the opposition parties is to point out the risks of a single-party rule. That is their job. But the job of the PAP (People's Action Party) is to make sure that Singapore continues to flourish. We will also point out the risks of a multi-party system and, most importantly, we must always keep out the ills of complacency, elitism and corruption."[20] In view of various challenges, both internal and external, "the Government has to make sure that the current system continues to work, and the PAP must ensure that it is open-minded and keeps up with the times, and comes up with policies that are rooted in the ground."[21]

OYK's views on one-party dominance in Singapore did not go unchallenged. Leon Perera, the Non-Constituency Member of Parliament (NCMP) from the WP disagreed with OYK's analysis and thought that it was something dangerous for Singapore's future. He argued that a one-party system made it very difficult for alternative parties to exist and the ruling party, with no viable competitors, may lose its way. There was also the danger that the ruling party in a one-party dominant system can change the Constitution to keep itself in power forever.[22] Perera also argued that there was no track record for one party that has thrived for 100 years or more as a developed country. Finally, if a one-party system cannot last forever, it may be too late for another good party to emerge if there is a time for change.[23] Worse still, a new, extremist party may fill the political vacuum when a crisis hits and steer Singapore into the abyss. Hence, a one-party dominant system was dangerous as it may fail one day with "no able, responsible and electable

---

18. Ibid.

19. Ibid.

20. Ibid.

21. Ibid.

22. Martino Tan, "WP & SDP respond to Ong Ye Kung's speech about risks of two- or multi-party system S'pore", *Mothership*, 26 January 2017.

23. Ibid.

Opposition to take its place if that happens."[24] Endorsing Perera's position, Gerald Giam, a former NCMP from the WP argued that a credible political party cannot appear overnight. Rather, it takes "years and many election cycles to build up this institution" and "anyone who thinks otherwise is clueless about political realities."[25]

The secretary-general of the Singapore Democratic Party (SDP), Chee Soon Juan also took issue with OYK's position on the need for one-party dominance in Singapore. Chee argued that OYK was clinging on to "out-dated and reality-free view that a one-party rule is the way forward."[26] Rather, he put forth that Singaporeans valued a vibrant and democratic society where an open exchange of ideas and freedom of expression was valued. It was mainly due to the PAP's unchecked political dominance that many mistakes had been made such as the influx of foreigners that have depressed the wages of Singaporeans. Hence, OYK's position was said to be "at complete odds with reality" and for "Singapore's future survival, multi-party system must replace one-party rule."[27]

Analysis

OYK's statement and position on the one-party dominant state and the subsequent rebuttals by the Singapore Opposition clearly show the debate and differences that exist on the directions of national politics in Singapore. That this debate is largely a moot point — only a debate with no prospects of change in the political status quo — is due to the predominantly strong position of the PAP which has ruled since 1959 and is omnipresent in Singapore politics. For a highly developed society, this may appear somewhat contradictory as political and economic development and advancement in education are believed to promote a culture and system of political pluralism and checks and balances, and not a one-party dominant state as in existence for more than five decades in Singapore. Why this is the state of affairs in Singapore will be analysed in this book.

---

24. Ibid.
25. Ibid.
26. Ibid.
27. Ibid.

INTRODUCTION: DEMOCRACY, POLITICS AND THE PUZZLE OF DOMINANCE

In his edited book titled *Uncommon Democracies: The One-Party Dominant Regimes*, T.J. Pempel analysed cases of one-party dominance in a number of advanced democracies. This included studying the dominance of the Labor Party in Israel (pre-independence to 1977), the Social Democratic Party in Sweden (1932–1976), the Liberal Democratic Party in Japan (1955–1990) and the Christian Democrats in Italy (1945–1980).[1] As a rule, in advanced industrial democracies, 'throwing out the rascals' during elections, the party that has lost public support, has been the hallmark of democracy. Yet, this is not always the case and there have been exceptions. According to Pempel:

> These exceptions are the presence, within the group of industrialized democracies, of one-party dominant states. In these countries, despite free electoral competition, relatively open information systems, respect for civil liberties, and the right of free political association, a single party has managed to govern alone or as the primary and ongoing partner in coalitions, without interruption, for substantial periods of time, often for three to five decades, and to dominate the formation of as many as ten, twelve or more successive governments.[2]

For Pempel, one-party dominance in advanced democracies is interesting because it is not supposed to happen: "What makes long-term rule by a single party among the industrialized democracies an enticing puzzle is not just that it is rare but it is not supposed to happen."[3] This would have been understandable if there was "social stagnation and rule by a limited oligarchy", which does not seem to be found in the advanced democracies. How such a phenomenon emerged in a non-

---

1. T.J. Pempel (ed), *Uncommon Democracies: The One-Party Dominant Regimes* (Ithaca, New York: Cornell University Press, 1990).

2. Ibid, pp. 2–3.

3. Ibid, p. 5.

authoritarian system was a puzzle that Pempel wanted to solve. These societies did not operate in a system with a sole legal party or for that matter, where the ruling party implemented rigid state controls over the society. Neither, as in many newly independent states, was there a presence of a "historical remnant of anticolonial movements that papered over social diversities as a means of achieving national independence."[4] Instead, these advanced industrialised societies were socially stable, characterised by democratic freedoms and liberties and "were built on the recognition rather than the denial of social diversity".[5]

For these reasons, Pempel argued that "most theories of voting behaviour or party systems are unequipped to deal with the regular and unswerving return of one party to office decade after decade in vigorous industrial democracies."[6] For Pempel, even from the perspective of organisational theory, one-party dominance was puzzling. Citing Robert Michels, Pempel argued that most organisations — political and non-political — found it difficult to adapt to changes. This is because over time, organisations "come to adopt their members' and their leaders' particularistic interests rather than the more general goals and interests to which they were originally pledged."[7] Hence, even though undertaking changes and adaptation is good for the organisation's interests, over time, its members and leaders tend to oppose these adaptations, despite changing socio-political conditions. This is because past successes tend to reinforce the attitude of not changing existing policies and programmes on grounds that these had worked in the past.

In view of these factors, Pempel put forward a number of queries relating to one-party dominance in advanced industrialised countries. These included:

a. How and why it occurs under situations of social dynamics and political openness?
b. How does a single party come to retain a plurality or a majority of a relatively free vote by a dynamic and fluid citizenry decade after decade?
c. Why don't at least some of its supporters desert it?
d. Why, with demographic changes, don't other voting blocs become more numerous, thereby reducing it to minority status?

---

4.   Ibid.

5.   Ibid.

6.   Ibid, pp. 5–6.

7.   Ibid, p. 6.

e. Why don't other parties or coalitions find it sufficiently desirable and possible at least once or twice to organise an alternative government?[8]

At the same time, Pempel's study attempted to understand the causes and consequences of one-party dominance in developed industrialised states. For him:

> The causes are puzzling because one-party dominance is at variance with most expectations about voting behaviour in complex and changing societies. It is also at variance with expectations of organizational behaviour by both the dominant party and its opponents. Both such literatures suggest the improbability of a single political party remaining uninterruptedly at the core of the government for three or four decades.
>
> The consequences of one-party dominance are also interesting. Long-term rule by a single party shows that political parties are of consequence not simply in their electoral, vote-getting mode but also in their governing and policy formulation modes. Long-term rule by a single party affords an opportunity to view parties in both veins simultaneously, winning elections and governing, and in ways that reinforce each other.[9]

The reference to Pempel's work on one-party dominance is highly relevant for the study of the resilience of one-party dominance in Singapore. While in the early years, say in the 1960s, 1970s and 1980s, Singapore could easily fit the status of one-party dominant states in the developing world, as found in Asia and Africa, this situation changed fundamentally from the 1990s. Singapore has developed on almost all fronts, especially economically, to become one of the wealthiest states in the world. Even though it has a relatively small population, its demographics are characterised by a populace that is highly educated, informed and technologically savvy. In short, it can easily qualify as an advanced state. Yet, politically, the one-party dominant state and system seems to be strengthening and not weakening. If Pempel's argument that this is not only rare but is not supposed to happen in developed society, then what explains Singapore as a strong one-party dominant state? This study will attempt to unravel this puzzle.

---

8. Ibid, p. 6.

9. Ibid, p. 7.

ONE-PARTY DOMINANCE: A FRAMEWORK FOR ANALYSIS

Introduction

By the turn of the 21st century, some works exist on the concept and praxis of the one-party dominant political system.[1] The term 'dominant' was popularised by Maurice Duverger in 1951.[2] This covers party systems in Europe, Latin America and Asia, with multiple case studies analysing the various dynamics of the emergence of a dominant political party in multi-party democracies. The one-party dominant state is different from a one-party state as is found in China, Cuba, Vietnam and North Korea today. The end of the Cold War and what Samuel Huntington described as the 'Third Wave of Democratization' did not preclude the rise of a one-party dominant party state.[3] This political system seems to have endured in many countries and in many ways even gained traction and legitimacy, especially with the ability of the one-party dominant state's government to score high on various aspects of governance, including providing goods related to national security, social stability and economic development. One state that stands out in this regard is Singapore, where the ruling party, the People's Action Party (PAP), though operating in a multi-party system, has been continuously returned to power since 1959. Following the 2015 General Elections on 11 September, the PAP was again returned to office with an even stronger mandate than what it gained in the previous elections in 2011. In order to understand the one-party dominant system in Singapore and its political resilience, it will be useful first to understand the concept of one-party dominance.

---

1. Some of the key works that will be referred in this study include: Giovanni Sartori, *Parties and Party Systems: A Framework for Analysis* (Cambridge, UK: Cambridge University Press, 1976; reprint in 2005); T.J. Pempel, (ed.), *Uncommon Democracies: The One-Party Dominant Regimes* (Ithaca, New York: Cornell University Press, 1990); Hermann Giliomee and Charles Simkins, (eds.), *The Awkward Embrace: One Party Dominance and Democracy* (Cape Town, South Africa: Tafelberg, 1999).

2. Maurice Duverger, *Political Parties: Their Organization and Activity in the Modern State* (New York: John Wiley and Sons, 1954).

3. Samuel P. Huntington, *The Third Wave: Democratization in the Late 20th Century* (Norman, Oklahoma: University of Oklahoma Press, 1991).

One-party dominance

Despite the existence of multi-racial and multi-religious societies in Asia and Africa, there were fears that following the end of the Cold War, multi-party democracy would bring about the fracturing of the national polity with a fractured and divided party system gaining dominance. Not only did this not happen but instead, in many instances, one-party dominant states emerged. There are many examples of such parties that have been dominant at one time or another, including the Congress Party in India, the Kuomintang in Taiwan, the African National Congress in South Africa, the United Malays National Organisation in Malaysia and the GOLKAR in Indonesia. And, it is not just a Third World phenomenon. The Social Democrats in Sweden were in power from 1936 to 1976, the Liberal Democratic Party (LDP) in Japan from 1955 to 1993 and now in power since 2012, and the Christian Democrats in Italy from 1945 to 1993. For many of these states, for a long time, these political parties enjoyed continuous electoral victories and their defeat was not just unlikely, it was also not even envisaged.

There is no such thing as a single mode or mould of what constitutes a 'one-party dominant state'. Neither are one-party dominant states static in the manner they are structured or function. Renske Doorenspleet and Lia Nijzink argued that "one-party-dominant systems do not follow the 'normal' or 'expected' pattern of party competition in a democracy."[4] A system of one-party dominance can exist in a democratic or non-democratic context. Hence, while one-party dominant systems tend to be exceptional, yet due to their persistence in a number of settings, it is worth studying what accounts for the phenomenon, especially the endurance of these systems and possibly too, why and when such systems collapse.

What is a one-party dominant state?

Maurice Duverger was among the first to discuss the issue of the one-party dominant state. In his seminal work published in 1951 in French which was later translated into English in 1967, Duverger defines a dominant party as follows:

> a party larger than any other, which heads the list and clearly out-distances its rivals over a certain period of time…A party is dominant when it is identified with an

---

4. Renske Doorenspleet and Lia Nijzink, "One-Party Dominance in African Democracies: A Framework for Analysis", in Renske Doorenspleet and Lia Nijzink (eds.), *One-Party Dominance in African Democracies* (Boulder, Colorado: Lynne Rienner Publishers, 2013), p. 2.

epoch; when its doctrine, ideas, methods, its style…coincide with those of the epoch…Domination is a question of influence rather than strength; it is also linked with belief. A dominant party is that which public opinion believes to be dominant… Even the enemies of the dominant party, even citizens who refuse to give it their vote, acknowledge its superior status and its influence; they deplore it but admit it.[5]

The other two of leading authorities on the subject of one-party dominant system are Giovanni Sartori and T.J. Pempel. In his study of political parties and party systems in 1976, Sartori described a one-party dominant system as one where the same party wins an absolute majority in at least three consecutive elections. Sartori's criteria injected a time frame dimension covering at least three elections. In Sartori terminology, this refers to the "predominant" party system. T.J. Pempel pointed out that despite free electoral competition, relatively open information systems, respect for civil liberties, and the right of free political association, in a number of states across Asia and Africa, a single party has managed to govern alone or as the primary and ongoing partner in coalitions, without interruption, for substantial periods of time.[6] According to Pempel, a political party is considered 'dominant' if it is dominant in numbers, securing at least a plurality of votes and seats but this counts if the party is electorally dominant for an uninterrupted and prolonged period; it must enjoy a dominant bargaining position, always setting the tone when it comes to government formation; and it must be dominant governmentally whereby it determines the public policy agenda.[7] Yet, Pempel argued that a one-party dominant system is "exceptionally rare, involving a serendipitous congruence of effort and luck."[8]

Clearly, from the aforementioned, there are political systems that are described as 'one-party dominant' states and these have been found in both the developed and developing world. While the concept of defining what is a one-party dominant state continues to be contested somewhat, what is clear is that it refers to a situation where political parties have successfully and continuously won election victories

---

5. Maurice Duverger, *Political Parties: Their Organization and Activity in the Modern State*, pp. 308–309.

6. T.J. Pempel (ed.), *Uncommon Democracies: The One-Party Dominant Regimes*, p. 1.

7. See Clemens Spiess, *Democracy and Party System in Developing Countries: A Comparative Study of India and South Africa* (Routledge Advances in South Asian Studies), 1st Edition (London, UK: Routledge, 2009), p. 12.

8. T.J. Pempel (ed.), *Uncommon Democracies: The One-Party Dominant Regimes*, p. 334.

and whose future defeat cannot be envisaged or is unlikely in the foreseeable time to come.[9] Scholars such as Patrick Dunleavy have argued that a dominant political party usually qualifies through three key criteria:

a. The party is seen as exceptionally effective by voters, so that it is set apart from all other parties.
b. It consequently has an extensive 'core' or protected area of the ideological space, within which no other party can compete effectively for voters' support.
c. At the basic minimum level of effectiveness that voters use to judge whether to participate or not, the lead party has a wider potential appeal to more voters than its rivals.[10]

In view of these factors, scholars have defined a 'dominant political system' either from the empirist or analytical perspective. Hence, Gary W. Cox defined "dominant parties are those which are uninterruptedly in government, either alone or as the senior partners of a coalition, for a long period of time (say three to five decades)."[11] For Alan Ware, "the predominant party system. This is a system where one party regularly wins enough parliamentary seats to control the government on its own."[12]

Probably, Brendan O'Leary provided a useful operational approach to unpack what a one-party dominant state is constituted of:

> [W]e know what we mean by a dominant party in democratic conditions. First, it must be a party which is dominant in number: it must regularly win more seats in parliamentary or congressional elections than its opponents...Secondly, this party must enjoy a dominant bargaining position. It must be able to stay in government on a regular basis. If it must share power with smaller parties,...it is nevertheless the key agent in the political system, with privileged access to the key executive and

---

9. Raymond Suttner, "Party Dominance 'Theory': Of What Value?", *Politikon*, December 2006, 33(3), p. 277.

10. Patrick Dunleavy, "Rethinking Dominant Party Systems", in Matthijs Bogaards and Françoise Boucek (eds.), *Dominant Parties and Democracy: Concepts, Measures and Comparison* (London, UK: Routledge, 2010), pp. 23–33.

11. Gary W. Cox, *Making Votes Count: Strategic Coordination in the World's Electoral Systems* (Cambridge, UK: Cambridge University Press, 1997), p. 238.

12. Alan Ware, *Political Parties and Party Systems* (Oxford, UK: Oxford University Press, 1995), p. 159.

legislative posts. Thirdly,...a dominant party must be chronologically pre-eminent. It must govern continuously for a long time, although analysts might differ over whether three or four general election victories, and whether a decade or a decade and a half are the crucial benchmarks of dominance. Finally, a dominant party must be ideologically dominant: it must be capable of using government to shape public policy so that the nature of the state and the society over which it presides is fundamentally changed.[13]

Clearly, when one speaks of a one-party dominant system, one takes into consideration the length of the political dominance, the margin of dominance and the repetition of electoral dominance. The point being, in a multi-party democracy, the fact exists that some political parties are more dominant than others in terms of electoral support, and uninterrupted and consecutive access to national power over many years, be it over three or four elections. Such political parties control the majority of legislative seats and control executive power over a period of time.

Why do one-party dominant systems arise and endure?

Many factors help to explain the endurance of the one-party dominant system and state. First, there is the role of history, as has been argued by scholars such as Huntington and others such as Hermann Giliomee and Charles Simkins. In systems that have a one-party dominant system, the states often have experienced colonialism, civil wars or repression under a civilian or military regime. Many of the ruling parties in such states emerged as nationalist movements that mobilised the citizens to fight for independence, for new political arrangements and even championed the democratisation movements. These parties become dominant as they are seen to be the progenitors of nationalism and the modern state, and often succeed in creating a new state and system in its image. As was argued by Duverger, "a dominant party is dominant because people believe it is so" as "the party is associated with an epoch."[14] A party is dominant when "its doctrines, ideas, methods, its style, so to speak, coincide with those of the people."[15]

---

13. Brendan O'Leary, "Britain's Japanese Question: 'Is There a Dominant Party?'", in Helen Margetts and Gareth Smyth (eds.), *Turning Japanese: Britain with a Permanent Party of Government* (London, UK: Lawrence and Wishart, 1994), p. 4.

14. Maurice Duverger, *Political Parties: Their Organization and Activity in the Modern State*, p. 308.

15. Ibid.

Similarly, Huntington believed that historical background of a party was critical as some parties derived their strength "from its struggle for power" and that "the longer a nationalist party fought for independence, the longer it was able to enjoy the power that came with independence."[16] This is especially true of political movements or parties that played a key role in the struggle for independence or democracy and where these parties were able to mobilise the political loyalties of its citizens. According to Giliomee and Simkins, even in an environment of multi-party democracy, "loyalty to the party is equated with loyalty to the nation or with patriotism, and criticism of especially the party leader is associated with disloyalty towards nation and state."[17] This was all the more so as these dominant parties played a distinct role in nation building and hence, the association of the state with the party. The role of history is important in determining the endurance of the one-party dominant state and the role played particularly in the struggle for its independence or democracy.

Second, most of the dominant parties emerged as 'national' or 'nationalist' parties, transcending national racial, religious, linguistic and economic fault lines. This is also in part due to the fact that these parties are also broad-based multi-ethnic, multi-religious and multi-linguistic parties, and representative of the national economic strata rather than a particular class. Most of the newer parties, however, partly due to the competitive nature of democracy, tend to be associated with a particular agenda and often tend to have a more particularistic following or support base. While the older nationalist or national parties tend to transcend multiple cleavages, its success in doing so also helps to ensure its staying power in politics. As was demonstrated by Giliomee and Simkins, the dominant parties in states such as South Africa, Taiwan and Malaysia successfully transcended class, religious and linguistic divisions, especially in highly heterogeneous societies. Hence, a party's ability to transcend complex national cleavages and attract support from different divergent social groups can play a big role in entrenching its dominant position. It is also in a strong position to co-opt other political forces, including from the opposition, thereby reinforcing its political dominance and power.

Third, as was argued by Duverger and Arend Lijphart, the nature of electoral systems and institutional arrangements can also play a part in instituting the endurance

---

16. Samuel Huntington, *The Third Wave: Democratization in the Late 20th Century*, p. 426.

17. Hermann Giliomee and Charles Simkins, *The Awkward Embrace: One Party Dominance and Democracy*, p. 350.

of a one-party dominant state. While proportional representation systems allow small parties to win seats in parliament, thereby causing party system fragmentation, the majoritarian first-past-the-post system tends to reinforce political dominance.

Fourth, a state's political culture can also affect and influence the emergence of a dominant party system, as has been argued by Frederic C. Schaffer, Donal B. Cruise O'Brien and Lawrence Schlemmer.[18] When a nation's political institutions like the dominant political party is fused with national cultural norms and where the party is seen as the personification of the state and its people, it can assist in the strengthening and maintenance of a one-party dominant state.

Fifth, no political party can remain in power unless it proves itself and gains performance legitimacy. A failed party is unlikely to survive and hence, governmental performance is an important factor in explaining the longevity of political parties and their dominance. While people may support a dominant political party due to emotional ties, support for its ideology and historical role, for many, it is because it is a performing party. In short, rationality and meritocracy are equally important factors in explaining the endurance of the one-party dominant state. As Arian Asher and Samuel Barnes noted, "so long as the dominant party performs intelligently, the opposition can do little that is effective. Even bad decisions will not be disastrous unless the opposition is in a position to take advantage of them and it seldom is."[19] The relationship between the state and party also plays an important role in explaining the endurance of one-party dominance. All being equal, the incumbent ruling party tends to have better access to resources and information compared to the opposition and this advantage, over a long period of time, can permanently disadvantage the opposition. The role of external influence is also important in helping the endurance of the one-party system, including a party being seen as the national bastion in the face of external threats and challenges.

In short, while there is no 'one size fits all' explanation, the context in which a single-party dominance takes place is vitally important. According to Jonas Pontusson, the political dominance of the Social Democrats in Sweden can be explained through "a virtuous cycle involving three essential features: capacity to

---

18. For instance, see Frederic C. Shaffer, *Democracy in Translation: Understanding Politics in an Unfamiliar Culture* (Ithaca, NY: Cornell University Press, 1998).

19. Arian Asher and Samuel Barnes, "The Dominant Party System: A Neglected Model of Democratic Stability", *Journal of Politics*, 36, p. 600.

mobilize voters, control of the political agenda, and control of the government."[20] In the case of Israel, Michael Shalev argued that Mapai's dominance of the Israeli political system can be explained from three inter-related factors: "1. The role of class and other economy-based interests and cleavages in shaping mass political mobilisation; 2. The importance of political control of the economy and effective political management of distributional conflicts for the success of governing parties, especially parties of the left; 3. The impact on the domestic political economy of its economic and political connections to the international system."[21]

Why do they collapse?

While the rise and sustenance of a one-party dominant system have been a fact, it is also true that many of these dominant parties have eventually been defeated at the ballot boxes. This is true of the LDP in Japan, the Congress in India, Mapai in Israel and GOLKAR in Indonesia. Why do one-party dominant systems collapse? There are a number of explanations for this. First, it is mainly due to the failure to perform economically, as was the case in Indonesia. Related to this is often the abuse of power after years of unchecked dominance in the system.

Second, is the ability of the opposition to gain legitimacy as a contender for government, often made possible by the manifold failures of the dominant party in power which often leads to national crises. Due to various failures and shortcomings, the dominant party is unable to maintain its power base. It suffers from being discredited and eventually loses legitimacy. Duverger argued that the failure of the dominant parties to adapt to changing times and legislative situations can lead to the collapse of the dominant party system. According to Duverger, "the dominant party wears itself out in office, it loses its vigour, its arteries harden. It would thus be possible to show…that every domination bears within itself the seeds of its own destruction."[22] Hence, due to it being in power for a long time, inertia and lack of a

---

20. Jonas Pontusson, "Conditions of Labor-Party Dominance: Sweden and Britain Compared", in T.J. Pempel (ed.), *Uncommon Democracies: The One-Party Dominant Regimes* (Ithaca, New York: Cornell University Press, 1990), p. 62.

21. Michael Shalev, "The Political Economy of Labor-Party Dominance and Decline in Israel", in T.J. Pempel (ed.), *Uncommon Democracies: The One-Party Dominant Regimes* (Ithaca, New York: Cornell University Press, 1990), p. 87.

22. Maurice Duverger, *Political Parties*, Second Edition (London, UK: Methuen, 1959), p. 312.

vigorous leadership structure in the face of challenges from new social forces and rival parties, the dominant party is likely to collapse.

It can also result from a maturity of the political society that believes in checks and balances, all the more, if credible alternatives are available. Hence, as was argued by Ellis S. Krauss and Jon Pierre, "in the face of social change for instance, the opposition in a one-party dominant state may respond with new political strategies and effectively take advantage of that change to legitimise themselves."[23] There is also the image aspect with the society as a whole wanting to demonstrate that it is in step with the global democratisation phenomenon, especially when the one-party dominant system is not working. All being equal, a functioning multi-party democracy is often seen as a superior global public image than a one-party dominant state.

What are the dangers of a dominant party system?

First, conceptually, there are some who argue that the notion of a 'one-party dominant' state is simply undemocratic as the same political party remains in power and there is no alternative party in power. The notion of a 'democracy' in such a state is a flawed one. This, however, is a very narrow definition of democracy as every other ingredients of democracy such as regular free and fair elections, a free press, freedom of association and expression, and the existence of a multi-party system are present. This narrow definition is too concerned with the presence of an opposition and the need for an alternative party to form the government. Opposition to the view that a one-party dominant state is a threat to democracy was articulated by Firoz Cachalia, an African National Congress (ANC) leader, in an article in a South African newspaper:

> Some academics and opposition politicians have, for a long time now, been making the argument that South Africa is developing a system of one-party dominance that is dangerous for democracy and that consequently South Africa needs an effective opposition to protect democracy...I will...argue that the ANC's dominance strengthens the prospects of democratic consolidation and is good for both economic growth and in the long term for greater social equity...for most

---

23. Ellis S. Krauss and Jon Pierre, "The Decline of Dominant Parties: Parliamentary Politics in Sweden and Japan in the 1970s", T.J. Pempel (ed.), *Uncommon Democracies: The One-Party Dominant Regimes* (Ithaca, New York: Cornell University Press, 1990), pp. 228–229.

of its history, the ANC has been committed to an inclusive nationalism and its values have been strongly shaped by the enlightenment's universalism. It achieved its position of dominance in liberation politics and in post-apartheid South Africa through the method of secular politics. Its dominance is thus the result of successful contestation, not the absence of it.[24]

Second, a far more serious danger of a dominant party system is the tendency to conflate the state with the party. While this is the practice in a single-party state, in a dominant party system where other political parties are also in existence, such a practice can have a deleterious effect on the state and society. Third, through continuous rule, a one-party dominant state may engineer rules and regulations in such a manner that it can permanently disadvantage an opposition from ever coming to power. This can be done through electoral fraud but more often through legal and repressive measures that totally marginalise the political alternative to the ruling dominant party.

Conclusion

Clearly, one-party dominant states in a system of multi-party plurality are political entities and forms that are worth analysing as they are an important part of the political landscape worldwide, though their numbers have declined and are declining, as these forms of governments and political arrangements came under challenge. What is meant by one-party dominant states, the reasons for their rise, endurance, collapse, and the benefits and dangers of these systems, were discussed from a general perspective. Eventually, the role of history, political culture, nature of threats facing the entity and how these elements can be mobilised to create a compact between the government and the governed are key considerations in understanding such a system. The following chapters will examine the phenomenon of a one-party dominant state in Singapore.

---

24. *Business Day* (South Africa), 31 May 1999. Cited in Clemens Spiess, *Democracy and Party System in Developing Countries: A Comparative Study of India and South Africa* (Routledge Advances in South Asian Studies) 1st Edition, p. 2.

THE SINGAPORE POLITICAL SYSTEM

Introduction

Following the Second World War when Singapore's politics entered an era of tailspin, continuous change has been its key hallmark. The first period from 1945 to 1955 was an era of change brought about by the British colonial authorities to bequeath its colony with a political system *a la British* in the hope that the successor state would continue to be politically relevant to London and that the leaders of the new state would remain politically, economically and strategically friendly to Great Britain. The second period, from 1955 to 1965, was also an era of continuous change with Singapore emerging as a self-governing colony with limited, and later full internal powers, and from September 1963 to August 1965 as a state in the Federation of Malaysia. This period, namely, from limited and full internal self-government, to being an independent entity in the sovereign state of Malaysia, saw three elections being conducted in 1955, 1959 and 1963. These elections signaled the type of politics that would emerge in Singapore in the post-1965 era. The third period covers when Singapore became a full-fledged independent state. Independent Singapore continued its culture of transformation that saw a near-total makeover of Singapore politically, economically and even socially. While the British bequeathed a system of Westminster parliamentary democracy, eventually due to a host of factors, a hybrid political architecture emerged over the next 50 years or so when various political changes were injected that fundamentally altered the political system that was inherited from the British colonialists.

The evolution of Singapore's political system is best made clear by undertaking a review of literature on what has been written on Singapore's political and party system. This will make evident the importance of the past in Singapore's politics, the importance of leadership, the key factors that shape Singapore's politics, the nature of political parties, and how elections have been contested over the years that culminated in a situation where the People's Action Party (PAP) has emerged as *primus inter pares* compared to other political parties in the Republic.

Writings on Singapore's politics and political dominance

There are works on Singapore's political and party system as well as on elections. Constance Mary Turnbull provided an overview of Singapore's constitutional developments covering the period 1819 to 1968.[1] Yeo Kim Wah's research covered the detailed political developments spanning the decade from 1945 to 1955. The study explored the rise of political parties, the politics of nationalism, communalism and communism, and the three elections that were held in 1948, 1951 and 1955.[2] The Labour Front government dominated Singapore's politics from 1955 to 1959 under David Marshall and Lim Yew Hock. Following the 1959 General Elections, when the PAP first came to power through a 'united front' arrangement with the left-wing elements, Singapore's politics has been essentially an issue of PAP and its dominance of the political system to this day. Chan Heng Chee described Singapore's first 24 months after independence as the 'politics of survival' with the 'ideology of survival' reigning supreme.[3] Since then, there have been many works on the PAP and its character. These include writings by Chan Heng Chee, Pang Cheng Lian, Thomas J. Bellows and Shee Poon Kim.[4] The thrust of the writings and the subsequent ones that followed was to examine and analyse what emerged as the rise of a one-party dominant parliament.[5]

Despite incremental changes to the political system and the end of PAP's monopolistic control of the parliament in 1981, the basic trend and status remains

---

1. Constance Mary Turnbull, "Constitutional Developments 1819–1968", in Ooi Jin Bee and Chiang Hai Ding (eds.), *Modern Singapore* (Singapore: Singapore University Press, 1969), pp. 181–196.

2. Yeo Kim Wah, *Political Developments in Singapore 1945–1955* (Singapore: Singapore University Press, 1973).

3. Chan Heng Chee, *Singapore: The Politics of Survival, 1965–1967* (Singapore: Oxford University Press, 1971), pp. 48–54.

4. See Chan Heng Chee, *The Dynamics of One Party Dominance: The PAP at the Grassroots* (Singapore: Singapore University Press, 1976); Pang Cheng Lian, *Singapore's People's Action Party: Its History, Organization and Leadership* (Singapore: Oxford University Press, 1971); Thomas J. Bellows, *The People's Action Party of Singapore* (New Haven, Connecticut: Yale University Southeast Asian Studies, 1970); Shee Poon Kim, "The People's Action Party of Singapore, 1954–1970: A Study of Survivalism of a Single-Dominant Party" (PhD Dissertation, Indiana University, 1971).

5. See Jon S.T. Quah, "Political Science in Singapore", in Basant K. Kapur (ed.), *Singapore Studies: Critical Surveys of the Humanities and Social Sciences* (Singapore: Singapore University Press, 1986), p. 94.

largely unchanged — the PAP's dominance remains unchallenged. A number of studies have focused on electoral politics in Singapore. This includes writings by Yeo Kim Wah, Ong Chit Chung, Frances L. Starner, Alex Josey and others.[6]

The Singapore political system

On attaining independence in August 1965, Singapore was faced with the task of establishing its own political system. The political system is about the sharing of political power between the various branches of government, namely, executive, legislative and judiciary, about the powers of the head of government and state as well as about the system of checks and balances to ensure accountability, including the role of citizens in politics. Singapore, although a newly independent state, was not devoid of political experiences which were critical in developing its own political system. From the period of self-government in the 1950s and Singapore's short inclusion in the Federation of Malaysia, concepts of the elected representative, the electoral processes and the mechanisms of governance have been exposed to Singapore's polity and elites.

As a former colony of Britain, it came as no surprise that Singapore adopted the Westminster parliamentary system. This system of government or at least its fundamentals had been already introduced to Singapore during the period of Singapore's self-rule in the form of the Legislative Assembly. However, upon Singapore's expulsion from the Federation of Malaysia, the contention was not centred on the choice of an institution of government but on the nature of governance. As Shee Poon Kim noted, "it was at this critical juncture, based on Singapore's immediate past experience that the political elite in Singapore was adamant in creating a multiracial polity and a modern mixed economy".[7]

---

6. Yeo Kim Wah, *Political Developments in Singapore 1945–1955* (Singapore: Singapore University Press, 1973); Ong Chit Chung, "The 1959 Singapore General Election", *Journal of Southeast Asian Studies*, March 1975, 6(1), pp. 61–86; Frances L. Starner, "The Singapore Elections of 1963", in K.J. Ratnam and Robert Stephen Milne (eds.), *The Malayan Parliamentary Elections of 1964* (Singapore: University of Malaya Press, 1967), pp. 312–358; Alex Josey, *The Crucial Years Ahead: Republic of Singapore General Elections 1968* (Singapore: Donald Moore Press, 1968).

7. Shee Poon Kim, "The Evolution of the Political System" in Jon S.T. Quah, Chan Heng Chee and Seah Chee Meow (eds.), *Government and Politics of Singapore* (Singapore: Oxford University Press, 1985), pp. 3–24.

The Westminster parliamentary system is widespread in many former colonial states under British rule. Upon independence, many of these former colonial states adopted this model of government from their British masters. Singapore is a typical example of such a state. In Singapore, the ceremonial head of state is the president and the prime minister is the head of government. Singapore has a unicameral house and since independence in 1965, it has held regular elections to elect members of parliament. As in most typical British democracies, there are three centres of power, namely, the Executive, Legislature and Judiciary. Although the Singapore government is modeled after that of the British, Singapore has introduced several innovations to the system of government leading many to question whether the system of government in place in Singapore today can still be referred to as a Westminster parliamentary system and what are the implications of these innovations to the government and politics of Singapore. The key innovations include the Non-Constituency Member of Parliament (NCMP), Nominated Member of Parliament (NMP), Group Representation Constituencies (GRCs) and the Elected President (EP).

The Non-Constituency Member of Parliament scheme

The NCMP scheme was introduced in 1984 to ensure the inclusion of the Opposition in parliament. Up to three of the 'best losers' in elections could be inducted into parliament as NCMPs with limited voting powers. The rationale of the introduction of this scheme was that the PAP felt that there was the need for debates in parliament, fuelled by the tacit acknowledgement of the impotency of the Opposition to win in general elections. The scheme was meant to provide a 'backdoor entry' for the Opposition into parliament. This system was at first received negatively by Opposition leaders who viewed this arrangement as an insult to the Opposition. However, the Opposition leaders finally accepted the offer after recognising the benefit of being in parliament. NCMPs, while having limited voting powers, are given the opportunity to raise questions in parliament. In January 2016, the government amended the constitution to give NCMPs that will be elected in the next general elections the same voting rights as MPs.[8]

Given that the PAP controls nearly all seats in parliament and that the NCMPs have only limited voting rights, the NCMPs' role is limited to merely being a 'voice'

---

8. Lee Min Kok, "NCMPs to get equal voting rights: 7 things to know about the current scheme", *The Straits Times*, 27 January 2016.

in parliamentary debate. Neither being able to influence the PAP MPs nor having the ability to tip the balance of the arguments, the NCMPs have effectively little impact on the voting patterns in parliament. This effectively makes the NCMP scheme as nothing more than a PAP's pacification of the electorate. The effective message sent by the PAP through this scheme was that if the electorate wanted an opposition in parliament, the PAP would provide it. There was thus no need for the electorate to vote for the Opposition and against the PAP.

This innovation to the parliamentary system was arguably done by the PAP to accommodate the need for a non-threatening Opposition in parliament. First, shocked and later, coming to terms with the electorate's choice in the 1981 by-election and the 1984 General Elections which saw the PAP's complete dominance of parliament broken, the PAP has been alleged to have introduced the scheme for two main purposes. First, since it interpreted the actions of the electorate as a vote of disgruntlement rather than disapproval of the PAP, this scheme would pacify the electorate's desire for alternative voices in parliament. Second, by admitting NCMPs into parliament with limited voting rights, the PAP was implicitly portraying the Opposition as an impotent force that needed the good graces of the PAP. By satisfying the wants of the electorate while holding a firm grip over parliament, the PAP was able to retain its hegemony of the government and politics of Singapore.

There was also the PAP's less known agenda, through a demonstration-effect, of showing the younger voters, who were seen as being attracted to the 'myth of the opposition' what it could and could not do, hoping to douse the attraction for them. As was argued by then Prime Minister Lee Kuan Yew, the younger generation, who had not lived through the 1950s and 1960s, "harboured myths about the role of an Opposition" and "had no idea how destructive an Opposition could be".[9] This was despite his belief that a limited opposition presence could also act as a check and balance against any governmental impropriety.

Reflecting on the NCMP scheme some 25 years later, Prime Minister Lee Hsien Loong noted that following the introduction of the scheme, the new team ministers and MPs concluded that "it was good for the government and good for the Singapore system that we have opposition in Parliament. The opposition members could express opposing views, could question and criticise the government, and

---

9. *Singapore Parliamentary Debates, Official Report* (24 July 1984), vol. 44, cols. 1724–1726.

could make Ministers justify their actions. The opposition provided Mr. Lee [Kuan Yew] and his team a 'foil' or backdrop against which they could set their ideas more clearly in contrast to what was being presented on the other side."[10] As opposition were seen as a good thing, whatever was the outcome in a general elections, there would at least be a certain minimum number of opposition in parliament, be it on their own merit or through the NCMP scheme. The government also believed that the best losers had the right to be in parliament compared to the proportional representation system as "the voters in the constituency which you contested have to have a sufficiently high regard to give you one of the highest votes among the losing candidates."[11] According to Prime Minister Lee, "you have got people who are really personally voting for you. I think that gives you legitimacy...."[12]

Believing that the NCMP scheme has done better than being counterproductive, on 27 January 2016, Singapore's Prime Minister Lee Hsien Loong proposed a constitutional amendment that would alter the status and rights of the NCMPs. The number of NCMPs would be increased from nine to 12 in the next general elections. The NCMPs would also be given the same voting rights as MPs. Clearly, the NCMP scheme is an innovation to the original Westminster parliamentary system. Given that in some cases of Westminster parliamentary systems some MPs are appointed rather than elected, the Singapore case is different as the NCMPs have only limited voting rights and the rationale of their inclusion is certainly in need of further questioning. Rather than serving as an expansion to the plurality of views in parliament, the NCMP scheme is often viewed as an attempt by the PAP to effectively neutralise any potential threat of Opposition members being elected into parliament as full-fledged members.

The Nominated Member of Parliament scheme

The NMP scheme was introduced in 1991 during Goh Chok Tong's tenure as Singapore's prime minister. Outstanding members of the public could be nominated to be non-partisan MPs with limited voting powers. NMPs are to provide feedback,

10. Walter Sim, "PM Lee Hsien Loong: More opposition MPs next GE, equal voting power for NCMPs", *The Straits Times*, 28 January 2016.

11. Ibid.

12. Ibid.

generate debates against MPs and contribute their individual talents and expertise in parliament. The scheme was part of Goh's desire to develop a more consultative form of governance. Realising that there may be talented individuals in society who may shun public office due to the consequences of political life and given Singapore's limited talent pool, the scheme would allow such individuals to serve a two-year term in parliament. Without the need to be a member of any political party and gain direct induction into parliament without the need to contest in elections, it was hoped that more talented individuals would be willing to step forth and serve as NMPs. The introduction of this political innovation was taken in positive light as it allowed for the increase in the diversity of opinion in parliament. However, since NMPs do not represent any political constituency, they too like NCMPs, have limited voting rights. Since its induction in the early 1990s, NMPs, though not directly challenging the PAP hegemony in parliament, have by their own right proved their worth by pushing for certain bills regarding social welfare issues to be passed in parliament.

The Group Representation Constituency scheme

The GRC scheme was first introduced in 1988 and further refined in 1991, 1997 and 2011. The rationale for the introduction of GRCs was to ensure ethnic minority representation in Parliament and enhance administration based on economies of scale.[13] The GRCs, which initially consisted of three-member groups, were later expanded to four-member groups, and later, to a maximum of six-member groups. In the formation of GRCs, it is also stipulated that at least one of the members of the group must be a minority candidate, which means that one of the candidates must be of either Malay, Indian or Eurasian descent. This potential candidate is required to apply to the Elections Department to obtain a certification that confirms the applicant's ethnic minority status.

Singapore's rigid housing quota policies have resulted in ethnic minorities losing their dominant enclaves and hence, the importance of constitutionally instituting minority representation in parliament through the GRC mechanism. Given the current demography of total Chinese electoral majorities in the electoral system, the PAP government was fearful that representatives of ethnic minorities may not be able

---

13. N. Ganesan, "Singapore: Entrenching a City-State's Dominant Party System", *Southeast Asian Affairs, 1998* (Singapore: Institute of Southeast Asian Studies, 1998), p. 230.

to be voted in and hence, be accused of not taking the ethnic minorities' views into consideration. While this action is consistent with the PAP government's pro-multi-ethnic governance, the Opposition has raised its objections against the GRCs. The GRC system is accused of favouring large political parties who have the necessary political machinery and funds to finance a tremendously enlarged constituency. Opposition parties who at the onset are already challenged by their limited talents, manpower and funds, find it difficult to organise a team to contest for a GRC. Even when they do contest in one, the Opposition is fearful of losing the candidates' electoral deposit, which in the 2011 General Elections stood at S$13,000 per candidate. A forfeit of their electoral deposit would certainly create a large dent in any opposition party's funds. Even Goh admitted that GRCs do favour large political parties.

It is common for PAP GRC teams to be anchored by a senior politician with the rest of the team being relatively new faces. This is often perceived as the new PAP candidates 'riding on the tailcoat' of their much senior colleagues, even though it is also an excellent strategic approach to bring new PAP members into parliament. The Opposition, which lacks a large pool of talent, has generally been unwilling to compete head on with senior PAP candidates. For long, key opposition leaders such as Chiam See Tong and Low Thia Khiang preferred to compete in Single Member Constituencies (SMCs) and to their credit, were successful. Still, to the credit of the opposition parties, the 2011 and 2015 general elections were much more vibrant as the Opposition made a credible effort of mounting a large-scale challenge against the PAP across the various GRCs, including succeeding, for the first time, by capturing a GRC at Aljunied. In the 2015 General Elections, the Workers' Party (WP) maintained control of the Aljunied GRC.

The government has also argued that the GRC system has compelled all political parties and MPs to be conscious of the multi-racial character of Singapore. According to Prime Minister Lee Hsien Loong, the GRC system "puts pressure on us [to think of multiracial Singapore] and the PAP but I think it is the right system."[14] For the government, the GRC has an added bonus: it works together with the system of town councils. Due to the linkage between the GRC and town council, Prime Minister Lee argued that it will ensure responsible politics and compel the voters to be realistic:

---

14. See "PM Lee Hsien Loong at the debate on President's Address on 27 January 2016", *The Straits Times*, 27 January 2016.

This makes sure that any party which aspires to form the Government of Singapore first has a chance to demonstrate in a town council what it can or cannot do. And if it can do, that is a base from which it can build and persuade Singaporeans. If it cannot do, it is as well that Singaporeans know this early and everybody is under no illusion.[15]

On 27 January 2016, when the Singapore Prime Minister proposed a series of constitutional changes, he also promised to reduce the size of GRCs and to increase the number of SMCs at the next general elections.

The GRC scheme clearly sets the Singapore model of government apart from the typical Westminster parliamentary system. The enlarged representation is a distinct political innovation that contrasts the traditional SMC which is a defining characteristic of the Westminster system. The electorate is unable to cast its vote for a particular candidate and has no choice but to accept all the candidates in a GRC team or reject the team entirely. Although accepting the merits of the GRC scheme to ensure minority representation, such a system also reduces the relationship between the electorate and its representatives, since the relationship has evolved from individual-to-individual to that of the individual-to-team. A counterargument to this, however, is that the electorate is still able to relate directly with the individual MP as the GRC is merely an electoral mechanism, with the normal MP-to-electorate relationship largely intact and unchanged in every other sense.

The Elected President scheme

The role of the president of Singapore has been traditionally ceremonial. Singapore had four presidents prior to the 1993 Presidential Election, namely, Yusof bin Ishak (1965–1970), Benjamin Sheares (1971–1981), Devan Nair (1981–1985) and Wee Kim Wee (1985–1993). Since 1984, with the Opposition's success in breaking the PAP's complete control of parliament, the ruling party began to seek active ways to limit the intrusion of the Opposition and neutralise its impact on Singapore politics. Chief amongst the PAP concern was to safeguard its vast national reserves in the event an irresponsible government came into power in Singapore (read Opposition). By 1991, the PAP government released a *White Paper* stating the

---

15. Ibid.

establishment of an Elected President (EP) tasked with the duty to guard Singapore's financial reserves. The analogy given from the EP was that a 'two-key' mechanism was needed for release of the Singapore's reserves. The prime minister as the head of government would hold one key while the EP would hold the second key to the lock.

However, the EP was greeted with much cynicism when Ong Teng Cheong, a long-time PAP deputy prime minister (DPM), resigned from the party to contest in the first EP in 1993. Although there was a contestation for the post in 1993, the other contender, Chua Kim Yeow, was very much a reluctant candidate, pushed into action "after some arm-twisting by PAP stalwarts Goh Keng Swee and Richard Hu."[16] The inaugural election appeared very much as a staged event and the general public did not receive the entire EP scheme with much enthusiasm as well.

To the credit of Ong as the newly elected EP, he was pushing for a much clearer role of the EP. Ong was at odds with his former colleagues over the level of information and authority over Singapore's reserves that he should have as the EP. Not surprisingly, the PAP government in 1994 began to cull the powers of the EP. In the later years of Ong's tenure, the differences that he had with the PAP government over the role, functions and independence of the EP intensified and were widely covered in the local press.[17] These disagreements and contestations between Ong and his former colleagues further diminished Ong's possibility of seeking a second term as the EP. However, Ong did not seek a second term due to ill health and the office of the EP was won uncontested by S.R. Nathan, a distinguished civil servant and former diplomat with close ties with the PAP leadership. Nathan held the office for two consecutive terms. Following Nathan, Tony Tan, another former DPM, won the presidential election albeit narrowly in 2011.

---

16. R.S. Milne and Diane K. Mauzy, *Singapore Politics under the People's Action Party* (London, UK: Routledge, 2002), p. 153.

17. In 2019, during the launch of his memoirs in Mandarin, when asked of any regrets during his tenure as prime minister, Goh Chok Tong referred to the clash his government had with Ong Teng Cheong. Ong wanted information on national assets that made up Singapore's reserves. In hindsight Goh concluded that "had we worked the system a bit better, I think we could have avoided that. Put it this way, the presidency ended up on a sour note because of that experience." See Cara Wong, "Singapore must have strong ruling party with clear majority: Goh Chok Tong", *The Straits Times*, 27 May 2019.

The EP, in essence, is clearly an innovation of the Singapore's government. However, the PAP, by limiting the discretionary powers of the EP has reduced the role of the EP and returned the role of the presidency to that of a predominantly ceremonial role. Even though the EP can act robustly under certain circumstances, this is something that has never been exercised and is yet to be tested. With a set of stringent criteria in place for the selection of EP candidates, few are able to fulfill the requirements and those who do, are mostly linked in one way or another to the PAP government. Moreover, the EP is compelled to accept the advice of the Council of Presidential Advisers, a committee appointed by the PAP government, essentially a check by the executive on the EP.

While for long, the PAP and probably the public assumed that the EP was a position created for the PAP to stamp its dominance on national politics, it came as a shock when its candidate for the presidential election in August 2011 was almost defeated. Four candidates, almost all, linked to the government in one way or another, contested and the former DPM, Tony Tan, essentially the PAP's candidate, only garnered 35.2% of the total votes. His closest rival, the highly popular Tan Cheng Bock, a former PAP MP, garnered 34.85% of the total votes. The other two candidates, Tan Jee Say and Tan Kin Lian, secured 25.04% and 4.91% of the total votes, respectively. While the public anger with the PAP, first expressed in the May 2011 General Elections was now translated into anti-PAP sentiments in the presidential election, it also signaled that Singapore and Singaporeans had politically arrived and the PAP could no longer take its dominance for granted.

On 27 January 2016, Singapore's Prime Minister Lee Hsien Loong proposed a constitutional amendment that would alter the status and rights of the EP. While the president would remain an elected office, a Constitutional Commission made up of nine members and chaired by the Chief Justice, would review three key areas relating to the EP. The three areas include: "updating the eligibility criteria for presidential candidates, strengthening the Council of Presidential Advisers and ensuring minorities have a chance to be elected."[18] The report of the commission had to be submitted quickly as Singapore's presidential election was due in August

---

18. Zakir Hussain, "Changes to political system to prepare Singapore for long term", *The Straits Times*, 28 January 2016.

2017. In 2017, Singapore conducted its first 'hiatus-triggered' EP election with Halimah Yacob as the first minority president via the route.

Analysis

By examining the four political innovations to Singapore's political system, it is undeniable that the current system differs from the system that was established in 1965. These institutional changes have altered the nature of elected representatives, created the degrees of differences between full-fledged MPs, NMPs and NCMPs and most importantly, differentiated the voting rights of each category. The NMP and NCMP schemes, although being new channels of representation and having increased the plurality of opinion in parliament, have limited impact on the decision-making process in Singapore. Due to the nature of PAP's hegemony in parliament and the constitutional constraints of NMP and NCMP voting rights, the powers of decision making still rest in the firm grip of PAP hands.

On the note of the GRCs, they are a distinct contrast to the typical SMCs of a Westminster parliamentary system. The key impact of the GRCs on the political system is the increase of disproportionate representation of the electorate in parliament. Traditionally, the first-past-the-post electoral system in Westminster parliamentary systems has been argued to produce a disproportionate representation in parliament. The number of seats a political party may win in parliament is not proportionate to the percentage of popular votes it receives. The GRC scheme further increases this disproportion, as the stakes in each enlarged constituency is no longer a single seat in parliament but may be as high as six seats in parliament.

At the same time, the EP appears to be moving the Singapore's parliamentary system into that of a hybrid system, that is, a combination of a presidential and parliamentary systems. In a full parliamentary system, the powers of the state rest in the hands of the prime minister and his cabinet. With the introduction of the EP, at least potentially, an alternative centre of power has been created in the Singapore system. Although the EP's powers are confined to the state's financial reserves, the huge size of Singapore's financial reserves makes it an important and critical appointment. The PAP government has, however, been reducing the powers of the EP immediately after it was instituted. This may be due to differences of the first directly elected EP, Ong Teng Cheong, and his former PAP colleagues over the management of Singapore's reserves, the status of the EP as an independent institution, or the position of the EP as PAP's final line of defence against a 'rogue' government. Nonetheless, due to these issues and controversies over the independence and role of the EP, marred by the apparent lack of real contestation for the post, the EP has been viewed by many as yet another mechanism of the PAP's entrenchment and control of Singapore's politics.

SINGAPORE'S ELECTORAL HISTORY, 1948–2015

Introduction

The concept of governance involves the notion of those who govern and those who are governed. Good governance fundamentally involves a theory of representation whereby the governed has the right to be represented often by a candidate of their choice. Elections and voting are closely linked to the understanding of the importance of representation in governance. In Singapore, political elections have been held since the Legislative Council elections in 1948. Prior to the Republic's independence in 1965, Singapore had a series of Legislative Assembly elections that contributed to the political education and experience of both the political parties and the electorate. It was during this period that Singapore saw the emergence and growth of many political parties. Upon independence in 1965, the Republic has conducted frequent general elections for parliament, the highest representative body in the city-state. The last being in September 2015 with the political forces now in the throes of readying for the next one. Beside parliamentary elections, Singapore has also carried out presidential elections since the introduction of the Elected President in 1993.

Presently the parliament has two different types of electoral divisions, the Single Member Constituencies (SMCs) and the Group Representation Constituencies (GRCs). There are 13 SMCs and 16 GRCs. In the current parliament, the GRCs vary from four to six seats totaling 76 parliamentary seats. The number of SMCs and GRCs has been changing since the GRC system was first introduced in 1988. In the 2011 General Elections, the PAP was returned to power with 81 seats with the Opposition, namely, the Workers' Party (WP) winning six seats. The WP won a five-member GRC of Aljunied and retained its SMC seat of Hougang. At the same time, due to the introduction of two other categories of members of parliament (MPs), namely, the Non-Constituency Member of Parliament (NCMP) and Nominated Member of Parliament (NMP), there were also seats allocated accordingly. In fact, the WP won two NCMP seats and another went to the SPP. In two by-elections held after the 2011 General Elections, the WP retained its Hougang SMC and added an additional seat of Punggol East SMC, becoming the most successful Opposition in Singapore's history since 1965. In the 2015 General Elections, the PAP won 83 seats with the WP winning six seats as well as three NCMP seats. The PAP also won a by-election following the resignation of its member in May 2016.

In the history of Singapore's elections, it is possible to disaggregate the electoral history into three distinct phases as follows: Phase 1 (1948–1967): Emergence of political parties and vibrant elections; Phase 2 (1968–1980): PAP's total hegemony at the polls; and Phase 3 (1981–2015): Reinvigorated Opposition. Each of these three phases displays distinct characteristics which have coloured the history of elections in Singapore.

Phase 1 (1948–1967): Emergence of political parties and vibrant elections

The dawn of political parties in Singapore began after the Second World War. The tumultuous years of war and the Japanese Occupation stirred political consciousness amongst the local population. With the desire of the British colonial masters to grant a certain degree of participation to the populace, local elections were first held for a partially elected legislature in 1948. These local elections paved the way for increased participation leading to self-government and a fully elected legislature by 1959 (Table 4.1). In the early 1960s, Singapore held a crucial referendum regarding the desire to merge with the then Malaya.

Table 4.1:	Singapore's Electoral Power, 1948–2015			
Year	**Party**	**Seats Contested**	**Seats Won**	**% Votes**
1948	PP	6	3	49.5
1951	PP	9	6	45.5
1955	LF	25	10	26.7
1959	PAP	51	43	53.4
1963	PAP	51	37	46.4
1968	PAP	58	58	84.4
1972	PAP	65	65	69.0
1976	PAP	69	69	72.4
1980	PAP	75	75	75.5
1984	PAP	79	77	62.9

(Continued)

Table 4.1: (*Continued*)

Year	Party	Seats Contested	Seats Won	% Votes
1988	PAP	81	80	61.7
1991	PAP	81	77	59.3
1997	PAP	83	81	63.5
2001	PAP	84	82	75.3
2006	PAP	84	82	66.6
2011	PAP	87	81	60.1
2015	PAP	89	83	69.8

Source: Author.

An important event, the merger and eventual separation, has severely impacted on the political developments and political culture of the Republic which is still evident to this day.

The political parties that emerged in the late 1940s and 1950s, clearly developed identities along social class structures. From leftist political parties such as the banned Malayan Communist Party to the left-leaning parties of the likes of the Labour Front (LF) and the more centrist party of the PAP, political parties in Singapore have their roots in typical ideological-based parties. While there were ethnic nationalist parties such as the *Persatuan Melayu Singapura* (Singapore Malay Association) in Singapore, the dominant parties, those who drew tremendous support tended to be those which had appealing ideologies to the post-war electorate. For example, in the Legislative Assembly elections of 1955, in which the LF emerged as the leading political party with 10 out of 25 elected seats, the main issues were regarding democracy, self-government, emergency regulations, education, housing and trade (see Table 4.1). Chief amongst the electoral issues were the directions available for complete independence. The LF's success and its ability to form a coalition with elements of the Alliance Party in Singapore warranted the invitation by the Colony's Governor to David Marshall to form the government.

In the 1959 General Elections for the first fully elected Legislative Assembly in Singapore, the PAP emerged as the dominant political party in Singapore. Winning 43 out of 51 seats, the PAP was in a commanding position to steer Singapore into the next stage of its desire for independence. The PAP, with a mix of English-educated intellectuals and left-leaning members, had a combination of visionary leadership as well as the ability to mobilise, in particular, the Chinese-educated workers.

However, the cooperation between the moderates and the pro-communists in the PAP was short-lived and by early 1961, the pro-communist faction broke away from the PAP to form the *Barisan Sosialis* or the Socialist Front. This posed a great challenge to the PAP as the defections of left-leaning PAP assemblymen left the PAP with a single seat majority in the Legislative Assembly. The PAP under the moderates clanged to power by controlling 26 seats while those opposing it led by the *Barisan Sosialis* had 25 seats. Despite the odds, the PAP pushed forth its proposal for Singapore to merge with Malaya. The left-leaning political parties were strongly against this proposal and it was mainly due to this disagreement that led to the breakup of the PAP in the first place. As Malaya had just successfully ended the Emergency, marking the Malayan Government's 12-year struggle against the communists, the *Barisan Sosialis* understandably feared for its existence in the Federation of Malaysia, as it was also labeled a pro-communist organisation. The victory in the merger referendum held in September 1962 gave the PAP the mandate to steer Singapore into Malaysia in which it did in 1963. In that year, the PAP faced its strongest challenge by the *Barisan Sosialis* in the Legislative Assembly elections. The PAP, despite numerous defections and loss of its machineries to mobilise, in particular, the Chinese working class, managed to return to office with 37 out of 51 seats and winning 47% of the popular votes.

Although the PAP remained in office, merger with Malaysia was short-lived. By 1965, Singapore peacefully seceded from the Federation of Malaysia and became an independent and sovereign state. The electoral contestation during this period was extremely vibrant and tough. This period of electoral history is important as it marked the beginning of Singapore's political system. The tumultuous events during this period, ranging from racial riots, political extremism and the failure of merger left indelible deep marks on the polity and politics of Singapore which remain up to this day.

Phase 2 (1968–1980): PAP's total hegemony at the polls

The second phase of Singapore's electoral history saw the PAP consolidating its grip over politics in Singapore as a result of its full and unbroken control of parliament from 1968 to 1981. The PAP's total victories at the polls were not due to the absence of political opposition but clearly something else which attracted the electorate to the PAP. The *Barisan Sosialis* after the 1963 Legislative Assembly elections had begun to adopt a strategy to disengage the PAP in parliament. This strategy culminated in the total boycott of the 1968 General Elections. The move which aimed to bring the 'fight' out into the streets was met with sufficient force of the law. However, the *Barisan Sosialis'* action to discredit the institution of elections and indirectly the PAP was unsuccessful. Although the WP and some other independent candidates contested in the general elections, the Opposition's presence was barely felt as the PAP was returned to power on Nomination Day by winning 51 of 58 seats by walkovers. The PAP secured approximately 87% of the popular vote for the remaining seven contested seats. Thus, this began the PAP's total domination of parliament for the next three general elections (namely, in 1972, 1976 and 1980).

The 1972 General Elections proved to be more interesting. The opposition parties only allowed the PAP walkovers in eight of the now expanded 65-seat parliament on Nomination Day. The chief oppositional forces were the United National Front and the WP which contested in 33 and 27 seats, respectively. The *Barisan Sosialis* returned to electoral contestation by competing in 10 wards. However, despite the presence of a significant opposition in the elections, the PAP was successful in keeping out the Opposition from parliament by winning all seats with 69% of the popular vote. This continued as the trend, with the PAP winning all the seats in the 1976 and 1980 general elections.

This period of electoral history that saw the parliamentary consolidation of the PAP gives rise to the fundamental question of what enabled the PAP to achieve such astounding victories. Was all this because of the *Barisan Sosialis'* failed attempt to delegitimise the 1968 General Elections that gave the PAP full control of parliament and how the PAP in power, managed to engineer its subsequent successes? Or did the PAP, when given the complete power to govern Singapore in 1968, capitalise on the situation and provided effective, efficient and growth-oriented governance that won it the approval of the general electorate? While historical evidence tends to support the latter suggestion, it is undeniable that the PAP's incumbency facilitated its growth as a hegemonic political party and enriched its political capacity to bring about its subsequent victories at the general elections. Arguably, this phase of the PAP's complete dominance of politics in Singapore enabled it to pursue its policies with no opposition. Policies and bills were able to be passed with ease in parliament, and the constancy of the PAP in office enabled its leaders to follow through policies to eventually achieve its desired goal. It was also during this phase that Singapore underwent drastic transformation. Singapore's economic growth and social stability can also be traced to PAP policies implemented from the late 1960s to the early 1980s.

Phase 3 (1981–2015): PAP's hegemony amidst the rise of a weak opposition

From 1968 to 1980, the PAP had the luxury of enjoying total victories in four consecutive parliamentary general elections. The party's share of popular votes had been rising and it appeared that the challenge that was mounted by the Opposition began to wane as evident from the number of seats each political party was able to contest. However, the PAP's privilege of maintaining an exclusive membership in parliament ended after 1980. The first Opposition presence came in the 1981 parliamentary by-election. Following this, in every subsequent general elections the opposition parties managed to maintain a token presence in parliament with the 2011 General Elections being a watershed in the Opposition's success. Although the opposition parties lost, they managed to retain, for a long time, their stranglehold on two SMC wards, Hougang and Potong Pasir. In 2011, while Potong Pasir was lost to the PAP, the Opposition made its first breakthrough in a GRC.

The 1981 Anson by-election came about due to the resignation of Devan Nair as the MP for Anson. There was a three-cornered fight between the PAP, WP and United People's Front. Despite efforts by many senior PAP members such as Goh Chok Tong and Ong Teng Cheong to assist the PAP candidate Pang Kim Hin, the victory eventually went to long-time opposition leader J.B. Jeyaretnam of the WP. Jeyaretnam's success marked the end of the era of PAP's complete control of all seats in parliament. The Opposition's new fervour was again rewarded in the 1984 General Elections when the WP managed to retain the Anson seat and the Singapore Democratic Party candidate, Chiam See Tong won in Potong Pasir. In 1988, the Opposition lost all except the Potong Pasir seat. In 1991, adopting a 'by-election' strategy, where the Opposition conceded sufficient seats to the PAP to be returned as the government on nomination day, the Opposition succeeded in winning four parliamentary seats.

While the Opposition had tried to implement the 'by-election' strategy in subsequent general elections in 1997 and 2001, the results had not been encouraging, with the Opposition holding on only to its Hougang and Potong Pasir seats. In the

2006 General Elections, the first under a new prime minister, Lee Hsien Loong, the 'by-election' strategy was not pursued by the Opposition but intensified its all-round challenge to the PAP. While the Opposition only retained its two seats, its overall performance was impressive, signposting of what was to come, especially with the WP doing relatively well wherever its candidates contested. The WP's losing candidate for the Aljunied GRC was offered the NCMP seat. It suggested that there was a renewed rejuvenation in the Opposition and this was fully realised in the 2011 General Elections with the WP winning six parliamentary and two NCMP seats, with another NCMP seat going to the SPP. This meant, for the first time in the history of independent Singapore, there was a presence of nine members on the opposition bench. Later, a 10th was added with the WP's victory in the Punggol East by-election in 2013. In the 2015 General Elections, the PAP performed admirably well. Even though there was an all-round dip in support for the Opposition, the WP managed to retain the Aljunied GRC and Hougang SMC seats even though it lost the Punggol East SMC. Hence, despite the hegemonic presence of the PAP, there was also a concomitant ascendancy of the Opposition in Singapore's politics in line with the increasing democratisation phenomenon taking place worldwide.

SEEDS OF THE PEOPLE'S ACTION PARTY'S HEGEMONY: THE IMPORTANCE OF THE 1955, 1959 AND 1963 LEGISLATIVE ASSEMBLY ELECTIONS

Introduction

While Chapter 4 on the electoral history of Singapore vividly made it evident that the People's Action Party (PAP) has been in power on a continuous basis from 1959 onwards and won every general elections (including the legislative elections in 1959 and 1963), until the latest one in 2015, the actual seeds of the PAP's political hegemony and dominance can be found in the pre-1965 period. For this, one needs to understand and appreciate the PAP's role, participation and what it stood for since the 1955 Legislative Assembly elections and the subsequent two, namely in 1959 and 1963, wherein the seeds of the PAP's political dominance in Singapore can be found. Had the PAP's fortunes in the three legislative elections been different, it is highly unlikely that the PAP would have been in the dominant position it finds itself today.

The 1955 General Elections

Singapore held its 1955 General Elections on 2 April 1955. It was a turning point for the nascent state's political journey, given that for the first time in its history, "a majority of legislators" was voted into office by the general public rather than being appointed by the British colonisers as was the case following the 1948 and 1951 elections.[1] This was among several changes that had resulted from the Rendel Constitution. Other reviews made to the existing system of governance in Singapore included "automating" the list of eligible voters, substituting the "Legislative Council" for the "Legislative Assembly", having a nine-minister "council", mandating

---

1. Cheryl Sim, "People's Action Party: Pre-independence years", in *Singapore Infopedia*, National Library Board (2015), http://eresources.nlb.gov.sg/infopedia/articles/ SIP_2015-02-04_094340.html

the Assembly to appoint a Speaker not part of itself and drawing the "electoral boundaries" to form 25 constituencies.[2]

As a result, the 1955 General Elections was the first in which the PAP and Labour Front (LF) had contested, alongside four other political parties, namely, the Progressive Party (PP), Democratic Party (DP), Singapore Alliance (SA) and Labour Party (LP). While only 25 seats in the Legislative Assembly were up for contest, there were 79 candidates, of which, 10 were independent and the rest belonged to the aforementioned political parties.[3] Out of the 300,199 voters that made up the electorate, only 52.7% casted their votes.[4] Yet, this was a spike in the number of voters in the 1955 Legislative Assembly elections; almost five times of that in the previous 1951 Legislative Assembly elections.[5]

The PP had the largest number of candidates, totalling 22 and had even won six seats in the previous Legislative Council.[6] Given these factors, the 1955 Legislative Assembly elections were expected to favour the PP, especially as it was also favoured by the British colonisers over others as most of its members were 'English-educated professional elites'.[7] The PP contested on a platform to "localise civil service"; provide — without charge — six years of "bilingual education" for children aged six onwards; deliver enhanced "medical services" with no fee or increase in "income tax"; and establish a "government housing authority" to make owning a house more affordable for the people.[8] However, the PP only won four seats, in Bukit Panjang, Paya Lebar, Serangoon and Tanglin.[9]

---

2. Lim Tin Seng, "1955 Legislative Assembly general election", in *Singapore Infopedia, National Library Board* (2014), http://eresources.nlb.gov.sg/infopedia/articles/SIP_2014-07-07_134339.html

3. Ibid.

4. "Legislative Assembly General Election 1955", in *Singapore Elections*, http://www.singapore-elections.com/general-election/1955/

5. Lim Tin Seng, "1955 Legislative Assembly general election".

6. Ibid.

7. Ibid.

8. Ibid.

9. "1955 Legislative Assembly General Election results", in *Elections Department Singapore*, http://www.eld.gov.sg/elections_past_parliamentary1955.html

The DP had the second largest number of candidates. In contrast to the PP, the DP candidates were largely Chinese-educated members and had the financial support of the 'wealthy Chinese', including the Singapore Chamber of Commerce.[10] The party contested on the manifesto of promoting the legislature and education system for "all races" and advocated "free trade" and "investment".[11] It also championed the need for more affordable housing through "housing development schemes".[12] The party won two seats at Changi and Tiong Bahru.

The PAP appeared to be a political party in between the PP and DP in terms of policies, being made up of 'English-educated' elites and prominent 'Chinese-educated trade unionists'.[13] The PAP championed the cause of "immediate independence" for Singapore and called for mandatory, free education for children up to 16 years old. It had also called for the abolition of "Emergency Regulations" and for a review of the Trade Unions Ordinance to permit "unions to set up political funds".[14] The PAP also brought up the idea of a Workers' Charter that had included the proposition for "minimum wage", welfare handouts for the unemployed, "equal pay" across genders, 14 days of annual leave, legitimising medical leave, funded-maternity leave and "workers' compensation".[15] Additionally, the party proposed an "economic policy" that would spur the expansion of local producers.[16] Being a new political party and a contender for the first time, the PAP appeared to be largely aspiring to be a credible opposition party. It fielded four candidates and won three, namely at Tanjong Pagar, Punggol-Tampines and Bukit Timah. Lee Kuan Yew won in Tanjong Pagar and Lim Chin Siong won in Bukit Timah, with Lee representing the 'Western-educated' elite and Lim, a leading trade unionist, representing the 'left-wing'.[17]

---

10. Ibid.

11. Ibid.

12. Ibid.

13. Ibid.

14. Ibid.

15. Ibid.

16. Ibid.

17. "Singapore Legislative Assembly General Election 1955, Bukit Timah", in *Singapore Elections*, http://www.singapore-elections.com/general-election/1955/bukit-timah.html

The SA, made up of members from the United Malays National Organisation (UMNO), the Malayan Chinese Association, and the Malay Union, was the mirror image of the Alliance Party in power in Malaya. The party championed the need for affordable housing via a "government housing trust", compulsory but free education for children, and greater medical services, but also the safeguarding and building of "local industries".[18] Like the PAP, it also wanted complete self-governance rather than one that was shared with the British as well as a reform in the Trade Unions Ordinance such that unions could "set up political funds".[19] Of its five candidates, three won in the constituency of Pasir Panjang, Southern Islands and Ulu Bedok.[20]

The LF and the PAP appeared to be similar parties as far as programmes were concerned. Like the PAP, the LF competed in the 1955 Legislative Assembly elections without expecting to dominate the domestic political scene. Both the PAP and LF wanted to establish themselves as a strong political opposition. In terms of policies, both had wanted immediate self-rule. The LF also advocated for social welfare handouts including unemployment benefits, housing subsidies, more affordable healthcare, and a price floor for "wages".[21] The LF supported the abolishing of the "Emergency Regulations" and reviewing of the Trade Unions Ordinance to grant unions the space to "organise" and "set up political funds".[22] Unexpectedly the LF won 10 seats at Cairnhill, Geylang, Havelock, Farrer Park, Kampong Kapor, Katong, Rochore, Queenstown, Stamford and Whampoa. The LF leader, David Marshall became Singapore's first chief minister.[23] There were also 10 candidates who contested as independents. Two of them were voted to the Legislative Assembly. Ahmad Ibrahim won in Sembawang and R. Jumabhoy won in Seletar.[24]

---

18. Lim Tin Seng, "1955 Legislative Assembly general election".

19. Ibid.

20. "1955 Legislative Assembly General Election results".

21. Lim Tin Seng, "1955 Legislative Assembly general election".

22. Ibid.

23. Cheryl Sim, "People's Action Party: Pre-independence years".

24. "1955 Legislative Assembly General Election results".

The 1959 General Elections

The 1959 General Elections was held on 30 May, where 51 seats were contested in the Legislative Assembly.[25] This was twice the number of seats contested in the 1955 General Elections and the number of voters increased to 590,000.[26] In addition to the 35 independent candidates, the rest came from 13 political parties with the PAP offering 51, the Singapore People's Alliance (SPA) 39, Liberal Socialists 32, and 38 others from 10 other parties.[27] While the 1955 General Elections was held under the Rendel Constitution, the 1959 General Elections were carried out under the 1958 State of Singapore Constitution. This constitution granted Singapore the freedom of self-rule, an elected *Yang di-Pertuan Negara* or head of state, as well as complete jurisdiction over the Legislative Assembly, although the British continued to intervene where domestic security and defence were concerned.[28]

Apart from the sheer increase in participation, the 1959 General Elections also saw a more intense campaigning from the different political parties as compared to the 1955 General Elections. Despite being only an opposition with three seats in the previous Legislative Assembly, in 1959 the PAP decided to contest all seats by fielding 51 candidates and asserting that it had the capacity and ability to give to the nation "a stable, honest, and just government, which could be truly called the government of the people for the people."[29] The party also compared its growing strength to the increasing factionalism within the other parties, arguing that the success of the PAP was due to its uncompromising hold onto its "political beliefs"

25. "194 to contest 51 seats", *The Straits Times*, 26 April 1959, http://eresources.nlb.gov.sg/newspapers/Digitised/Article/straitstimes19590426-1.2.2

26. "The day of decision", *The Straits Times*, 30 May 1959, http://eresources.nlb.gov.sg/newspapers/Digitised/Article/straitstimes19590530-1.2.2

27. "1959 Legislative Assembly General Election, 30th May 1959", in *History SG*, http://eresources.nlb.gov.sg/history/events/bad3de1d-21ce-48de-99b6-6e717e47328e#4

28. "1959 Legislative Assembly General Election, 29th May 1959", in *History SG*, http://eresources.nlb.gov.sg/history/events/bad3de1d-21ce-48de-99b6-6e717e47328e#1

29. "PAP leader: We can give an honest government", *The Straits Times*, 29 April 1959, http://eresources.nlb.gov.sg/newspapers/Digitised/Article/straitstimes19590429-1.2.4

that were in the best interest of the people.[30] The other political parties like the Liberal Socialists[31] and SPA[32] in turn responded by accusing the PAP of employing Communist tactics and ways, thus subjugating the people and denying them the right to individual freedom.

Despite the significant increase in number of participating political parties and seats available for contestation, the profiles of the winners were not as diverse: they were either from the PAP, the SPA, UMNO, or an independent candidate. From its 39 candidates, the SPA won three seats, in Cairnhill, Joo Chiat and Mountbatten. Lim Yew Hock was one of its notable winners. The *Pertubuhan Kebangsaan Melayu Singapura* (PKMS, also known as Singapore UMNO) won four seats, in Geylang Serai, Kampong Kembangan, Southern Islands and Tanglin. Only one independent candidate, A.P. Rajah, won in the 1959 General Elections, namely, in Farrer Park. In every other constituency, the PAP swept to victory. Compared to 1955, in the 1959 General Elections, the party had a landslide victory, winning 43 out of 51 seats, and so went on to become the ruling party. Some of the key victories included Lee Kuan Yew's win in Tanjong Pagar, Hoe Puay Choo in Bras Basah, Kenneth Byrne in Crawford, Chan Choy Siong in Delta, Ong Eng Guan in Hong Lim, Chan Chee Seng in Jalan Besar, S. Rajaratnam in Kampong Glam, Goh Keng Swee in Kreta Ayer, Toh Chin Chye in Rochore, Wong Soon Fong in Toa Payoh and Sheng Nam Chin in Nee Soon.[33] The overwhelming support for the PAP led then Chief Minister Lim Yew Hock along with the other ministers to resign from the government on 1 June 1959, passing the mandate of government to Lee Kuan Yew, PAP's secretary-general, who assumed the position of Singapore's first prime minister.[34]

---

30. Ibid.

31. "Lib-Soc candidate accuses PAP of Red methods", *The Straits Times*, 13 May 1959, http://eresources.nlb.gov.sg/newspapers/Digitised/Article/straitstimes19590513-1.2.63

32. "Lim: PAP still rides Red tiger", *The Straits Times*, 30 May 1959, http://eresources.nlb.gov.sg/newspapers/Digitised/Article/straitstimes19590530-1.2.98

33. "Legislative Assembly General Election 1959", in *Singapore Elections*, http://www.singapore-elections.com/general-election/1959/

34. "1959 Legislative Assembly General Election, 29th May 1959".

The 1963 General Elections

The third and final Legislative Assembly elections for Singapore was held on 21 September 1963 and was called on a "short notice"[35] by Lee Kuan Yew, who was the then prime minister. For him and the PAP, it came at an opportune time — just five days after the PAP had successfully led Singapore to merge with the Federation of Malaya on 16 September, collectively becoming the Federation of Malaysia. For the 1963 Legislative Assembly elections, there were 51 seats up for grabs. There were 16 independent candidates[36] as well as seven competing political parties that included the PAP (fielded 51 candidates)[37], the *Barisan Sosialis* (fielded 46 candidates)[38], the United People's Party (fielded 42 candidates)[39], the SA, which was a coalition of the SPA, the UMNO, the Malayan Chinese Association, and the Malayan Indian Congress (fielded 42 candidates)[40], the *Partai Rakyat* (fielded four candidates)[41], the Pan-Malayan Islamic Party (fielded two candidates)[42] and the Workers' Party (fielded three candidates)[43]. While the PAP contested in all 51 seats, it only won

---

35. Stephanie Ho, "History of general elections in Singapore", in *Singapore Infopedia* (National Library Board: 1 September 2014), http://eresources.nlb.gov.sg/infopedia/articles/SIP_549_2004-12-28.html

36. "Legislative Assembly General Election 1963, Ratings", in *Singapore Elections*, http://www.singapore-elections.com/general-election/1963/ratings.html

37. "People's Action Party", in *Singapore Elections*, http://www.singapore-elections.com/political-parties/pap.html

38. "Barisan Sosialis", in *Singapore Elections*, http://www.singapore-elections.com/political-parties/barisan.html

39. "United People's Party", in *Singapore Elections*, http://www.singapore-elections.com/political-parties/upp.html

40. "Alliance Party Singapura — Singapore Alliance", in *Singapore Elections*, http://www.singapore-elections.com/political-parties/sa.html

41. "Partai Rakyat, Singapore State Division", in *Singapore Elections*, http://www.singapore-elections.com/political-parties/pr.html

42. "Angkatan Islam Singapura — Pan-Malayan Islamic Party", in *Singapore Elections*, http://www.singapore-elections.com/political-parties/ai-pmip.html

43. "Workers' Party", in *Singapore Elections*, http://www.singapore-elections.com/political-parties/wp.html

in 37 constituencies, six less than in 1959. Ong Eng Guan, who was expelled from the PAP, managed to continue representing the Hong Lim constituency as he did in the previous elections but in a new party, the United People's Party (UPP). The remaining 13 seats in the Legislative Assembly were won by the *Barisan Sosialis*.

Out of the seven political parties that contested in the 1963 General Elections, only three were represented in the Legislative Assembly, namely, the PAP, the UPP, and the *Barisan Sosialis*. The *Barisan Sosialis* was made up of 13 former PAP members who were dismissed from the party, and the single representing candidate for the UPP, Ong Eng Guan, was also a previous member of the PAP. Ong was part of the PAP but was expelled in 1960, on grounds of disavowing the "principles of collective leadership", along with two others in the Assembly who had sided with him.[44] Ong then formed the UPP in 1961 after he had won in the Hong Lim constituency by-election despite being dismissed from the PAP.[45] Even though the UPP contested in 42 constituencies, only Ong won in the 1963 General Elections.[46]

The *Barisan Sosialis* was formed after the 13 members from the PAP were expelled. Lim Chin Siong and Lee Siew Choh, who were part of the 13, then formed the *Barisan Sosialis*, which is noted as the most formidable opposition to the PAP even till date.[47] Even though the 1963 General Elections was the first that the party contested in, it fielded a total of 46 candidates to compete for the 51 seats, and it won 13 seats.[48] The *Barisan Sosialis* won in Bukit Merah, Bukit Panjang, Bukit Timah, Choa Chu Kang, Crawford, Havelock, Jalan Kayu, Jurong, Nee Soon, Paya Lebar, Tampines, Thomson and Toa Payoh.[49]

---

44. "Ong: The full story", *The Straits Times*, 21 June 1960, http://eresources.nlb.gov.sg/newspapers/Digitised/Article/straitstimes19600621-1.2.2

45. Jamie Koh, "Ong Eng Guan", in *Singapore Infopedia* (National Library Board: 2016), http://eresources.nlb.gov.sg/infopedia/articles/SIP_2013-07-12_154519.html

46. "1963 Parliamentary Election Results", in *Elections Department Singapore*, http://www.eld.gov.sg/elections_past_parliamentary1963.html

47. "Barisan Sosialis", in *Singapore Elections*, http://www.singapore-elections.com/political-parties/barisan.html

48. Ibid.

49. "1963 Parliamentary Election results", in *Elections Department Singapore*, http://www.eld.gov.sg/elections_past_parliamentary1963.html

While the PAP won 43 seats in the previous general elections, this number dropped to just 41 seats by the end of the two by-elections in April and July 1961.[50] The two by-election losses in 1961 as well as the intra-party factionalism were a series of blows to the party's initial confidence in 1959. The PAP timed the 1963 General Elections to coincide with Singapore's merger with the Federation of Malaya as those who favoured merger were also predisposed to vote for the PAP and not the *Barisan Sosialis*, which opposed merger. Some have argued that the 1963 General Elections was the PAP's most tumultuous and "toughest election battle in history".[51] This was because there were three other parties that had fielded over 40 candidates, a sizable number to threaten the PAP's position as the government. The PAP, however, managed to garner 46.9% of popular votes, which translated to it having won a two-thirds majority as the government.[52]

Significance of the 1955, 1959 and 1963 Legislative Assembly elections for the PAP

The 1955 Legislative Assembly elections were significant from a number of perspectives. The elections can be viewed as the herald of a more politically active and conscious population, highlighting a growing appetite for decolonisation and self-governance. With the significant jump in the number of voters who had participated in the elections that year, it became clear that the people knew for themselves whom they had wanted to be governed by, thus implying that the elected was all the more obligated to fulfil their duties and promises to the people. This included providing affordable housing, paving the way for a higher "standard of living", generating economic growth, ensuring that the public service had sufficient manpower, providing for greater social welfare, and making education more inclusive.[53]

---

50. "Legislative Assembly By-Election July 1961 seats", in *Singapore Elections*, http://www.singapore-elections.com/by-election/1961-7/seats.html

51. "Legislative Assembly General Election 1963", in *Singapore Elections*, http://www.singapore-elections.com/general-election/1963/

52. "People's Action Party", in *Singapore Elections*, http://www.singapore-elections.com/political-parties/pap.html

53. Lim Tin Seng, "1955 Legislative Assembly general election".

The ruling LF, however, was faced with many challenges. Its determination for immediate and "complete" self-rule was not well received by the British, and the pro-communists in Singapore also disrupted stability and order through strikes and demonstrations.[54] This resulted in intra-party factionalism in almost all political parties and even David Marshall was forced to resign as chief minister on 7 June 1956. Despite this quick descent for the party, the LF had nonetheless made several noteworthy political contributions that Singapore continues to hold on till today. More specifically, Marshall implemented and conducted 'meet-the-people sessions', promoted 'multilingualism' in the Legislative Assembly as a way to encourage greater public participation in domestic politics, supported bilingual education in schools and was also a critical figure in the enactment of the Labour Ordinance which placed a cap on working hours.[55] Lim Yew Hock succeeded David Marshall and was eventually successful in the constitutional negotiations with the British which led to full internal self-government in 1959.

The other key personality to emerge from the 1955 Legislative Assembly elections was Lee Kuan Yew. Even though the PAP only had three members in the Legislative Assembly, through the sheer power of political debates, Lee was effectively the leader of the Opposition, putting pressure on the LF government on various issues involving political and constitutional reforms, and more importantly on issues of domestic politics relating to housing, education and labour reforms. Together with David Marshall, they were the leading lights in the Legislative Assembly and held some of the most memorable debates in the legislature, which makes the present parliament more like a university debating team.

While Lee Kuan Yew was debating David Marshall about the future of Singapore, he and his colleagues were also involved in a life-and-death struggle within the PAP. The PAP was born as a united front between the English- and Chinese-educated intellectuals with moderates, and pro-communist and leftists found in both camps. While Lee Kuan Yew, Toh Chin Chye, Goh Keng Swee and S. Rajaratnam represented the English-educated 'moderates', Lim Chin Siong, Fong Swee Suan, Samad Ismail and Devan Nair represented the pro-communist and leftist camp. Later, Devan Nair joined Lee Kuan Yew's camp.

---

54. Ibid.

55. Ibid.

The key to Lee Kuan Yew's and PAP's eventual victory and *imprimatur* on Singapore's politics was their ability to defeat the pro-communists and leftists in the various Central Executive Committee (CEC) elections. When the PAP was established in 1954, the Malayan Communist Party chief, Chin Peng, instructed many of his cadres to join the PAP.[56] When the PAP was established in November 1954, three of the CEC members were communists, Fong Swee Suan, Devan Nair and Chan Chiaw Thor. In the 1956 PAP CEC, there were four, namely, Lim Chin Siong, Devan Nair, Chia Ek Tian and Goh Boon Toh. It was following these developments that the communists and their supporters tried to capture the PAP from within. Through the sub-committee responsible for redrafting the party's constitution that was led by James Puthucheary, the party branches were allowed to vote in members of the CEC. However, before the communists could implement their plans, the Lim Yew Hock government detained key communists and leftists such as Lim Chin Siong, Fong Swee Suan, Devan Nair and James Puthucheary.

On 4 August 1957, the pro-communists again tried to capture the PAP. At the annual party conference, packed largely by pro-communist supporters, six pro-communists were voted into the CEC. Lee Kuan Yew and his five other colleagues voted into the CEC refused to take up their posts. The new PAP chairman was Tan Chong Kin and Lee Kuan Yew's successor, T.T. Rajah. However, on 22 August 1957, the Lim Yew Hock government arrested all the pro-communist members of the PAP CEC except T.T. Rajah, who fearing arrest, resigned as secretary-general. Following this, the party fell back to the hands of the moderates and to prevent future takeovers from within, the PAP instituted two new classes of membership — cadre and ordinary members, and it was formalised that only the former could vote for members of the CEC. Hence, since August 1957, the largely anti-communist but moderate members of the PAP have been in control of the party, ensuring that the leftists would not be in a position to control the party.

The pro-communist and leftist members, nevertheless, through Fong Chong Pik or the Plen, continued to work closely with Lee Kuan Yew and his colleagues as this was the only way to operate politically in Singapore, where the Malayan Communist Party was deemed illegal. This was the principal reason, despite internecine conflicts in the PAP from 1954 to 1958, in 1959, the PAP's 'united

---

56. Bilveer Singh, *Quest for Political Power: Communist Subversion and Militancy in Singapore* (Singapore: Marshall Cavendish, 2015), p. 121.

front' remained intact, allowing it to contest as a powerful political party aiming to capture power in self-governing Singapore.

Even though the PAP won resoundingly in 1959, capturing 43 out of the 51 seats, the differences between the moderates and leftists did not abate. If anything, it got worse. Following the PAP's victory, the leftist camp was hoping that all political detainees would be released but this did not happen following the release of only eight detainees including Lim Chin Siong, Devan Nair, Sandra Woodhull, James Puthucheary, Fong Swee Suan, Tan Chong Kin, Chen Say Jame and Chan Chiaw Thor. While releasing political prisoners was one of Lee Kuan Yew's electoral promises in 1959, Lee also wanted assurances that these detainees would not promote communist causes, which he was not convinced. Failing to capture the CEC of the PAP, the pro-left members tried other machinations to bring down the Lee Kuan Yew government. There was the struggle to gain control of the trade unions. Eventually, the Singapore Trades Union Congress was split into the National Trades Union Congress led by pro-Lee Devan Nair and the Singapore Association of Trade Unions supporting Lim Chin Siong and his leftist comrades.

However, it was the battle over merger with Malaysia and the Security Ordinance that brought the brinkmanship of the two factions within the PAP to the fore and ultimately led to the split in the PAP — that has continued to affect Singapore's politics to this day. Beijing, the Malayan Communist Party's mentor, opposed merger and this opposition was carried out vigorously by Lim Chin Siong. When Tunku Abdul Rahman proposed the merger of Singapore with Malaya (with Borneo, Brunei and Sarawak) to form Malaysia on 27 May 1961, the battle lines within the PAP were openly drawn. Lee Kuan Yew and his colleagues had championed merger since the establishment of the PAP in 1954. The Left feared that the anti-communist Tunku, who had earlier declared Emergency in Malaya from 1948 to 1960 and successfully defeated the communist insurgency, would crush the communists in Singapore once Singapore was part of Malaysia. The communists also believed that this was something Lee Kuan Yew and his moderate colleagues in the PAP favoured. Similarly, the Left believed that the security ordinance regulations, if they continued in operation, would be used to cripple and destroy the Left, as had been done by the British in the past and the David Marshall and Lim Yew Hock governments from 1955 to 1959.

In view of these differences, the pro-communist Left tried to weaken the PAP politically. This was undertaken through industrial and student strikes. When two by-elections took place in 1961, in Hong Lim and Anson, the Left supported the

anti-PAP candidates, namely, Ong Eng Guan and David Marshall, in an attempt
to weaken Lee Kuan Yew and his government. But when Lee and his colleagues
held a referendum on merger, Lee's proposal was given an overwhelming support.
In July 1961, Lee called for a vote of confidence in his government and he narrowly
survived. He received 27 votes (26 from the PAP and one from an independent).
Eight opposition members voted against him and 16 abstained including 13 from the
PAP, who belonged or supported the Left. According to Lee Kuan Yew, "had we lost
the vote, the government would have had to resign. Then either the pro-communists
could form the government with more defections from the PAP or there would be a
general election, which they [pro-communists] believed they could win".[57]

Following the vote of confidence, the 13 PAP members who abstained were
expelled from the party and they went on to form the *Barisan Sosialis* on 30 July
1961 under Lim Chin Siong. The battle between the moderates and the leftists
culminated in the launch of Operation Coldstore on 2 February 1963 that led
to the detention of prominent leftist politicians and trade unionists such as Lim
Chin Siong, Fong Swee Suan and others. This was a death-knell blow to the Left
and ended any challenge the leftists could pose to the moderates. Hence, by the
time the 1963 Legislative Assembly elections were held, most of the leftist leaders
were already incarcerated and despite this, the Left still performed admirably,
with the *Barisan Sosialis* winning 13 seats. However, slowly but surely, the days
of the *Barisan Sosialis* and the Left were numbered, partly due to the political
environment in Malaysia that was largely anti-communist, and also due to strategic
mistakes made by the *Barisan Sosialis*, such as taking the 'fight to the streets' and
abandoning parliament, which literally surrendered political power to the PAP.
Since mounting on the 'political horse' due to its sheer attractive policies and
better leaders, and strategic mistakes by the pro-communist Left and especially
the *Barisan Sosialis*, the PAP has not dismounted from power ever since. This
is especially since August 1965 when Singapore was expelled from Malaysia and
where the PAP's leadership has been able to lead the independent Republic to a
successful political and economic entity.

Interestingly, the 1963 Legislative Assembly was made up of what can be
described as an all PAP cast — those who remained loyal to the PAP and who

57. Lee Kuan Yew, *The Singapore Story: Memoirs of Lee Kuan Yew* (Singapore: Times Books
International, 1998), p. 377.

won the majority in the 1963 General Elections and the former PAP members who became members of the *Barisan Sosialis* or United People's Party. In many ways, this signposted the beginning of the irrelevance of all other political parties in Singapore and also largely explained the character and nature of Singapore's politics since the 1963 elections. At the same time, there appears to be 'two PAPs' that should be noted in Singapore politics — the PAP of 1959 to 1963, which largely represented a 'united front' of the Left and moderates, and the post-1963 PAP, that was largely anti-Left and one that continues to dominate Singapore's politics to this day, and one that is known more for being to the 'centre' and 'right' of the political spectrum.

SINGAPORE AS A ONE-PARTY DOMINANT STATE: CASE STUDY OF THE 2011 AND 2015 GENERAL ELECTIONS

The 2011 General Elections

Politically speaking, in the context of the one-party dominant system in Singapore since 1963, on 8 May 2011 Singaporeans woke up to a slightly new Singapore. Prime Minister Lee Hsien Loong described the General Elections as "a new phase in its [Singapore's] political development."[1] On 19 April 2011, the government had announced that Singapore's 14th elections since 1955 will be held on 7 May 2011. Prior to the announcement of the polling date, there were many electoral reforms introduced on how the next general elections would be conducted. This included updating the voter rolls three times, announcing rules involving election advertising on the internet and amending the Films Act for political films. In May 2009, Prime Minister Lee announced sweeping changes to the composition of the next parliament with at least 18 Members of Parliament (MPs) (about 20%) that would not be from the ruling party. This involved the Nominated Member of Parliament (NMP) scheme with nine members. The Non-Constituency Member of Parliament (NCMP) scheme was expanded to include the possibility of the nine of the 'best losers' from the opposition entering the parliament.[2]

The government also promised to reduce the average size of the Group Representation Constituencies (GRCs) with the overall percentage dropping from 5.4 MPs to less than five. There would also be fewer six-member GRCs, smaller GRC sizes and a minimum of 12 Single Member Constituencies (SMCs) from the previous nine. In December 2009, a 'cooling off' period of 24 hours with no political campaigning except party political broadcast was announced. This was rationalised

---

1. "Pledge to work together for a just and fair society", *The Straits Times*, 22 May 2011.

2. "Changes to electoral system to encourage wider range of views in Parliament", *Channel NewsAsia*, 27 May 2009.

on the need "to calm down, reflect on the issues and the arguments, and analyse what's at stake, logically, rationally" as well as to reduce potential "public disorder".[3] A critical pre-General Elections development was the redrawing of the electoral boundaries. In the past, hotly contested constituencies in preceding elections were usually subsumed into other GRCs or massively rearranged. For instance, the SMC seat of Anson, as did the Eunos and Cheng San GRCs, disappeared. Following the 1997 General Elections, eight of few wards in which PAP fared the worst in the elections were absorbed into safer GRCs. This time round in the lead up to the 2011 General Elections, while there were major changes, the most important was probably the increase of constituencies from 84 to 87. Also, compared to 2006, the number of SMCs was increased from nine to 12. As for the GRCs, while there were no four-member GRCs in 2006, in 2011, there were two. The number of five-member GRCs increased from nine to 11 with the number of six-member GRCs decreasing from five to two. According to the ruling party, electoral boundary changes were necessitated by the changing demographics and the need to create smaller GRCs.

The electoral changes introduced in 2011 left the number of GRC seats unchanged at 75 while reducing their percentage slightly in an expanded House. The SMC seats were raised by three. The electoral boundaries are important as this plays a key role in determining how the voters in a particular constituency relate to the candidate, be it from the ruling PAP or, the Opposition. From the PAP's perspective, the electoral changes were critical due to the "need for ministers to anchor GRCs, population shifts following the sprouting of new housing estates, the performance of incumbent MPs, and the prime minister's promise that there would be at least 12 SMCs and that GRCs would have an average of no more than five member wards".[4] Also, if the eight new SMCs were analysed, they were carved out of GRCs where the PAP had performed well, making them relatively safe single seats.

The state of the parties

The PAP, the hegemonic ruling party since 1959, continued its dominance unchallenged as it prepared for the 14th General Elections. While the Opposition

---

3. Chua Chin Hon, "24 hours to cool off before Polling Day", *The Straits Times*, 1 December 2009.

4. Chua Lee Hoong, "Commentary: Few surprises despite the many changes", *The Straits Times*, 25 February 2011.

continued to argue that the PAP cannot be equated with Singapore and vice versa, what cannot be ignored was that the PAP's *imprimatur* and hold on national power remained unshakeable with the electorate continuing to trust the party with the nation's future. This was something even the Opposition agreed on during the 2011 General Elections campaigns.[5] Still, the single most important feature characterising the PAP as it prepared for the polls was the 'politics of renewal' that the party underwent. By April 2011, when the national polls were announced, there were many 'political goodbyes' and 'political welcomes' in the PAP, reflecting the fundamental generational change the PAP was undertaking. This became even more pronounced following the 2011 General Elections when Prime Minister Lee announced his cabinet.

In total, the PAP introduced 24 new candidates with 18 PAP MPs retiring. Senior PAP leaders such as Lee Kuan Yew and Lee Hsien Loong also indicated that there were up to five 'heavyweights' in the new PAP line-up who were slotted for key leadership positions in the coming years.[6] Of the 24 'new faces', the five potential office holders included Chan Chun Sing, Tan Chuan-Jin, Heng Swee Keat, Lawrence Wong and Ong Ye Kung.[7] Thus, just prior to the 2011 General Elections, the PAP revamped itself and positioned a leadership that was likely to be around for another generation or so. Equally important, many key leaders were tipped to emerge from the 'Class of 2011' possibly including a future prime minister (something that the prime minister and his 3G team delivered later by naming Heng Swee Keat as the most likely next prime minister of Singapore in November 2018).

As for the Opposition, what was undeniable was the intense activism in terms of who, what and where they would position themselves in the hustings. Historically, the opposition in Singapore had a dismal showing at the general elections. In the 2006 General Elections, two seats were won by the Opposition, Chiam See Tong in Potong Pasir and Low Thia Khiang in Hougang, with a third seat provided for NCMP Sylvia Lim. In terms of popular vote, however, the opposition parties have collectively

---

5. For example, see speech by Low Thia Khiang at the Workers' Party Rally at Serangoon Stadium on 29 April 2011.

6. "PAP banks on the future with new line-up", *The Straits Times*, 18 April 2011; also see Lee Kuan Yew, "Voters should look at the fundamentals", *Today*, 26 April 2011.

7. The Shi Ning, "At least 5 potential ministers in new slate", *Business Times*, 18 April 2011.

captured on average a third of the votes. However, due to the first-past-the-post system, the maximum number of seats the opposition had held since 1965 was four in 1991. In view of the hype about the 2011 General Elections, the Opposition also started canvassing in selected areas, stepping up their walkabouts and door-to-door visits, selling newsletters, and recruiting quality candidates as well as identifying potential wards to be contested.

The Opposition also tried to project itself as being made up of qualified individuals rather than being anchored by one or two personalities. As argued by Low from Hougang, "what we're trying to do now is to introduce a certain depth to the party — depth in the sense that the WP is not led just by Low Thia Khiang and Sylvia."[8] Also, in terms of strategies and manifestation of political maturity, Low argued that it was imperative that the Opposition "rely less on anger against the PAP for votes and do more to articulate their convictions and policy directions." By showcasing multiple capable candidates, Low argued that it would help the Opposition to perform better when contesting in a GRC. Low also stressed on leadership renewal in the Opposition. This was necessitated by the need to signal that the Opposition was also renewing itself, to be in touch with the voters and the new environment, and more important, to position the younger generation "to lead opposition movement in the future."[9] The Opposition also hoped to present a united front to avoid three-corner fights as well as to contest, not just in the SMCs but also in most of the GRCs. Prior to the polls, both Low and Chiam indicated their desire to lead a GRC. As was indicated by Low, "I have declared to the press long ago that the option is open."[10]

While none of the opposition parties were trouble-free, still the Workers' Party (WP) appeared the strongest, most compact and most connected with the ground. The WP also proved to be the party with the greatest potential amongst all the opposition parties in Singapore. The WP was able to field many credible candidates who were seen to be comparable or even more impressive than the PAP candidates. Its secretary-general, Low Thia Khiang, had held his Hougang seat since 1991.

---

8. "Low: GRC win a boost for opposition", *The Straits Times*, 14 March 2011.

9. "Low Thia Khiang: Opposition renewal an important issue for voters", *The Online Citizen*, 13 March 2011, http://www.theonlinecitizen.com/2011/03/low-thia-khiang-opposition-renewal-an-important-issue-for-voters/

10. "Show-cause letter widens rift in SDA", *The Straits Times*, 11 February 2011.

Since the 2006 General Elections, together with Sylvia Lim as the NCMP, there have been two WP representatives in parliament. Prior to the 2011 General Elections, the second most important party was the Singapore Democratic Alliance (SDA), an alliance between Singapore People's Party (SPP), Singapore Malay National Organisation (PKMS) and Singapore Justice Party (SJP), and formerly including the National Solidarity Party (NSP), which left the coalition in 2007. For the most part, its public face was Chiam See Tong, the long-time MP for Potong Pasir and leader of the SPP. However, in the lead up to the 2011 General Elections, the SDA was riddled with internal conflicts with Chiam eventually replaced as chairman, mainly on health grounds. There were also important policy issues, amongst the most important being Chiam's desire to bring the Reform Party (RP) into the SDA, a move opposed by the senior members of the coalition.[11] In early 2011, Chiam pulled the SPP from the SDA, further weakening the SDA.[12]

Pre-general elections issues

By any yardstick, the PAP, on most scores, except for embracing democracy *a la the West*, can be credited for transforming Singapore from a 'Third World' to a 'First World'. The only question has been at what cost? Politically, economically, socio-culturally and from the military-security point of view, the PAP-led government had achieved a great deal all-round, thereby emerging as a model in various developmental arenas and domains. Despite this, as no society or government is perfect, there have always been issues of governance, and this continued to be raised at various forums, with a significant segment of the population (about 30–35%) voting against the PAP in every general elections. Here, even minister mentor Lee Kuan Yew warned that the PAP should not take its good fortunes for granted as it might lose power one day. According to the late elder statesman, "there will come a time when eventually the public will say, look, let's try the other side, whether because the PAP has declined in quality or the opposition has put up a team which is equal to the PAP and they say, let's try the other side. That day will come."[13]

---

11. See "GE: SDA says Chiam pulling SPP out of alliance", *ChannelNewsAsia.com*, 2 March 2011; "Chiam pulls party out of alliance", *Today*, 3 March 2011.

12. See "Chiam pulls party out of alliance", *Today*, 3 March 2011.

13. "PAP will be voted out one day: MM Lee", *AsiaOne News*, 21 January 2011, https://www.asiaone.com/News/AsiaOne%2BNews/Singapore/Story/A1Story20110121-259459.html

Just as in the past, the 2011 General Elections was preceded by a discussion of a number of issues. The bread-and-butter issues continued to bedevil the PAP's leadership as the Republic was hurt by the Global Financial Crisis in 2008 and even though it did well in recovering, the consequences of the downturn continued to affect the masses, especially the lower-income groups. In some ways, the Republic found itself positioned at the tip of a bull's horn as it embraced globalisation but could not always control and mitigate its negative fallouts. As the Republic continued to plug itself into the global economic grid, it became even more vulnerable to vagaries of the open global market with both positive and negative consequences at home. Inflation and fare hikes were also political issues as they tended to affect the lower-income Singaporeans more than others. This undermined the PAP's legitimacy to some extent, making it pay during the 2011 General Elections as many voters did not benefit from what would have been advertised as a high-growing economy. As was admitted by Minister Mentor Lee Kuan Yew two days before Nomination Day, "The cost of living is a current problem. I know that the inflation is higher this year because petrol and electricity prices have gone up and so have some food prices."[14] However, the minister mentor also reminded Singaporeans that "we import all our energy and food, and our standards of living have also gone up. We are not buying the same basket of food and daily necessities we were five or 10 years ago."[15]

However, income inequality and the standard of living were issues that persisted and continued to be a point of aggravation for many members of the public. One of the biggest concerns to emerge prior to the polls was the growing income gap. Singapore's Gini coefficient measures the degree of inequality of income distribution, and in 2009, the figure stood up at 42.5. A United Nations Development Programme Report released in 2009 ranked Singapore second amongst the countries with the highest income inequalities with Hong Kong being first at 43.4.[16] The top 10% of

---

14. S. Ramesh and Imelda Saad, "GE: MM Lee says Singapore is not Disney World", *Channel NewsAsia*, 25 April 2011, http://www.channelnewsasia.com/1124752/1/. html. Reference cited in *MyCarForum*, 25 April 2011, https://www.mycarforum.com/topic/2662569-ge-mm-lee-says-singapore-is-not-disney-world/

15. Lee Kuan Yew, "Voters should look at the fundamentals".

16. See Human Development Reports (HDR), United Nations Development Programme, 2009. Available at hdrstats.org/en/indicators/161.html; also see "Singapore ranked 2nd highest on Gini coefficient score in UN Report", *Singapore News Alternative*, http://www.singaporenewsalternative.blogspot.com/2009/10/spore-ranked-2

households in Singapore experienced a 110.8% increase in real income between the years 1995 and 2007, while for the lowest 10%, the increase was only 7.7%, contributing to a strong skewing effect.[17] Between 2000 and 2005, the bottom 30th percentile of wage earners also experienced an income decline.[18] In 2009, Singapore had a gross domestic product (GDP) per capita of S$51,656.[19] The average monthly wage in the same year was S$3,872, rising to S$4,089 in 2010. In 2009, the median income was S$2,400.[20] This indicated that more than half of the workers earned only two-thirds of the average wage or less. This data suggested a strong polarisation between high-wage earners and low-wage earners. Implicitly, this also signalled that in addition to the primordial fault lines of race and religion, a new potentially divisive issue that could surface was a class divide that cut across the traditional racial and religious fault lines. Mainly due to rising costs of living and income inequalities, Senior Minister Goh Chok Tong admitted that "the ground is not so sweet for election", something similarly echoed by Health Minister Khaw Boon Wan when he lamented that "the ground is not as sweet" as it was in 2006 in Sembawang GRC.[21]

In addition to cost of living and bread-and-butter issues, a number of other issues also dominated the 2011 General Elections. First, there was the credibility of the opposition candidates. The PAP tried to cast aspersions on a number of opposition candidates such as Chen Show Mao of the WP and Vincent Wijeysingha from the Singapore Democratic Party (SDP).[22] This was tantamount to political mudslinging, quite rare in Singapore's politics. Other election hot buttons included housing, foreign

---

17. Table: Average Monthly Household Income from Work per Household Member among Employed Household by Decline in Real Terms, DOD, Key Household Trends.

18. For additional information, see Ishita Dhamani, *Income Inequality in Singapore: Causes, Consequences and Policy Options*, National University of Singapore, May 2008, http://www.scribd.com/doc/3661870/Income-Inequality-in-Singapore

19. "MCYS social statistics", Ministry of Community Development, Youth and Sports Strategic Planning, Research and Development Division, Singapore.

20. "Earning and wages 2009 and 2010", Ministry of Manpower, Singapore.

21. See Maria Siow, "GE: Ground 'not so sweet' for elections, says SM Goh", *Channel NewsAsia*, 18 April 2011, http://www.channelnewsasia.com/stories/singaporelocalnews/view/; also see Salma Khalik, "Ground less sweet, says Khaw but he's confident", *The Straits Times*, 25 April 2011.

22. See Neo Chai Chin, "PAP: Will Wijeysingha pursue gay agenda? SDP: No, we will not", *Today*, 27 April 2011.

workers and the issue of race and religion. In view of the rising cost of housing since the 2006 General Elections, many Singaporeans have had difficulties purchasing cheap public housing, worsened further by the long waiting period. The minister for national development, Mah Bow Tan, defended the rising costs of public housing on grounds that "you cannot expect that in a situation where the economy is growing at 14 per cent, that you know housing prices will not go up."[23] However, almost all the opposition parties, especially the WP, contended that it was possible to provide cheap public housing but the PAP government was unwilling to do so.[24] Another hot issue was Singaporeans' attitudes towards the large number of foreign migrants and workers, particularly those who came from China and India. With Singapore hosting 1.2 million foreign workers in 2008 alone, these workers were viewed not just as job competitors but as 'overcrowders' in an already dense environment, competing for resources in housing, transport, hospitals and education.[25] Furthermore, cultural and language differences created tension in terms of social dynamics. In a survey, two out of three people were concerned about the impact of foreigners on community relations.[26]

The election results

On Nomination Day on 27 April 2011, of the 87 seats that were to be contested, only five seats were won by walkovers by the PAP, all belonging to Tanjong Pagar GRC. The five-member team that entered parliament through walkover comprised of Lee Kuan Yew, Indranee Rajah, Chia Shi-Lu, Lily Neo and Chan Chun Sing. What stood out on Nomination Day was the decision by opposition incumbents, Low Thia Khiang and Chiam See Tong, to contest a GRC as they had subtly indicated earlier. For the 2011 General Elections, the *battle royale* was focused on the Aljunied GRC. Midway in the campaign, sensing that the public anger against the PAP was

---

23. "Housing remains a hot election issue, says Mah", *The Straits Times*, 31 January 2011.

24. Fiona Chan and Robin Chan, "Housing not a 'make-or-break' election issue", *The Straits Times*, 25 April 2011.

25. See Brian J. Shaw and Rahil Ismail, *Good Fences Make Good Neighbours? Geographies of Marginalisation: Housing Singapore's Foreign Workers*, Paper presented for Southeast Asian Geography Association (SEAGA), Hanoi, Vietnam, 23–26 November 2010, http://www.seaga.xtreemhost.com/seaga2010/CS2A-ShawIsmail.pdf?i=2

26. *Citizens and the Nation: National Orientations of Singapore Survey* (Singapore: Institute of Policy Studies, 2010).

mounting, Prime Minister Lee Hsien Loong admitted that his government had made mistakes and apologised publicly. On 3 May 2011, at a lunchtime rally, the prime minister argued that no government was perfect:

> We made a mistake when we let Mas Selamat run away. We made a mistake when Orchard Road got flooded. And there are other mistakes which we've made from time to time and, I'm sure, occasionally will happen again. I hope, not too often. But when it happens, then we should acknowledge it, we should apologise. Take responsibility, put things right. If we have to discipline somebody, we'll do that and we must learn from the lessons and never make the same mistake again…We are sorry we didn't get it exactly right, but I hope you understand and bear with us because we're trying our best to solve the problems.[27]

In the end, on 8 May 2011, the PAP was returned to power for the 13th time, winning 60.14% of the votes, compared to 66.6% it won in 2006 (see Table 6.1). However, it suffered on a number of counts. The general elections results represented a major game changer in Singapore politics, with most, including the PAP top leaders, believing that Singapore had entered a new era as far as politics was concerned.

The PAP had won a landslide victory in terms of the number of seats, 81 out of 87 seats, due to the first-past-the-post system. However, in terms of the proportion of votes and the number of seats, this was the worst result in PAP's history since Singapore's independence in 1965. The PAP got a popular vote of 60.14%,

Table 6.1: 2011 General Elections: Parliamentary Seats and Percentage of Votes by Political Parties

Party	Seats Won	Total Votes	Percentage of Votes
PAP	81	1,212,514	60.14
WP	6 [+2 NCMPs]	258,510	12.82
NSP	0	242,682	12.04
SDP	0	97,362	4.83
RP	0	86,294	4.28
SPP	0 [+1 NCMP]	62,639	3.11
SDA	0	55,988	2.78

Source: Author.

27. Leong Wee Keat, "We have made mistakes: PM Lee", Today, 4 May 2011.

down from 66.6% and 75% for the 2006 and 2001general elections, respectively. Moreover, the party lost four more seats than in the 2006 General Elections, most significantly losing the Aljunied GRC. The PAP, however, reclaimed the Potong Pasir SMC by 114 votes, and won the Joo Chiat SMC by 388 votes. While Prime Minister Lee called the victory a "clear mandate", he and several others, including Senior Minister Goh, later expressed disappointment over the results. He revealed, "I was expecting, to be frank, slightly better results."[28] In addition to a lower popular vote, many key cabinet ministers helming GRCs scored below average, snatching narrow victories. Some of these include the following:

- East Coast GRC with 54.53%, helmed by Lim Swee Say (Minister in Prime Minister's Office) and Raymond Lim (Minister for Transport);
- Bishan-Toa Payoh GRC with 56.93%, helmed by Wong Kan Seng (Deputy Prime Minister and Coordinating Minister for National Security) and Ng Eng Hen (Minister for Education);
- Marine Parade GRC with 56.64%, helmed by Goh Chok Tong (former Prime Minister and then incumbent Senior Minister);
- Nee Soon GRC with 58.40%, helmed by K. Shanmugam (Minister for Home Affairs, Minister for Law);
- Moulmein-Kallang GRC with 58.55%, helmed by Yaacob Ibrahim (Minister for Environment and Water Resources) and Lui Tuck Yew (Minister of Information, Communications and the Arts).

The message from the ground, in delivering the PAP only 60% of the popular votes, was clear. As the outgoing foreign minister George Yeo in his final rally speech acknowledged, the PAP needed to transform and stay in touch with the voters. If it did not reinvent itself in becoming more consultative and more accountable for its actions, it would become a party in slow decline, as indicated by the 2011 General Elections results. In fact, in an election rally on 4 May 2011, Yeo stated that, "the PAP must be transformed", that there was "resentment against the government" and the party needs to exercise "flexibility" and treat its citizens as "human beings".[29] The WP, for the time being, emerged as a clear competitor to the PAP, although the road had been a long one

---

28. "SM Goh: 'Heart and head' the way to go", *AsiaOne*, 9 May 2011. See https://www.asiaone.com/News/Elections/Story/A1Story20110509-277767.html

29. See Alicia Wong, "Minister George Yeo: We need a 'transformed' PAP", *The Singapore Scene (Yahoo News)*, 5 May 2011.

and the challenge to PAP's hegemony is still only a long-term goal. While achieving small wins in the SMCs in previous years, it created history by winning a GRC and forcing out one of the PAP's most celebrated ministers, George Yeo. The GRC had been designed with the idea that the public was unlikely to vote against a minister in favour of untested opposition candidates. In 2011, the WP proved this wrong. Aljunied was won not simply because of public discontent for the PAP, but because the five members fielded by WP had proven themselves to be strong and credible leaders, including two of the party heavyweights in Low Thia Khiang and Sylvia Lim, WP's secret weapons of Chen Show Mao and Pritam Singh, who surprised many with their eloquence and conviction in delivering their rally speeches, as well as Muhamad Faisal Manap, a family consultant who promised to assist families in trouble. Despite Low leaving Hougang in the hands of his prodigy, Yaw Shin Leong, the Hougang voters clearly trusted the leadership handover and gave a resounding affirmation during the polls.

Implications of the 2011 General Elections

The one critical thing which the 2011 General Elections results led to was the enhancement of the ruling party's democratic credentials, at home and internationally. At a time when entrenched 'soft' and 'hard' authoritarian regimes were struggling for survival and legitimacy, as in North Africa, the Gulf and parts of Asia, the PAP government relaxed and allowed the freest reins ever for the Opposition and their supporters. This resulted in big wins, relatively speaking, for the Opposition but even more importantly, in heightening the legitimacy for the long-established PAP rule, which continues to maintain its hegemonic control of Singapore's politics. Certainly, the Opposition had made great strides. However, at the end of the hustings and when all the dust had settled down, the PAP's control of the parliament remained unchallenged, controlling 81 out of 87 seats minus three seats reserved for NCMPs. This meant that 93.1% of parliamentary power remained in the hands of the PAP, permitting it a free hand to literally to legislate changes as it has the mandate from the people to do so even though it has also signalled its intentions to pay greater heed to public demands. In short, it was a win-win general elections with the PAP continuing to maintain near-total and dominant control of parliament while the Opposition is given greater room to manoeuvre but which in reality means little in terms of policy making and implementation. Still, the Opposition's numerically minuscule presence cannot be ignored as it represents 40% of the Singapore electorate.

Even before the general elections results were announced, the elections was already an important milestone on a number of counts. First, it was clear that the PAP and the Opposition found themselves in a totally new environment with many domestic and international changes affecting the electorate. This was worsened by the fact that many national issues had not been resolved before Polling Day. As was argued by Prime Minister Lee Hsien Loong, "there are more issues which are not completely settled this time,"[30] leading him to ponder whether his party would be able to match the 66.6% of the popular vote it garnered in 2006. In his words, "I think 66 per cent is a very high number…whether we'll reach that I can't say."[31] The unresolved issues included inflation, cost of living, public housing, income gaps, immigration and ministerial salaries. This also included the parliament's approval of an S$890,700 increase in the president's salary from S$4,267,500.[32] Minister Mentor Lee Kuan Yew's remarks on the Malay-Muslim community also did not help.

Second, the 14th General Elections did not see the PAP return to power on Nomination Day. Not only did the Opposition mount its biggest challenge, contesting 82 out of 87 seats, or more specifically, 14 GRCs and all the 12 SMCs, it also for the first time gave many Singaporeans a chance to vote, since there were a large number of walkovers in the past. This, as well as the final results, signalled a significant shift in public support for the opposition parties. The invigorated Opposition was also able to collectively field a slate of credible and capable candidates, dispelling the argument that the Opposition was only able to field weak candidates that lacked credibility.

When the 2011 General Elections results were announced, Prime Minister Lee stated that this would be a watershed election. He was totally right but not in the manner he framed it. For Prime Minister Lee, 'watershed' implied the recognition of the PAP's success and most important, permitting the PAP to position key leaders for future leadership position. In the past, 'watershed' was usually associated with a sudden or major fall in votes for the PAP and losses in key constituencies. Instead, it was a watershed election on the following counts:

---

30. Chua Lee Hoong, "Cost of living: We are doing what we can", *The Straits Times*, 22 April 2011.

31. Ibid.

32. "Parliament approves increase in President's salary, expenditure", *Today*, 11 March 2011.

- **Quality of the Opposition.** Despite regular diatribes that the Opposition was incapable of recruiting credible and talented individuals into its ranks, the 2011 General Elections proved otherwise. The opposition parties showed that they were capable of attracting talented and highly qualified individuals into their ranks, especially younger Singaporeans such as Nicole Seah, Glenda Han and Gerald Giam, just to mention three.

- **Intensive use of the new media.** Unlike the past, what distinguished the 2011 General Elections was the pervasive use of the new media, with blogs, Twitter, Facebook, The Online Citizen and Temasek Review, representing a very powerful alternative to the largely state-controlled mainstream media. More importantly, the new media formed a critical bridge between the Opposition and the younger voters, especially those from Gen Y.

- **Importance of younger voters.** The 2011 General Elections clearly dispelled the long-held view that the younger voters were highly apathetic. Instead, the general elections demonstrated a heavy involvement and participation of younger Singaporeans, many of whom felt disadvantaged by the ruling party's policies, especially in the areas of cost of living, housing, jobs and migration, leading many to believe that the 'Singapore Dream' appeared very distant. Their resentment often translated into participation and support for the Opposition, culminating in a shift away from the traditional support for the PAP.

- **Issue-intense mood.** This was one of the most issue-intense general elections. Even before the 2011 General Elections results were announced, senior PAP politicians were already admitting that the "ground was not sweet." Probably even more importantly, the ability of the Opposition to identify, articulate and frame issues by blaming the PAP for failing to solve various issues that hurt Singaporeans such as immigration, cost of living and housing, greatly resonated with the electorate, leading to the PAP's losses across the board. While there were various local and municipal issues, what hurt the PAP were national issues that all were able to identify with. As was candidly admitted by one of the losing PAP candidates in Aljunied GRC, "the national mood, the national issues just swept us from under our feet. When we realised that, in fact, it was not just the local issues but national issues that had taken a kind of different priority, I thought it was rather too late."[33]

- **Resilient support for the PAP.** In many ways, the PAP's electoral support had never been fully and effectively tested for a long time, as in the past it had always

---

33. See Leong Wee Keat, "Many remain hurt by MM's Lee's remarks", *Today*, 13 May 2011.

managed to form a government on Nomination Day. It was a rare occurrence indeed, when almost all the seats were contested in the 2011 General Elections. After more than 50 years in power, the PAP leaders could take heart that there was much public support for them despite the multiple issues that were being debated. In the end, when the PAP was tested, especially in an environment of great anger and unhappiness, the PAP, though winning only 60% of the valid votes, still succeeded in winning 81 out of the 87 seats. This was a great achievement, showing the resilience of the PAP in Singapore's politics.

- **Great strides by the Opposition in national politics.** On the whole, the Opposition, almost for the first time since political independence in 1965, made tremendous political strides in national politics. Unlike the past, the leadership programmes and ability to connect with the electorate improved markedly, gaining much public respect and support. In many ways, the opposition parties appeared to have matured, signalling their ability to cooperate amongst themselves, to articulate issues responsibly and more importantly, to demonstrate that they are a responsible political force working for the good of Singapore and Singaporeans. This largely explained their improved electoral performance with only one opposition candidate losing his deposit and that too, in a three-corner fight.

- **Emergence of the WP as an important player in national politics.** In many ways, the WP maintained its momentum as the leading opposition party in Singapore politics, especially following its more than credible performance in the 2006 General Elections. In the 2011 General Elections, it stamped its dominance and emerged as *primus inter pares* among the parties competing against the PAP, eventually winning eight out of nine (six MPs and two NCMPs) seats in parliament with more than 40% of popular support for the party wherever it contested.

- **PAP and Opposition's success in political rejuvenation.** Just as the PAP did, the Opposition contested the 2011 General Elections in the hope of demonstrating that political rejuvenation was taking place in various parties. Thus, while the PAP retired many experienced MPs and introduced what was slated as 'fourth-generation leaders', the Opposition did likewise, with many new and younger leaders emerging in the forefront. This was true of almost all opposition parties, signalling that a younger group of leaders have been positioned to shape national politics for many years to come. By all counts, the PAP's dominance is unlikely to be challenged for quite some time. Singapore's next prime minister will most probably be picked from the 'fourth-generation leaders' who have been 'helicoptered' into cabinet, with most Singaporeans evaluating closely the performance of anointed appointees, especially the 'heavyweights' such as Heng Swee Keat, Chan Chun Sing and Tan Chuan-Jin. It will be 'make or break' for these fast trackers.

- **Dominance of national issues over local (municipal) ones.** Traditionally, the outcome of the general elections was largely a function of both national and local issues. However, what stood out in the 2011 General Elections was the overall importance of national issues that tended to overshadow the local ones. This meant that even though the PAP might have been working hard to address what was identified as local issues, eventually, the ability of the Opposition to frame the contest as one where national issues such as immigration, cost of living, income disparity and housing crunch that affected everyone proved to be very powerful and appealing, and largely accounted for the swing of most of the floating votes against the PAP. Thus, despite the national economy performing well with double-digit growth, it was insufficient to hold down the general public's unhappiness on many counts, resulting in the drop in the PAP's performance compared to that of the Opposition.

- **Triumph of political mobilisers over technocrats.** If there was one significant development in national politics that manifested in the 2011 General Elections, it was the public craving and support for political mobilisers over technocrats. Here, the PAP performed badly compared to the Opposition. Since the 1970s, it was almost axiomatic that technocratic leaders were a necessity for peace and prosperity, leading the PAP to recruit most of its top leaders with these qualities. This was largely true in circumstances of rising growth, minimal domestic issues and strong connection between the government and the governed. However, at a time of multiple crises, the rise of a new generation of voters and new political leaders trying to connect with the voters, the role and significance of political mobilisers became increasingly important. Here, the Opposition did extremely well, compared to the PAP, largely accounting for the better than expected performance of the Opposition. This was because winning the electoral support in the general elections can be a very emotional event and the Opposition succeeded in framing issues that connected the opposing parties with the masses, something the PAP had great difficulties in doing. While the PAP had a powerful track record, successful policies on most counts and highly credible leaders, these were insufficient to face the juggernaut of public unhappiness which the Opposition succeeded in articulating through eloquent leaders, resulting partly in the swing against the ruling party on Polling Day.

- **Fall of political giants.** If there was one observable outcome in the 2011 General Elections, it was the fall of political giants. The PAP lost three outstanding individuals, namely, the highly affable George Yeo, minister for foreign affairs, Lim Hwee Hua, the only full female minister in the cabinet, and Zainul Abidin Rasheed, a highly respected and able individual, and one slotted as the next speaker of parliament. Falling with the PAP's GRC team at Aljunied was Ong Ye Kung, a new face, who had been touted as one of the future heavyweights of the PAP, being a former principal private secretary to then Deputy Prime Minister Lee Hsien Loong. For the Opposition, the 2011 General Elections marked the political exit of Chiam See Tong, who together with the late J.B. Jeyaretnam, had symbolised political opposition to the PAP since the 1970s. They were the ones who had succeeded in breaking through the PAP's hegemonic political stranglehold since the early 1980s. In many ways, they were the pathfinders, paving the way for the Opposition, eventually culminating in the opposition movement gaining a respectable stake in Singapore's national politics today.

- **Singapore politics after the stepping down of Lee Kuan Yew.** The 2011 General Elections was a watershed one as it would, by all counts, represent the last general elections for Lee Kuan Yew, the one man who had played such a decisive role in national politics since 1955, first as a member of the opposition bench from 1955 to 1959, then as prime minister from 1959 to 1990 and since then as senior minister and minister mentor. He is the architect and 'father' of modern Singapore. Generations of Singaporeans have grown up politically identifying Lee Kuan Yew as the face of not just the PAP but also of Singapore. This would fundamentally change, not just due to his ripe age but also his retirement from the cabinet in May 2011, being a prelude to his exit from national politics. All being equal, come the next general elections, which happened in 2015, Lee Kuan Yew, was not expected to figure in any line-up, totally terminating his association with Tanjong Pagar since 1955 — the longest record for a Singaporean politician to be associated with a single constituency. While his political *imprimatur*, creation and transformation of Singapore from a 'Third World' to a 'First World' will remain etched in the national psyche, it will, nevertheless, mark the entry of Singapore politics into a new era, especially with rising expectations and challenges from a younger electorate. Lee Kuan Yew's retirement from the cabinet also signalled that the Republic has, *de facto*, entered into a post-Lee Kuan Yew era. Challenging questions as to what would happen to the PAP and Singapore after the elder Lee leaves the political scene will be more easily answered as a truly post-Lee Kuan Yew era will have emerged, though with Lee Kuan Yew still around.

The big question on everyone's mind, including the PAP and the Opposition, was whether the PAP would slide backward and the Opposition's forward could be stalled. For this, the political competitors, especially the PAP went on an overdrive. Three main scenarios were possible by the time the country entered into its 15th General Elections in 2015. First, the slightly dented PAP would reinvent itself and re-emerge as a dominant political party. This would require the newly appointed key PAP leaders and their backbenchers to successfully address the concerns and grievances of the electorate and, more importantly, to connect emotionally with the younger voters who now constitute the political majority. Prime Minister Lee Hsien Loong indicated that the newer leaders at the helm would do just that and how effectively this was undertaken could determine the status of the PAP in national politics in a largely post-Lee Kuan Yew era. In fact, the transformation of the PAP from a largely conservative party, believing that material benefits could satisfy the electorate, to a political party being connected to the internet and digital-driven generation, and one reaching out and listening to the majority of the electorate, would eventually determine the power, position and status of the party in national politics.

Second, despite its respectable performance in the 2011 General Elections, the Opposition's emergence might have only been a temporary phenomenon. This could be because the upsurge of support for the Opposition might have been more a protest vote against the unpopular policies of the PAP. Also, the traditional divide amongst the opposition parties might be too difficult to bridge. Thus, just as in the 1991 General Elections when the Opposition won four seats, it merely represented a slight dip in support for the PAP and following this, from 1997 to 2006, the Opposition failed to garner more than two parliamentary seats. If the Opposition failed to get its act together, it could be *déjà vu* as far as the Opposition's parliamentary standing was concerned.

Third, the Opposition would consolidate and emerge as a major political force in national politics. This could be through two major routes: first, not as an immediate alternative to the PAP but by providing a strong voice where it could act as a check and balance by highlighting the weaknesses of various PAP policies whenever given the opportunity; and second, as an alternative to the PAP either with the emergence of the WP as the dominant opposition party, or through a united front strategy where the Opposition consolidated itself in either a loose or tight coalition. Whatever the mechanics, it would mean the emergence of the

Opposition as an important part of the national political landscape, truly befitting the status of Singapore as a First World state.

The 2015 General Elections

On 25 August 2015, the rumour mill that had been working at full speed was rested on when Singapore's 15th General Elections would be held. Through the press release from the Elections Department under the Prime Minister's Office, it was announced that the president had issued the Writ of Election. Parliament was to be dissolved, the Nomination Day was set for 1 September and the Polling Day was set for 11 September 2015.

While the 2011 General Elections was path-breaking in denting in a limited way the dominance of the ruling People's Action Party (PAP), there was more continuity than a major shift in the numerical makeup of the parliament. The PAP still controlled 93% of the seats and Singapore's political course was not altered. The parliamentary decibel level increased but not its direction. Still, the 2015 General Elections was noteworthy for a number of reasons. From the 1959 General Elections to the one held in 2011, Lee Kuan Yew had been the leading protagonist, capturing the imagination of the voters bar none. This situation changed with the passing of the independent nation's founding prime minister. For the first time, the PAP and the nation were without the anchor personality that had shaped the Republic's politics for more than 50 years. The PAP, the opposition parties and the Singapore electorate had never faced such a situation.

The 2015 General Elections also marked the passing of two political generations — that of Lee Kuan Yew and Goh Chok Tong even though the latter contested in the Marine Parade GRC. The 2015 General Elections ensured that political power was vested in the hands of the third- and fourth-generation leaders led by Prime Minister Lee Hsien Loong. This elections introduced the fourth and fifth generations of PAP's political leaders and was also about passing the baton from Prime Minister Lee to the next leader. It was also evident that a failure to signal who would helm Singapore's politics after Lee Hsien Loong could call into question the future of the PAP, and possibly the nation.

The then minister for law and minister for foreign affairs, K. Shanmugam, had noted that hardly any political party has remained in power for more than

Table 6.2: Comparing the 2011 and 2015 General Elections Facts

	The Bare Facts	
	2011	2015
Voters	2,350,257	2,460,977
		110,720 [4.71%+]
Wards	87	89
		2 [2.2%+]
SMCs	12	13
		1 [8.3%+]
GRCs	15	16
		1 [6.6%+]
	6 member: 2	6 member: 2 [no change]
	5 member: 11	5 member: 8 [27.2%+]
	4 member: 2	4 member: 6 [200%+]

Source: Author.

70 years. A key question was whether the PAP could confound this seven-decade jinx? For this, it would need at least 10 years for the new leader of the PAP to consolidate himself in the party and win public support. As no prime minister-in-waiting has been discernible prior to the 2015 General Elections, would the time frame be fast-forwarded?

The 2015 General Elections also saw the largest number of voters entering the fray. Compared to the 2,350,257 registered voters in February 2011, there were 2,460,977 registered voters eligible for the 2015 hustings, an increase of 4.7% (see Table 6.2). Most of these were young first-time voters with some new citizens. The 2015 General Elections also saw the largest number of electoral wards, 89. There was one more Single Member Constituency (SMC) (13) and Group Representation Constituency (GRC) (16) compared to the last general elections but more four-man GRCs, with all seats being contested. As expected, the PAP contested all constituencies.

Despite difficult relations among the opposition parties, negotiations were held to avert three-cornered fights but this failed. The much-expected opposition unity in contesting against the PAP evaporated even though only a minimal number of three-cornered contests took place. Even more interesting was the ability of the SPP led by opposition veteran Chiam See Tong and the Democratic Progressive Party (DPP), to jointly contest a GRC under a single party banner — something never seen in the past. However, the WP, the largest opposition party, contested for 28 seats including defending the constituencies it held.

The 2015 General Elections was also expected to be one of the most competitive in recent years. With the rise of new political leaders, two new political parties, a more discerning political generation and most importantly, issues that affect almost every political generation, this was a political contestation that was to determine how dominant the PAP would be and how much support the Opposition could garner. Perennial 'bread and butter' issues such as cost of living, housing, health care, education, income gap and role of foreigners were expected to dominate the campaign trail. How the PAP managed them and how the Opposition exploited the issues were expected to be the key determinants of the electoral outcome. There was also the belief that if the issues remained local in nature, then the Opposition's march could be contained. However, if national issues took centre stage as happened in 2011, then the PAP's electoral votes could possibly fall below 60% and the Opposition's parliamentary presence increased. However, there was no question that the PAP would be returned as the government. The ruling party was also advantaged by global developments that tended to temper public anger against the government. With the global economy undergoing tectonics shifts, especially in Europe, United States, China and India, and uncertain political developments in Malaysia and Indonesia, the tried and tested steady hand of the PAP was favoured, to the disadvantage of the Opposition.

The PAP's track record also advantaged the ruling party. While the PAP had cemented its relationship with the electorate, especially with the SG50 (Singapore 50 Years) anniversary celebrations, the party was also expected to reap public goodwill for a job well done. There was also the expectation of public sympathy over the passing of Lee Kuan Yew who would have been 92 on 16 September 2015, five days after the Polling Day. The changed political terrain, new leaders, wide-ranging challenges of a developed society and matured electorate's mindset provided the sinews for a sea change to occur. The elections, it was postured, would decide how Singapore innovated politically and economically through greater democratic space and welfare programmes that would set the road ahead for the next 50 years. Most importantly, it would also signpost as to who was likely to be the prime minister-in-waiting for a state where leadership was the key driver of politics and development. Yet, at the same time, an effective Opposition was desired by the electorate as a check and balance to the PAP as well as something positive for Singapore's international image. Hence, the key question was — by what margin would the ruling PAP win?

The 2015 General Elections results

Even before the final results were announced in the early hours of 12 September 2015, it became clear that the ruling PAP would not only win but stamp its political dominance even more strongly. By the time all the results were in, the PAP had won 83 out of the 89 seats, securing 69.86% of the valid votes. This increased the PAP's seats in parliament by two. More important, there was a 9.7% swing in favour of the PAP compared to the 2011 General Elections. The 2015 results were the best for the PAP since 2001 when it captured 75.3% of the valid votes. The PAP even won the Punggol East SMC that it had lost to the WP in the 2013 by-election. All the opposition parties suffered a dip in their results, especially in comparison to the 2011 election results (Table 6.3).

Accounting for PAP's robust win in the 2015 General Elections

In many ways, while the win for the PAP was expected, the margin and emphatic nature of its victory were not. The strong victory for the PAP and general decline

Table 6.3: 2011 and 2015 Election Results Compared

Political Party/Alliance	Seats Won in 2011	Seats Won in 2015	% of Valid Votes in 2011	% of Valid Votes in 2015
PAP	81	83	60.14	69.86
WP	6	6	12.83	12.48
NSP	0	0	12.04	3.53
SDP	0	0	4.83	3.76
RP	0	0	4.28	2.63
SPP	0	0	3.11	2.17
SDA	0	0	2.78	2.06
SFP	Did not Contest	0	Did not Contest	2.25
PPP	Did not Contest	0	Did not Contest	1.13

Source: Author.

of support for the Opposition came as the surprise to all, including to the ruling party and its political opponents. Why then did the PAP win big? There have been many post-mortems on the 2015 General Elections and broadly speaking, there is a consensus as to why the PAP did well.

Retired PAP Member of Parliament for Ang Mo Kio GRC Inderjit Singh, in his Facebook post, explained the results as being a function of a number of factors. As to whether one should be surprised with the results, the former veteran parliamentarian noted:

> Given that GE2015 was called at a time when the ground could not have been any "sweeter", are the results a good reflection of the PAP's real support from voters? Ordinarily, given the timing and the fact that the previous government did many things to ensure the ground was as "sweet" as it can get, we should have expected that the PAP should have done significantly better than GE2011 with GE2015 perhaps delivering a score of around 64% to 65% of overall national vote, with the same number of 6 seats lost as in 2011.

However, the ruling party did far better than that, upping its performance from the previous elections by a 10 percentage point. Singh reasoned the PAP's robust performance being due to the following factors:

1. SG50 where the country celebrated in a very good mood and the government gave away good things to all Singaporeans
2. Mr. Lee Kuan Yew's passing was sad, but it did rally Singaporeans together and many would have reinforced their support for the PAP and realised the vulnerability we faced and continue to face as an unlikely nation
3. Pioneer Generation Package (PGP) of $8b would have won over most pioneer citizens above the age of 65. The PAP should have gotten a vote boost from this group
4. The government started its term after the 2011 election by making many changes, starting with the reduction of ministerial salaries and shifting its policies to be more inclusive and also addressing all the issues that Singaporeans were upset with before GE2011:
    a. Housing availability and cost (has improved tremendously but there is still room for improvement)
    b. Transport infrastructure (which people can see the efforts made but the true impact of these efforts will only be felt around 2020)

c. Building more hospitals (full effect yet to be felt)

d. Tightened the intake of foreigners (which had a double-edged effect — making small and medium-sized enterprises (SMEs) upset that they cannot get enough workers while trying to please Singaporeans). But the effect of this was also not fully felt as many foreigners are still here and people are more upset with the increase of Permanent Residents (PRs) and citizens more than the lower level foreign workers. Also, Professionals, Managers, Executives and Technicians (PMETs) continue to worry about their jobs

e. MediShield Life to take away worries of medical bills in the future

5. The government changed its position from a "growth at all cost" economic policy to an "inclusive growth" economic policy, therefore shifting more to the left to implement many schemes to rebalance income equality

6. There was also the instability factor in the region and the global economy which may have made some voters still wanting a more stable political environment in Singapore. This is especially with the governance and racial politics issues just across the Causeway.[34]

In the same vein, Professor Tommy Koh shared his 'reflections' on 10 factors that could have directly and indirectly affected the 2015 polls.[35] These were:

First, 2015 is not an ordinary year. It is our Golden Jubilee year. Singaporeans from all walks of life, and of different political persuasions, are very proud of what we have achieved in the past 50 years.

Second, I think that the Lee Kuan Yew factor played a part in the electoral success of the PAP. Mr Lee's passing triggered a spontaneous outpouring of love and respect for him by Singaporeans. The people of Singapore acknowledged that the success of Singapore was due, in large part, to the vision, courage and determination of Mr Lee and the other founding fathers.

Third, the opposition made a big mistake in contesting all 89 seats in Parliament. Although many of the candidates, from parties other than the Workers' Party (WP) and the Singapore Democratic Party (SDP), had no prospect of winning, the fact that all seats were contested made it possible for the PAP to warn against a freak election.

---

34. Inderjit Singh, *Facebook*, 16 September 2015.

35. Tommy Koh, "10 reflections on GE 2015", *The Straits Times*, 17 September 2015.

Fourth, since 2011, the Government has done several very significant things to win the hearts and minds of senior citizens. The Pioneer Generation Package, MediShield Life, and the Silver Support Scheme have been very well received. The belated recognition of the pioneers and their contributions to Singapore has touched the hearts of many older Singaporeans. My hypothesis is that the majority of the half a million voters, over the age of 65, would have voted for the PAP.

Fifth, the PAP has brought relief to three of the pain points that emerged in the 2011 General Election. These are housing, immigration and transport. National Development Minister Khaw Boon Wan has increased the supply of public housing, and cooled the overheated property market. The Government has also reduced the intake of foreign workers. Transport Minister Lui Tuck Yew worked very hard on both the bus system and the MRT system. He has brought relief to the bus system. The problem of the frequent breakdown of our train system has, however, not yet been solved, in spite of his best efforts.

Sixth, the PAP has also responded to the growing concerns about inequality in Singapore. It has introduced schemes like Workfare and the Progressive Wage Model...Therefore, although Singapore continues to be a very unequal society, and life is hard for the bottom 30 per cent of our population, the Government was given credit by the electorate for the many initiatives it has taken to address the problem.

Seventh, the ascendance of the WP was seriously affected by the PAP's allegation that it had mismanaged the Aljunied-Hougang-Punggol East Town Council, and that it had exposed an integrity issue.

Eighth, the PAP did a better job managing the electoral campaign this year than in 2011. PAP organising secretary Ng Eng Hen proved to be a capable campaign manager. Although the PAP was outgunned by the opposition in the staging of rallies, it devoted more manpower and resources to door-to-door campaigning and retail diplomacy. The party also decided to capitalise on the popularity of PM Lee by putting up his poster in every constituency. It was like a referendum on him, and it could have backfired. Fortunately for the PAP, the strategy seemed to have paid off.

Ninth, the sentiments of the electorate have always been affected by the external environment. The 2001 GE is a case in point. Following the Sept 11 terrorist attacks in the United States, the electorate rallied to the PAP, which has a good track record of keeping peace at home, and a strong defence against any external threat. In that election, the PAP's popular vote was 75.3 per cent. In this election, the PAP's narrative about the terrorist threat from the Islamic State of Iraq and Syria (ISIS) and the uncertain global economy worked to its advantage.

Tenth, I am glad that the PAP leader whose team scored the highest popular vote of 79 per cent was Deputy Prime Minister and Finance Minister Tharman Shanmugaratnam. He was always calm and measured. He never uttered an insult or a threat. Instead, he explained the PAP's policies and rebutted the alternatives put forward by the opposition in a clear and rational way. He was intellectually brilliant but came across as humble and open-minded.

Finally, on 13 September 2015, some 48 hours after the PAP's resounding victory, two analysts from *The Straits Times*, Jeremy Au Yong and Tham Yuen-C posited "8 reasons for surge of support" for the PAP. These were:

1. The SG50 factor
Observers had expected Singapore's Golden Jubilee to weigh heavily in the People's Action Party's (PAP) favour. And it looks like the all-year-round SG50 festivities, with the biggest National Day Parade on August 9, did have a feel-good effect on voters. But, more than that, celebrating Singapore's 50th year of independence and harking back to the country's early, more turbulent days, could also have reminded Singaporeans of just how unique their country is — a little red dot that not only existed, but also thrived against all odds.

2. The LKY effect
The death of the founding prime minister Lee Kuan Yew in March reminded Singaporeans of his key role in the country's progress. While it evoked a sense of gratitude and sympathy, some pundits were unsure if it would translate into votes for his PAP. But what is certain, though, is how the week of mourning galvanised Singaporeans, especially the silent majority, who turned up in the hundreds of thousands to pay respects outside Parliament House, at tribute sites around the country, and on the streets as his hearse passed by on the day of his funeral. The sense of solidarity and patriotism could have swung votes the PAP's way. And the story of how he and his pioneer generation of leaders built Singapore could have driven home the importance of a good leadership, which was a key plank of the PAP's campaign this election.

3. Policy changes
The Workers' Party (WP) had campaigned on it, telling voters that the Government's policy "U-turns" over the past four years were the result of a stronger opposition

presence in Parliament. It turns out though, that voters could have given the PAP credit for the policy changes instead. In areas such as immigration and property prices, the Government took quick, decisive actions to tighten the tap on foreigners and bring down property prices. These policy changes have, possibly, defused a number of hot button issues that turned up the heat in the 2011 elections and given voters fewer reasons for protest. Over the past four years, the leftward shift that the party had taken had also become more obvious, drawing praise from opposition parties and activists alike.

4. The AHPETC controversy

The issue of the WP's Aljunied-Hougang-Punggol East Town Council (AHPETC) dominated the first half of this election's campaign for both the opposition party and the PAP. On the one side, the PAP had attacked the WP for lapses at its town council, saying it exposed a deeper integrity problem at the party. On the other side, the WP had painted itself as a victim of the ruling party's bullying, saying the PAP was using the town council system to hobble opposition parties. But, in the second part of its campaign, the WP had moved away from the issue, seemingly confident that voters would not care. As it turns out, voters may not have bought the opposition party's story — that the whole issue was just being stirred up unnecessarily by the PAP. Perhaps the surest sign of this is the party's results in Aljunied GRC, most associated with the town council issue. The party barely clung onto the constituency, polling just 50.95 per cent of valid votes.

5. Fear of the 'what-ifs'

At the final Workers' Party (WP) rally of the campaign period, Hougang MP Png Eng Huat made a call for sweeping change. He said a fundamental overhaul of Singapore's political landscape was needed and that it could only be realised with a wave of support for the WP. Singapore needed "big change" at the polls, he said, or "nothing else will change at all". Those comments — taken in the context of this campaign and opposition leaders openly talking about the need for at least 20 opposition MPs — may have presented undecided voters with too much of a change all at once. While it was unlikely that anyone seriously bought into the PAP warning that it might fail to form the government, the opposition might have offered a vision of the future they were not yet ready to embrace.

6. Quality of the opposition

While the 2011 General Election was marked by excitement over a series of "star-catches" by opposition parties, there was a comparatively muted response to this year's slate. Part of it was simply because the voters had seen it all before. Highly qualified former government scholar with stellar academic credentials?…It is unclear if these star catches made all that much difference. PM Lee's criticism that the opposition was a "mouse in the House" may have found agreement with some voters. Opposition parties seemed less prepared for battle in 2015 than four years ago, when they presented a more thought-out strategy. The NSP was hurt by its constant flip-flopping on its decision to contest MacPherson SMC; the Singapore People's Party and Democratic Progressive Party could not agree on a joint team until the 11th hour; and the Internet had a field day with two separate Reform Party candidates who accidentally called on voters to support other parties.

7. PM Lee's likeability

Prime Minister Lee Hsien Loong may be one of the PAP's most popular politicians, but many observers still felt that his decision to place himself at the heart of the campaign was a risk. Posters of his smiling face were everywhere during this campaign, much to the chagrin of the opposition candidates. PM Lee also made campaign stops in various constituencies and sent e-mails to voters that were signed by him. The results are evidence that the gamble paid off. The PAP made gains across the board and PM Lee ended up with one of the best-performing wards in the election. Voters also rewarded him with the strongest mandate of his tenure.

8. External environment

In a departure from recent years, Prime Minister Lee Hsien Loong spent a significant chunk of this year's National Day Rally talking about global issues. "We have to be alive to our external environment, that's a fundamental reality for a 'little red dot'," he said, as he explained how instability in Singapore's neighbourhood could affect the nation. For voters who had kept up with global affairs, they might have seen that all is not well with the world at the moment. Even as Singapore's election campaign was picking up steam, its closest neighbour, Malaysia, was contending with growing unrest over corruption allegations involving the prime minister and China's massive stock market crash captured headlines around the world.[36]

The aforementioned assessment on why the ruling PAP enhanced its dominance at the 2015 General Elections basically pointed to a number of key considerations, namely, the silver jubilee celebrations, the government's generous handouts, especially for the 'silver citizens', the 'reduce-the-pain' policies since the 2011 General Elections, the relatively poor quality of the Opposition (except for the WP) and the sympathy factor following the passing on of Lee Kuan Yew. Clearly these were important contributory factors that worked in favour of the ruling PAP. However, it still does not convincingly explain why there was a strong surge by 10% in favour of the PAP compared to the last general elections in 2011.

Most probably, this had very much to do with the commissions and omissions of the opposition parties rather the strengths of the ruling PAP itself. In a way, it was a freak election in favour of the PAP and a protest vote against the Opposition. Already, much has been said of the poor quality of the Opposition's leadership and policies. The inability of the Opposition to work out a 'united front' indicated the poor and weak strategic position of the opposition parties, something which has coloured the Opposition's DNA for the last 50 years or so, and shun the public away from the Opposition in favour of the PAP. The opposition parties had difficulties agreeing on which wards to contest and more importantly, to prevent three-cornered fights. Having agreed upon this ostensibly wise strategy of not contesting with each other, the NSP suffered an internal leadership split on the issue leading its acting secretary-general, Hazel Poa, to resign just prior to Nomination Day. Following this, the NSP reneged on its stance to avoid a three-cornered fight. In the elections, the NSP and WP challenged the PAP candidate at the MacPherson SMC ward and lost, signalling the poor state of affairs in the NSP and the Opposition as a whole.

Except for the WP, the rest of the seven opposition parties could not boast of any star candidate or policy that could gain traction with the public. This largely explained the massive wins of the PAP against non-WP candidates as evident in Table 6.4. Of all the opposition parties other than the WP, the SDP came next best.

---

36. See Jeremy Au-Yong and Tham Yuen-C, "8 reasons for surge of support", *The Straits Times*, 13 September 2015.

Table 6.4: **PAP's Scores against Non-WP Contestants in the 2015 General Elections**

Wards	PAP's % Votes	Opposition's % Votes
Ang Mo Kio GRC	78.63	21.37
Bishan-Toa Payoh GRC	73.59	26.41
Chua Chu Kang GRC	76.89	23.11
Holland-Bukit Timah GRC	66.62	33.38
Jurong GRC	79.28	20.72
Marsiling-Yew Tee GRC	68.73	31.27
Pasir Ris-Punggol GRC	72.89	27.11
Sembawang GRC	72.28	27.72
Tampines GRC	72.06	27.94
Tanjong Pagar GRC	77.71	22.29
West Coast GRC	78.57	21.43
Bukit Batok SMC	72.99	26.40 (SDP); 0.60 (IND)
Hong Kah SMC	74.76	25.24
Mountbatten SMC	71.84	28.16
Pioneer SMC	76.34	23.66
Potong Pasir SMC	66.41	33.59
Radin Mas SMC	77.25	12.71 (SFP); 10.04 (IND)
Yuhua SMC	73.54	26.46

Source: Author.

Otherwise, all the other opposition parties were defeated by the PAP where they secured votes in the 20-plus percentage range. The only other party to stand out in defeat was the SPP where its candidate lost to the PAP incumbent in Potong Pasir SMC by securing 33.59% of the votes. This was a clear signal by the Singapore voters that they categorically rejected the candidates from the SDA, NSP, RP, SFP (Singapore First Party), PPP (People's Power Party), SDP, and SPP. Since 1965, the political culture in Singapore has never endorsed independent candidates and hence, their rejection was expected.

In contrast, of all the opposition political parties, the WP as in the 2011 polls, emerged as the 'star' party even though its performance dipped compared to the 2011 General Elections (Table 6.5). In terms of the number of seats won, the WP maintained the status quo, retaining its Aljunied GRC and Hougang SMC that it

Table 6.5: PAP's Scores against WP Contestants in the 2015 General Elections

Wards	PAP's % Votes	WP's % Votes
Aljunied GRC	49.05	50.95
East Coast GRC	60.73	39.27
Jalan Besar GRC	67.73	32.27
Marine Parade GRC	64.07	35.93
Nee Soon GRC	66.83	33.17
Fengshan SMC	57.52	42.48
Hougang SMC	42.31	57.69
MacPherson SMC	65.58	33.60 (WP); 0.82 (NSP)
Punggol East SMC	51.76	48.24
Sengkang West SMC	62.11	37.89

Source: Author.

also won in the 2011 elections. However, the Punggol East SMC that the WP won in a by-election was lost to the PAP.

In general, the 2015 General Elections showed a nationwide swing against the Opposition largely explaining the 10% surge in the PAP's votes compared to the 2011 General Elections. The PAP was expected to win, probably by around 60%, plus or minus, 1 to 2 percentage points. However, it was definitely not expected to romp home with a 10-percentage point compared to the 2011 General Elections. This was brought about by a number of factors. First, the Opposition did not benefit from a 'by-election effect' as every seat was contested. While by itself it did not create a fear that the ruling party would lose, mainly due to the general weakness of the Opposition, still, it made the voters cautious with their votes.

Second, while the public preferred to have opposition presence in parliament, it was not prepared for an opposition government. Somehow there was a sentiment, mainly stemming from the overwhelming public attendance at the opposition rallies of the WP and to some extent, the SDP, the discourses in the social media about the desirability of a strong opposition to punish the ruling party for its failures and the betting by bookies that created perception that there was a chance that the WP might perform exceptionally well, winning not just in its Aljunied GRC, Hougang and Punggol East SMC seats but also possibly in East Coast GRC, Jalan Besar GRC, Marine Parade GRC, MacPherson SMC and Sengkang West SMC. As the public was not prepared for this big swing that would have cause a serious dent to the ruling PAP government's power standing which the public was rather comfortable with, most of the voters became conservative with their voting, casting votes for the 'devil they knew' than the 'devil they did not really know'. It would appear that Singaporeans developed a 'cold feet syndrome', fearing that the PAP may lose badly and deciding to support it, reversing their earlier political behaviour of giving more support to the Opposition so that an effective system of checks and balances would develop in the political system.

This was especially so with regard to the third factor that swung the electoral support in favour of the PAP, namely, the floating voters. All being said, about 25% of the voters tend to be anti-PAP. The PAP's permanent support bank stands at around 45%. This leaves about 30% of floating voters, mostly made up of the middle and lower middle class. This is the group that always tends to suffer permanently and is sandwiched as it cannot move up and is always in fear of being downgraded to the lower end of the economic strata. This is also the group that tends to be daring and is prepared to express its anger at the ballot box. However, due to various factors such as SG50, the passing of Lee Kuan Yew, the popularity of the prime minister, the public support for PAP's 'left of centre' policies since 2011 and the fear that the WP might perform exceptionally well (something unpalatable for many conservative-oriented Singaporeans, including those in the middle class), there appeared to be a backlash against the WP, in particular, and all opposition parties, in general. This developed into a 'national tsunami' of support for the PAP in almost all constituencies, accounting for the 10% surge in PAP's support compared to the 2011 General Elections. Even in WP-held constituencies, there was a big swing against the incumbent, greatly benefitting the ruling party and entrenching further the one-party dominant state in Singapore at a time when democratic consolidation seems to be the norm in First World states and even in developed states in Asia such as Taiwan, Hong Kong, Japan and South Korea. Somehow, Singapore's exceptionalism in this regard stands out and the question is — why is the one-party dominant system so resilient in Singapore?

POST-2015 GENERAL ELECTIONS DEVELOPMENTS (THE BUKIT BATOK BY-ELECTION AND THE 2017 PRESIDENTIAL ELECTION)

Introduction

While there was much expectation that Singapore's politics would mature and a more robust democracy would emerge in the Republic, the whittling away of the People's Action Party's (PAP) support was strongly reversed in the 2015 General Elections. The May 2016 Bukit Batok by-election, followed by the 'selection' of Halimah Yacob as Singapore's seventh president in September 2017, sealed and reinforced the growing predominance of the PAP in Singapore's politics and hence, the continued resilience and entrenchment of the one-party dominant state, which some say, is a predominant state in the Republic.

The May 2016 Bukit Batok by-election

By and large, by-election results in Singapore have mirrored the outcomes of general elections. Since independence, out of the 31 by-elections, the PAP has only lost three, namely, in October 1981 in Anson, in May 2012 in Hougang and in January 2013 in Punggol East. All the PAP's defeats were at the hands of the Workers' Party (WP). PAP's electoral victories, both at the general elections and by-elections, since the mid-1960s were largely undertaken in an environment of PAP's dominance and where the Opposition was in a weak position with little public support.

Generally, Singapore voters tend to be less cautious in a by-election, as there is already a PAP as the government. Still, until 1981, the Opposition could not make electoral headways, due to its weakness and the asymmetrical power that the PAP exercised nationally on all fronts in the Republic. With a more matured and sophisticated electorate by the 1980s, the Opposition has been able to make some inroads in Singapore's politics by exploiting electoral grievances on various issues, partly accounting for the historic, first-ever opposition parliament seat in 1981 since 1965 that was garnered through a by-election. Despite the WP's successes in the three by-elections in 1981, 2012 and 2013, the Opposition was unable to defeat the PAP in the 2016 Bukit Batok by-election.

The Bukit Batok by-election was called following the resignation of David Ong, the serving PAP Member of Parliament (MP) on grounds of personal indiscretion. The 7 May 2016 contest was between PAP's Murali Pillai and Chee Soon Juan of the Singapore Democratic Party (SDP). The WP, together with the Democratic Progressive Party (DPP), Singapore Democratic Alliance (SDA), Singapore First Party (SFP) and the People's Power Party (PPP), ruled themselves out of contesting in the by-election. While Chee campaigned on the slogan that it was the right time to send another opposition member to parliament, the PAP focused on various municipal issues and upgrading that its designated member would undertake. Even more interesting was the fact that Bukit Batok was a matured housing estate with a Chinese majority population. Clearly, despite the much-talked about the importance of race being a determinant in Singapore's politics, in the Bukit Batok by-election, this was nowhere to be seen. When the results were announced, Murali won 61.21% of the votes compared to Chee's 38.79%.

The 2017 Presidential Election

Following what was described by some as a highly divisive 2011 Presidential Election and where the office of the EP was believed to have been misunderstood, especially where there was a belief that the EP could function as an 'alternate government', the government announced that there would be changes to the role and functions of the EP. Foremost among these changes was the need to allow minorities to be elected to the post, especially if someone from a minority group had not held the post for a long time. This led to the appointment of a nine-member Constitutional Commission in August 2016, headed by Chief Justice Sundaresh Menon, to address the issues. In September 2016, the government published a *White Paper* on the EP, broadly accepting the recommendations of the Constitutional Commission. The *White Paper* was debated in parliament in November 2016. The *White Paper* proposed a number of changes: raising the qualifying criteria for presidential candidates, introducing provisions to ensure that ethnic minorities are elected to the office from time to time, and to enhance the role of the Council of Presidential Advisers, whom the EP was obliged to consult when exercising the latter's executive powers. When the bill was passed in parliament, Prime Minister Lee Hsien Loong announced that the next presidential election would be held in August 2017 and that it would be reserved for a qualified candidate from the Malay community. This would mean that Singapore was destined to have a Malay president after 46 years, the last one being President Yusof Ishak who served as president from August 1965 to November 1970. The presidential election was later held in September 2017.

In the 2017 Presidential Election, three Malay candidates, namely, Halimah Yacob, Salleh Marican and Farid Khan, filed their application for the Certificate of Eligibility on 4 September 2017. Halimah, a long-serving PAP MP and a speaker of parliament, was clearly the PAP's choice. Salleh and Farid were successful businessmen. On 11 September 2017, the Presidential Election Commission announced that only Halimah was eligible and hence, won the presidency, like S.R. Nathan, through a walkover. Thus, this ended the much anticipated 2017 Presidential Election through a walkover and the selection of Singapore's first female president.

The public's reaction to the selection of President Halimah on 13 September 2017 through a walkover was not totally forthcoming. Many felt that the PAP had long planned and loaded the 'dice' before the Nomination Day of the presidential election to ensure Halimah's victory. This was partly by raising the 'bar', namely, eligibility criteria, so high that no Malay candidate from the community could qualify except for a political office holder.[1] This suspicion was all but confirmed when Chan Chun Sing, then minister in the Prime Minister's Office and in-charge of the National Trades Union Congress (NTUC), twice addressed Halimah as 'Madam President', described by some as a 'Freudian' slip.[2] During the parliamentary debate on the Presidential Election (Amendment Bill) on 6 February 2017, Chan referred to Halimah, then the speaker, as 'Madam President'. This was 220 days before Halimah, the PAP's endorsed candidate won the presidency through a walkover as her two competitors were disqualified.

---

1. Tessa Wong, "Why Singaporeans aren't all glad to get the president they wanted", *BBC News*, 13 September 2017.

2. Terry Xu, "Why Chan Chun Sing's 'freudian slip' of Mdm President, is not funny at all", *The Online Citizen*, 7 February 2017, https://www.theonlinecitizen.com/2017/02/07/why-chan-chun-sings-freudian-slip-of-mdm-president-is-not-funny-at-all/

That the PAP would pay a political price for this innovation was articulated by none other than Chan Chun Sing himself. Chan, during a discussion at the Institute of Police Studies forum on the Reserved Presidential Election, stated that he and his party decided to undertake the innovation for the good of Singapore's future, something that can be defended today in view how racial and religious politics have torn apart other diverse societies. Chan argued that "no good politician would sacrifice his political capital for a problem that may arise in future generations. Most good politicians in the world would try to preserve their political capital for themselves to manage their current problems."[3] However, "we are prepared to pay the political price, because we think the future of our country is much more important than any political capital that we may have."[4] The political price that Chan is talking about is probably public anger of being 'cheated' and denied of a right to express themselves and vote on the elected presidency, which may instead be expressed negatively during the forthcoming general elections.

It is thus clear that the hiatus-trigger Malay-only candidate election for the presidency in Singapore in 2017 was not without controversy. The criticisms were, not so much against the innovation per se but the manner it was implemented. Some of the anger against the government over the issue include:

- That the hiatus-trigger mechanism for Malays only was a red herring as the real aim was to deny Tan Cheng Bock from winning the presidency;
- Singaporeans were denied the right to vote as the government had disqualified two other potential candidates;
- Some felt that the PAP government did not trust voters or have confidence in the voters to choose their head of state;
- Some felt that the right to vote was violated;
- Some felt that the very core principle of meritocracy was ignored by the government; and

---

3. Lianne Chia, "Govt prepared to pay political price over changes to Elected Presidency: Chan Chun Sing", *Channel NewsAsia*, 8 September 2017, https://www.channelnewsasia.com/news/singapore/govt-prepared-to-pay-political-price-over-changes-to-elected-9199326

4. Ibid.

- Some felt that the government was signalling to the voters that it can ignore ground sentiments and do whatever it wants regardless of the public's choice and voice.[5]

How exactly the manner President Halimah was elected as the sixth Elected President (EP) will become an issue in the forthcoming general elections remains to be seen even though many also think that there may be more pressing and urgent issues that this controversy may be swept to the backwaters for the time being. This is also partly because President Halimah is highly popular among Singaporeans and well-liked.

Analysis

Even though the EP has been in operation since 1993 and its powers have been systematically whittled away, the PAP government has continued to insist that the EP is still a critical office to safeguard the interests of Singapore. In a 2006 public forum on governance, Lee Kuan Yew reiterated the need for the EP to counter a rogue government. In the same forum, Lee argued, "even with an Elected President, if they (the opposition) win a second time, the reserves are open, because they can then arrange for their president to be elected and the country comes to a grinding halt."[6] This statement demonstrates clearly the poor opinion that Lee and the PAP have for Singapore's political opposition. More importantly, the statement while referring to the inability of the Opposition to install its selected candidate for the role of the EP, implicitly reveals the same ability of the PAP to install the EP of its choice and do its bidding.

---

5. See Neyla Zannia, "Criticisms of Elected Presidency persist despite explanations and justifications", *The Online Citizen*, 26 September 2017, https://www.theonlinecitizen. com/2017/09/26/criticisms-of-elected-presidency-persist-despite-explanations-and-justifications/; Kumaran Pillai, "Like how we predicted! Halimah Yacob, our 3rd Indian President and 2nd from the Malay Community", *The Independent*, 23 July 2017, http://theindependent.sg/halimah-yacob-our-3rd-indian-president-and-2nd-from-the-malay-community/; Kirsten Han, "How Singapore elected a president without a vote", *CNN*, 12 September 2017, https://edition.cnn.com/2017/09/11/asia/singapore-race-presidential-election/index.html

6. See "Singapore must preserve its system of government: MM", *The Straits Times*, 16 September 2006.

Still, from the perspective of political dominance in Singapore, the office of the Head of State is vitally important, all the more, one vested with new executive powers. In whatever form, following various amendments and changes, the PAP continues to totally control the presidency, showing clearly its political dominance in the Republic. Despite the somewhat lethargic increase in support and presence of the Opposition in parliament since 1981, political power remains overwhelmingly in the hands of the prime minister and the PAP.

This was further reinforced by the by-election victory by the PAP in Bukit Batok in May 2016. What was significant about the May 2016 victory was the fact that this was the PAP's first by-election win in a Single-Member Constituency since 1981. Even though the PAP has been in power since 1959 and the Republic has made rapid all-round progress on all fronts and with the rise of an educated middle class, politically Singaporeans still remain largely conservative, preferring to 'live with the devil they know than the devil they do not know', thereby playing an important role in the continued entrenchment of the PAP in Singapore's politics at the expense of the Opposition to this day.

THE 2018 MALAYSIAN GENERAL ELECTIONS AND THE FALL OF THE NATIONAL FRONT GOVERNMENT: WILL THERE BE A CONTAGION-EFFECT ON SINGAPORE?

Introduction

In politics, a contagion-effect describes a development where something happening in one geographical area or even within a state can spread out and affect others in a similar manner. In short, it can have a bandwagon effect on State B as a result of an event happening in State A. With regard to the 2018 General Elections in Malaysia, the contagion-effect discussed with regard to Singapore is whether the collapse of the 61-year-old *Barisan Nasional* (BN) or National Front [Alliance from 1957– 1969] government can similarly induce a domino-effect and lead to the collapse of the PAP government in Singapore that has been in power since 1959. The answer to the question is — *no* — *except under one circumstance.*

The collapse of the BN government in 2018

Until May 2018, in non-communist Southeast Asia, Malaysia was the longest-serving one-party dominant state.[1] The continued existence of the Communist Party of Vietnam does not qualify as it operates in a one-party state, unlike Malaysia which has been practising a thriving and robust multi-party democracy since 1957. While the Alliance and BN have had challenges in the past, the tell-tales that something was terribly wrong with the 'political framework' became evident in the 2008 and 2013 general elections when the BN not only lost its two-thirds majority but in 2013, also lost the popular vote even though it remained in government. From 2013 to 2018, the BN faced many irreversible challenges that eventually ended its 61-year reign in Malaysia.

---

1. While describing Malaysia (Malaya before 1963) as a one-party dominant state may not be theoretically correct, in reality, it was a coalition in power with the United Malays National Organisation (UMNO) as the senior partner, be it from 1957 to 1969 in the Alliance or from 1969 to 2018 in the BN.

Reasons for the collapse of the BN government

While no single factor was responsible for the BN's collapse, eventually many *mini-tsunamis* combined to form a mega destructive wave on 9 May 2018 that toppled the ruling coalition, largely against the expectations of most analysts.[2] This Malaysian elections was akin to Donald Trump's victory in the November 2016 US Presidential Election and the UK Brexit vote on 23 June 2016, with the voters deciding in one way while pundits were largely predicting the opposite outcome. Clearly, Malaysian and non-Malaysian observers, and analysts were caught off guard by the 2018 General Elections results.[3]

According to Alex Capri, however, Malaysia's 14th General Elections "results should come as no surprise. This latest event is affirmation, yet again, of the convergence of powerful forces that are sweeping the world: digital disruption and its economic and social consequences; a middle-class backlash against entrenched and corrupt elites; and, like it or not, the growing influence of China."[4] For him, "just like the Brexit and Trump election outcomes, data analytics, social media and digital platforms played a major role in determining the winners in this historic election."[5] This is a reality that is often ignored. Capri noted that "Malaysia has a smartphone penetration rate of over 75%, with over 40% of the country's 15 million voters under the age of forty — meaning, 'digital natives,'" and "they get their news almost exclusively via social media."[6] According to Capri, while many social media platforms such as Facebook, Twitter and YouTube dominate the Malaysian scene, some 97% of social media users are active on Facebook, making "Malaysia one of the world's most digitally connected and internet-savvy countries."[7] What this also

---

2. See Chua Mui Hoong, "Malaysian General Elections: 5 takeaways for Singapore", *The Straits Times*, 13 May 2018.

3. For example, see Simon Tay, "Malaysia votes: What the General Election means for Malaysia's stability and Singapore–Malaysia Ties", *Singapore Institute of International Affairs*, 20 April 2018, http://www.siiaonline.org/malaysia-votes-what-the-general-election-means-for-malaysias-stability-and-singapore-malaysia-ties/

4. Alex Capri, "Why Malaysia's surprise election result should be a wake-up call for global leaders", *Forbes*, 10 May 2018, http://www.globaladvisors.biz/blog/2018/05/11/why-malaysias-surprise-election-result-should-be-a-wake-up-call-for-global-leaders/

5. Ibid.

6. Ibid.

7. Ibid.

means is that the 2018 General Elections was effectively a cyberspace election with bots and fake news being played out and where through artificial intelligence and data analytics, the opposition coalition was able to "target specific voters with laser-accuracy via social media" at the expense of the largely complacent, out-of-touch-with-the-public ruling coalition.[8]

While the role of the social media and technology was critical, however, in what is often dubbed as 'conservative Malaysia', real and hard issues relating to cost of living and unacceptable blatant high-level corruption doomed the ruling BN.[9] While digital technology provided a power multiplier-effect for a small wealthy elite, the blatant corruption and existence of dysfunctional institutions controlled by the same elites led to an electoral backlash. According to a Malaysian analyst, "concerns over cost of living was the single most compelling issue for Malaysians — particularly for 1.4 million young voters" that led to the political tsunami against the ruling coalition. This was mainly because these young voters were uncertain of their economic future, despite Malaysia being touted as a rich state.[10]

In this environment of uncertainty, salt was added to the national wounds when Prime Minister Najib Razak became embroiled in a mega corruption scandal surrounding the 1Malaysia Development Berhad (1MDB), something the ordinary citizens could not stomach any longer.[11] While corruption and the outbreak of scandals are not new issues, the scale of the 1MDB and the continued denial and mismanagement of the issue by the ruling coalition, especially the Prime Minister,

---

8. Ibid.

9. Following former Prime Minister Najib Razak's arrest on 3 July 2018 and where he was charged on three counts of criminal breach of trust and using his position for gratification, allegations have surfaced that he used his official position to plunder state funds, especially through the Malaysian state fund 1MDB with the money used to buy real estate overseas, artefacts, etc. However, much anger has also been directed at the spending spree of Najib's wife, Rosmah Mansor, including the publicity on her trove of luxury items such as handbags, jewellery, etc. worth more than US$273 million. This has greatly damaged Najib in the eye of the public. See "Former PM Najib arrested", *The Business Times*, 3 July 2018.

10. Cited in Alex Capri, "Why Malaysia's surprise election result should be a wake-up call for global leaders".

11. Randeep Ramesh, "1MDB: The inside story of the world's biggest financial scandal", *The Guardian*, 28 July 2016, https://www.theguardian.com/world/2016/jul/28/1mdb-inside-story-worlds-biggest-financial-scandal-malaysia

sounded his political death knell, including allegations associated with his wife, Rosmah Mansor, who was seen to be flouting her ill-gotten wealth over global brand luxury items such as diamond rings, designer bags and shoes.[12] Rosmah was painted as 'Malaysia's Imelda Marcos' and that was enough to fatally hurt the ruling coalition.[13] Thus, even though the ruling BN was always successful due to the votes from the majority Malay-Muslims, and especially in view of the fear of racial tensions and issues, in the 2018 General Elections, there was a national swing away from the party that brought about its downfall.

Malaysia's opposition also criticised the BN government for 'selling' the country to China and Chinese investments through the launch of multi-billion dollars mega projects. Prime Minister Najib was said to have 'tilted' towards China mainly for economic reasons and where massive corruption was also alleged. According to one analyst, between 2009 and 2018, Malaysia had signed 14 Memorandums of Understanding (MOUs) with China worth US$34 billion. In addition to the Kuala Lumpur–Singapore high-speed rail link that was opposed by the Opposition, many of the projects were linked to China's One-Belt-One-Road initiative and where China was both the financier and contractor, such as the US$13 billion East Coast Rail Link connecting Malaysia's east and west coasts, with China Exim Bank providing the funds and the China Communications Construction Company building the rail link.[14]

From the ruling party's side, it was eventually Najib's loss of credibility that hurt him within the United Malays National Organisation (UMNO), the BN and the nation. Somehow, even though he was in national politics for more than four

---

12. See A. Ananthalakshmi, "Malaysia's first lady linked to $30 mln worth of jewelry bought with IMDB funds", *Reuters*, 16 June 2017; Nor Arlene Tan, "Inside the lavish world of Malaysia's Rosmah Mansor", *Arab News*, 9 June 2018.

13. Danielle Ann, "Rosmah vs Imelda Marcos? Who is the true Southeast Asian First Lady of seized luxury?", *Alvinology.com*, 24 May 2018, https://alvinology.com/2018/05/24/rosmah-vs-imelda-who-is-the-true-southeast-asian-first-lady-of-seized-luxury/; on 4 October 2018, Rosmah was arrested and charged with 17 counts of violating money-laundering laws, including tax evasion. See Yantoultra Ngui and Ben Otto, "Rosmah Mansor, Wife of former Malaysian leader, charged with money laundering related to 1MDB scandal", *The Wall Street Journal*, 4 October 2018, https://www.wsj.com/articles/rosmah-mansor-wife-of-former-malaysian-leader-arrested-in-connection-with-1mdb-scandal-1538560162

14. See Tham Siew Yean, "Chinese investments in Malaysia: Five years into the BRI", *ISEAS Perspectives*, 11, 27 February 2018.

decades, he appeared to be out of touch with ground sentiments, or for that matter, the grassroots leaders were not communicating the toxic ground feelings towards him. Before the general elections, Najib even had hopes of not just winning but also the possibility of regaining the two-thirds majority in parliament, showing how badly disconnected he was from political realities of Malaysia. In this regard, some of Najib's fatal failings included[15]:

a. Not appreciating or understanding the intense infighting in the UMNO divisional branches country-wide with about 78 branches affected by this problem. This greatly weakened UMNO on the ground during the elections.

b. Allowing key decisions about the elections and other national matters, including sacking of top UMNO officials, to be in the hands of a cabal made up of five to six individuals who were not grounded in party politics but only keen in ensuring that Najib remains as the prime minister as well as continuing the kleptocratic practices of garnering more megaprojects that would yield massive corruption monies. This included officials such as Abdul Azeez Abdul Rahim (Tabung Haji) and Bustari Yusof, a leading businessman close to Najib's family.[16]

c. Being badly advised that Najib-led BN would win around 140 seats in the general elections.

d. Being advised to choose 9 May 2018 as the polling date, in the belief that it would strike fear in the Chinese voters, reminding them of the 13 May 1969 racial riot and where five days after the polling, the fasting month of Ramadhan would begin and even if there was unhappiness with Najib's 'expected win', the likelihood of street demonstrations would be minimal.

e. Deciding to ban *Parti Pribumi Bersatu Malaysia* (BERSATU) and forcing it to contest under the PKR banner, a highly fatal move that not only publicly eventuated the Mahathir–Anwar reconciliation but showed to the public the level Najib and BN would go to harm 'democracy' just to ensure that the BN wins.

---

15. Interview on 18 June 2018 in Kuala Lumpur with a key *Pakatan Harapan* (PH) grassroots activist who was heavily involved in the Malaysian May 2018 General Elections.

16. See Royce Tan, "Abdul Azeez: I'm a victim of name dropping", *The Star*, 3 March 2018; *Malaysians Must Know the Truth*, 23 May 2018, http://malaysiansmustknowthetruth. blogspot.com/2018/05/as-macc-chief-exposes-king-of-cash-mp.html; Clare Rewcastle Brown, "Bustari The Bag Man? How Najib bought the Sarawak election", *The Sarawak Report*, 29 May 2017; also see "Najib's circle of family, friends and cronies", *Reddit*, https://www.reddit.com/r/malaysia/comments/8lkzxm/najibs_circle_of_family_friends_and_cronies/?st=jllsagxc&sh=16504bc6

f.   When reports started to surface that the *Pakatan Harapan* (PH) was doing very well and likely to win, Najib was convinced that these reports were false (or fake news) and only surfaced because those supporting the PH were 'bought' and as such, the reports were not to be believed. When three days before polling, on 6 May, Najib was told that West Malaysia was effectively lost to the Opposition, he did not believe it and continued confidently to behave as if he would be returned to office again on 9 May.[17]

It was in this context that Nur Jazlan, a UMNO Supreme Council member commented that Najib "should have seen the collapse of UMNO and *Barisan Nasional* (BN) coming and that there were issues with his leadership."[18] He blamed BN's defeat on Najib's "failure to address allegations of corruption made against him and issues related to 1Malaysia Development Berhad (1MDB)" and that "UMNO's approval rating was beginning to diminish since the issue of 1MDB surfaced beginning 2014."[19] Nur Jazlan opined that "in politics, he, as the leader of a party, should have known that all these negative perceptions against him and the family would eventually cause UMNO and BN's defeat. We lost because of these perceptions, because they are all tied to him."[20]

A key question was, if the ground was 'sour' and 'toxic', why was this not communicated to Najib and why did the feedback mechanism of the dominant party fail? Nur Jazlan stated that this was partly due to the party's respect for Najib and probably even more important, "many of the party members chose to remain quiet and not speak up previously due to the respect they had towards Najib as the son of former prime minister Tun Abdul Razak Hussein."[21] UMNO Youth Chief, Khairy Jamaluddin, however, stated that there was a problem with Najib's leadership as he and the top leaders were detached from reality and thought that

---

17. Many of these points were garnered by the author's interview with individuals in Kuala Lumpur who were working closely with the PH leadership prior to Polling Day on 9 May 2018.

18. "Nur Jazlan: Najib should have foreseen BN's collapse". *The Sun Daily*, 21 May 2018, http://www.thesundaily.my/news/2018/05/21/nur-jazlan-najib-should-have-foreseen-bn%E2%80%99s-collapse

19. Ibid.

20. Ibid.

21. Ibid.

the BN was invincible. He said that UMNO and BN failed "to acknowledge that the grassroots had rejected the party. What happened was we became delusional; we got drunk on our own Kool-Aid and we got carried away. We didn't want to bell the cat. Nobody, after former deputy Tan Sri Muhyiddin Yassin was purged, after Datuk Seri Shafie was purged...Nobody wanted to acknowledge we had a problem. That was a terrible mistake on our part."[22]

For Khairy, the general elections results were indicative of not just the rejection of Najib but also the rejection of UMNO and BN. It was a "systemic rejection of what we stand for and if we can accept that, then we can start to rebuild this party."[23] For Khairy, a fatal mistake that eventually dismantled the BN's power structure in the country was the party members' failure to speak the truth and their sole interest in defending Najib. This was especially after Muhyiddin, the deputy prime minister and Shafie Apdal, a federal minister and UMNO's vice president, were removed from cabinet for publicly criticising Najib over the IMDB scandal.[24] Hence, for Khairy, there were signs that the BN was in trouble: "Was there a signal? Yes, there were clear signals but we became oblivious to the signals...This must not happen again, we must not ever allow UMNO leaders to be detached from reality and not ask tough questions. If we continue with our feudal mindset of protecting the leader from the truth, UMNO will go extinct."[25] For Khairy, "the mistake of failing to speak the truth in order to protect Najib is one he will personally have to live with for the rest of his life."[26] In a way, as was predicted by pollster Ibrahim Suffian from the Merdeka Centre, "in the short term, this [July 2015 sackings] has thwarted the intentions

---

22. "'Nobody wanted to acknowledge we have a problem': UMNO youth chief Khairy on BN's defeat", *Channel NewsAsia*, 15 May 2018, https://www.channelnewsasia.com/news/asia/khairy-umno-ge14-defeat-barisan-nasional-malaysia-10234396

23. Ibid.

24. 28 July 2015 was the day of Najib's long-knives. He sacked his key critics in cabinet. In addition to Muhyiddin Yassin and Mohammad Shafie Apdal, three senior ministers were also removed, namely, Palanivel Govidasamy, Hasan Malek, Ewon Ebin, as well as two key national officers, Gani Patail, the attorney-general investigating the 1MDB case and the Special Branch director.

25. "'Nobody wanted to acknowledge we have a problem': UMNO youth chief Khairy on BN's defeat".

26. Ibid.

of those trying to unseat him [Najib]. However, it is a long road to regain the political capital [lost] by the economic issues, GST [goods and services tax] and the 1MDB saga." This proved to be prophetic and in reality, not only did Najib fail to regain the political capital, he also galvanised those opposing him into a political force that eventually unseated Najib's government.[27]

However, what brought all these grievances and unhappiness together, and convinced Malaysians to undertake a regime change was the presence of Malaysia's controversial and yet iconic all-season, perennial political leader, Mahathir Mohamad, who provided the centre of gravity to oppose Najib and the BN. Mahathir became the Opposition's centripetal force uniting all anti-Najib and anti-BN forces together into an unstoppable juggernaut that toppled the 61-year ruling alliance. Mahathir cobbled a multi-racial coalition called PH or Alliance of Hope, formed in September 2015, consisting of the Democratic Action Party (DAP), People's Justice Party (PKR), Malaysian United Indigenous Party (BERSATU) and the National Trust Party (AMANAH), that was allied with two local political parties in Sabah, namely, the Sabah Heritage Party (Warisan) and the UPKO (United *Pasokmomogun Kadazandusun Murut* Organisation). Following the 2018 General Elections in Malaysia, the PH not only holds the majority in the national parliament but also controls eight of the 13 state assemblies in Kedah, Penang, Perak, Selangor, Negeri Sembilan, Malacca, Johor and Sabah. Sarawak is also likely to switch alignment even though it had not joined the PH. In June 2018, four political parties aligned to BN in Sarawak formed a new coalition called *Gabungan Parti Sarawak* (Coalition of Sarawak Political Parties) by leaving BN but not joining the PH yet.[28] With a tried and tested national leader albeit somewhat controversial, Mahathir, at 92 then, campaigned tirelessly to change Malaysia. He promised to repeal the Goods and Services Tax of 6%, re-examine the mega infrastructure projects such as the Singapore–Malaysia High Speed Rail, review Malaysia's business contracts with China, and manage the country based on the rule of law. If the 2008 and 2013

27. Shannon Teoh, "Najib sacks DPM, four ministers and A-G", *The Straits Times*, 29 July 2015.

28. See Mohd. Latif Ahmad, "Sarawak BN not joining Pakatan Harapan: Abang Johari", *New Straits Times*, 14 May 2018; Stephen Then, "Sarawak Pakatan Harapan will fight new GPS coalition of former BN parties in the next state polls", *The Star*, 12 June 2018; "Departure of Sarawak parties from Barisan Nasional is Pakatan Harapan's gain, analysts say", *The Straits Times*, 13 June 2018.

dipping of the BN votes was due to the 'Chinese tsunami', then the BN's defeat in 2018 can definitely be attributed to a 'partial Malay tsunami' against the BN and this was primarily due to the Mahathir factor. Malaysian Malays continue to believe that Mahathir would champion and safeguard Malay rights, and hence, the preparedness to abandon UMNO for a group of leaders who were formerly with UMNO such as Mahathir and even Anwar Ibrahim.

In a way, if the public was attracted to the Opposition that was in the past principally made up of the DAP, PKR and PAS, the BN would have long lost power, especially in the 2013 General Elections. However, what was different in 2018 was the Mahathir factor as well as the support Mahathir received from former UMNO stalwarts. As one report stated before Polling Day, "The opposition has also banked on Dr Mahathir's star power, with many flocking to rallies to catch a glimpse of a leader they had held in awe during his 22 years at the helm."[29] Similarly, a *New York Times* report elucidated the Mahathir factor in the following terms:

> Mr. Mahathir is not just the only Malaysian politician today who can hold the fractious opposition together; *he is also the only one who stands any chance of defeating Mr. Najib at his own game, namely by appealing to the Muslim-Malay majority.* [emphasis added]
>
> The opposition has long been a motley assortment, usually of the Malay party led by Mr. Anwar, a predominantly ethnic-Chinese party and some Islamists. Partly because of their association with, say, the Chinese party, even Muslim-Malay opposition leaders like Mr. Anwar have been accused of betraying their own ethnic group and religion. And UMNO has consistently framed any challenge to it as a threat to Muslim-Malays' political power, their preferential quotas and even Islam itself. Such charges can't stick against Mr. Mahathir.[30]

Mahathir also gained much public sympathy, especially from the perspective of a then 92-year-old former prime minister who was taking on Najib, whom he had backed in the past for the post of prime minister. As Mahathir said in a campaign rally on 5 May 2018, "It is very tiring but still I survive. Now I'm old.

---

29. See Lim Ai Leen and Shannon Teoh, "Malaysia election: Mahathir calls for change at Reformasi rally site", *The Straits Times*, 7 May 2018.

30. See Wong Chin-Huat, "Why Malaysia's opposition picked an old foe as its leader", *The New York Times*, 11 January 2018.

I still can speak for one hour. I would like to find out any other 92-year-old willing to speak for one hour."[31] Mahathir's willingness to admit that he made many mistakes in the past, was prepared to reconcile with his former political adversaries such as Anwar and that he would like to put the country and its politics right as he "does not have much time left", resonated powerfully with the electorate that not only made Mahathir the oldest head of government in the world today but is likely to prolong his record as the longest-serving prime minister in Malaysia. Mahathir's appeal was across-the-board but was strategically powerful among Malay voters that eventually won the elections for the PH.[32]

In addition, many former UMNO stalwarts also backed Mahathir's leadership of PH and his rallying cry to topple Najib, whom Mahathir described as a 'thief',[33] and the BN. Both Mahathir and Anwar were former UMNO leaders. Muhyiddin was similarly like Anwar, was not only an UMNO vice president but also the country's DPM. Additionally, Daim Zainuddin, Rais Yatim and Rafidah Aziz also openly campaigned and supported Mahathir and the PH. Rafidah, for instance, who was attending an election rally after more than 10 years, justified her support for Mahathir's campaign as follows: "While I was in my retirement, I was watching what the government was up to. The time has come for me to do the right thing, especially when the country is falling apart."[34] The current chief minister of Sabah, Shafie Apdal, was formerly an UMNO federal minister and its vice president. The former chief minister of Johor, Osman Sapian, was formerly an UMNO state assemblyman in Johor before he was dropped by UMNO and he later became the Johore secretary for BERSATU. In April 2019 Osman was replaced by Sahruddin Jamal. Malaysia's former foreign minister and a senior UMNO member, Hamid Albar, also supported Muhyiddin and Mahathir.

---

31. See Jack Board, "Mahathir brings together old brigade, doubles down on Najib in Melaka", *Channel NewsAsia*, 5 May 2018, https://www.channelnewsasia.com/news/asia/mahathir-melaka-malaysia-ge14-najib-10204378

32. Ibid.

33. See "Under Najib, many became thieves, says Dr Mahathir", *Today*, 26 August 2018; "Tun Mahathir: 'When Najib became a thief, everyone under him became a thief' — your days are numbered", *The Coverage*, 30 August 2018, https://thecoverage.my/news/tun-mahathir-najib-became-thief-everyone-became-thief-days-numbered/

34. See Jack Board, "Mahathir brings together old brigade, doubles down on Najib in Melaka".

Mahathir, Muhyiddin, Shafie and Osman's former UMNO links are also critical in explaining the collapse of the UMNO-led BN government. While many Malaysians have been critical of the BN in the last decade or so, best evident in the 2008 and 2013 general elections, there was somehow a reluctance to overthrow a discredited political system for something unknown. In short, there was a fear of change for the unknown, especially in a country that had experienced inter-racial conflicts and bloodshed in the past. There was always the fear that the Malays would perceive the attempt to overthrow UMNO as a direct challenge to Malay supremacy and power in the country, a compact championed by UMNO since its formation and formalised through the Alliance and BN structure. However, with former UMNO stalwarts such as Mahathir, known as champions of 'Malay rights', this fear was largely allayed. As a *New York Times* report in January 2018 stated, "and because Mr Mahathir represents continuity in change, his nomination [as leader of PH and possibly the next prime minister] has just made change more acceptable — for voters in this election perhaps but far more important, for eventually reforming Malaysia's deep state."[35] While some analysts have argued that Mahathir was a factor but not the only factor in the BN's defeat, the point remains that the role of Mahathir was extremely critical, even the keystone, in creating a momentum and a political setting where Najib and the BN could not defend themselves and hence, the historic defeat.[36]

Some have even argued that the new party that Mahathir leads, BERSATU, that admits only Malays and natives of Sabah and Sarawak, represents "a clear attempt to steal some of UMNO's ethnic thunder."[37] If anything, many Malays voted for Mahathir as he was seen as the real representative and symbol of UMNO compared to Najib and this also made supporting the PH far more easy and palatable compared to the past, and hence, the downfall of Najib and the BN in May 2018.[38] If Khairy Jamaluddin, the UMNO Youth Chief was lamenting the rejection of Malay support at the grassroots, by the converse, it also meant that Mahathir and his party came

---

35. See Wong Chin-Huat, "Why Malaysia's opposition picked an old foe as its leader".

36. "Yoursay: Harapan win a 20-year effort, not just due to Dr M", *Malaysiakini*, 20 July 2018.

37. See Wong Chin-Huat, "Why Malaysia's opposition picked an old foe as its leader".

38. Uihua, "Is Muhyiddin's new party a rebranded UMNO? Or could it be a stroke of genius?", *Cilisos.my*, 17 August 2016, https://cilisos.my/is-muhyiddins-new-party-a-rebranded-umno-or-could-it-be-a-stroke-of-genius/

to be seen as the real champions of the Malays and hence, as the 'new UMNO', whatever the party label it carried. Mahathir argued that UMNO has betrayed the trust of the people, especially of the Malays and they should abandon the party. According to Mahathir, UMNO leaders and members should leave the party as it was not worth being associated with it: "When a leader has betrayed the party, and he can't be removed, then the only option for you is to leave, there's no point staying."[39] UMNO stands for United Malays National Organisation and BERSATU stands for Malaysian United Indigenous Party. Both political parties look similar. When the party was launched in January 2017 in Shah Alam, Selangor, its president, Muhyiddin Yassin called on the opposition parties to put aside their differences to form a viable alternative. He argued, "we have to save the nation, this is the reason why we are here, to save the nation...we will never win if we can't come together. It must be one-on-one fight. This is just the beginning, the work starts now, there must be a sense of urgency to put together a people's front, or barisan rakyat."[40] Mainly due to the shift of loyalties of the Malaysian population and especially of the Malays, the May 2018 elections was akin to a bloodless coup that toppled the pro-Malay party, UMNO as well as dismantled a consociational ethnic-based power sharing framework that largely operated in Malaysia since 1957. Interestingly, when UMNO celebrated its 72th anniversary on 11 May 2018, Mahathir's message to the party was a simple one: "go back to your roots", implying that the party had deviated from its promises and mission, and hinted that someone else, probably BERSATU, was the new champions of the Malays in Malaysia.[41]

Implications of the BN collapse for Singapore's PAP

A key question following the BN defeat and the victory of PH was whether the People's Action Party (PAP) would suffer the same fate as the BN in the coming elections. Prior to May 2018, there had been two major discourses about the manner the PAP would be defeated in Singapore and dislodged from power. The first discourse involved themes relating to the rising rejection of the PAP due to

---

39. See Melissa Goh, "Mahathir launches new party; promises to abolish GST if opposition wins", *Channel NewsAsia*, 15 January 2017, https://www.channelnewsasia.com/news/asia/mahathir-launches-new-party-promises-to-abolish-gst-if-oppositio-7579242

40. Ibid.

41. Annabelle Lee, "Dr M birthday message to UMNO — 'Go back to your roots'", *Malaysiakini*, 11 May 2018, https://www.malaysiakini.com/news/424240

the party's failures on various fronts, especially performance legitimacy, arrogance, increasingly being elitist and out of touch with the voters as well as fatal mistakes that would motivate voters to reject the party at the ballot box. In Singapore's context, this would involve issues relating to corruption, cronyism and nepotism, something that the public rejects in toto. The second discourse relates to the rise of the Opposition's credibility and voters' willingness to give the Opposition, either as a single party or a coalition of parties, a chance to rule Singapore in place of the PAP. Since May 2018, though somewhat related to the first and second discourses, a new narrative has surfaced, arguing that what happened to the BN can and should transpire in Singapore. This stems from the view that this is something 'that can be done' and is doable, compared to the view that it was an impossible task, that what is needed is an acceptable leader and a coalition to topple the PAP, that the electorate, especially the young, is increasingly unhappy with the ruling party and what has stopped it from voting the party out of power was the lack of a credible alternative, and finally, the view that is being spread, is that PAP's longevity in power has bred all kinds of abuses, inefficiencies and negative consequences that have harmed the State and society, and that a change, at the right time and to the right group of alternative political leadership, would be a good thing for Singapore and its people, and its international image as a developed and democratic political entity.

The supporters of the PH's victory and aspiring for a similar contagion in Singapore have premised their arguments on the notion that if the PH can do so in Malaysia, so can the Opposition in Singapore even though the timeline is a factor that needs to be considered, say may be, two more elections from the forthcoming 2019/2020/2021 General Elections. The issues on which to galvanise the anti-PAP campaign are manifold, including:

1. The unabated rising cost of living and largely stagnant salaries of the majority of Singaporeans, especially if compared to the rate of inflation and costs of basic goods and services in the Republic.
2. The economy seems to be largely straddling along on an old formula and the talk of a new skill-based economy is just that, talk, with bulk of the citizens not benefitting from the so-called new economy, and if there are any benefits, these seemed to have accrued to non-citizens and have been systematically creamed off by foreigners.
3. The continued culture of the PAP to use state organs, including the civil service, government-linked companies (GLCs), etc. and most blatantly of all, the People's Association, to promote the PAP's interests that are juxtaposed as the

interest of the state, is seen as an abuse of power that is increasingly viewed as unacceptable by most voters and is looked upon as a violation of the principles of fair play and justice.

4. The rising criticism of the ruling party, be it of its leaders, such as the prime minister who suffered a backlash over the handling of Lee Kuan Yew's house at Oxley Road, and the prime minister's public quarrel with his siblings over many aspects of Lee Kuan Yew's political and other inheritances.

5. The view that Singapore under the PAP, despite the rhetoric of upholding meritocracy, violated it blatantly by organising the 'election' of a Malay-only elected presidency, through a 'selection' and not an 'election' as was promised by the prime minister. This was seen as re-writing the rules of the political game to benefit the ruling party, as and when it desires, as the PAP is in control of parliament and hence, the non-existence of any checks and balances, to the detriment of the public interest at large at any one time under the present political paradigm.

6. Despite the PAP lambasting the Workers' Party (WP) for mismanagement of town council's funds,[42] the PAP administered government itself, through its GLCs, is seen to be involved in, at least indirectly, corrupt practices, as was discovered, followed by the prosecution in the US of Keppel, Jurong and Sembawang Shipyards[43] but where these officials were not punished by the state.[44] This 'Animal Farm' approach to politics is seen as a double-standard and unacceptable as the electorate becomes more matured, informed and demands fair play.

7. In short, the PAP is said to be suffering from a rising credibility crisis that will chip away, albeit slowly, its political control and legitimacy, and lead eventually

---

42. On 5 October 2018, a civil case was brought against three WP leaders, namely, Low Thia Khiang, Sylvia Lim and Pritam Singh, for mismanagement of Aljunied-Hougang Town Council funds. See Selina Lum, "Checks and balances at AHTC lacking and flawed, court told", *The Straits Times*, 6 October 2018.

43. Vincent Low, "What happens now to Sembcorp Marine after Keppel pays US$422m in fines for corruption?", *The Online Citizen*, 26 January 2018; John Geddie, "Keppel bribery fine shines spotlight on peer Sembcorp, shares slide", *Reuters*, 26 December 2017, https://www.reuters.com/article/us-keppel-corp-stocks/keppel-bribery-fine-shines-spotlight-on-peer-sembcorp-shares-slide-idUSKBN1EK09I; Tang See Kit, "Keppel O&M bribery case: What you need to know", *Channel NewsAsia*, 7 January 2018, https://www.channelnewsasia.com/news/business/keppel-o-m-bribery-case-what-you-need-to-know-9836154; "Singapore firm Keppel Offshore to pay $422 mn in corruption fines", *AFP News*, 23 December 2017, https://sg.news.yahoo.com/singapore-firm-keppel-offshore-pay-422-mn-corruption-104858672-finance.html

44. See Walter Woon, "Punishing Corporate Corruption", *The Straits Times*, 30 April 2018.

to its loss of power, *a la BN* in Malaysia. It will be the many *mini tsunamis* that will eventually accumulate and once the tipping point is reached, bring the PAP down once the conditions are right.

Singapore watcher and Australian academic, James Chin from the University of Tasmania argued that, following the BN defeat "the PAP could lose power as its brand was fast becoming 'toxic.'"[45] He stated that the PAP's astounding electoral victory in 2015 was "primarily due to the death of Lee Kuan Yew six months earlier" and "voters wanted to give LKY a last hurrah."[46] However, beneath the PAP's excellent performance was the presence of strong public discontent and unhappiness, mainly due to the "disconnect between the ruling party and the masses and costs of living" as "ordinary Singaporeans already have a negative view of the PAP elite, who graduate from the best-known universities, hold the most prestigious scholarships and serve in the Singapore Armed Forces before entering PAP politics. They are seen as totally removed from the hard lives of ordinary Singaporeans."[47] Since the 2015 General Elections, Chin noted that Singaporeans were subjected to higher costs, including: a 30% hike in the prices of water — which the prime minister deems as "absolutely necessary"; increase in tuition fees for university students despite huge surpluses in the universities' endowment funds; gas tariffs were continuously increased despite Singapore Power making an average profit of S$1 billion a year for the past 13 years; parking charges at Housing and Development Board (HDB) and Urban Redevelopment Authority (URA) carparks, despite URA and HDB making almost S$600 million in profits from car park charges; a S$13.30 airport tax for passengers flying out of Changi Airport which took effect on 1 July 2018 to fund the new Terminal 5; and possible e-commerce GST imposed on goods purchased online.[48] To these grouses can be added the HDB leasehold issue that has gripped Singapore and which the prime minister and key leaders have tried to address but without satisfying everybody and which will probably be a hot potato issue in the

45. See Kwok Fangjie, "Mahathir: Singaporeans must be tired of having the same government since independence", 29 May 2018, *The Online Citizen*, https://www.theonlinecitizen.com/2018/05/29/mahathir-singaporeans-must-be-tired-of-having-the-same-government-since-independence/

46. Ibid.

47. Ibid.

48. Ibid.

coming general elections.[49] In October 2018, the government announced further hikes in electricity charges for the population.[50]

However, supporters of the PAP have argued that the PH victory will not have an impact on PAP's future and longevity as the malaises suffered by BN and UMNO, in particular, are not characteristics of the PAP. Rather what happened in Malaysia was a one-off development and due to BN's shortcomings that do not apply to the PAP. If anything, Singaporean voters believe that the regime change experienced by BN will not happen in Singapore as this would be disastrous for Singapore and its people, a narrative the PAP has been socialising the public for some decades now, even though this was similarly pandered in Malaysia as far as UMNO's role was concerned and still the people eventually decided to dispense with UMNO and its rhetoric. The key reason argued by PAP's supporters and the detractors of the contagion-effect is the better job done by the PAP since 1965 compared to UMNO and the BN. From this perspective, the statement made by Malaysia's new prime minister, Mahathir Mohamad in his interview with *The Financial Times* on 29 May 2018, that "I think the people of Singapore, like the people in Malaysia, must be tired of having the same government, the same party since independence" does not hold water, as far as supporters of the PAP are concerned.[51] Clearly, from the perspective of personal credibility of the incumbent, Prime Minister Lee Hsien Loong, and the fourth-generation leaders such as Heng Swee Keat, Chan Chun Sing and Ong Ye Kung, whom the incumbent prime minister has groomed to take over the reins of government and the all-round political, economic and socio-cultural performance of the PAP, the standing and legitimacy remain very high and cannot be compared with UMNO or BN, and hence, one should not expect what transpired in May 2018 in Malaysia to repeat in Singapore. This is analogous to comparing apples to oranges.

---

49. See Wong Pei Ting, "The Big Read: No easy answers to HDB lease decay issue, but public mindset has to change first", *Today*, 5 June 2018.

50. On 28 June 2018, SP Group announced that electricity tariffs would rise by an average of 6.9% from July to September. Later, on 30 September 2018, SP Power again announced that electricity prices would go up by 2.1% from October to December 2018. Both hikes were justified on grounds of high cost of natural gas that is used for generating electricity in Singapore. See *The Straits Times*, 29 June 2018 and 30 September 2018.

51. See John Lim, "Singaporeans are tired of the same government too, says Tun M", *SAYS*, 31 May 2018, http://says.com/my/news/tun-m-like-malaysians-singaporeans-are-tired-of-the-same-government-too

In July 2018, Ho Kwon Ping, an active public intellectual, warned against assuming that the 2018 Malaysian General Elections results will have a spill-over effect in Singapore. He argued that Singaporeans will be "drawing the wrong lessons if we look at Malaysia and think that the fall of the PAP is imminent for whatever reasons that are happening across the Causeway."[52] He argued that it was the "the unbridled, egregiously blatant and massively enormous corruption" that brought Najib down rather than the absence of full democratic institutions and human rights, putting down of dissent or presence of paternalistic governance.[53] For Ho, the PAP will only fall if there is widespread corruption among its leaders. He also cautioned against the rise of nepotism and cronyism in the government.[54] Ho's position is something that can be endorsed as it signposts that one should not over-read what happened in Malaysia to be easily repeated in Singapore.

While the arguments of the pros and cons of the change of regime in Malaysia in May 2018 can be expected to continue, to return to the question of whether this type of regime change can happen to Singapore is not a moot point. Clearly, the PAP has spoken about the possibility of losing power on a number of occasions. The PAP, under Goh Chok Tong talked of splitting the PAP into Team A and Team B, whether to reflect the factions within the PAP or try to control the destiny of Singapore politics by being the government and opposition at the same time, but this idea was eventually dismissed. Later, K. Shanmugam talked about the difficulties political parties face in ruling a state beyond seven decades. This was followed by Lee Kuan Yew's warning that the PAP would collapse if it does not keep reinventing itself and keep winning public trust and confidence. This was followed by Ong Ye Kung's argument that Singapore will always be ruled by 'one dominant party' but it need not always be the PAP. Hence, whether one would agree or disagree with the

---

52. Faris Mokthar, "'Foolish mistake' to think PAP will suffer the same fate as Malaysia's former government: Ho Kwon Ping", *Today*, 12 July 2017.

53. Kayla Wong, "Foolish to think PAP will suffer the same fate as Barisan Nasional: Ho Kwon Ping", *Nikkei Asian Review*, 20 July 2018; "Najib-BN's 'blatant corruption' led to gov't change, 'won't happen to Singapore'", *Malaysiakini*, 13 July 2018.

54. Kayla Wong, "Foolish to think PAP will suffer the same fate as Barisan Nasional: Ho Kwon Ping"; similarly, in January 2017, at an Institute of Policy Studies discussion on Singapore in 2065, Ho argued that the issues such as nepotism, cronyism and corruption have the potential to bring about the PAP's downfall in future. See "Loss of confidence in the PAP? Possible if complacency sets in", *The Straits Times*, 25 January 2017.

thesis of PAP's perpetual rule, the idea of the PAP losing power is no longer alien or new. The question would be — how would the PAP eventually lose power?

While this may be due to PAP's weaknesses or the Opposition's strengths, what happened to the BN was extremely instructive, especially in view of the extremely close historical, political, economic and socio-cultural ties between Singapore and Malaysia. What is often missed in the BN's defeat was the fact that eventually what defeated the BN was the defection of key UMNO leaders from the party who went on to become key leaders of the Opposition. Whatever incarnations Mahathir Mohamad, Anwar Ibrahim, Muhyiddin Yassin, Daim Zainuddin, Rais Yatim, Rafidah Aziz, Shafie Apdal, Hamid Albar and Osman Sapian may have become today, they were formerly UMNO stalwarts. If the UMNO-led BN has been in power in Malaysia for 61 years (1957–2018), and Mahathir Mohamad led the government from 1981 to 2003, almost one-third of the tenure, who can be more UMNO than Mahathir Mohamad in Malaysia today? Eventually, the defections and splits within UMNO doomed the party and the BN. While the PKR, DAP and even PAS tried jointly to dislodge the BN on two occasions in 2008 and 2013, they failed. But once Mahathir came on board and led the coalition, the BN was defeated. This was because Mahathir was seen as a source of continuity from the past and in fact, many saw Mahathir as the 'true' representative of UMNO and BN compared to Najib and his close associates.

What this informs us is that the PAP will remain in power for as long as it keeps its unity. The Opposition in Singapore is likely to grow in strength and will capture more parliamentary seats and electoral support but forming the alternative government to the PAP is likely to be an 'Everestian' and 'Herculean' task. The Opposition in Singapore remains weak all-round — be it from the perspective of an alternative narrative to the PAP, its credibility to work together and the fact that various opposition parties suffer from problems that have made the public cautious about supporting them. The PAP has also achieved unthinkable success and this will be difficult to deny and ignore, and hence, difficult to dislodge such a high-performing ruling party. Still, if the PAP continues to inflict pain on the voters, its days will also be numbered. At the same time, dislodging the PAP will be greatly eased if the Opposition is led by a former PAP stalwart. In short, the dominance of the PAP is unlikely to be challenged by the Opposition for a long time to come. This has become a political given in Singapore thus far. However, if former PAP members, for one reason or another, join the Opposition or establish the Malaysian version of 'Pakatan Harapan' in Singapore, then the days of the PAP could be near its end. Anyway, historically, the biggest challenge and enemy of the PAP has always been the PAP itself, as seen in the splits, internal challenges, internecine struggles and dissensions from the mid-1950s to the early 1960s, culminating in the setting up of the Barisan Sosialis.

What can cause the PAP to split in the coming years? First, it can be due to sharp policy differences, especially over the political order and economy. Will Singapore have a more open and somewhat greater liberal order, or will things remain as they are? Will the economy be as it is, with foreign capital and workers dominating it, especially with Singapore's future being a hostage to the world's economy? Second, a major debate that can split the party would be the extent and type of welfare system Singapore may want to adopt in future in view of the rising poverty and challenges facing lower-income Singaporeans. This is an extremely sensitive issue and one that will become even more divisive with more Singaporeans being marginalised economically and unemployed. If foreigners are seen to be the main beneficiaries of Singapore and the government's policies, there will be a big political price to pay for the ruling elites. Third, internal dissensions can emerge if there are sharp and irreconcilable differences over who will lead the PAP after Lee Hsien Loong and probably even after that? If for some reasons, the choice of the prime minister is not based on the 'best and brightest' individual but determined by the curse of cronyism and nepotism, then the probability of an internal split will be even more imminent. Fourth, what is meant by meritocracy in Singapore in future can also split the party, especially with more Singaporeans opposing the 'paper-first qualification', PAP-structured and sanctioned approach to promotions and placement of people in key positions, especially government scholarship holders who have been treated as first-among-equals. Finally, the outbreak of scandals, especially corruption, can also weaken and hurt the ruling party a la Najib in Malaysia.

Until and unless these mistakes and shortcomings take place, the one-party dominant state in Singapore under the PAP is likely to persist. Singaporeans view the PAP not just as a ruling party to be elected every four to five years but a long-term governing compact that has successfully delivered political, economic and social goods since 1959. Singaporeans have also been with the PAP, through various landmark challenges, be it in or out of Malaysia, British military withdrawal, etc. and this has created a unique bond that is difficult to severe. As long as the PAP keeps delivering the public goods to the satisfaction of the majority of voters for every generation, then the chances of remaining in power will be strong. In a way, the voters' DNA has become used to the PAP and this habit of supporting and being governed by the PAP has become almost psychologically natural and unquestioned, creating a Pavlovian-type transactional ruler–ruled pact. However, as the late Lee Kuan Yew warned in 2011, one day the PAP will be voted out of office. He predicted that Singaporeans "will get tired of a stable government and say let's try the opposition." According to Lee, "There will come a time when eventually the public will say, look, let's try the other side, either because the PAP has declined in quality or the opposition has put up a team which is equal to the PAP and they say, let's try the other side. That day will come…No system lasts for forever, that's for sure. In the next 10 years to 20 years, I don't think it'll happen. Beyond that, I cannot tell. Will we always be able to get the most dedicated and the most capable, with integrity to devote their lives to this? I hope so, but forever, I don't know."[55] Citing the example of the Liberal Democratic Party in Japan, which held power from 1955 to 2009 and later, succeeded in regaining power in 2012, Lee stated that its downfall was because "it carried on with old ideas."[56]

Hence, the 2018 Malaysian General Elections will only have a contagion-effect on Singapore if it inspires and provokes a split within the PAP. The split can eventuate for any one or more reasons, especially if a strong personality emerges who disagrees with the existing policies of the party, and worse, if the future prime minister is deemed to be weak, corrupt, nepotistic and crony-oriented. If for one reason or another, there is a Mahathir, Muhyiddin or Shafie in the PAP and Singapore, then this can create the setting for these individuals to either join the Opposition or establish a broad-based coalition to challenge the PAP in a general elections. Only under these circumstances will there be a successful domino-effect *a la Malaysia* in 2018 on Singapore and result in the collapse of the PAP-entrenched political order in Singapore.

---

55. *AsiaOne News*, 21 January 2011. The ideas were contained in Lee Kuan Yew's book titled *Lee Kuan Yew: Hard Truths to Keep Singapore Going*.

56. Ibid.

POST-MALAYSIAN 2018 GENERAL ELECTIONS DEVELOPMENTS AND SINGAPORE'S POLITICS

The 2018 Malaysian General Elections ushered in a notion that a one-party dominant system can be terminated. While this was not a new development, the fact that it happened in Malaysia, almost unexpectedly, makes its understanding and ramifications important, especially for its southern neighbour, Singapore, which has a similar political history of a one-party dominant state. The interesting part of the 'dialogue' is that both Malaysia and Singapore have been described as 'one-party dominant states' even though Malaysia's dominance is through a coalition, hence, a collection of political parties, while Singapore's dominance is through a single political party. With the UMNO-led *Barisan Nasional* (BN) being dislodged after 61 years, a 'big idea' that emerged in the region, including in both Malaysia and Singapore, was "whether Singapore can do a Malaysia", namely, whether what happened in Malaysia can transpire, spill-over or be repeated in Singapore. This was dealt with in Chapter 8 of this book. However, more pertinent, since the May 2018 Malaysian General Elections, a number of other developments have also taken place that will have a bearing on the future of Singapore as a one-party dominant state.

The establishment of an opposition coalition-of-willing in Singapore

A key reason the Opposition has languished in Singapore since 1965 has been its inability to get its act together, be it on an individual party basis and more sensibly, as a coalition, whether it is an electoral pact or as a tighter pact, say along the lines of coalition politics in Malaysia and Indonesia where all political parties agreed to a coalition leader, on an election manifesto, consensus on where and how to allocate seats, etc. These are things that have not really been undertaken in Singapore even though there have been attempts in the past to establish opposition pacts and during an election, to collaborate in order to prevent three-cornered contests, even though this has not always worked.

According to a *Straits Times* report, there have been a number of attempts to establish opposition coalitions in the past but there has been no lasting impact.[1] On 28 June 2001, four opposition political parties, namely, the Singapore People's Party (SPP), National Solidarity Party (NSP), Singapore Justice Party (SJP) and Singapore Malay National Organisation (PKMS), with the Singapore National Front, a breakaway group from the PKMS, as the fifth element, established the Singapore Democratic Alliance (SDA). The alliance was led by Chiam See Tong, the secretary-general of the SPP and Member of Parliament for Potong Pasir. In 2007, the NSP pulled out of the SDA on grounds that it wanted to "explore new possibilities through wider latitude to manoeuvre, re-engineer and rebuild the NSP."[2] In 2010, the Reform Party (RP) indicated interest in joining the SDA but disagreements over the terms of the RP's membership into the alliance led to the effort being futile. This also opened up differences within the SDA as there were disagreements between Chiam and SPP member, Desmond Lim.[3] In March 2011, the SDA decided to relieve Chiam of his role as the chairman of the alliance, partly due to his inactivity following his stroke. Following this announcement, Chiam pulled the SPP out of the alliance. Meanwhile, Lim who left the SPP to join the SJP as its secretary-general, was appointed as the SDA's secretary-general.

Since the formation of the SDA, it has contested in elections. In 2001, it fielded 13 candidates to contest in two Group Representation Constituencies (GRCs) and three Single Member Constituencies (SMCs). Chiam won under the SDA banner in Potong Pasir with Steve Chia elected as a Non-Constituency Member of Parliament (NCMP). Unofficially, the SDA was the leader of the Opposition with two MPs (Chiam and Chia). In 2006, the SDA contested in three GRCs and four SMCs with Chiam winning in Potong Pasir. In the 2011 General Elections, with the SPP having left the alliance, the SDA contested in the Pasir Ris-Punggol GRC and Punggol East SMC but failed to win any seat. In the 2013 by-election in Punggol East SMC, the

---

1. See Seow Bei Yi, "Tan Cheng Bock yet to decide on role in opposition coalition, says small window to effect political change", *The Straits Times*, 29 July 2018.

2. Loh Chee Kong and Derrick A. Paulo, "Seeking 'room to manoeuvre', NSP leaves SDA", *Today*, 19 January 2007.

3. See "GE: SDA says Chiam pulling SPP out of alliance", *ChannelNewsAsia.com*, 2 March 2011, http://channelnewsasia.com/stories/singaporelocanews/view/1113966/1html; Cheow Xin Yi, "Chiam pulls party out of alliance", *Today*, 3 March 2011, http://www. todayonline.com/Singapore/EDC110303-0000259/Chiam-pulls-party-out-of-alliance

SDA leader, Desmond Lim, contested in the by-election and finished fourth with only 0.57% of the vote share, being the lowest percentage garnered in an election in Singapore since 1965.[4] In the 2015 General Elections, the SDA contested in one GRC in Pasir Ris-Punggol but lost.

As a result of the SDA's coalition experience, opposition cooperation has largely pertained to preventing three-cornered fights in a general elections even though some by-elections have seen opposition parties competing with each other, as happened in the 2013 by-election in Punggol East SMC. In October 2001, the opposition political parties worked out a deal to prevent three-cornered fighting in the Bukit Timah SMC contest seeing one involving the PAP, SDA and an independent candidate, Tan Kim Chuang. In December 2005, the opposition political parties met to discuss cooperation and in the 2006 General Elections, there were no three-cornered fights. In March 2011, the opposition political parties again met to prevent three-cornered fights. This was largely successful except for Punggol East SMC where a three-cornered fighting involving the PAP, WP and SDA took place. In September 2011, Tan Jee Say, a former presidential candidate said that he would like to unite the Opposition and build a coalition for the 2015 General Elections. The SPP, NSP and RP indicated interest but nothing came out of it.[5]

In the Hougang SMC by-election in May 2012, the Opposition stayed united in allowing the WP to contest the seat that the opposition party had held since 1991. However, in the Punggol East SMC by-election in January 2013, the Opposition could not agree among themselves and a four-cornered fight ensued involving the PAP, WP, RP and SDA, which was won by the WP. In August 2015, the opposition political parties met to prevent three-cornered fights but in the general elections, there were three three-cornered fights: in the Bukit Batok SMC involving the PAP, SDP and an independent candidate; in the MacPherson SMC involving the PAP, WP and NSP; and in the Radin Mas SMC involving the PAP, RP and an independent candidate. Needless to say, whenever there has been a three-cornered contest in a general elections, the PAP always triumphed except in the Punggol-East SMC

---

4. Toh Yong Chuan and Joyce Lim, "SDA scores worse result in post-independence history", *The Straits Times*, 27 January 2013, http://www.asiaone.com/News/Latest+News/Singapore/Story/A1Story20130127-398101.html

5. See Seow Bei Yi, "Tan Cheng Bock yet to decide on role in opposition coalition, says small window to effect political change".

by-election. Following the September 2015 General Elections, four opposition political parties, the NSP, RP, People's Power Party (PPP) and Singapore First Party (SFP) met to establish a coalition but nothing came out of it.[6] Since early 2016, Tan Cheng Bock has also been meeting opposition political parties bilaterally to discuss collaboration but these discussions remained inconclusive.[7]

It was against this backdrop, where all the opposition political parties did badly in the 2015 General Elections and the success of coalition politics in the 2018 Malaysian General Elections that a new lease of life was given to the possibility of opposition coalition in Singapore. Some two months after the BN defeat in May 2018, the SDP invited Chua Tian Chang, vice-president and Chief of Information of the *Parti Keadilan Rakyat* (PKR), who was barred from contesting in the 2018 Malaysian General Elections and a *Pakatan Harapan* (PH) politician, to Singapore to speak on 7 July 2018 to the opposition political parties on how coalition politics succeeded in Malaysia.[8] Chua's dialogue with the SDP-organised event was almost a 'coaching session', about what the Singapore opposition can learn from the Malaysian experience in toppling a one-party dominant state. For some, however, it was an 'invitation to subvert' as this was a key politician from the ruling government in Malaysia attempting to interfere in Singapore's politics.

At what was dubbed a 'private talk' by Chua to the SDP, he explained the PH's success in the following terms:

> What the people are interested in is whether we were willing to come together and whether we were ready to provide an alternative, like a shadow cabinet. We had the advantage of Mahathir and Anwar coming together despite their misgivings for each other. They understood that there was a bigger agenda.
>
> The NGOs were also at a crossroads. They knew they were wasting their time with a BN government who did not care about their agenda. They knew they had to either join the opposition or mobilize their resources to help the reformation.
>
> Political parties knew that they had to respect civil society and empower them to speak up and to lead in whatever they were passionate about. As for the BERSIH

---

6. Ibid.

7. See Elgin Toh and Tham Yuen-C, "Singapore opposition take lessons from Malaysian election result", *The New Paper*, 31 July 2018, https://www.tnp.sg/news/singapore/singapore-opposition-take-lessons-malaysian-election-result

8. Ibid.

movement, it was the parties that called on the members [of NGOs] to attend protests in the beginning as NGOs in Malaysia were weak. The support for each other was crucial for reform and PH's eventual success at the polls.[9]

Following Chua's 'private talk' on 28 July 2018 at the invitation of Chee Soon Juan, the SDP secretary-general, seven opposition political parties in Singapore convened for a luncheon meeting to discuss the possibility of opposition coalition for the forthcoming general elections scheduled for 2020 or 2021 even though some pundits predict that it may be held as early as late 2019 to coincide with Singapore's 200th anniversary of British rule and the PAP's 60-year rule of Singapore. The participating political parties included the SDP, NSP, PPP, SFP, RP, DPP (Democratic Progressive Party) and a then party-in-the-waiting, People's Voice Party (PVP). Tan Cheng Bock, the five-term PAP MP for the Ayer Rajah constituency and a candidate in the 2011 Presidential Election, was also invited and attended as an observer.

As the *Pakatan Harapan* that won the 2018 Malaysian General Elections was an "an inspiring underdog story", many in Singapore thought that it was worth emulating it.[10] According to Goh Meng Seng, the PPP secretary-general, "The Malaysian election was an important catalyst. It opened our minds to the possibilities of coalition politics. We also saw the need for a steady hand leading the coalition — someone voters can trust as prime minister."[11] All the participating members agreed that it would be an uphill task to establish a political coalition, what more defeat the PAP. Still, the 2018 Malaysian catalyst was seen as important and where there was a need to change the way the Opposition operated in Singapore. As was argued by Lim Tean, the leader of the PVP, clearly, the coalition would need a centralised form of leadership.[12] However, what was

---

9. Quoted in Andrew Loh, "Opinion: Opposition alliance 'on the cards': Are Cheng Bock and WP the key to unity?", *The Independent*, 15 July 2018, theindependent.sg/opinion-opposition-alliance-on-the-cards-are-tan-cheng-bock-wp-the-key-to-unity/

10. Seow Bei Yi, "Tan Cheng Bock yet to decide on role in opposition coalition, says small window to effect political change".

11. Ibid.

12. "An Opposition alliance under Tan Cheng Bock", *Under the Angsana Tree*, 1 August 2018, https://undertheangsanatree.blogspot.com/2018/08/an-opposition-alliance-under-tan-cheng.html

more important was the need to think differently as a political opposition in Singapore. He argued:

> The message that the opposition should be voted into Parliament to be a check and balance on the government is no longer relevant or enough. Unfortunately, this was always the message by the opposition in the past and that relegated the opposition to be second best...We have no time for futile concepts such as not contesting all seats and have the PAP returned to power on Nomination Day.[13]

He also stated that the Opposition should strive to be the next government of Singapore:

> Our alliance must strive to form the next Government in the upcoming General Election. The winds of change are here and they have buffeted the world for the past two years...Those who try to suggest that what happened in the West and now Malaysia cannot possibly happen in Singapore are myopic and in denial.[14]

Yet, at the same time, the 'reality bites' cannot be ignored.[15] First, establishing a 'Pakatan Singapore' would not be easy as the political, economic and socio-cultural situations in Singapore differ from those in Malaysia. Singapore does not have the chronic corruption that exists in Malaysia, best exemplified by the 1MDB saga. The cost of living in Malaysia has ballooned and eroded the purchasing power of ordinary Malaysians. While Singapore faces the same problem, the severity is not as serious as in Malaysia. Singapore also is devoid of a Dr Mahathir, who is probably Malaysia's most successful prime minister, in addition to being its long-serving head of government from 1981 to 2003. While there has long been opposition presence in Singapore, this differs greatly from the Malaysian landscape. Unlike in Singapore, in Malaysia, the component political parties of the PH, especially

---

13. Seow Bei Yi, "Tan Cheng Bock yet to decide on role in opposition coalition, says small window to effect political change".

14. See Kenneth Cheng and Cynthia Choo, "The Big Read: Opposition parties banding together — a grand plan or a last throw of the disc?", *Today*, 4 August 2018. This sentiment was echoed by Goh Meng Seng who argued that "fundamentally, we feel the PAP should not be in power anymore", claiming that the country is not running well compared to the past. Ibid.

15. Seow Bei Yi, "Tan Cheng Bock yet to decide on role in opposition coalition, says small window to effect political change".

the DAP and PKR, have been around for a long time, have a long history of parliamentary victories and experience, including governing states such as Penang, Selangor, etc. not to mention PAS that had ruled Kelantan and Terengganu for a long time. Clearly, if the Opposition in Singapore is to make any impact at all, it has to produce high-quality candidates, be engaged on the ground for a long time, need a clear and alternative political narrative and message, and must demonstrate the ability to govern Singapore, as well as, or better than the PAP and more importantly, convince the public of its ability to do so.

Still, the idea of having an opposition coalition in Singapore was a refreshing and realistic one, especially if any dent was to be made in the one-party dominant system in Singapore. What was particularly encouraging and a sign of a 'sea change' was the involvement of Tan Cheng Bock in the 28 July 2018 meeting. It represented, formally at least, the first time a leading and credible PAP member had 'crossed over' to the Opposition, what more, to lead it. This was the closest one could compare to what Mahathir Mohamad did in Malaysia when he abandoned UMNO and BN, and joined forces with the PH. For Tan, the need for a coalition was obvious. It would allow the smaller political parties such as the SFP, PPP and RP to stand under a more prominent unified banner, assist in unifying the fragmented parties under one umbrella, provide for the possible sharing of resources and most important, not only put up a 'united front' politically against the 'PAP Leviathan' but demonstrate to the public of the Opposition's rising political maturity.

The 78-year-old Tan, who is a highly popular and credible political figure in Singapore, stated that he had "a small window of opportunity" to effect change in Singapore.[16] According to him, he "may only have a short time to mentor a team to work for the good of the nation. I want to put my last years to good use. I want to pass all that I have acquired and learnt in the political arena to the next generation."[17] He admitted that he was invited to lead even though he had not decided "in what capacity", a decision he claimed he had not yet finalised.[18] Yet, at the same time, he remarked that "I would regret it if I had the chance to make a difference but did nothing."[19] He made it clear that "if you want me to lead, then we must think

---

16. Ibid.

17. Ibid.

18. Ibid.

19. Ibid.

of the country first. If we go in, we must go in as a team."[20] He also observed that most of the political parties present in the July 2018 meeting had participated in elections for many years but not won a seat.[21] In his view, "to be fair, many from the seven parties stood in past elections because they believed they acted in Singapore's best interests. But I think some may also need to stand down and serve from the backroom if it is for the good of the country."[22] He also dismissed Derek da Cunha's observation which stated that Tan was "mixing with this particular crowd — which in the pecking order of non-PAP parties rank as third, fourth and fifth-raters, will not do anything for Dr Tan's reputation."[23] Tan responded by saying that "I believe the men and women I met yesterday were more than willing to make way for better men and women who should stand in their place. They have guts. They have put themselves out there."[24]

While Tan did give the Opposition a boost, at the same time, there is no denial that the challenges ahead are colossal. There remain the perennial issues of personality differences and different approaches to politics. This led the then DPP leader,[25] Benjamin Pwee to remark "whatever differences that exist — must be submerged. There must not be ego politics within such a [coalition] framework."[26] Goh Meng

---

20. Teng Yong Ping, "Tan Cheng Bock open to leading proposed opposition coalition", *Yahoo News Singapore*, 28 July 2018, https://sg.news.yahoo.com/tan-cheng-bock-expresses-interest-leading-opposition-coalition-113957990.html

21. The SDP was present and organised the 'opposition get-together' but last held a seat in the Singapore parliament in 1991 when it captured three parliamentary seats under the leadership of Chiam See Tong. However, following the split in the party between 1993 and 1995, its leader, Chiam, set up a new party, the SPP and it contested and retained the former SDP's seat in Potong Pasir. Since 1991, the SDP has never won a parliamentary seat.

22. Seow Bei Yi, "Tan Cheng Bock yet to decide on role in opposition coalition, says small window to effect political change".

23. Ibid.

24. Ibid.

25. In February 2019, it was reported that Benjamin Pwee had applied to join the SDP. See Linette Lai, "Former DPP chief Benjamin Pwee applies to join SDP", *The Straits Times*, 19 February 2019.

26. Ibid. Goh Meng Seng was somewhat optimistic when he argued "If we are all egomaniacs, we won't be sitting on the same table...All the leaders have their differences in their ideologies, policy-wise and how things should be done, but I do not think they are so egoistic

Seng also stated that it was "premature to say this coalition will definitely be formed as there will be a lot of issues to be discussed and sorted out."[27] However, he was also realistic about the need for a new game-changing approach for the Opposition: "We are at rock-bottom. When we come to that stage, nothing could be worse than to try...a new approach to get a different result. If we don't change, the results won't change."[28] In a similar vein, Goh stated that "The fact is that our fortunes and destinies are linked...We cannot do without each other. If you don't try, you won't know. It cannot be worse than the status quo."[29] Still, Goh Meng Seng stressed the need for close cooperation as "without discipline such a coalition equals trouble."[30]

The key to a successful opposition coalition would be its universality, namely, whether it would able to embrace all the key opposition political parties in Singapore. The SDA did not participate as its leader, Desmond Lim, was not in Singapore. He later stated that he would be prepared to join the coalition.[31] However, most glaring was the absence of two successful opposition political parties, namely, the WP and SPP. Even though both were invited, they did not attend. The WP excused itself by stating that it was going through a leadership transition and was concentrating on building its organisation, partly in response to the election of a new secretary-general, Pritam Singh in place of Low Thia Khiang.[32] Similarly, the SPP stated that its priority was to undertake an intensive ground engagement to understand the feelings and sentiments of Singaporeans. However, Lina Chiam, the SPP leader stated that the party was "open to having a conversation with Dr Tan Cheng Bock to

as to say they can do it all by themselves." See Kenneth Cheng and Cynthia Choo, "The Big Read: Opposition parties banding together — a grand plan or a last throw of the disc?".

27. See Kenneth Cheng and Cynthia Choo, "The Big Read: Opposition parties banding together — a grand plan or a last throw of the disc?".

28. Ibid.

29. Ibid.

30. Seow Bei Yi, "Tan Cheng Bock yet to decide on role in opposition coalition, says small window to effect political change".

31. Wong Pei Ting, "Dr Tan Cheng Bock open to role in opposition, says he wants to effect change", Today, 29 July 2018.

32. Wong Pei Ting, "Dr Tan Cheng Bock open to role in opposition, says he wants to effect change"; Seow Bei Yi, "Tan Cheng Bock yet to decide on role in opposition coalition, says small window to effect political change".

hear his views and thoughts about the future of Singapore."[33] If the WP and SPP do not join the Tan-led coalition, it would weaken the coalition even though there can still be an electoral pact for the coming elections to avoid three-cornered contests.

Whatever the real impact and achievement of the opposition coalition will be in the next general elections, clearly, if the coalition does not disintegrate before the elections, the ruling PAP would be facing a serious challenge after a long time. Tan Cheng Bock's credibility will greatly uplift the Opposition's image and status, all the more, if Tan decides to helm a GRC, say in West Coast, where his traditional Ayer Rajah electoral constituency was located. According to Spencer Ng, the NSP secretary-general, it is also hoped that Tan's presence will draw more talented Singaporeans to the Opposition's cause and side. He argued, "having the leadership of Dr Tan Cheng Bock, I hope more talented Singaporeans are willing enough to step out of their comfort zones to really fight for what is right and beneficial for the country."[34]

This is especially so as there are serious political issues facing the ruling party and government. Since the PAP resoundingly won in the 2015 General Elections, Singapore has faced many challenges that have hurt the PAP's standing, especially the prime minister, Lee Hsien Loong. These challenges include: all round price increases and cost of living that have hurt the majority of Singaporeans on a day-to-day basis, especially at a time when PAP stalwarts are still justifying and defending the need to pay ministers so highly that many consider it as ignominious, especially when politics should be a calling and not be 'monetised'; the housing worries as leasehold will depreciate to zero, not to mention the high cost of public housing for first-time buyers; problems with the non-stop Mass Rapid Transit (MRT) breakdowns, including forged maintenance records; the controversial compulsory CareShield Life policy; the controversial 'selection' of the Elected President (EP); the corruption charges abroad against government-linked companies such as Keppel, Jurong and Sembawang Shipyards and where they were made to pay millions of dollars in fines to the United States; and finally, the politicisation of what was a family feud involving the prime minister over the late Lee Kuan Yew's property at 38 Oxley Road. These issues were well-captured by a *Straits Times* op-ed by Chua Mui Hoong in February 2018:

---

33. Ibid.

34. See Kenneth Cheng and Cynthia Choo, "The Big Read: Opposition parties banding together — a grand plan or a last throw of the disc?".

The intellectual and achievement gap between the ruler and the ruled has narrowed. Meanwhile, news and images of frequent train delays, lift malfunctions, decaying trees and bursting water pipes, widely shared on social media, all add to a sense that government agencies are falling short even on maintenance matters. If performance forms the bedrock of a trusting people-government relationship, alas, in some people's minds, even that is faulty.

Worse, when things go wrong, so the whispers go, blame is pushed down to the lower rungs.

Both Keppel Corp and SMRT have been in the news for what appear to be systemic issues. A Keppel subsidiary was fined by the US authorities for giving bribes in Brazil. The corruption trial lasted 14 years, from 2001 to 2014.

In SMRT, pumps were not maintained; worse, maintenance reports were falsified for over a year. These were discovered only after MRT tunnels were flooded last October when a pump failed to work.[35]

All these issues have the potential to greatly hurt the PAP's image and will provide the Opposition with strong arguments to hold the government to account. With a more demanding and discerning younger voters with no links to the past and no sense of hardships of their forefathers, they are less likely to be forgiving of the ruling party and its leaders. This will make the next general elections an important one, especially once Heng Swee Keat was named the first assistant secretary-general of the PAP in November 2018, and later, from 1 May 2019 onwards, as the sole deputy prime minister, effectively making him the prime minister-in-waiting. Whether the new prime minister will be a centrifugal or centripetal force in national politics also remains to be seen. That the government was and should be worried of an opposition coalition was evident from the fact that someone quickly posted a 'fake news' item of what the 'election manifesto' of the coalition for the forthcoming election would be, something that was meant to frighten the voters by highlighting the 'revolutionary', destabilising and unreasonable nature of the Opposition. This was debunked and dismissed by Chee Soon Juan as he was alleged to have met Tan to draft the so-called 'election manifesto', something that did not transpire.[36]

---

35. See Chua Mui Hoong, "Has trust in the government been eroded? It's time to talk frankly", *The Straits Times*, 1 February 2018.

36. Tanya Ong, "Chee Soon Juan debunks as 'not true' text message with details of opposition coalition manifesto", *Mothership*, 7 August 2018, https://mothership.sg/2018/08/chee-soon-juan-opposition-coalition-manifesto-fake/; Ethan Rakin, "Dr Chee Soon Juan discredits the contents of an election manifesto allegedly written by a coalition made

Still, by July 2019, there was no sight of an opposition coalition emerging in Singapore. Lim Tean, who was highly supportive of the coalition and had set up his own political party, the PVP, commented in April 2019, that "for (several) months, I held out hope for an alliance. Nothing has materialised. And I think it's best that we each develop our own party and do what we think is best in the interest of the Singapore people. If after eight months, nothing has come out of it, it's hard to imagine (it would happen)."[37] The lack of progress on opposition coalition-building has led the other opposition political parties in Singapore to opt for 'Plan B'. As was stated by the RP chairman, Andy Zhu, "there were no updates before or after he [Dr Tan] started his party. We didn't probe him further because it is up to him individually to decide."[38] From this development, it would appear that what was touted as a possible game-changer in Singapore politics after the PH's victory in May 2018 has somewhat dissipated even though some form of cooperation among the opposition political parties can be expected in the coming general elections in Singapore.

The role of Malaysian civil society groups in promoting the concept of 'doing a Malaysia in Singapore'

Earlier, the role of Chua Tian Chang, the PKR vice-president and a known civil society activist, was mentioned, where he spoke to the SDP and others who were present, on how opposition coalition politics succeeded in Malaysia in ending the 61 years of BN rule. There have also been many writings arguing along the same line since then, especially after the new Malaysian prime minister, Mahathir Mohamad, also weighed in and said that Singaporeans were similarly wanting to end the one-party dominant rule of the PAP. In an interview with *The Financial Times* on 30 May 2018, Mahathir is reported to have said that the impact of the Malaysian electoral earthquake on Singapore was clear: "I think the people of Singapore, like the people in Malaysia, must be tired of having the same government, the same party since independence."[39]

---

up of opposition parties in Singapore", *Business Insider*, 8 August 2018, https:// www.businessinsider.sg/chee-soon-juan-discredits-the-contents-of-an-election-manifesto-apparently-written-by-a-coalition-made-up-of-opposition-parties-in-singapore/

37. Kenneth Cheng and Wong Pei Tong, "With no Tan Cheng Bock-led alliance in sight, opposition parties turn to plan Bs", *Today*, 8 April 2019.

38. Ibid.

39. Cited in Jewel Stolarchuk, "Mahathir boldly states: 'The people of Singapore must be

On 18 August 2018, ENGAGE,[40] a Malaysian civil society group, organised a public forum in Johor Bahru, in a city bordering Singapore on a topic titled "Can Singapore do a Malaysia?". The speakers at the forum were Hassan Karim, a PKR MP for Pasir Gudang in Johor, Hishamuddin Rais, a veteran civil society activist, Tan Wah Piow, a former student leader from Singapore who lives in London and Thum Ping Tjin, a Singaporean historian based in London. In general, all four speakers were political activists and the forum was attended by nearly 200 people, many from Singapore, including from the opposition political parties.

Key points of the forum

Thomas Fann, as the chairperson of the panel and the lead man of ENGAGE, opened the session by arguing that the 9 May 2018 'mega shock' in Malaysia, which was brought about through the ballot box and peacefully, replaced a 61-year old regime and this democratic transition was an inspiration for others, especially where a one-party dominant system had existed, as in Singapore. Hassan Karim, the first speaker, stated that while no country should dictate to another on its domestic politics, the fact that Singapore and Malaysia were neighbours and with so much in common, meant that what happened on 9 May 2018 was bound to have an impact on Singapore's politics. There was also much to learn from the Malaysian experience, where the opposition political parties established a united coalition and had a shared manifesto with a common logo, symbol and leader. That proved to be the undoing of Najib Razak and the BN. He also noted that the overthrow of the BN system did not happen suddenly but took some 10 years, beginning with the 2008 General Elections.

Hassan argued that for the Opposition to topple the ruling PAP in Singapore, it must develop itself as a credible alternative. He also observed that in Southeast

---

tired of having the same government since independence'", *The Independent*, 30 May 2018, http://theindependent.sg/mahathirs-boldly-states-the-people-of-singapore-must-be-tired-of-having-the-same-government-since-independence/

40. ENGAGE, a civil society group was established in September 2013 with Thomas Fann as the chairperson. Fann has been active in civil society activities, championing democracy, human rights and citizen participation. He has been an active member of BERSIH and CAGED (Citizen Action Group on Enforced Disappearance), a coalition of 48 civil society groups which was formed at the beginning of May 2017 to monitor cases of enforced disappearances and assist families of missing victims. The contact details of ENGAGE are as follows: 55-A, Jalan Molek 2/4, Taman Molek, Johor Bahru 81100.

Asia, one-party dominant systems had collapsed in the Philippines, Indonesia and Malaysia when the leading political party suffered internal splits. Hence, the implosion, entropy and breakdown of the ruling party were important in bringing it down, almost the *sine qua non*, to provide the necessary and sufficient condition for the collapse of such political orders. Also, what made bringing the BN down far easier was the presence of a 'familiar face', namely, Mahathir, which the Malaysian people could recognise and identify with. He wondered whether there was anyone in the PAP who could perform the role of a 'Mahathir' in Singapore? In other words, was a leading PAP figure prepared to breakaway and lead the Opposition against the PAP? Finally, he also observed that modern technology played a crucial role in de-legitimising the BN as there was a constant barrage of attack on Najib, UMNO and the BN, and over time, it severely damaged the image, credibility and reputation of the ruling party and its officials, making it easy to dislodge them from power from the perspective of the electorate. This was something Singapore could learn from Malaysia.

Thum Ping Tjin argued that while it was good to have political change in Singapore, the ruling PAP was too deeply entrenched from the structural and institutional perspective. The systemic architecture and social controls made it difficult to 'do a Malaysia in Singapore'. While Malaysia as a federal state had diverse centres of powers and where the control of the centre was never total, in Singapore, this was totally different. As a small city-state, the PAP had penetrated every layer of society and this made it difficult to overthrow it. While Malaysia had political, economic, socio-cultural, religious and even military elites, and the sultans, with clear powers delineated in the Federal Constitution, in Singapore, power was centralised in the PAP, with its tentacles reaching every political, economic and socio-cultural domains of the Republic. In short, there was only one centre of power and this was totally in the hands of the PAP, making for Singapore to be an 'absolute republic' and 'an overwhelming government', in the hands of the PAP.

In a way, it did not really matter when there was a change of leaders in Singapore as the system was deeply established and more importantly, functioning under a PAP-structured order. Through various political innovations such as the GRC, NMP (Nominated Member of Parliament), NCMP and even the EP, the PAP had changed the rules of the game and 'loaded the dice' to make political, and especially regime change, next to impossible in Singapore. However, what can change the political landscape and loosen PAP's hold on Singapore would be an internal split in the party, as had transpired in other one-party dominant states that eventually led to their downfall. For this to happen, the factor of 'timeline' needs to be appreciated as this is a distant possibility. For the time being, for Thum, it is not a question of 'Singapore doing a Malaysia' but more a 'Singapore doing a Singapore'.

For the third speaker, Hishamuddin Rais, the need for political change in Singapore was obvious and long overdue. For him, what happened in Malaysia that toppled UMNO and the BN, was a long time in the making. He traced this to the 1940s and 1950s when the Malay Nationalist Party was formed to fight British colonialism and following this, to oppose what he regarded as a neo-colonial order under UMNO and its partners, placed in power, to protect British colonial interest in independent Malaya, something which the Malayan Communist Party also campaigned on. In view of this long struggle and the success that was achieved on 9 May 2018, he argued that Singapore could not escape the consequences of what happened in Malaysia as it was 'part of the Malayan peninsular', being not just geographically close but also having close political, economic and socio-cultural ties. He argued that even though the PAP's control of Singapore was much tighter than was the case under BN, such control can still be broken, as was evident in the collapse of UMNO's stranglehold in the Federal Land Development Authority (FELDA) areas. For him, there was the need to exchange experiences so that Singapore could learn how to topple a highly centralised political elite that was all-round dominant.

Also, historically, Singapore could learn from the fact that one-party dominant system does not survive for too long, as was evident in the collapse of similar regimes in the Philippines, Indonesia and Malaysia. He also wondered whether Singaporeans would be daring enough to take risks and challenge the political power wielders by organising public demonstrations, as happened in Malaysia through the *Gabungan Pilihanraya Bersih dan Adil* (Bersih). Finally, he admitted that Najib, UMNO and the BN were toppled by the assistance from the Western states and their agencies that were uncomfortable with the Najib government that was veering too close to China at the expense of the West. In this regard, the continuous dose of anti-Najib tirades in the mainstream and social media of the West, created the setting that made it easy to topple Najib and his government in May 2018, something which can be described as Western subversion and where many of Najib's opponents colluded with these Western agencies. He mentioned the role of *The New York Times* in exposing the 1MDB scandal, the continuous attacks by other media outlets and even the US government that wanted to see Najib toppled as the West and many in PH, including himself, had a common interest in seeing the fall of Najib and BN, even if it meant colluding with external actors.

Finally, Tan Wah Piow, a long-time critic and opponent of the Singapore government, believed that 'Singapore could do a Malaysia' and this must be done for the good of Singapore and Singaporeans. What happened in Malaysia was significant for Singapore as regime change could take place peacefully through the ballot box. However, while there was a need for political change in Singapore, this was unlikely to be easy, due to the strength of the PAP and its system of all-round control, including its draconian laws that could neutralise its political opponents. He referred to the Internal Security Act and detention without trial as examples of these laws. The PAP had used the state and its agencies, such as the People's Association, to dominate Singapore. He thought that the key impediment to toppling the PAP was the idea and the key source of PAP's legitimacy that has been socialised to the electorate, was the first-rate performance of the government over the past five decades. This was something that was difficult to challenge as the ruling party was very adept in delivering the economic and other social goods due to its control of the massive wealth of the state. Singaporeans also feared losing the comfort zones that they were living in and even though they may not agree with the government, being pragmatic, they preferred to live 'with the devil they knew and disliked' than the 'unknown'. Hence, the fear of the unknown and the untested Opposition, had worked to the advantage of the ruling party and prolonged its stay and longevity. As such, the concept of the 'alternative' to the ruling party has never really gained a foothold and this has made it difficult to topple the PAP.

He also contended that in Singapore there was the 'rule by law' and not the 'rule of law'. This has made it difficult to challenge the ruling party as the government had hijacked the constitution to serve its political needs, the primary one being, to perpetuate its power at the expense of the people, who are both pliant and fearful. As a lawyer, he argued that the idea of people's sovereignty has been lost in Singapore and in many ways, Singaporeans have lost their state to a ruling elite. Hence, for him, doing 'a Malaysia in Singapore' is not just about toppling the PAP (say, by getting an ex-prime minister to topple the PAP) but much more, so as to change the political system that will place the people at the centre of the political system and not where the people are subservient to the ruling elites and party. However, as Singapore lacks many of the ingredients that brought the BN down, such as non-governmental organisations (NGOs) and active opposition political parties, it will take a much longer period to topple the ruling PAP. As the system is generally tailored to assist the ruling party to perpetuate its political stranglehold, what needs to be done is to change the voters' mindset about their role in the political system and once this can be done, there will be change and the ruling party can be toppled. Hence, while there was a need to 'do a Malaysia in Singapore', the PAP's deep control of the system meant that it would be 'mission impossible for the time being'.

Clearly, the Johor Bahru forum was an attempt to bring it one notch higher from what Chua Tian Chang had earlier tried to undertake at the SDP's luncheon talk. The Johor Bahru forum was a clear case of a highly active Malaysian political NGO trying to provide a platform in Malaysia for Singaporeans and the Singapore opposition to undertake a regime change in Singapore. While the conditions of both Malaysia and Singapore are totally different, still the attempt of 'coaching', some say, 'subversion', was a clear indication that there was a Malaysian government and non-government support not just to interfere in Singapore's politics, but more importantly to wreck the political contract that has existed between Singaporeans and its government for a long time.

Dr Mahathir and attempts by Singaporean and Malaysian activists to bring political change in Singapore

Following the public forum in Johor Bahru, on 30 August 2018, five activists, namely, Tan Wah Piow, a former Singaporean who is exiled in London and four other Singaporeans, Thum Ping Tjin, Kirsten Han, Jolovan Wham and Sonny Liew, together with Hishamuddin Rais, a celebrated Malaysian activist who was arrested for links with the Malayan Communist Party in the past, met Mahathir at the Perdana Leadership Foundation in Putrajaya, the political capital of Malaysia.[41]

---

41. See Wong Pei Ting, "Former political dissident, Singapore civil activists meet Dr Mahathir", *Today*, 30 August 2018; Augustine Low, "What does it say when Singaporeans look to Mahathir to bring change in Singapore?", *The Online Citizen*, 31 August 2018, https://www.theonlinecitizen.com/2018/08/31/what-does-it-say-when-singaporeans-look-to-mahathir-to-bring-change-to-singapore/; Sumisha Naidu, "Malaysia PM Mahathir invited to speak at democracy conference by political activists", *Channel NewsAsia*, 31 August 2018, https://www.channelnewsasia.com/news/singapore/mahathir-tan-wah-piow-thum-ping-tjin-democracy-conference-10668618; Andrew Loh, "Spore exile Tan Wah Piow meets Mahathir; says M'sia is a beacon for democracy", *The Independent*, 31 August 2018,

According to the Malaysian Prime Minister's Office, this was a meeting between Mahathir, Tan Wah Piow and four Singaporean "non-governmental individuals".[42] The ostensible reason for meeting Mahathir was to invite him to speak at a conference on building democracy in Southeast Asia to be organised by Tan Wah Piow in the first quarter of 2019 by his organisation called Forces for the Renewal of Southeast Asia. Mahathir was invited to give the keynote address at the conference and the Malaysian prime minister accepted the invitation in principle subject to availability. The Singaporeans also presented Mahathir with a document titled "People's Charter for Southeast Asia".[43]

According to Tan Wah Piow, "as far as I am concerned, the most important thing that Tun Mahathir brought about through his victory is this positiveness and aspiration for a freer society...Personally, I am very grateful for this open, democratic space that Tun Mahathir's government has opened and it is a beacon for many who are struggling for democracy. Not just Singapore but in other parts of Southeast Asia."[44] Thum added that he "urged Dr Mahathir to take the lead in lobbying for the promotion of democracy and freedom of expression and inquiry in Southeast Asia during the meeting."[45] He also "felt that Malaysia is in a unique opportunity to really be a beacon of democracy in the region."[46]

That the meeting between Mahathir and the Singaporean activists was more than a conference invitation was evident from the subsequent statements by the activists. Tan Wah Piow stated that "I hope the May 9 polls can influence Singaporeans. Malaysia has pointed the way to Singaporeans that change is possible and not frightening.[47] The *Malay Mail* reported Tan Wah Piow's

---

http://theindependent.sg/spore-exile-tan-wah-piow-meets-mahathir-says-msia-is-a-beacon-for-democracy/

42. Sumisha Naidu, "Malaysia PM Mahathir invited to speak at democracy conference by political activists".

43. Andrew Loh, "Spore exile Tan Wah Piow meets Mahathir; says M'sia is a beacon for democracy".

44. Sumisha Naidu, "Malaysia PM Mahathir invited to speak at democracy conference by political activists".

45. Ibid.

46. Ibid.

47. Andrew Loh, "Spore exile Tan Wah Piow meets Mahathir; says M'sia is a beacon for democracy".

comments in a slightly more different tone: "Malaysians have shone a light to Singaporeans, that change is possible, that change is not frightening, and any kind of narrative that a change of government will lead to racial riots is wiped out."[48] Agreeing with Tan Wah Piow, Thum also stated that the Malaysian template can be used to help other Southeast Asian nations, presumably even Singapore.[49]

That Singaporean politicians would react negatively to Mahathir's meeting with Singaporean activists and dissidents was not unexpected. As was argued by Augustine Low, a writer for *The Online Citizen*, "for the PAP, Mahathir is the elephant in the room."[50] For Low, Mahathir's electoral victory "could prove to be a nightmare for the PAP. True enough, this nightmare is now being played out. The 93-year-old Dr Mahathir is the one person that the PAP absolutely does not want its critics and opponents to tango with."[51] Hence, when Tan Wah Piow was asked on how he expected the Singapore government to respond to the meeting with Mahathir, he replied: "I think they will be very concerned, not because I met Dr Mahathir but the fact that the prime minister is prepared to share his views about democracy and to enhance the development of democracy in the region." Tan Wah Piow also argued that "Malaysia is now shining this beacon which is probably stealing the limelight from Singapore. I think that is what worries them. Singapore is becoming an outdated, archaic society with its dominant party controls."[52]

Among the first PAP member to respond was Seah Kian Peng, an MP for Marine Parade GRC. In his Facebook post, Seah stated that it was "quite clear to me that PJ Thum does not wish Singapore well."[53] Seah questioned Thum's motive for inviting Mahathir to "bring democracy to Singapore" even though this was not exactly what

---

48. Danial Dzulkifly, "May 9 polls prove change is possible for Singapore too, says exile", *The Malay Mail*, 30 August 2018.

49. Ibid.

50. Augustine Low, "For the PAP, Mahathir is the elephant in the room", *The Online Citizen*, 3 September 2018.

51. Ibid.

52. Sumisha Naidu, "Malaysia PM Mahathir invited to speak at democracy conference by political activists".

53. MP Seah Kian Peng urges netizens not to get 'personal or abusive' in debate over Thum's comments.

Thum stated publicly.[54] In the same Facebook post, Seah also questioned Thum for suggesting that Singapore should also rejoice on Malaysia's Independence Day. Seah also responded to Teo Soh Lung's post on the public forum in Johor Bahru where she wrote, "Singapore is part of Malaya la," with Seah commenting, "Really? This is what PJ Thum and Teo Soh Lung and the SDP believe in their heart of hearts."[55] As the SDP had not commented on the Singapore activists' meeting with Mahathir, and Seah was mistaken, he apologised, stating that he made the wrong assumption, thinking that Teo was still an SDP member as she stood on the SDP ticket in the 2011 General Elections.[56] This was also in response to the SDP's critique of Seah, where the opposition party stated that "Dr Thum and Teo Soh Lung are not members of the SDP, thus do not speak for the party or represent us in any way."[57]

Bertha Henson, a former *Straits Times* journalist later wrote that "a missive by a PAP MP Seah Kian Peng practically" denounced "them as traitors."[58] Seah's criticism of Thum, however, was shared and supported by K. Shanmugam, the minister for law and home affairs, who had crossed swords with Thum for more than six hours during a Select Committee hearing on fake news in March 2018. Shanmugam, referring to the meeting between Tan Wah Piow, Thum and other Singaporeans with Mahathir, described "the whole conduct" as being "a little sad, quite regretful." According to him, "We can have political differences within Singapore. That is normal, it is people's right. But we should never go out and invite someone foreign, foreign politician to intervene in our domestic politics. I think that is an absolute no-no."[59]

---

54. A fellow Singaporean who accompanied Thum to meet Mahathir, Kirsten Han, denied that there was any invitation for Mahathir to "bring democracy to Singapore". See "Seah Kian Peng — retract your Facebook post and issue an apology", *The Online Citizen*, 3 September 2018.

55. Royston Sim, "MP Seah Kin Peng urges netizens not to get 'personal or abusive' in debate over Thum Ping Tjin's comments", *The Straits Times*, 3 September 2018.

56. Ibid.

57. Ibid.

58. Bertha Henson, "And the winner of that KL meeting is...Dr M", *Today*, 2 September 2018.

59. Terry Xu, "K Shanmugam masterfully links photo and comment of Thum Ping Tjin as him inviting foreign politician to intervene in Singapore politics", *The Online Citizen*, https://www.theonlinecitizen.com/2018/09/02/k-shanmugam-masterfully-links-

In response to Seah's vitriolic response to the Thum and Tan's meeting with Mahathir, with some suggesting that this tantamount to an act of treason and betrayal, the social media was rife with accusations and counter-accusations.[60] Kirsten Han, who was one of the activists who met Mahathir, later posted that Seah's remarks had triggered "a torrent of accusation of treason against the group" and that "we are also getting death threats."[61] This led Seah to remark that "whilst we have different points of views...we can all agree to disagree and be civil about it."[62] He also stated that "it was regretful that I see all kinds of abusive remarks that are made by different individuals (and trolls) against each other. I do not support such type of comments regardless of what views or positions they take."[63] To the flak that Thum drew from netizens, he responded by saying, "I love my country and my people" and that he was proposing "Singapore to do a Singapore" as far as political change was concerned, and that it did not "preclude us from learning from others' experience to make our country better" as "we can always aspire to improve the quality of our democracy."[64]

The diatribe got worse with retired diplomat and a seasoned public commentator and intellectual, Bilahari Kausikan joining the fray. In response to Thum's Facebook post about his love for "my country and my people", Bilahari questioned Thum's loyalty by asking "which is his country and who are his people? Not a straightforward issue when dealing with a slippery character."[65] Bilahari raised this question, not just

photo-and-comment-of-thum-ping-tjin-as-inviting-foreign-politician-to-intervene-in-singapore-politics/; also see Nisha Abdul Rahim, "A little sad, a bit regretful: Shanmugam on activists' move to engage Mahathir", *Channel NewsAsia*, 2 September 2018, https://www.channelnewsasia.com/news/singapore/shanmugam-on-tan-wah-piow-thum-ping-tjin-meeting-mahathir-10676820

60. See Royston Sim, "Thum refutes notion he is a traitor: MP calls for calm online", *The New Paper*, 4 September 2018.

61. Ibid. MP Seah Kian Peng urges netizens not to get 'personal or abusive' in debate over Thum Ping Tjin's comments.

62. See Royston Sim, "Thum refutes notion he is a traitor: MP calls for calm online"; Royston Sim, "MP Seah Kin Peng urges netizens not to get 'personal or abusive' in debate over Thum Ping Tjin's comments".

63. Ibid.

64. See Royston Sim, "Thum refutes notion he is a traitor: MP calls for calm online".

65. Royston Sim, "Ex-diplomat Bilahari Kausikan asks historian Thum Ping Tjin to make clear his loyalties", *The Straits Times*, 4 September 2018.

due to the allegation that Thum invited Mahathir to "interfere in Singapore's internal politics" but also his consistent, but somewhat unnationalistic remarks of wishing "Singapore a happy 50th illegal independence day" on 31 August 2013 and repeating it in 2014 as well as reference to Malaysia as 'Malaya'.[66] On 9 August 2016, Thum wrote that "it is my fervent wish that we will overcome narrow politics and one day return to our rightful place alongside our brothers and sisters in Malaya."[67] This begged the question whether Thum is proposing Singapore's merger with Malaysia.

In the same vein, with netizens attacking Tan Wah Piow and other Singaporeans meeting with Mahathir, activist Jolovan Wham defended their action as something normal and acceptable.[68] Wham argued that "lobbying an overseas politician on political and civil rights in your country is nothing new" as "activists all over the world do it."[69] He argued that it was alright for Thum to invite Mahathir "to bring democracy to Singapore" as it was "a purely strategic question and has nothing to do with 'foreign interference' or subversion."[70] Instead, Wham argued that "if there was anyone who is being divisive, it is Shanmugam and Seah for their irresponsible comments and for unleashing a mob on PJ Thum and Kirsten Han."[71]

In the midst of the 'exchange', Thum, Han and Wham sent a letter to Prime Minister Lee Hsien Loong, urging him to look into the conduct of Seah and Shanmugam whom they accused of having made allegations "without adequate substantiation or evidence."[72] The purpose of writing to Prime Minister Lee, who

---

66. Ibid.

67. Ibid.

68. On 29 November 2017, Jolovan Wham was charged on seven counts, including vandalism and organising a public assembly without permit and refusing to sign police statements. As of mid-October 2018, the trial was still ongoing. See Shaffiq Idris Alkhatib, "Civil rights activist Jolovan Wham charged with organising public assemblies without permit and vandalism", *The Straits Times*, 29 November 2017; Tan Tam Mei, "Jolovan Wham trial adjourned with defence failing to call witnesses", *The Straits Times*, 2 October 2018.

69. Yasmine Yahya, "No harm in asking foreigners to influence local politics: Activist Jolovan Wham", *The Straits Times*, 5 September 2018.

70. Ibid.

71. Ibid.

72. "MHA responds to activists' letter of complaint to PM Lee Hsien Loong", *The Straits Times*, 6 September 2018.

is also secretary-general of the PAP was to persuade him to "take leadership in promoting responsible behaviour among members" of his party.[73] The trio also sent a letter to Charles Chong, who chairs the Select Committee on Deliberate Online Falsehoods, alleging that Seah and Shanmugam were "themselves making public allegations without adequate substantiation or evidence."[74] Prime Minister Lee forwarded the letter to Shanmugam and the reply came from Shanmugam's press secretary, Sunny Lee. In defence of Shanmugam, Sunny Lee stated: "The three individuals claimed that they are patriots. It is not patriotic to invite any foreign leader to intervene in Singapore politics, especially the leader of a country who has declared his desire to increase the price of water to Singapore by more than 10 times, and with whom we seek to maintain close and friendly relations."[75] The Ministry of Home Affairs' response also stated that the purpose of the trio to write the letter was to "divert attention from the conduct of the writers."[76] Sunny Lee concluded his letter by stating that "we can have vigorous debates within Singapore about our own affairs. But you cross a red line when you invite foreign powers or foreign leader into Singapore politics."[77] In view of these factors, Sunny Lee stated that Minister Shanmugam stood by his comments with regard to the trio's meeting with Mahathir and what was said about promoting democracy in Singapore.

Analysis

Clearly, the old belief that developments in Singapore and Malaysia are indivisible have been proven true and remain as relevant in the past as they are today. While both Singapore and Malaysia have many issues that divide them as well as there are many areas of cooperation and convergence, the preparedness of Mahathir to articulate his views about the need for a regime change in Singapore is new. No Singaporean and Malaysian leader has publicly called for this and interfered in the domestic politics of each other until the May 2018 General Elections in Malaysia. In addition to Mahathir's statement, the willingness of Malaysian NGOs linked to the

---

73. Ibid.

74. Ibid.

75. Ibid.

76. Ibid.

77. Ibid.

ruling party, in this case, PKR, to organise public forums about "doing a Malaysia in Singapore" is also politically novel. Following this, those who participated in the forum, especially Tan Wah Piow, Thum Ping Tjin and Hishamuddin Rais met Mahathir and called on him to promote democracy in Singapore as well as participate in a conference on spreading democracy in the region that was eventually held in February 2019, to which Mahathir had earlier accepted in principle.

While these Malaysian developments have tried to shape the political agenda of Singapore in the coming months and years, there was also an attempt to form a 'coalition of willing' among the opposition parties in Singapore. While a meeting of seven political parties took place, progress has been rather slow, signalling that serious differences exist among these political parties, especially on the modus operandi of cooperation in a general elections. Probably, the past ghost of personality differences, inability of the political parties to cooperate and agree on where the political parties will contest are issues that are yet to be surmounted. There is also the old mistrust and hence, antagonism that if political party A is in the coalition, political party B will not want to be part of the coalition due to intense ideological and personal differences as well as past conflicts, say between the SDP and SPP. Tan Cheng Bock's decision to launch his own political party rather than join an existing one or lead a coalition of existing political parties is also a clear indication of continued differences among the opposition political parties in Singapore, something that is likely to further advantage and reinforce the current state of PAP's dominance in Singapore.

NEW ISSUES AND DEVELOPMENTS IN SINGAPORE AS THE PRE-DOMINANT PAP PREPARES FOR THE FORTHCOMING GENERAL ELECTIONS

Introduction

While many issues have surfaced since the People's Action Party (PAP) romped to victory in the 2015 General Elections, many new developments have also taken place and many of these have the potential to impact the forthcoming general elections. Several old issues continue to bedevil the PAP as it prepares for the upcoming general elections. These include the rising cost of living, healthcare costs, costs and availability of housing, breakdown in transportation especially the Mass Rapid Transit (MRT), rising unemployment and concerns about limited jobs in the near future for the youth, especially school leavers and graduates. As Singapore's 13th General Elections since independence in 1965 must be held by January 2021 and could be held as early as September 2019, a number of new issues and developments have also surfaced both in domestic and international politics.

Domestic issues and developments

The Workers' Party and the Aljunied-Hougang-Punggol East Town Council saga

The Aljunied-Hougang-Punggol East Town Council (AHPETC) issue surfaced in 2013 and got heated prior to the 2015 General Elections.[1] In February 2015, the Auditor-General Office reported that the AHPETC was found to be in default of the Town Councils Act and Town Councils Financial Rules.[2] The issue was frequently discussed in parliament and outside, especially by top PAP leaders to discredit the WP and its top leadership. It was also a major issue that surfaced

---

1. Amelia Teng and Karamjit Kaur, "WP not being upfront on issue: Shanmugam", *The Straits Times*, 4 September 2015.
2. See "Analysts and the AHPETC and the voters", *The New Paper*, 1 September 2015.

during the 2015 General Elections that the PAP used to insinuate that the voters stood to lose under the Workers' Party (WP) leadership as residents' interests would be compromised. For instance, the then minister for law and minister for foreign affairs, K. Shanmugam argued, "they [WP] haven't produced unqualified accounts in a single year. Why are you holding back information from your own auditors? Why are you saying that you are refusing to give information on the key issues? Why is the High Court saying you misled Parliament? That's not me saying that."[3] The minister further stated, "the High Court said that Ms Sylvia Lim misled Parliament, was dishonest. She has not responded to that. Yeah, you don't go to jail for that. I suppose that is all right? Another observation the High Court made was that if this kind of conduct had taken place in a public company, it probably would attract criminal sanctions."[4] Many analysts also believe that part of the reason, relatively speaking, for the WP's poorer performance in the 2015 General Elections compared to the 2011 General Elections, was due to the town council saga. Less than a year later, Shanmugam alleged that "AHTC's leadership has neither upheld or enforced integrity, nor ethical values. The rot is at the top."[5]

The town council saga reached a new crescendo when in July 2017, the AHTC, which had appointed an independent panel of three lawyers at the behest of the Ministry of National Development (MND) and Housing and Development Board (HDB), announced that it would be suing Aljunied-Hougang Town Council (AHTC) chairman, Pritam Singh, the vice-chairman Sylvia Lim and the then secretary-general of the party, Low Thia Khiang, as well as three former managing agents, for improper payments made to the managing agent.[6] Following the WP's victory in the Aljunied Group Representation Constituency (GRC) in the 2011 General Elections, FM Solutions & Services (FMSS) was appointed, without tender, as the managing agent and FM Solutions and Integrated Services (FMSIS)

---

3. See Amelia Teng and Karamjit Kaur, "WP not being upfront on issue: Shanmugam".

4. Ibid.

5. Charissa Yong, "WP MPs 'have not shown integrity'", *The Straits Times*, 24 July 2016.

6. The three independent members were Philip Jeyaretnam, N. Sreenivasan and Ong Pang Thye. The three former managing agents were Chua Zhi Hon, Kenneth Foo Seck Guan and Koh Weng Kong, who worked closely with How Weng Fan and Danny Loh. See Alfred Chua, "AHTC trial: Town councillors grilled over not raising questions about managing agent's appointment", *Today*, 29 October 2018.

as the service provider.[7] The civil lawsuit against the WP alleged that it breached its fiduciary duties in administering the AHTC. It centred around S$33.7 million that AHTC paid to FMSS and FMSIS between 2011 and 2015.[8] Added to this suit, there is another legal suit by Pasir Ris-Punggol Town Council (PRPTC) that aims to recover whatever losses the Punggol East constituency may have incurred when the town council was led by the WP.[9]

In the legal suit that started in October 2018, it was argued that Sylvia Lim and Low Thia Khiang had breached their fiduciary duties and failed to act in good faith when FMSS was appointed as the town council's managing agent in 2011. This is because the leaders of FMSS, namely How Weng Fan and her husband, Danny Loh, were long-time WP supporters. It was also alleged that insufficient efforts were made to disclose the conflict of interest of this relationship to other town councilors.[10] The fact that no tender was called for the appointment of FMSS was viewed as unjustifiable and a breach of trust. AHTC was also accused of failing in its financial duties when it awarded a contract to a much more costly architect, leading to a fee differential of more than S$2.8 million.[11]

In defence, the WP Members of Parliament (MPs) argued that they had acted in good faith and in the best interest of the Aljunied-Hougang residents. As MPs are given a degree of latitude to run town councils, they believed that they did not violate any rules of the Town Councils Act and Town Councils Financial Rules. The WP MPs also claimed that the claims sought by the AHTC and PRPTC respectively were totally based on the reports provided by Klynveld Peat Marwick Goerdeler (KPMG) and PricewaterhouseCoopers (PwC), two of the top auditors in the world, and that they did not take into consideration the special circumstances of the time when the WP MPs made the decisions to engage FMSS and FMSIS.[12] For instance,

---

7. The WP argued that no tender was called as "urgent taking over work was needed". See "The AHTC lawsuits against Workers' Party MPs explained in 5 minutes", *The Must Share News Team*, 2 October 2018, https://mustsharenews.com/ahtc-lawsuits/

8. Adrian Lim and Rachel Au-Yong, "AHTC wrap-up: What are the 2 lawsuits about?", *The Straits Times*, 4 November 2018.

9. Ibid.

10. Ibid.

11. Ibid.

12. Ibid.

Chelva Rajah, the WP town councillors' lawyer argued that the "ruling PAP had a track record of making things difficult for opposition town councils."[13]

Following the November 2018 hearing, the lawyers for the two town councils and the WP MPs would make their final statements in March 2019 and it will be many more months before the final verdict is made by the sitting judge, Kanan Ramesh. If the WP MPs are found to have breached their duties and made improper payments, a new round of hearing would commence on how much ought to be paid, which can take up much more time. If, after all these hearings, the WP MPs are found liable and are unable to pay, they will be declared bankrupt and could lose their parliamentary seats, that is, if they are still sitting MPs. Interestingly, in November 2018, the WP MPs were able to raise more than S$1 million within four days from public donations.[14]

According to long-time political observer and the former chief editor of *Today* and *The New Paper*, P.N. Balji, "the last chapters of the Aljunied-Hougang Town Council magnum opus are being written with the end game still anybody's guess. If it is dragged till the very bitter end, the long-running saga is likely to end with three MPs of the Workers' Party (WP) losing their seats in parliament. Should the scenario pan out, Singapore would be poorer for it while opposition politics would take a long time to recover after a short burst of optimism when the ruling party was ejected out of a GRC for the first time in the 2011 general elections."[15] For Balji, "WP miscalculated big time that the government had moved away from the knuckle-duster approach of the Lee Kuan Yew era providing an important marker for those who want to challenge the government: Make sure your dealings are beyond reproach. The WP's troubles are likely to mean that the opposition party and Singapore will pay a heavy price if the end game is to punish the party severely."[16]

---

13. Ibid.

14. On 28 October 2018, the WP announced that "we are closing the appeal for now, as the amount raised substantially covers the legal fees required at this point in time. We would like to ask you to hold your contributions if you have not transferred them." Rachel Genevieve Chia, "People donated over S$1 million in 4 days to the Workers' Party MPs embroiled in a multi-million dollars lawsuit", *Business Insider*, 29 October 2018, https://www.businessinsider.sg/workers-party-mps-embroiled-in-multi-million-dollar-lawsuits-raise-more-than-s1-million-in-4-days/

15. P.N. Balji, "Aljunied-Hougang Town Council saga: What is the end game?", *Yahoo News Singapore*, 31 July 2017, https://sg.news.yahoo.com/comment-aljunied-hougang-town-council-saga-end-game-101158627.html

16. Ibid.

Registration of two new political parties

In the 2015 General Elections, two new political parties, namely, the Singapore First Party (SFP) and the People's Power Party (PPP) contested in the elections. For the forthcoming general elections, it would appear that there would also be two new political parties joining the fray, namely, the People's Voice Party (PVP) and the Progress Singapore Party (PSP). The former leader of the National Solidarity Party (NSP), Lim Tean who resigned from the party in May 2017 on grounds of having a fundamentally different approach to politics from his party, set up the PVP on 29 October 2018 and it was formally registered on 31 October 2018, becoming "the eleventh [active] political party in the country" even though historically more than 40 political parties have existed with 11 having being dissolved.[17]

Through his Facebook video, Lim Tean announced a number of promises his new party would make, including: return the Central Provident Fund (CPF) to citizens age 55; not to increase the Goods and Services Tax (GST) by 2%; make basic goods zero GST — baby milk, diapers, rice, books, etc.; slash prime minister's pay by 70%; introduce a Living Wage; bring in a Direct Democracy which involves referendums; look into the true accounts of Temasek Holdings and GIC (Government Investment Corporation); address the HDB ownership/tenant situation; call for a referendum to overturn the Elected President and cast fresh votes for a new one; break up the monopolies that do not serve Singaporeans (Real Estate, Telco's, Banks, Supermarkets etc.); protect Singaporeans and New Citizens jobs; scrap the PAP's march towards a 10 million population; and examine recent water, electricity and transport hikes and dial back and reduce where necessary.[18] Lim Tean also stated that the PVP was not formed to "act as a check-and-balance to the PAP, but to actually form the government."[19] For him, "it is evident the PAP are [sic] long past caring for our people and their lease on possession of their office must be brought to an end. I want to assure you that there is not a single mess the PAP has made that we cannot undo."[20]

---

17. Anna Maria Romero, "Lim Tean debuts new political party — People's Voice", *The Independent*, 31 October 2018; "8 promises that Lim Tean made as leader of People's Voice", *The Must Share News Team*, 30 October 2018.

18. Ibid.

19. Ibid.

20. Ibid.

Following closely the footsteps of Lim Tean, on 16 January 2019, Tan Cheng Bock applied to the Registry of Societies to have the PSP registered and on 16 March 2019, he announced that his party had been given an in-principle approval.[21] On 1 April 2019, Tan announced that his party had been officially registered on 28 March 2019.[22] The 78-year-old Tan, who was the former PAP member for Ayer Rajah for 26 years and a presidential candidate in the 2011 Presidential Election (who lost narrowly to Tony Tan), announced his re-entry into national politics in order to add a new voice in parliament and stated that some of the party members were former PAP cadre members.[23] In a public conversation, Tan said that he did not want his political party to be known as an opposition party but rather as the 'alternative party' to the PAP, arguing that he wanted to revive the earlier ideals of the PAP which the current PAP had somewhat forgotten and deviated from.[24] He argued that there was clearly an 'old PAP' that was highly respected and a 'new PAP' which was facing many problems and wanted to restore the rising 'trust deficit' in the government.[25] As the 'grand old man' of national politics, Tan stated that he had many options confronting him, including "joining an existing opposition party, taking over an existing opposition party or running independently" but decided to form a new party as the best option.[26] He stated that even though he was setting up a new political party, "we still look forward to working with others in the opposition who are passionate about putting country first — before either party or self".[27]

---

21. See "Tan Cheng Bock's application to form political party approved 'in principle'", *Channel NewsAsia*, 16 March 2019, https://www.channelnewsasia.com/news/singapore/tan-cheng-bock-s-application-to-form-political-party-approved-in-11351438/

22. See "Tan Cheng Bock's Progress Singapore Party officially registered", *Channel NewsAsia*, 1 April 2019, https://www.channelnewsasia.com/news/singapore/tan-cheng-bock-s-progress-singapore-party-officially-registered-11398996

23. Faris Mokhtar, "Exclusive: Revealed — the people behind Tan Cheng Bock's proposed new party and its election plans", *Today*, 8 February 2019.

24. Tan Cheng Bock's conversation with students at the National University of Singapore on 3 April 2019.

25. Ibid.

26. See Matthias Ang, "Tan Cheng Bock announces return to politics with new Progress Singapore Party (PSP)", *Mothership*, 18 January 2019, https://mothership.sg/2019/01/tan-cheng-bock-returns-new-political-party/

27. Ibid.

From the perspective of the PAP's institutional history and legacy, Tan Cheng Bock represented and symbolised a nightmare scenario. This was because it reminded the PAP's leadership of the potential of splits and divisions from within, something that had eventually led to the downfall of one-party dominant states elsewhere, the latest being in Malaysia. From the time of PAP's founding in late 1954, right to 1968, the PAP suffered from the consequences of splits from within, be it from the right or left of the political spectrum. For the PAP, amid the difficult and divisive coalition between the pro-Communists and Left, and the moderates since its founding, two of its key leading members were responsible for the split that destroyed the party's unity and almost led to its loss of power. On 18 June 1961, Ong Eng Guan, the former mayor of Singapore and the former minister of national development in the first PAP cabinet in 1959, formed the United People's Party (UPP), which was registered on 14 July 1961.[28] After being sacked by the PAP, Ong challenged the ruling party in the Hong Lim by-election and won resoundingly. Following this, the UPP was formed. Ong again won in the 1963 Legislative Assembly elections. The PAP only regained the seat when Ong resigned his seat on 16 June 1965, arguing that the PAP-controlled Legislative Assembly served "no useful purpose".[29]

The influential leader of the pro-communist Left, Lim Chin Siong, who played a key role in the founding of the PAP in November 1954, was a source of serious division in the PAP and he tried to unseat the moderates by trying to capture power from within. Failing this, he split with the PAP and on 21 June 1961, founded the *Barisan Sosialis* that was officially registered on 13 August 1961. Despite Operation Coldstore that decimated the Left in Singapore in February 1963, in the September 1963 Legislative Assembly elections the *Barisan* won 13 seats, with the PAP capturing 37 of the 51 seats. This was despite the fact that the PAP's electorate vote was only 46.9%, the lowest ever in its history as a ruling party.

This brought home to the PAP what splits can potentially lead to and hence, the importance of the Tan Cheng Bock phenomenon. Historically, by leaving the party and competing in the 2011 Presidential Election, it was clear that he would represent a political force that was largely antithetical to the PAP. The same can be

---

28. "New party now registered", *The Straits Times*, 22 July 1961.

29. "Mr Ong quits the Assembly", *The Straits Times*, 17 June 1965.

said of his efforts to cobble together an opposition coalition in July 2018. However, it was the setting up of an opposition political party that was the clearest sign yet of a former leading member of the PAP who was bent on challenging the ruling party's hold on power. From that perspective, the establishment of the PSP would be the third key attempt in 58 years by a former PAP member (after Ong Eng Guan and Lim Chin Siong) to form a new political party that wanted to challenge and possibly unseat the PAP and the first ever since August 1965. Even more ominous for the PAP was the willingness of five opposition political parties in Singapore to form a coalition with Tan Cheng Bock, especially for the forthcoming general elections even though how it will actually turn out remains to be seen.[30] On 27 May 2019, through his Facebook, Tan announced that he intended to launch the PSP on 15 June 2019 at the Singapore Expo Hall 5 and was awaiting a police permit to do so.[31] Later, he announced a further postponement of his party's launch.

The finalisation of the 4G PAP leadership

Since Lee Hsien Loong assumed the office of prime minister in Singapore in August 2004, a central theme that has accompanied his leadership has been the need to add 'new blood' to the political leadership and some 15 years later; this promise was near to fruition. This was the culmination of the PAP's 35th Central Executive Committee (CEC) meeting in November 2018 when the 'new faces' that had been groomed since the 2011 and 2015 general elections came to dominate the CEC with only three members from the 3G still left in the CEC (Lee Hsien Loong and K. Shanmugam, with Ng Eng Hen co-opted as a member). The party's key leaders announced on 23 November 2018 are presented in Table 10.1.

That the 4G leadership was taking shape became clear in January 2018 when a group of 16 PAP's ministers and senior ministers of state, responded to Emeritus Senior Minister Goh Chok Tong's call, in December 2017, to settle the issue of

---

30. Victor Loh and Faris Mokhtar, "The leaders of at least five opposition parties told TODAY that they are open to an alliance with Dr Tan", *Today*, 19 January 2019.

31. See Sulaiman Daud, "Tan Cheng Bock's Progress S'pore Party to launch on June 15 at Expo", *Mothership*, 27 May 2019, https://mothership.sg/2019/05/tan-cheng-bock-psp-launch/ ; also see Tan Cheng Bock's Facebook at https://www.facebook.com/pg/TanChengBock/posts/

Table 10.1.   35th PAP CEC Office Holders

Chairman	Gan Kim Yong
Vice-Chairman	Masagos Zulkifli Bin Masagos Mohamad
Secretary-General	Lee Hsien Loong
1st Assistant Secretary-General	Heng Swee Keat
2nd Assistant Secretary-General	Chan Chun Sing
Treasurer	K. Shanmugam
Assistant Treasurer	Ong Ye Kung
Organising Secretaries	Grace Fu
	Desmond Lee#
Members	Christopher de Souza#
	Indranee Thurai Rajah
	Ng Chee Meng
	Ng Eng Hen*
	Tan Chuan-Jin
	Josephine Teo*
	Sitoh Yih Pin#
	Vivian Balakrishnan
	Lawrence Wong#

* Co-opted on 11 Nov 2018
# Co-opted on 23 Nov 2018
Source: "PAP New CEC", People's Action Party, 23 November 2018, https://www.pap.org.sg/pap-new-cec

the Singapore's fourth prime minister within the next six to nine months.[32] The 16 'young PAP leaders' included the following: Chan Chun Sing, Chee Hong Tat, Grace Fu, Heng Swee Keat, Koh Poh Koon, Desmond Lee, Masagos Zulkifli, Ng Chee Meng, Ong Ye Kung, Janil Puthucheary, Indranee Rajah, S. Iswaran, Sim Ann, Tan Chuan-Jin, Josephine Teo and Lawrence Wong. The somewhat rare January 2018 declaration by the 'Group of 16' stated inter alia that in view of Prime Minister Lee Hsien Loong's decision to step down after the new elections, the younger generation leaders were keenly aware of the 'pressing issue'. However, as a retort to

32. According to ESM Goh, "Every succession is different, but one thing remains the same: each cohort will have to pick one amongst themselves to lead, and support him. I hope the current cohort will do so in 6 to 9 months' time. Then PM (Lee Hsien Loong) can formally designate their choice as his potential successor before 2018 ends." See Elgin Toh, "ESM Goh Chok Tong says settling 4G leadership an urgent challenge, hopes next PM can be designated 'before 2018 ends'", The Straits Times, 31 December 2017.

ESM Goh, the 'Group of 16' also stated that "we are conscious of our responsibility, are working closely together as a team, and will settle on a leader from amongst us in good time."[33] On 26 January 2018, Prime Minister Lee stated, in response to the 'Group of 16' that "my assessment is, it probably will take a little bit longer" and that "ESM (Goh) is speaking with the privilege of watching things rather than being responsible to make it happen. I think we know it's a very serious matter."[34] A key leader of the 4G leadership, Ong Ye Kung, confirmed the sentiments of the 'Group' when he stated on 28 January 2018 that "I think the PM has made it quite clear [on the issue of not rushing through to name a successor]. Don't get constrained by an artificial deadline [to name a successor]."[35]

The most important decision of the 35th CEC meeting was the consensus to appoint Heng Swee Keat and Chan Chun Sing as the first and second assistant secretary-general of the PAP respectively, signalling vividly that Heng and Chan are the PAP's anointed successors as prime minister and deputy prime minister (DPM), respectively. When exactly this transition will take place remains to be seen even though Prime Minister Lee has indicated that it will be 18 to 24 months after the next general elections. For some, the choice of Heng as Singapore's prime minister-in-waiting came as a surprise, partly due to his age, which means that he would be 60 years old when he becomes the next prime minister, and also stemming from the uncertainties of health, as a result of the stroke he suffered in May 2016. However, due to his personality traits, of which his amicable character, his sterling public service, among others as being one of Lee Kuan Yew's best principal private secretaries and his ability to keep the 4G leaders together, were the key assets that channelled him as Singapore's next prime minister. Ong Ye Kung's decision in January 2018 not to contest for the top position among the 4G leaders also played a critical role, even being the decider to a large extent, in ensuring Heng's victory as he emerged as *primus inter pares* among the 4G

33. "Singapore's younger office holders will settle on a potential leader 'in good time'", *Channel NewsAsia*, 4 January 2018, https://www.channelnewsasia.com/news/singapore/singapore-s-younger-office-holders-will-settle-on-a-potential-9832326

34. Ng June Sen, "PM Lee Hsien Loong responds to ESM Goh Chok Tong's 'watching' FB posts", *The Straits Times*, 5 February 2018.

35. "Good for 4G ministers not to be constrained by 'artificial deadline' to select leader: Ong Ye Kung", *The Straits Times*, 29 January 2018.

leaders, especially in the 'Group of 16' that was informally formed in response to ESM Goh's challenge.[36]

The key question that remains to be answered will be — can Heng Swee Keat do two things: (a) keep the party's unity; and (b) help the PAP win elections and lead the party to continue performing as it has in the past? These were the two benchmarks Prime Minister Lee highlighted during his interview with Singapore journalists in Buenos Aires, Argentina in early December 2018 for political transition to take place in Singapore. He argued, "it depends on the party staying together and the party winning elections. And the first thing to do will be to win the next election."[37] While the second part of the key question remains to be seen, what was interesting was the few months before and after Heng's election as first assistant secretary-general that issues of 'party unity' came to dominate the PAP leadership's public discourse.

For instance, at the PAP's annual conference and biennial elections in November 2018, Prime Minister Lee talked of the need for the party to win the next general elections by "uniting Singaporeans".[38] Similarly, the PAP's designated successor to Lee Hsien Loong, Heng Swee Keat, hinted of possible divisions within the PAP during his interview with journalists in Buenos Aires. He said that after his 4G colleagues had informed him of their decision to choose him as their leader, he had a "very nice discussion" with Chan Chun Sing and asked him to be his deputy and "he readily accepted...I want to ensure that we maintain that unity in the team and that's why I had such a good discussion with Chun Sing, not just on being the leader and deputy, but also on what we need to do to take Singapore forward. We are both very clear that it is not about lobbying younger office-holders for a

---

36. When Ong Ye Kung told reporters "I am shaping up in my mind someone who can be the leader amongst us. I am sure my colleagues are thinking of the same issue too" but ruled himself out of the race, not many took him seriously. Yet, this was a key decision that helped to reduce the three-man race to a two-man one that eventually led to Heng clinching the race. See Tham Yuen-C, Seow Bei Yi, and Elgin Toh, "4G ministers say they will settle on a leader 'in good time'; Ong Ye Kung says he has someone in mind", *The Straits Times*, 4 January 2018.

37. Charissa Yong, "Cabinet reshuffle to take place sometime after Budget 2019: PM Lee Hsien Loong", *The Straits Times*, 4 December 2018.

38. "PM Lee calls on PAP to unite Singaporeans, continue with pragmatic and centrist approach", *The Straits Times*, 11 November 2018.

particular position, but about reaching agreements on how we can do this well and the agenda for taking Singapore forward."[39] In whatever context Heng was talking about "lobbying for positions", be it about positions within the PAP CEC or even in the various ministries, it is not something that is healthy for PAP's unity and does not bode too well for the future of Singapore if its ends up with a breakup of the party, something senior leaders such as Lee Kuan Yew had warned in the past.[40]

In this regard, most interesting of all was the observation by Zakir Hussain, the *Straits Times* news editor and senior journalist who wrote a commentary article titled, "PAP unveils new leadership: Key challenge will be keeping party cohesive and united" on 24 November 2018. In it, he observed:

One theme clearly stood out from yesterday's People's Action Party (PAP) announcement of its new leadership slate: The numerous references to the need for the team to be cohesive and united. "United" was a word repeated no fewer than a dozen times throughout the evening — and it would appear to have been intentional. Shortly after the party's top decision-making body, the Central Executive Committee (CEC), met and released a statement on the PAP's new line-up at 4.30pm, two other statements followed. The first, on the PAP's Facebook page, was by its secretary-general, Prime Minister Lee Hsien Loong, who endorsed the decision of the fourth-generation (4G) team to have Mr Heng Swee Keat as their next leader, and Mr Chan Chun Sing as his deputy. PM Lee gave his vote of confidence to Mr Heng and Mr Chan, and pledged that "all of us in the new CEC, older or younger, will work together to build a strong and united party that will continue to serve the people and lead Singapore forward".

A statement signed by 32 younger office-holders — including Mr Heng and Mr Chan — followed and endorsed the move to name both of them as their leaders. "We will continue to work cohesively as a team," it said. "We are united in our purpose of serving Singaporeans to the best of our abilities". There is no reason to expect that the PAP — which has stayed cohesive for most of the 59 years it has been in power — might not one day face such divisions. It has had splits in the past, notably in 1961, when left-leaning members broke away to form the Barisan Sosialis.

---

39. See Charissa Yong, "4G ministers will start discussions with Singaporeans next year: Heng", *The Straits Times*, 4 December 2018.

40. "PAP will be voted out one day: MM Lee", *AsiaOne*, 21 January 2011, https://www.asia one.com/News/AsiaOne%2BNews/Singapore/Story/A1Story20110121-259459. html

Hence the many references yesterday to the need for cohesion and unity. While it appears aimed at reassuring those Singaporeans who may be concerned about whether the PAP will stay united, it is also for those party members who saw distinct differences between contenders for the party posts — and who might now be tempted to scale back their involvement, or even back another party, as the chosen leader may not be someone they preferred.

The need for unity and the assurances that they will work as a team were underlined by Mr Heng and Mr Chan in their statements at a media conference an hour after their new posts were announced. Mr Heng said Singaporeans "like to see a strong and united political leadership working in close partnership with our people". And while there is natural interest in who will be the fourth prime minister, "it is just as important that we have a strong, united and cohesive team in the Cabinet". Mr Chan, too, echoed the point on teamwork, saying: "Teamwork is critical to us. Our team must be greater than the sum of our individual parts. As a team, we will complement one another, leveraging our respective strengths to do our best for Singapore," he added.

Mr Chan, too, emphasised that teamwork was a key takeaway for him from older political leaders. "No matter how good we are individually, it (excelling) is necessary but not sufficient," he said. "What distinguishes the Singapore team from the others who we are competing against... is the fact that we have a very cohesive team, and that is the hallmark of our leadership style".[41]

Interestingly, during a visit to Switzerland in early May 2019, Heng Swee Keat revisited the 'unity theme' when he said that this was one of the key challenges confronting Singapore. Heng said, "our biggest challenge that we need to address is to build a sense of unity amidst these tremendous changes that are going on around us. This can be done with good governance, keeping politics constructive and making hard decisions for the long run, rather than short-term benefits. Together with good governance and a sense of unity among our people, Singapore can remain strong".[42]

---

41. See Zakir Hussain, "PAP unveils new leadership: Key challenge will be keeping party cohesive and united", *The Straits Times*, 24 November 2018.

42. See "Singapore's biggest challenge is to build 'a sense of unity' amid 'tremendous changes': DPM Heng", *Channel NewsAsia*, https://www.channelnewsasia.com/image/11522958/0x0/960/720/72a3329ff2e0cfe1327ff5961726b3e2/di/dpm-heng-in-switzerland.jpg

A major opportunity for Heng Swee Keat to make his presence felt nationally as the anointed successor of Prime Minister Lee and the leader of the 4G was his dialogue with 700 students at Nanyang Technological University on 28 March 2019. He made a number of important points signalling that there would be more continuity than change under him, at least, in the short term. Among others, he spoke of the need to be open and welcoming of foreigners, of the need to work towards an optimum population for Singapore in the future, the importance of artificial intelligence and technological disruptions and in response to the question whether it was Singapore or the PAP that was unprepared for a prime minister from a minority community, Heng said that "at the right time, when enough people think that way, we would have, we may have, a minority who becomes the leader of the country."[43]

As part of the preparation to get the 4G leaders to take over the reign of political leadership, the single most important signal was the announcement by the Prime Minister's Office on 23 April 2019 that Heng Swee Keat would be appointed as the DPM on 1 May 2019. As the DPM, he would continue as the Finance Minister and continue chairing the Future Economy Council and National Research Foundation. He would also be the acting prime minister in the absence of Prime Minister Lee.[44] The incumbent DPMs, Teo Chee Hean and Tharman Shanmugaratnam, would relinquish their posts and remain in the cabinet as senior ministers. Teo would continue as coordinating minister for national security while Tharman, who helmed the coordinating minister for economic and social policies, would be re-designated as coordinating minister for social policies. Tharman would also take on a new responsibility as the deputy chairman of Singapore's sovereign wealth fund, the GIC and continue to advise Prime Minister Lee on economic policies.[45]

---

43. Adrian Lim, "Heng Swee Keat on S'pore staying open: We don't want a world where people build walls", *The Straits Times*, 29 March 2019; Adrian Lim, "Singapore will have ethnic minority PM at right time, says Heng Swee Keat", *The Straits Times*, 29 March 2019.

44. "Heng Swee Keat to be promoted to DPM in Cabinet reshuffle", *Channel NewsAsia*, 23 April 2019, https://www.channelnewsasia.com/news/singapore/heng-swee-keat-promoted-deputy-prime-minister-cabinet-2019-11470768; Martino Tan, "PM Lee's Cabinet reshuffle offers clarity to S'pore's leadership transition with solo DPM", *Mothership*, 24 April 2019, https://mothership.sg/2019/04/why-is-heng-swee-keat-new-dpm/; Low Youjin, "Heng Swee Keat's elevation to DPM leaves no doubt on succession plan: Analysts", *Today*, 24 April 2019.

45. Ibid.

On 23 April 2019, Tharman, in his Facebook post, endorsed the appointment of Heng as DPM in the following terms:

> We took a major step today in leadership succession, and it is a plus for Singapore's future. Swee Keat is the best person to move up to become DPM and take over as PM during the next term of government. He has exceptional ability, mettle and the confidence of the 4G team…We have avoided sudden change. It may be unexciting and predictable, but it works for Singapore.[46]

The appointment of Heng as the DPM was the culmination of political changes initiated in November 2018 when the PAP's new CEC was announced with Heng and Chan as the first and second assistant secretary-general positions respectively, paving the way for them to be appointed as the next DPMs in place of Teo and Tharman. Most poignantly, the appointment of Heng as the next and sole DPM was a clear sign that he was set to become Singapore's next prime minister.[47] However, what was surprising was that Chan was not appointed as the second DPM. Historically, there were only three other times when there was one DPM, from 1959 to 1968 (Toh Chin Chye), 1973 to 1980 (Goh Keng Swee) and 1993 to 1995 (Lee Hsien Loong).

According to Gillian Koh, "with the appointment of just one Deputy Prime Minister, what is being signalled is that there is a clear pecking order, and there should be no confusion, there should be no sort of questions raised as to whether the previous group of contenders for the premiership post will be given more duties, more responsibilities, such that they are still in the running for the position."[48] While Chan, as long as he remains as the PAP's second assistant secretary-general, stands the chance of becoming the second DPM in the very near future, in the

---

46. Jewel Stolarchuk, "If only you could be our PM" — Singaporeans tell Tharman as he lauds Heng Swee Keat", *The Independent*, 24 April 2019, http://theindependent.sg/if-only-you-could-be-our-pm-singaporeans-tell-tharman-as-he-lauds-heng-swee-keat/

47. Kevin Kwang, "Heng Swee Keat's appointment as next DPM sends 'clear signal' of succession: Analysts", *Channel NewsAsia*, 24 April 2019, https://www.channelnewsasia.com/news/singapore/heng-swee-keat-next-dpm-clear-signal-succession-analysts-11472142; Martino Tan, "PM Lee's Cabinet reshuffle offers clarity to S'pore's leadership transition with solo DPM", *Mothership*, 24 April 2019, https://mothership.sg/2019/04/why-is-heng-swee-keat-new-dpm/; Low Youjin, "Heng Swee Keat's elevation to DPM leaves no doubt on succession plan: Analysts".

48. Kevin Kwang, "Heng Swee Keat's appointment as next DPM sends 'clear signal' of succession: Analysts".

short term, the political contestation among the 4G leaders was put to rest, with the 4G leaders now busying themselves for the role of governing Singapore as well as preparing for the next general elections that must be held by 15 January 2021.

Later, Heng stated that as the sole DPM he would be supporting Prime Minister Lee in reviewing Singapore's longer-term policy measures to take the country forward in the next decade, including issues involving ageing population, economic restructuring and dealing with social issues that may arise as Singapore goes through a faster and more challenging pace of change. For Heng, it also includes strengthening Singapore's relations with its major external partners.[49] Stating that Heng may have 'understated' his duties as DPM, Prime Minister Lee said that "as a DPM, he is not just a minister but also carrying more of the political responsibilities."[50] According to Prime Minister Lee, as a DPM, it "means setting the agenda, pitching the Government's stance and policies to the public, building the younger team and being ready in all respects to take over from me and my older ministers as soon as possible."[51]

And since then, Heng has been doing just that — becoming 'prime-ministerial' as seen from his comments on national politics and policies. For instance, on Tan Cheng Bock's decision to form a new political party, Heng said that it was "a development that is not totally unexpected." However, "Singaporeans will have to decide on who can serve them better, and I will leave Singaporeans to make that judgment."[52] As the next general elections is something most analysts are buzzing about, Heng has also joined in the fray by stating that while there is still "some time" before the next poll, the PAP has already found some very good candidates, and that he was working with Chan to prepare for the next general elections. Heng

---

49. See "Heng Swee Keat to support PM Lee in longer term policy review as DPM", *Today*, 28 April 2019.

50. See Tang See Kit, "As DPM, Heng Swee Keat will take on more political responsibilities: PM Lee", *Channel NewsAsia*, 29 April 2019, https://www.channelnewsasia.com/news/singapore/dpm-heng-swee-keat-will-takep-on-bigger-political-role-11488330; Janice Lim, "Heng Swee Keat to hold more political responsibilities as my deputy: PM Lee", *Today*, 29 April 2019; Danson Cheong, "Heng Swee Keat will bear more political responsibilities as Singapore's No. 2: PM Lee Hsien Loong", *The Straits Times*, 29 April 2019.

51. Ibid.

52. "Heng Swee Keat: Tan Cheng Bock's move to form party 'not unexpected'", *Today*, 21 January 2019.

has talked about how he and Chan are working on the party manifesto that will signal how to bring Singapore forward in the next five years and beyond.[53]

Heng has also stated that Singapore had to evolve its own democratic model and that "the fact that the ruling party has been able to win elections is not because we have been suppressing. The fact is that we have…delivered on what we promised, and that we have won the trust and confidence of Singaporeans."[54] He argued that "it is not a given that having an opposition party (in government) and multiple parties will result in the best outcomes."[55] He cautioned against 'auction politics' where political parties made promises for a better life only to win votes by trying to score political points. Rather, he argued that "it is very important for us not to fall for that…We have built our society to be so vibrant, successful and cohesive over these years because we are prepared to do difficult things. We are prepared to take hard decisions and many Singaporeans know that…it is the outcomes that matter."[56]

Finally, for him, on the nature of Singapore's economy, the role of the government is important, just as it is vital to have evolved from a 'confrontational' to a 'collaborative' trade union system in the Republic.[57] In the face of challenges brought about by globalisation, Heng has said that the 'people' and 'workers' should be the centre of a state's policy.[58] On the sensitive topic of corruption, cronyism and nepotism, Heng has

---

53. "Singapore's biggest challenge is to build 'a sense of unity' amid 'tremendous changes': DPM Heng", *Channel NewsAsia*, 19 May 2019, https://www.channelnewsasia.com/news/singapore/singapore-heng-swee-keat-st-gallen-switzerland-biggest-challenge-11547090; also see Jaime Ho and Kevin Kwang, "PAP working on party manifesto, selecting candidates ahead of next General Election: DPM Heng", *Channel NewsAsia*, 5 May 2019, https://www.channelnewsasia.com/news/singapore/dpm-heng-swee-keat-on-pap-ge-preparations-11503786

54. "Singapore's biggest challenge is to build 'a sense of unity' amid 'tremendous changes': DPM Heng".

55. Kenneth Cheng, "Going beyond consultations: Heng wants to cultivate leaders in every corner of society", *Today*, 5 May 2019.

56. Ibid.

57. "Protecting workers, not jobs key to economic transformation: Heng Swee Keat", *Channel NewsAsia*, 19 May 2019, https://www.channelnewsasia.com/news/singapore/heng-swee-keat-protect-workers-not-jobs-economic-transformation-11519640

58. "Singapore's biggest challenge is to build 'a sense of unity' amid 'tremendous changes': DPM Heng".

also made his view very clear. During his May 2019 trip to Switzerland, he was asked how a one-party dominant state ensured that there was no corruption, nepotism and cronyism as many of the top policymakers, from the prime minister down to key ministers, such as himself, the finance minister, were sitting in the leadership positions of Singapore's sovereign wealth funds such as Temasek Holdings and GIC. While many one-party dominant states have been associated with corruption, nepotism and cronyism, Heng said that Singapore had very clear and strong rules against these vile practices. Hence, "for example, we have our sovereign funds, Temasek and GIC. Not once did I intervene as Minister of Finance in their investment decisions. Because if I did, I would not be able to hold her responsible for her performance. Under the Constitution, as Finance Minister, I am responsible to Parliament for its performance, and I, in turn, must hold the leadership of the SWF accountable. We have very strict rules against nepotism, very strong anti-corruption rules."[59]

While Heng is trying to project himself as the next focal point of the PAP and hence, the national leader for at least two terms, how exactly this will be worked out remains to be seen. At the same time, while the PAP has not publicly demonstrated any signs of an open split, the very fact that the 3G and 4G leaders are talking about the need for unity would signal that there is a serious imperative to ensure that this does not happen to the ruling party of Singapore and hence, an area of concern that will be of great importance to the forthcoming leaders of the PAP, the Singapore public and political observers as a whole.[60] This is because PAP's unity will ensure the durability of its one-party dominance in Singapore and a split could well sound PAP's death knell as the political rulers of Singapore.

Singapore Budget 2019

With the talk of a general elections around the corner, especially after the PAP leaders had settled the issue of the 4G leadership and possible transfer of power, the 2019 budget was expected to be an 'election budget', all the more as this was

---

59. Jewel Stolarchuk, "'We have very strict rules against nepotism' — DPM Heng on Temasek and GIC", *The Independent*, 23 May 2019, http://theindependent.sg/we-have-very-strict-rules-against-nepotism-dpm-heng-on-temasek-and-gic/

60. See P.N. Balji, "Comment: How Heng Swee Keat can return the favour to PAP cadres", *Yahoo News Singapore*, 25 November 2018.

delivered by Heng Swee Keat, the finance minister and who was also the party's new first assistant secretary-general.[61] If this was what was expected, then the budget was definitely not a rollout of sweeteners to entice the voters. It was far from being an election budget even though there were important indications as to where Singapore would be heading under the 4G leadership in the coming years.

Heng also signposted of the tough economic year ahead, something he made public while on a trip to Argentina in December 2018 during the Group of 20 (G-20) Summit.[62] Heng stated that Singapore's economy grew by 3.2% in 2018 with a budget surplus of S$2.1 billion but expected to suffer a budget deficit in 2019 of S$3.5 billion. Heng attributed the unexpected surplus in 2018 due to the two-year suspension of the Kuala Lumpur–Singapore High-Speed Rail Project and higher than expected stamp duty collections. Heng also blamed the expected deficit in 2019 being caused by S$6.1 billion that will be expended on the Merdeka Generation Package and the S$5.1 billion that will be expended on long-term care support for Singaporeans, signposting of the aging population that Singapore is likely to face in the coming years and where the situation is likely to worsen.

A number of important landmark policies were also announced, demonstrating the power of incumbency that has always aided and benefitted the PAP as a ruling party and where the Opposition, other than being bystanders can only criticise policies as something unfair and beyond their mandate as an opposition party. Heng announced the Bicentennial Bonus of S$1.1 billion that will help Singaporeans, especially the lower-income families. The Merdeka Generation Package was also announced for those born between 1950 and 1959 and those who became Singapore citizens before 1997 or those who were born in or before 1949, became a Singaporean citizen before 1997, but did not receive the Pioneer Generation Package. The Community Health Assist Scheme (CHAS) scheme was extended to cover all Singaporeans for chronic conditions regardless of income with S$200 million a year set aside for CHAS subsidies. Heng also announced the setting up of a S$5.1 billion Long-Term Care Support Fund to provide for CareShield Life subsidies

---

61. Martino Tan, "S'pore's Budget 2019 is definitely not an election budget. The one coming next year will be", *Mothership*, 21 February 2019; Janice Heng, "Budget 2019 could be generous — election or not: analysts", *Business Times*, 21 January 2019; Anna Maria Romero, "#SGBudget2019 an election budget?", *The Independent*, 19 February 2019.

62. Charissa Yong, "G-20 finance ministers concerned about preparing for risks, strengthening global system: Heng Swee Keat", *The Straits Times*, 2 December 2018.

and other long-term support measures such as ElderFund, etc. The government also announced that greater support for workers would be provided through existing schemes such as Career Support Programme and Workfare Income Supplement (WIS) Scheme. The government also announced the reduction of GST import relief for travelers for goods purchases abroad with the relief for those spending more than 48 hours outside Singapore reduced from S$600 to S$500, and for those who spend less than 48 hours outside Singapore reduced from S$150 to S$100.

If Heng's budget had certain attractions, two policy announcements during the Committee of Supply (COS) debates would certainly strengthen the PAP's appeal during the forthcoming elections. The two policies pertained to a tweaking of the Ministry of Education's (MOE) streaming policies as well as the institution of some kind of a minimum wage policy in Singapore. During the debate on issues relating to the MOE, the minister, Ong Ye Kung announced that the government would do away with secondary school streaming which has been in place for the last 40 years. By 2024, the Normal (Academic), Normal (Technical) and Express streams in secondary schools would be replaced by full subject-based banding, where students would be taking subjects at a lower or higher level based on their respective strengths and interest.[63] Ong used the following metaphor to describe the new education policy: "So from three education streams, we will now have one secondary education, many subject bands. We will no longer have fishes swimming down three separate streams, but we have one broad river, each fish negotiating its own journey."[64] The transition will be done over a five-year period with an initial 25 schools participating in the scheme beginning in 2020.

From the government's standpoint, as to whether the new approach would eradicate stigmatisation of students in secondary schools would depend very much on society, given its success in primary schools when similar subject-based banding was introduced since 2008. For Ong, "labels are everywhere, we are categorised in everything we do. Whether we want to create a wall between different people,

---

63. Zhaki Abdullah, "No reason why ending streaming won't remove stigma if society plays its part: Ong Ye Kung", *The Straits Times*, 10 March 2019; Lianne Chia, "Current approach to streaming in secondary schools to be phased out by 2024", *Channel NewsAsia*, 5 March 2019, https://www.channelnewsasia.com/news/singapore/streaming-secondary-schools-o-n-levels-ong-ye-kung-11312252

64. Lianne Chia, "Current approach to streaming in secondary schools to be phased out by 2024".

it is really up to us as a society."[65] However, Ong believes that there is no reason as to why Singapore cannot succeed in ending stigmatisation as this has been largely successful in primary school as "stigmatisation is not a government policy" but rather a "societal response".[66] Despite the intense debate surrounding the announcement by Minister Ong, the initiative was a political winner as the much detested and hated policy of streaming appears to be phased out.[67] This will be one ammunition the PAP will be able to use in the forthcoming general elections to its advantage, demonstrating that it is responsive to both public and societal needs.

The second policy to surface was the concretisation of some kind of a minimum wage policy in Singapore. During the COS debate involving the Ministry of Manpower, Josephine Teo stated that the local qualifying salary, which stipulates the basic minimum amount companies must pay the local workers each month if they wish to hire foreign workers would be raised from S$1,200 to S$1,300 from July 2019 onwards.[68] This, however, did not mean that Singapore was adopting an anti-foreign worker policy. On the contrary, Teo stated that there was a need to change mindsets about certain service jobs in the country. The manpower minister argued that "there is no question in my mind (that) we will continue to need foreign manpower in services but over-reliance carries risks and is not sustainable. As their home countries develop, will all the foreign workers today always be willing to take up these jobs in Singapore? More critically, should we as a society accept that many jobs in services are unattractive to locals? Should we not invest effort to uplift some of these jobs to be more appealing to locals?"[69] The minister also stated that the policy was incremental in nature, aimed at avoiding "sweeping changes". The reasons for this were twofold: "First, it is in the services sector where most restructuring is needed. Second, beyond moves already set in motion, we are not making further changes to quotas in other sectors and levies this year."[70] The policy

65. Zhaki Abdullah, "No reason why ending streaming won't remove stigma if society plays its part: Ong Ye Kung".

66. Ibid.

67. Ibid.

68. Tan See Kit, "Higher salary threshold for local workers from July under rules for hiring foreigners", *Channel NewsAsia*, 5 March 2019, https://www.channelnewsasia.com/news/singapore/higher-salary-threshold-local-workers-foreigners-11313012

69. Ibid.

70. Ibid.

change announced would certainly boost the government's standing as this was another move to assist the lower-income Singaporeans on top of the other policies that had been announced over the years.

Challenges stemming from data breaches at the Ministry of Health and the Hyflux issue

While the 2019 budget announced by Heng Swee Keat was supposed to boost the government's standing, two issues that surfaced during this period brought into question the government's handling of certain critical issues such as cybersecurity and water as a strategic resource that has the possibility of denting the PAP's image and standing.

Between 28 June and 4 July 2018, Singapore's largest data breach took place, with hackers targeting a government data depository, SingHealth, at the Ministry of Health (MOH) and where medical records of even the prime minister and cabinet members as well as 1.5 million Singaporeans were breached. Medication records of nearly 160,000 patients were also accessed. Gan Kim Yong, the health minister, apologised for what he called an 'unprecedented' cyberattack and said, "we must learn from this and emerge stronger and more resilient from this incident."[71] According to the minister of communications and information, S. Iswaran, the cyberattack was "deliberate, targeted and well-planned", not the work of casual hackers, with only a few countries having the level of sophistication to do the type of attacks that occurred on MOH's data.[72] A Committee of Inquiry later submitted a report on what happened and what to do to prevent a similar attack in future. The Personal Data Protection Commission fined the Integrated Health Information System (IHiS) S$750,000 and SingHealth S$250,000 for failing to take adequate security measures to protect the personal data in its possession.[73]

---

71. Kevin Kwang, "Singapore health system hit by 'most serious breach of personal data' in cyberattack; PM Lee's data targeted", *Channel NewsAsia*, 18 October 2018, https://www.channelnewsasia.com/news/singapore/singhealth-health-system-hit-serious-cyberattack-pm-lee-target-10548318

72. Ibid.

73. See Matthew Mohan, "PDPC fines IHiS, SingHealth combined S$1 million for data breach following cyberattack", *Channel NewsAsia*, 15 January 2019, https://www.channelnewsasia.com/news/singapore/ihis-singhealth-fined-1-million-data-breach-cyberattack-11124156; Irene Tham, "Singapore's privacy watchdog fines IHiS $750,000 and SingHealth $250,000 for data breach", *The Straits Times*, 15 January 2019.

Earlier, in 2016, the then Singapore's largest data breach involving 14,200 people happened, when the MOH HIV registry data was downloaded by Mikhy Farrera-Brochez, the same-sex partner of Ler Teck Siang, the then head of MOH's National Public Health Unit but where the breach was only disclosed in January 2019.[74] Minister Gan defended the government's decision not to inform the public and the HIV registry patients on grounds of a 'judgement call'. Gan argued that the police thought they had deleted all copies of the HIV registry data from Farrera-Brochez's devices and since there was no evidence that the data had been published, there was no need to inform those affected because informing them would cause distress and emotional harm.[75]

In February 2019, MOH stated that a computer error had resulted in 7,700 people receiving inaccurate healthcare subsidies when they applied for or renewed their CHAS cards in September and October 2018.[76] The mistake involved 17% of people who made applications and renewals from 18 September to 10 October 2018. Due to the mistake, 1,300 individuals received lower subsidies and 6,400 individuals received higher subsidies.[77] The NCS, the IT firm that managed the system, admitted that the mistake was due to an "isolated case of human error" that resulted in an incorrect version of a software being deployed during a system migration exercise.[78]

In mid-March 2019, the Singapore public was told that Secur Solutions Group (SSG), a vendor of the Health Sciences Authority (HSA) had mishandled the data of more than 808,000 blood donors and personal data had been accessed illegally and extracted. By this time, this made the lapse the second largest after the SingHealth failure. Despite all the emphasis about the importance of cybersecurity

---

74. See Vernon Chan, "Does Singapore's Ministry of Health deserve immunity for data breach?", *The Independent*, 17 February 2019; Mohit Sagar, "Singapore Ministry of Health reveals details of another serious medical data breach", *Opengov*, 30 January 2019, https://www.opengovasia.com/singapore-ministry-of-health-reveals-details-of-another-serious-medical-data-breach/

75. See Vernon Chan, "Does Singapore's Ministry of Health deserve immunity for data breach?".

76. Ng Huiwen, "Chas subsidies for about 7,700 people miscalculated due to IT error: MOH", *The Straits Times*, 16 February 2019.

77. Ibid.

78. Adrian Lim, "IT error led to wrong Chas subsidies for 7,700", *The Straits Times*, 17 February 2019.

in Singapore by the authorities, the personal data was uploaded on the internet in January 2019 and was left there for nine weeks.[79] SSG stated that "subsequent forensic analysis has now shown that between October 22, 2018 and March 13, 2019, the server was also accessed suspiciously from several other IP addresses. Based on this new information, SSG cannot exclude the possibility that registration-related information of donors on the server was exfiltrated. The database referred to above contains no other sensitive, medical or contact information. There had been earlier attacks on the same server that had occurred in 2017. These attacks are unrelated to the current incident, and there is no evidence to suggest that they compromised any HSA data."[80]

Clearly, cyberattacks have been taking place rather frequently on MOH platforms and where highly personal and confidential data of patients are stored. For a country that boasts of adding digital defence, which mainly focuses on cybersecurity, as its new pillar of Total Defence, these lapses are definitely troubling.[81] Clearly, someone very senior in the chain of command needs to take responsibility for these unacceptable lapses. As was argued by Aloysius Cheang, the Asia-Pacific executive vice-president of the Centre for Strategic Cyberspace + Security Science, a London-based think-tank, the frequency of the data leaks was indeed worrying. According to him, "this is not the first time; it's the third time [since January 2019, which excludes the HSA lapse revealed in mid-March 2019]. And when there's a third time, there's bound to be a fourth, a fifth, and so on." [82] He further said that there was a serious need for Singapore to send a strong signal that its sovereign control over its digital assets has not been compromised, especially since the nation prides itself on being a safe and secure place to do business. According to him, "You have to show people you can protect these things. If you can't even protect your own

---

79. "Personal data of 808,000 blood donors compromised for nine weeks; HSA lodges police report", *Today*, 15 March 2019.

80. "Blood donor data leak: HSA's vendor says information that went online was accessed illegally and possibly extracted", *Channel NewsAsia*, 30 March 2019, https://www.channelnewsasia.com/news/singapore/personal-data-of-800-000-blood-donors-accessed-illegally-hsa-ssg-11395364

81. Hariz Baharudin, "Digital Defence to be sixth Total Defence pillar, signalling importance of cyber security", *The Straits Times*, 14 February 2019.

82. Timothy Goh, "800,000 blood donors' personal data accessed illegally and possibly stolen; police investigating", *The Straits Times*, 30 March 2019.

citizens' data, how can you be trusted to protect that of companies like Google, Amazon, and private banks?"[83]

Over and above the downside of personal data being breached at the MOH, the public was exposed to another development surrounding the high-profile water treatment firm, Hyflux Limited. While it may appear about a business that had gone sour and involved the strategic commodity of water, public anger was easily evident when more than 100 retail investors of Hyflux perpetual securities and preference shareholders, many of whom were elderly, held a rare public protest at Hong Lim Park on 30 March 2019 against the company's restructuring plan and developments involving the beleaguered water treatment firm. Hyflux is believed to owe about S$900 million to some 34,000 perpetual securities and preference shareholders with investors expected to suffer heavy losses from the company's restructuring plan, which many recovering around only 3% in cash and 7% in equity.[84]

Impact of the other Lee: Hsien Yang's support for the Opposition

For most ordinary Singaporeans, steeped in an Asian political culture and having grown up to respect and revere Lee Kuan Yew, the founder-architect of modern Singapore, watching the spat between his children, including his eldest son, who also happens to be the prime minister, was shocking enough, with many thinking that such personal matters should be settled in the realm of the private and not publicised, what more, 'parliamentarised'. This 'shock' and the apparent 'split' in the Lee family reached a new height when Prime Minister Lee's younger brother, Lee Hsien Yang, decided to openly support his brother's political opponents. When the debate over the future of Lee Kuan Yew's house at 38 Oxley Road entered parliament in July 2017, former prime minister, Goh Chok Tong was reported as saying that it was clear "that Lee Hsien Yang's goal is to bring his elder brother Lee Hsien Loong down as Prime Minister."[85] From the subsequent actions of Lee Hsien

---

83. Ibid.

84. Grace Leong, "More than 100 Hyflux investors protest at Hong Lim Park", *The Straits Times*, 31 March 2019.

85. "Lee Hsien Yang aiming to bring PM Lee down, says ESM Goh", *Channel NewsAsia*, 4 July 2017, https://www.channelnewsasia.com/news/singapore/lee-hsien-yang-aiming-to-bring-pm-lee-down-says-esm-goh-9002198

Yang, Goh clearly appeared spot on. Lee Hsien Yang's feud with his brother was not just over the interpretation of the last will of Lee Kuan Yew and the future of the house at 38 Oxley Road but also where Lee Hsien Yang's son, Li Shengwu, now staying in the United States, was accused of contempt of court by the Attorney-General's Chambers (AGC) and Lee Hsien Yang's wife, Lee Suet Fern, had a complaint registered against her by the AGC. In short, it is not just a brother to brother conflict but something much wider, and hence, complex.

Lee Hsien Yang has openly supported not all opposition political parties but only Tan Cheng Bock's PSP. Hsien Yang had breakfast with Tan on two occasions, first on 4 November 2018 at a hawker centre in West Coast and the second on 2 February 2019 at a food centre in Teck Ghee, where his brother is the MP.[86] Lee Hsien Yang told reporters that "We were just here to have breakfast."[87] Tan, however, said in his Facebook that "we wanted to catch up with each other as we have not met for quite a while…It was a good breakfast, not only the food, but (also) the sharing we had on world affairs and the current state of politics in Singapore."[88] When Tan announced his decision to launch a new political party, Lee Hsien Yang praised Tan for consistently putting "the interest of the people first" and opined that "we are fortunate that he has stepped forward to serve Singapore…Cheng Bock is the leader Singapore deserves", supporting Tan's bid to contest in the coming general elections.[89]

Later, when his brother, Prime Minister Lee sued blogger Leong Sze Hian for defamation, Lee Hsien Yang was among the first to donate to his legal fund. Leong was defended by lawyer-turned-politician Lim Tean. Leong was sued by the Singapore prime minister after Leong shared an article alleging that Prime Minister Lee had helped Malaysia's former prime minister Najib Razak to launder money from the country's state fund, 1Malaysia Development Berhad (1MDB).[90]

---

86. Faris Mokhtar and Kenneth Cheng, "Tan Cheng Bock meets Lee Hsien Yang for the second time, amid talk of a growing alliance", *Today*, 2 February 2019.

87. Tee Zhuo, "Tan Cheng Bock meets Lee Hsien Yang for breakfast in Ang Mo Kio hawker centre", *The Straits Times*, 2 February 2019.

88. Ibid.

89. "Lee Hsien Yang backs Tan Cheng Bock's return to politics", *Today*, 25 January 2019.

90. Kenneth Cheng, "Lee Hsien Yang donates money to blogger facing defamation suit", *Today*, 27 December 2018.

Following this, when Singapore activist Jolovan Wham made a court appeal for a case against him, Lee Hsien Yang put up a S$20,000 security deposit for him, for which Wham need not repay Lee Hsien Yang. When asked for his motivation to do so, the prime minister's brother replied, "surely, it needs no explanation."[91]

The big question in the minds of many Singaporeans is — and if Goh Chok Tong is really right that Lee Hsien Yang is out to bring his brother down politically — then what will be Lee Hsien Yang's next move? Why is Lee Hsien Yang supporting the political rivals of Lee Hsien Loong and the PAP? Next, the bigger question is — will Lee Hsien Yang join an opposition political party, say the PSP and contest in the coming elections against the PAP? If that happens, this would mark a new development and a major departure in Singapore's politics, and where it is not just a question of a split in the PAP but more importantly, a split in one of the most important political families in Singapore and its ramifications and implications for national politics can be immense, with Singapore entering into uncharted political waters. This is all the more as the national, social and the international media have been reporting the spat between the two brothers and this will largely come to rest in the coming general elections with implications for both the Lees.

Resurfacing of the 'fear factor' in Singapore politics

During the prime ministership of Lee Kuan Yew, the fear factor was seen as a given, partly explaining the reasons for Singapore being described as an authoritarian state. Lee Kuan Yew also did not hide his preparedness to inject fear in the populace so that the Republic's hard-won stability and development would not be derailed. Many analysts and observers have highlighted the various occasions he had made public his preparedness to adopt a fisted approach towards his political opponents and keep the populace under control. Some of his more well-known quotes include:

> "Between being loved and being feared, I have always believed Machiavelli was right. If nobody is afraid of me, I'm meaningless."
> "Anybody who decides to take me on needs to put on knuckle-dusters. If you think you can hurt me more than I can hurt you, try. There is no way you can govern a Chinese society."

---

91. Jewel Stolarchuk, "Lee Hsien Yang said he doesn't need to be repaid for contribution towards court appeal: Jolovan Wham", *The Independent*, 23 May 2019.

"If you are a troublemaker...it's our job to politically destroy you...Everybody knows that in my bag I have a hatchet, and a very sharp one. You take me on, I take my hatchet, we meet in the cul-de-sac."[92]

Over time, especially under the prime ministership of Goh Chok Tong and Lee Hsien Loong, a less fisted and more consultative approach to politics is believed to have surfaced. This was partly in response to a more maturing electorate, a political leadership that was less inclined to be iron-fisted and also in the belief that the populace opposed this approach. Hence, partly fearing the counter-productive reaction and a popular backlash, the use of fear by the political leadership was believed to be on the decline though not totally ended.

Yet, over the last few years, there is a new discourse that the 'politics of fear' has returned to Singapore. In May 2019, leader of the PVP, Lim Tean observed that he was concerned that the government may use the new anti-fake laws to "to clamp freedom of speech and expression in the country."[93] For him, people who are concern about the country and want a better future for all, must admit that a society ruled by fear and where only the government propaganda is allowed to proliferate, can never create "a vibrant, innovative and enterprising citizenry".[94]

In early May 2019, Tan Cheng Bock is believed to have said that the politics of the PAP was nothing more than the politics of "fear and reward". Tan said that the public has been told not to vote the Opposition in Singapore as the Opposition represents the "politics of anger and envy".[95] To counter this perception and image of the Opposition, Tan believes that Singapore needs to "evolve a trusted political system based on transparency, accountability and independence."[96] Endorsing Tan's

---

92. See "Lee Kuan Yew: His most memorable quotes", *The Telegraph*, 23 March 2015, https://www.telegraph.co.uk/news/worldnews/asia/singapore/11489177/Lee-Kuan-Yew-his-most-memorable-quotes.html

93. Kiara Xavier, "Lim Tean says Singapore will have authoritarian 'democracy' with the 'Fake News' Bill, urges public to oppose it", *The Online Citizen*, 9 April 2019.

94. Ibid.

95. Jewel Stolarchuk, "'PAP is the politics of fear and reward' — Dr Tan Cheng Bock's speech to supporters goes viral", *The Independent*, 29 May 2019.

96. Ibid.

views, on 30 May 2019, former WP NCMP, Yee Jenn Jong stated that "fear is the politics that the ruling party had been playing for so long."[97] According to Yee, the PAP has been subtly and at times openly arguing that support for the Opposition and any change of government in Singapore would adversely affect Singapore's progress and the well-being of Singaporeans. For him, "people fear for lack of knowledge or from stereotypes painted" must be countered and the public is to be told that "the government agencies are obligated to make things right regardless of which party the MP is from"[98] and hence, the public should never fear of suffering the consequences of voting for the Opposition.

Clearly, two types of 'politics of fear' exist in Singapore. The first is the more blatant 'knuckle-duster' type of the Lee Kuan Yew era, something that is not really prevalent today and where Lee Kuan Yew's successors must be credited for implementing a more civil and less authoritarian political system in Singapore. However, it is the 'politics of fear' of the second type that is difficult to erase as this stems from PAP's successes over the last 60 years as well as the generally lacklustre performance and capability of the Opposition. To that extent, if the opposition political leaders such as Lim Tean, Tan Cheng Bock and Yee Jenn Jong are expressing the 'politics of fear' in Singapore, they are not totally wrong. However, this is also largely due to the successes of the PAP and the general dismal performance of the Opposition, and the public cannot be blamed for fearing the loss of the 'good life' if a change of government is to take place in Singapore, a narrative and belief system that will further help to entrench the PAP in Singapore. At the same time, the collapse of established political administrations, as in Indonesia and Malaysia, and the ensuring instability and uncertainties, have also created the 'fear of the unknown', thereby deterring many Singaporeans from abandoning the PAP and its established rule.

International developments

While the US–China competition and rivalries have emerged as a permanent part of the Asia-Pacific political, economic and strategic architecture and hence, the need

---

97. Jewel Stolarchuk, "WP politician echoes Dr Tan Cheng Bock's sentiment that fear is the politics of the PAP", *The Independent*, 29 May 2019.

98. Ibid.

for Singapore to navigate astutely to prevent being 'burned', it is the geopolitics of the Southeast Asian region, especially involving Malaysia and Indonesia, that have emerged as key immediate concerns, in turn, affecting the image, credibility and performance legitimacy of the PAP government. While China punished Singapore for allegedly drawing close to the US over the South China Sea dispute, when nine Singapore-bound 'Terrex' armoured infantry vehicles and military equipment were seized by Hong Kong customs in November 2016,[99] in June 2018, Singapore stole the international diplomatic limelight by acting as the host for the generally successful Donald Trump–Kim Jong Un Summit.[100]

The same, however, cannot be said of Singapore's relations with Malaysia, which have soured since the *Barisan Nasional* (BN) government was overthrown and Mahathir Mohamad led a new government under the *Pakatan Harapan* (PH) in May 2018. Since, Mahathir became Malaysia's prime minister again, a number of issues have emerged, including the Malaysian prime minister supporting political activists critical of the PAP,[101] cancellation of the Kuala Lumpur–Singapore High Speed Rail without officially informing Singapore and most importantly of all, reviving the price of water and territorial issues. For Mahathir, he has always complained that Singapore was literally 'stealing' water from Malaysia by paying 3 Malaysian cents (about 1 Singapore cent today) per 1,000 gallons of fresh water from Malaysia. He has maintained that the deal, which was made in 1962, was on weak legal standing and Singapore will lose if the issue is to be brought to the International Court of Justice (ICJ). In August 2018, Mahathir indicated that he

---

99. Jermyn Chow and Joyce Lim, "SAF armoured vehicles seized in Hong Kong port, Mindef expects shipment to return to Singapore 'expeditiously'", *The Straits Times*, 24 November 2016.

100. Tham Yuen-C, Seow Bei Yi and Ng Jun Sen, "Trump-Kim summit: The making of a last-minute meeting in Singapore", *The Straits Times*, 17 June 2018.

101. Mahathir had earlier promised the Singapore political activists of his support for a human rights conference, which was eventually organised under the auspices of Forces of Renewal for Southeast Asia and which was held in Kuala Lumpur from 16 to 17 February 2019. The key Malaysian government officials in attendance included Prime Minister Mahathir, Malaysia's defence minister, Mohamad Sabu and the chief minister of Selangor, Amirudin Shari. Many Singaporeans and ex-Singaporeans also attended, including Tan Wah Piow, P.J. Thum and Kirsten Han. For details, see "Conference Celebrating Democracy in Malaysia", Inaugural Conference of FORSEA, 16–17 February 2019, Kuala Lumpur. See https://forsea.co/human-rights-for-all/

would like to see the price of water that Singapore pays increased by 10-fold in order to reflect the higher cost of living.[102] Hence, following his return as prime minister in May 2018, he has criticised the 1962 water agreement as being 'too costly' and 'ridiculous' for Malaysia and wants it to be renegotiated.[103] Singapore's high-gear response to Mahathir's claims and position on water has been clear and consistent. The Singapore Ministry of Foreign Affairs stated in July 2018 that Malaysia lost the right to review water price in 1987.[104] Singapore also stated that it would continue to honour the 1962 Water Agreement and expect Malaysia to do the same, something Malaysia's new foreign minister, Saifuddin Abdullah, said he would.[105]

A probably more serious issue that surfaced in October 2018 was the territorial dispute involving aviation and maritime rights of the two states. This harked back to the maritime dispute between Singapore and Malaysia over Pedra Branca that existed throughout the prime ministership of Mahathir from 1981 to 2003, and was only resolved, albeit partially, by the ICJ decision in May 2008. When Mahathir returned to power in May 2018, one of the first things he did was to declare that it would not pursue the BN's policy to challenge the ICJ 2008 ruling on Pedra Branca, thereby ceding for good its right in seeking to revise the decision to award sovereignty of the island to Singapore.

Yet, it unexpectedly announced changes to the port limits for the Johor Bahru port on 25 October 2018 and this was followed by the Malaysian Marine Department issuing a Notice to Mariners on 22 November 2018 detailing an extension of the port limits that brought it closer to the Tuas area in Singapore, an area that has also been designated for Singapore's port expansion in the coming years. On 30 November, Singapore's Maritime and Port Authority issued a circular

---

102. "Malaysia PM Mahathir Mohamad wants to raise price of raw water sold to Singapore by more than 10 times", The Straits Times, 14 August 2018.

103. Ibid.

104. "Singapore has been clear and consistent that Malaysia lost its right to review water price in 1987: MFA", The Straits Times, 31 July 2018.

105. Yasmine Yahya, "Parliament: S'pore will honour 1962 Water Agreement and expects Malaysia to do the same, says Vivian Balakrishnan", The Straits Times, 9 July 2018; "Shannon Teoh, "Malaysia will honour water deal with Singapore, says Foreign Minister", The Straits Times, 25 July 2018.

that instructed ship masters and owners to disregard Malaysia's Notice to Mariners. Malaysia also deployed its ships in the disputed waters with the then Johor chief minister, Osman Sapian, visiting one of the ships, MV Pedoman, on 9 January 2019, which Singapore protested. In response, Singapore also suspended the Joint Ministerial Committee for Iskandar Malaysia (JMCIM) talks that were scheduled for 14 January. In March 2019, both disputing states agreed to mutually suspend the implementation of their overlapping port limits, which did to some extent, lower the tensions in the region since the dispute first erupted in October 2018. With the escalating claims and counter-claims and tensions, Singapore's new maritime dispute with Malaysia erupted under Mahathir's second tenure as prime minister. Since then, there have been mutual recriminations as well as many meetings held to resolve the issue, and it is quite clear that this will be a protracted maritime dispute. In mid-March 2019, the two countries' foreign ministers met in Kuala Lumpur and agreed to de-escalate the dispute even though by mid-April 2019, two Malaysian vessels remained anchored in Singapore's territorial waters which Malaysia claims are its.[106] With the onset of the bilateral talks at the prime minister's level, the Singapore Ministry of Foreign Affairs announced that "as of midnight on Tuesday [2 April 2019] no Malaysian government vessels were found to be anchored in the area previously covered by the overlapping Johor Baru port limits off Tanjung Piai and Singapore's port limits off Tuas", indicating some progress being made in the dispute.[107]

Adding to the litany of differences and disputes between Singapore and Malaysia under the PH government, on 4 December 2018, the Malaysian Transport Minister Anthony Loke announced that Malaysia intended to 'reclaim' the airspace over southern Johor that was previously accorded to Singapore in 1974 and that this would begin in phases between 2019 and 2023. He also stated that his government would be sending a protest note to Singapore over Singapore's plan to implement an instrument landing system (ILS) at Seletar Airport, arguing that this violated Malaysian sovereignty and caused restrictions on building heights and port activities that had the possibility of stalling the development of the Pasir Gudang industrial

---

106. Adrian Lim, "Parliament: Two Malaysian government vessels remain anchored in Singapore waters, says Vivian", *The Straits Times*, 2 April 2019.

107. Kenneth Cheng, "Singapore, Malaysia to begin talks on delimiting maritime boundaries in a month: PM Lee", *Today*, 9 April 2019.

area in eastern Johor. Singapore rejected Malaysia's claims of the negative impact the ILS would have on Johor. On 25 December 2018, the Civil Aviation Authority of Malaysia issued a Notice to Airmen (NOTAM) stating that it would be establishing an area of permanent restricted airspace over Pasir Gudang from 2 January 2019, to which Singapore protested on grounds that the restricted area was in a "controlled and congested airspace" and that it would affect aircrafts travelling in the area.

The outbreak of aviation and maritime disputes between the two states led to a plethora of high-level meetings between Singapore and Malaysia to calm the situation and resolve the fast deteriorating bilateral relations. The meeting of the two states' foreign ministers in January 2019 led to an agreement to a suspension of the implementation of ILS by Seletar Airport and the permanent restricted airspace by Malaysia. In the first week of April 2019, further breakthrough in bilateral negotiations occurred when both states reached an agreement on air issues which will allow Malaysian carrier Firefly to resume its services to Singapore. In the negotiations, Singapore agreed to withdraw the ILS for Seletar Airport and Malaysia agreed to indefinitely suspend its permanent Restricted Area over Pasir Gudang.[108]

An important factor facilitating the improvement in bilateral ties was probably due to the holding of the Leaders' Retreat scheduled for 8 and 9 April 2019 in Putrajaya, Malaysia. That was the first such bilateral meeting between Mahathir Mohamad and Lee Hsien Loong, which was initially scheduled for November 2018 but was postponed. At a press conference on 6 April 2019, Mahathir stated that "all of the things that are still unresolved, including the water problem, the central provident fund, (and) the borderline with our waters. What is Singapore waters? What is Malaysia waters? (Also) the flight over our area, who is going to control it. All these things will be discussed in a friendly manner. We are not going to confront them. But I believe that even Singapore understand(s) the need to revise the price of water" would be discussed at the retreat.[109] Clearly, both leaders had

---

108. Karamjit Kaur, "Firefly to resume flights to Singapore from week of April 22; Singapore withdraws ILS for Seletar Airport, Malaysia suspends restricted area over Pasir Gudang", *The Straits Times*, 6 April 2019.

109. "Malaysia-Singapore leaders' retreat next week to discuss 'unresolved' issues: PM Mahathir", *Channel NewsAsia*, 5 April 2019, https://www.channelnewsasia.com/news/asia/malaysia-singapore-leaders-retreat-unresolved-issues-11416774; also see Trina Leong, "Mahathir to discuss all unresolved issues with Singapore at leaders' retreat", *The Straits Times*, 6 April 2019.

decided to keep their channels of communications open as part of their efforts to solve bilateral issues and reduce tensions.[110]

The bilateral retreat was significant as both sides agreed to begin negotiations to delimit their maritime boundaries as well as to implement various measures to de-escalate the situation on their maritime borders. By the time the Leaders' Retreat ended, both Malaysia and Singapore had suspended the extensions of their overlapping port limits and ceased to anchor government vessels in the disputed area. Discussions also took place involving airspace, water and connectivity issues. Malaysia has indicated its intention to review the existing arrangement that gives Singapore air traffic controllers the right to manage the airspace over southern Johor with Malaysia intending to take over control over the airspace in stages from the end of 2019 to 2023. While Malaysia is keen to increase the price of water, Singapore has also expressed concerns over the sustainability of water supply from Johor River as well as issues relating to pollution. While the agreement to negotiate these difficult issues was a positive sign, equally significant was Mahathir and his wife, Siti Hasmah Mohamad Ali's decision to accept an invitation to them by Prime Minister Lee to attend Singapore's National Day Parade at the Padang on 9 August 2019.[111] The limited success at the 2019 Leaders' Retreat will definitely be an important factor in the improvement of bilateral ties that have been soured since the PH government came to power in May 2018.

The Mother of all issues — trust and confidence in the ruling party and government

Since June 1959 and through the trials and tribulations that followed, especially as a state in Malaysia and as an independent state, what has been largely responsible for the success of the PAP is primarily the trust, faith and confidence the Singapore voters have in the ruling party. Singapore's founding prime minister, Lee Kuan Yew has been quoted as saying that "trust between the government and people" was

---

110. See "Dr M and Hsien Loong to meet over bilateral issues", *The Star Online*, 8 April 2019, https://www.thestar.com.my/news/nation/2019/04/08/dr-m-and-hsien-loong-to-meet-over-bilateral-issues/

111. "Singapore, Malaysia to start talks on maritime boundaries within a month", *The Business Times*, 10 April 2019.

the single "greatest asset".[112] Similarly, Prime Minister Lee Hsien Loong said that "the PAP has earned the people's trust the hard way and we must never take it for granted or fritter it away."[113] Yet, on 1 February 2019, a leading Chinese daily in Singapore, *Lianhe Zaobao* published an editorial calling on the government to restore the public's confidence following several lapses by public service providers and government agencies.[114]

The *Lianhe Zaobao* editorial listed the following lapses as evidence of what was described as rising complacency of the Singapore system: MOH's HIV Registry data being leaked affecting 16,600 individuals; the SingHealth hacking, the biggest ever hacking incident in Singapore's history, that led to the theft of 1.5 million patient records; five deaths in the last 18 months during Singapore Armed Forces (SAF) training; Tan Tock Seng Hospital personnel failing to properly sterilise dental equipment used on patients; a Hepatitis C outbreak in Singapore General Hospital due to gaps in infection prevention and control practices; the "deteriorating" quality of SingPost's service, which includes the recent incident of a postman throwing away letters; increasing frequencies of large-scale power outages; "improper" management of SMRT which led to several major breakdowns, death of maintenance crew, and flooding of a tunnel.[115] This list did not include mistakes in distribution of the CHAS subsidies, the mishandling of blood donors' data by its vendor and the Hyflux saga, not to mention the corruption involving government-linked companies such as Keppel, Jurong and Sembawang shipyards and fines meted out in the United States.

Lianhe Zaobao argued that these mistakes and lapses were not accidental but probably had more to do with "the deterioration of our work ethic and a culture of 'muddling along' taking root."[116] Also, "with the society becoming too comfortable, people have become complacent, unwilling to improve the system, choose to ignore

---

112. Chua Mui Hoong, "Has trust in the government been eroded? It's time to talk frankly", *The Straits Times*, 1 February 2018.

113. Ibid.

114. "Zaobao: Recent major lapses involving public services may be result of a 'muddling along' culture taking root", *Mothership*, 2 February 2019, https://mothership.sg/2019/02/zaobao-editorial-major-public-service-lapses/

115. Ibid.

116. Ibid.

what's happening outside, and have become too self-satisfied."[117] Finally, it may also have to do with the problem of how rewards and punishments are meted out. The editorial noted that the culture and practice of "punishing the rank and file, while senior management takes little to no responsibility, reinforces negative attitudes and leads to a collective mentality of not taking their work seriously."[118] Exactly a year earlier, Chua Mui Hoong noted that there are Singaporeans with "deep-seated gripes" against the government. Chua argued that "for this group, maintaining trust in Government is not the issue because it has already been eroded. They may be a minority but they are vocal and with social media and technology, their views spread quickly and are amplified."[119]

Chua also quoted Goh Choon Kang, a former PAP MP's commentary in *Lianhe Zaobao* in December 2017 about the consequences stemming from the loss of trust between the elite and the masses, referring mainly to developments in Western societies. Goh Choon Kang also warned Singaporean leaders about turning their backs on the masses. He argued,

> they lose touch with the masses even though they are in leading positions. They feel that their achievements today are based solely on their own capabilities and talent within the meritocracy implemented by society. They bask in their own successes, sing their own praises and no longer have the slightest empathy for the people with the political parties fighting for power but unable to understand and sympathise with the public feeling. The system becomes such that it is your own problem if you cannot keep up with the times or are left behind. As a result, many pressing issues do not get proper attention. For example, jobs being outsourced or becoming short-term hired labour because of globalisation, job losses, workers facing job instability, wage stagnation, uneven distribution and a widening gap between the rich and the poor.[120]

Goh Choon Kang, in conclusion warned, "like mainstream political parties in other countries, the PAP may encounter issues of being too comfortable, of arrogance, slackness and losing touch with the grassroots because of its long-term rule, if it

117. Ibid.

118. Ibid.

119. Chua Mui Hoong, "Has trust in the government been eroded? It's time to talk frankly".

120. Cited in Ibid.

does not have sufficient awareness of potential problems or is unable to correct some possible problems in time", something Chua advised, where Goh's "warning should be heeded."[121]

In view of the warnings about the possible 'loss of touch' by the PAP with the masses in general and the criticisms raised in the February 2019 *Lianhe Zaobao* editorial, Singapore's prime minister-in-waiting, Heng Swee Keat, on 9 February 2019, responded by defending the government. He argued that he and his cabinet colleagues needed to respond to questions raised about the increasing complacency of the Singapore system. He said that the government will "not shirk from tackling problems" and dismissed suggestions that the political leadership and government have gone below the high standards.[122] Heng said, "we will not flinch from taking a hard look at ourselves each time there is a failure and doing whatever is necessary to put things right. But I reject the suggestion by some that the political leadership has allowed the whole system to go slack. And worse still, that we have gone soft on ourselves and the public service, failing to hold senior people accountable when things go wrong."[123] On the issue of accountability, Heng noted that "in serious cases, independent committees of inquiry are convened, and their findings, however awkward, are made public. Individuals found culpable will be held responsible and disciplined. If the lapse shows that the leader has been slack, negligent or incompetent, then serious consequences must follow, including removal."[124]

Clearly, while Heng was compelled to respond to criticisms and observations raised by observers and analysts such as Chua Mui Hoong, Goh Choon Kang and the editorial leaders of *Lianhe Zaobao*, the important point is that the issues of the capabilities of political leaders and the growing divide between the political elites and the masses have become mainstreamed. This is all the more so as political office holders and senior civil servants are extremely highly paid, and where there is a perception, as stated in the *Lianhe Zaobao* editorial, there are serious issues of rewards and punishment in the public service. As more issues of governance

---

121. Ibid.

122. Rachel Au-Yong, "Leaders will do what it takes to put things right: Heng Swee Keat", *The Straits Times*, 9 February 2019.

123. Ibid.

124. Ibid.

surface, especially those associated with 'public service failures' such as hacking into the MOH, MRT breakdowns, power outages, training deaths in the SAF or even the Hyflux saga, commentators and the public will view the ruling elites and the party with concern, and raise the question, has the PAP declined in quality? This is all the more as the PAP has been so focussed on selecting the right type of leaders for Singapore and where the survival of Singapore is often said to impinge on the quality of leaders in the PAP. Notwithstanding these issues, the PAP still, in comparison, has been able to recruit the best and brightest, and has been good in problem solving. To that extent, will issues relating to the credibility of the PAP and whether there is a growing trust deficit between the rulers and ruled in society become hotly discussed in the coming general elections remains to be seen. Also, the more such issues are raised, the better it will be in forcing not just the PAP but also the Opposition to recruit and deploy leaders who will best serve Singapore and its interests.

Conclusion

Without doubt, the PAP will not be plunging into the next general elections from a very big comfort zone as it did in 2015, what more, to repeat its unexpectedly resounding victory to the general demolition of the Opposition as whole. If the major issues remain unresolved and the ground remains sour, the chances are the ruling party will defer the forthcoming elections to a later date as it still has a big window till January 2021. Still, as elsewhere, Singapore politics, and for that matter, opposition politics, is not a simple plus-minus issue. This is because many factors go into how the public perceives the role, place and importance of the ruling party and the Opposition. While the majority of the public continues to believe that the PAP as the government is good for Singapore, at the same time, it also wants a respectable and effective opposition to be positioned in parliament to act as a check and balance than to give the PAP an unchecked and unfettered free reign.

At the same time, the status of the Opposition has enhanced since 2015 while that of the government has suffered some dent as evident from the various mini-crises it is facing — the four cyberattacks on MOH and the Hyflux issues being just some of the more recent ones. The forthcoming rise of the GST also hangs like a sword of Damocles over the PAP, just as many in the public are wary about the government's newly minted bill on the Protection from Online Falsehoods and

Manipulation Bill that was tabled in parliament on 1 April 2019, leading many to believe that the government may have acquired too much power on deciding what is fact and what is fake?

At the same time, while there may be a new window of opportunity for the Opposition to increase its presence and role in Singapore politics, the minor and fringe parties also need to find their place in the political landscape. If these largely ineffective political parties are in existence for decoration purposes or to stoke personal alter egos, then the PAP will continue to score between 70% to 80% of votes in certain GRCs, as it did in 2015, thereby bumping up the overall performance of the Singapore dominant party. Hence, while the challenges are manifold, whether the Opposition has the capacity to work together and behave as a team to challenge the PAP remains to be seen. If it does, the PAP will be stretched and a new modus operandi will emerge; if not, it will be more or less the same as in the past, with the one-party dominant system in Singapore largely unchanged even though similar systems have or are collapsing elsewhere.

EXPLAINING PAP'S POLITICAL DOMINANCE IN SINGAPORE'S POLITICS

Introduction

A one-party dominant state exists when one political party in a non-authoritarian multi-party system is able to continuously out-distant other political competitors and capture political power, being the majority in the legislature and executive, and is in a position to set the national political agenda. Singapore is a soft authoritarian state with clear democratic features. In Singapore, since the 1959 General Elections, the People's Action Party (PAP) has been in a position of hegemonic majority and dominance (see Table 11.1). Even at a time of its worst political fortunes, following the split in the PAP in 1961, in the 1963 General Elections, the PAP secured 72.5% of parliamentary power. Since then, the PAP has always controlled parliament with a dominance ranging from 93.26% to 100%. This is simply not a case of a one-party dominant state but rather a case of a one-party hegemonic state.

In the literature on a one-party dominant state in non-communist states, many factors have been discussed as being the source of dominance of this exceptional nature. The role of history has been discussed by many scholars with dominant parties often associated with political epochs of states. Parties of this nature are often perceived as 'historical parties', having been involved in the construction of a 'historical project' that characterises a particular state and its citizens. This often includes gaining political independence from a colonial power or overthrowing a dictatorship and installing a democratic system in its place. Second is the status of a political party as a truly national and nationalist party that transcends all types of fault lines in a state. It is often seen as the integrator and not representative of particularistic components of society. Third, is the role of the electoral system and institutions that determine the rules of political engagement and which may advantage the dominant political party. A state's political culture is also an important determinant of the voters' behaviour and their continued identification with a political party. Ideological factors also benefit a particular party and ensure

Table 11.1:   PAP's Parliamentary Power, 1959–2015

Year	Seats Contested	Seats Won by PAP	% of Parliament Power
1959	51	43	84.31
1963	51	37	72.55
1968	58	58	100
1972	65	65	100
1976	69	69	100
1980	75	75	100
1984	79	77	97.47
1988	81	80	98.77
1991	81	77	95.06
1997	83	81	97.59
2001	84	82	97.62
2006	84	82	97.62
2011	87	81	93.10
2015	89	83	93.26

Source: Author.

its continuous dominance due to its high legitimacy based on ideas of what it stands for, its achievements and the future it promises the electorate. Finally, no party can remain in power if it is devoid of performance legitimacy. Hence, successful all-round political, economic and social developments can ensure a political party's long-term longevity.

Explaining PAP's dominant position

While there are nearly 30 political parties registered in Singapore, how is it possible that the PAP has been the dominant, if not, the hegemonic political party in Singapore for nearly six decades [1959–2019]? Of all the opposition political parties, there are only a few which have contested regularly in Singapore's general elections. For the most time, only the numerically larger opposition political parties such as the Workers' Party (WP), the Singapore Democratic Party (SDP) and the Singapore Democratic Alliance (SDA) have been able to field candidates for most general elections since the 1990s. Moreover, no opposition party has on its own ever contested all the seats in a general elections except through an electoral pact, as happened in 2015. The 2015 General Elections was also the first time that

Singapore saw all seats being contested since 1965. Since 1965, the Opposition has never managed to win more than six parliamentary seats in any general elections. Presently, as in the 2011 General Elections, there are six opposition members in parliament after the 2015 General Elections. Following the 2011 General Elections, the WP increased its tally from six to seven seats in parliament following a by-election victory in Punggol East in January 2013.

However, the first point to note that it is not true that the PAP has always been in a dominant position. As Table 11.2 shows, from 1955 to 1959, the PAP was a member of the Opposition even though it performed remarkably well. Next, electoral politics in Singapore is a function of a number of factors. First, it has much to do with the political history of Singapore as a former colony of Britain and where it inherited a Westminster parliamentary system. This meant that regular elections have been held in Singapore and Singapore's parliamentary democracy can trace its origins to 1948 when the first elections for local representatives were held.

A good starting point to understand and explain the PAP's dominance in Singapore would be to analyse briefly general elections from 1991 to 2006, as the 2011 and 2015 polls have already been dealt with in Chapter 6. The PAP won the 1991 General Elections, under the leadership of a new prime minister, Goh Chok Tong, by winning 77 out of the 81 seats. It also captured 59.3% of the valid votes. The PAP's victory was due to the good timing the elections was called, Goh's popular policies and style, the PAP's past track record, the credible candidates the ruling party offered as well as the efficient party machinery. Since

Table 11.2:   Results of 1955 Legislative Assembly Elections

Political Party	No. of Seats	% of Votes
Labour Front	10	27.1
Progressive Party	4	24.8
People's Action Party	3	8.7
Democratic Party	2	20.5
Malayan Chinese Association	1	4.0
United Malays National Organisation	1	3.7
Malay Union	1	0.8
Labour Party	0	0.8
Independents	3	9.7

Source: Author.

1968, this was, nevertheless, the Opposition's best electoral performance, capturing four parliamentary seats. The Opposition's slow but forward movement was a function of a number of factors, including the electorate's unhappiness with PAP's unpopular policies such as educational streaming, the by-election strategy where the Opposition transformed the general elections into a by-election by allowing the ruling party to form a government on Nomination Day, the presence of some weak candidates in the PAP, the perennial 'bread and butter' issues and the ability of the Opposition to offer some relatively good candidates.

In the 1997 General Elections, the PAP reversed its earlier partial setback by winning 81 out of the 83 seats. The valid votes for the ruling party increased from 59.3% to 63.5%. The key issues in the elections were the persistence of the 'bread and butter' issues, the Opposition's call for alternative voices in parliament and the ruling party's threat of linking 'local government upgrading' to votes which some saw as 'blackmail politics'. The PAP won resoundingly due to its excellent track record since 1959, the existence of good programmes, the appeal of the prime minister, the effectiveness of the 'local government strategy', PAP's electioneering tactics of using the Group Representation Constituencies (GRCs) and electoral redrawing of boundaries, and the powerful political machinery of the PAP. In contrast, the regression of the Opposition's performance and appeal was due to the fact that it was not a match for the mammoth PAP, had no answer to the 'local government strategy' of the PAP, did not have appealing programmes and there were concerns with the Opposition's credibility, particularly to leaders such as Tang Liang Hong and Chee Soon Juan, especially in comparison to the PAP's slate of candidates, new and old.

The PAP won the 2001 General Elections resoundingly, capturing 82 of the 84 seats with 75% of the electoral votes. This was brought about by the massive electoral boundary redrawing that affected 91% of the voters as well as the global insecurity brought by the September 11, 2001 terrorist attacks on the United States. Against this backdrop, the uncertain international security and economic environment, the tried and tested PAP's political machinery, the credible candidates put up by the PAP and the disarray in the Opposition helped the PAP to win emphatically. The Opposition's rout was due to its inability to match the Herculean PAP, the intense divisions within the Opposition and the general weak candidates that the Opposition put up.

In the May 2006 General Elections, the PAP won convincingly even though there was a drop in the PAP's performance compared to that of 2001. As in the past, the PAP's track record, strong leadership and candidates, credible policies, and support given to the then new prime minister, Lee Hsien Loong, explained the PAP's victory. The Opposition's defeat was due to its inability to match the PAP in terms of policies and leaders as well as the public's confidence in the PAP, especially to bring the Republic forward in challenging times ahead.

Overall, the PAP's successes over the years can be explained on a number of counts. The party is well-organised, well-led and has the benefit of being in power since 1959, thereby capturing the political imagination of a few generations so far. Incumbency has thus been a crucial factor. The PAP has its branches in all constituencies in Singapore. The PAP has also been able to provide many social welfare services. One of its most successful programmes includes the PAP's childcare and pre-school facilities. These PAP childcare and pre-school centres are conveniently located in nearly all housing estates and cater mostly to the middle- and lower-income Singaporean families. The ability of the party to provide such basic services has earned it the support and loyalty of most middle-income Singaporeans. At the same time, the presence of such PAP services continues to boost the presence of the PAP and retain its image as a party being able to provide for Singaporeans.

The PAP, relative to other political parties in Singapore, also has massive funds. In the late 1990s, each PAP Member of Parliament was required to contribute S$600 per month to party coffers while PAP ministers were required to contribute S$1,000 per month.[1] In 2012, it was publicly stated that the MPs' annual allowance was S$192,500. For PAP's MPs, they contributed 10% of their allowance to the party, which amounted to a hefty S$19,250 annually. Since, following the 2015 General Elections, the PAP had 83 MPs, this would amount to an annual total of S$1,597,750 even though the actual amount is much higher as all ministers are required to contribute much more. Besides the contributions from elected MPs and ministers, the PAP also receives political donations from other groups and individuals.

Using Richard Gunther and Larry Diamond's observations of the functions of a political party, the PAP clearly excels in each and every category.[2] In candidate

1. R.S. Milne and Diane K. Mauzy, *Singapore Politics under the People's Action Party* (London, UK: Routledge, 2002), p. 43.

2. Richard Gunther and Larry Diamond, *Political Parties and Democracy* (Baltimore, MD and London, UK: The Johns Hopkins University Press, 2001), pp. 7–8.

recruitment, the PAP has been able to constantly recruit high-quality individuals. Just looking at the current third-generation leaders, the PAP's status is clearly boosted and enhanced by individuals such as Lee Hsien Loong, Tharman Shanmugaratnam, Teo Chee Hean and K. Shanmugam. Even more promising is the slate of fourth-generation PAP leaders that have been put into key portfolios at present, including Heng Swee Keat, Chan Chun Sing, Ong Ye Kung, Ng Chee Meng, Lawrence Wong, Desmond Lee, Chee Hong Tat and Janil Puthucheary. In Singapore's Asian setting, the role and importance of personality trumps over other key factors, largely explaining PAP's staying power. Clearly, the Opposition has no answer to this 'candidate power' which the PAP has the advantage of drawing from the civil service, military and private sector. Given Singapore's small population and a smaller pool of top talent, the ability of the PAP to recruit most, if not all of the available talent means that the Opposition is deprived of enlisting these talents into the opposition ranks. The PAP is also extremely successful in electoral mobilisation. This is due to the incumbency of the PAP in government, having the edge to prepare for elections way ahead of other political parties as the Elections Department is under the Prime Minister's Office. Since it knows precisely when elections would be held and with its strong presence in all electoral constituencies [including Opposition-held], the PAP has won convincingly in every general elections.

The PAP is also adept in structuring issues and providing not only effective leadership, but PAP leaders, in particular the Old Guards, who as visionaries were able to steer Singapore in the direction of their goals. Being a secular political party, the PAP, with its calls for a multi-ethnic and meritocratic society, has been able to represent the general populace in Singapore without much controversy. The PAP's ability to aggregate interest, compounded with its stellar track record of forming and sustaining the government of Singapore are critical keys to PAP's longevity in power. The party's unbroken grip over Singapore has allowed it to structure Singapore's social integration along the lines of the party leadership's vision and expectations. This has effectively tied the fate of Singapore to the party's continued governance of the island Republic. Clearly, the PAP as a well-structured and grounded political party, with established norms and links to the electorate, has been able to ensure its primacy in Singapore. With healthy party funds and success in recruiting new talent as well as generating new leaders in the party ranks, the PAP is able to provide a multitude of services and offer top-quality candidates during elections which the Opposition is unable to match.

Over the years, it has become more difficult to distinguish the PAP as a political party and the PAP as the government. The PAP's excellent track record in governing Singapore gives the party an added, some say unfair, advantage, over all other political parties. The government of Singapore is essentially a creation of the PAP and has remained the exclusive institution and preserve of the PAP. Typical of many political parties in power, the PAP has access to the machineries of state, including control over media and has used it to benefit the party. Ranging from electoral innovations, the longer the PAP is in power, the more it is able to formulate, create and raise barriers against other political opponents.

PAP's longevity in power, being 60 years in 2019, has also given it the ability to make long-term plans to foresee the challenges and needs facing her in the future. That this was a crucial factor was made clear by Goh Chok Tong, the former prime minister, in an interview with *Lianhe Zaobao* in May 2019. He argued that it was important for the PAP to always have a clear majority in parliament and it would be alright if the Opposition were to gain between 20% to 25% of the seats in the next 20 years. This is because with a clear majority, the government can afford to look at issues from a long-term view rather than being worried about the next elections. In Goh's words, "If there are 75% to 80% of the seats, you don't need to worry about the election alone. You can plan for the long run."[3]

The presence of certain institutions and mechanisms has also advantaged the incumbent PAP. The Scenario Planning Office (SPO) in the Prime Minister's Office, which began in 1995, was tasked to make these predictions and to come up with recommended solutions and plans to take on these future challenges.[4] PAP leaders, by default, as the incumbent prime minister and the cabinet, have access to these scenarios and can co-opt them into their party platforms. Political

---

3. See Anna Maria Romero, "Goh Chok Tong says ruling party must have clear majority of Parliamentary seats in 20 years", *The Independent*, 27 May 2019, http://theindependent. sg/goh-chok-tong-says-ruling-party-must-have-clear-majority-of-parliamentary-seats-in-20-years/

4. The Scenario Planning Office (SPO) was to come up with scenarios from the perspective of a whole-of-government approach to problem solving. In 2003, the office was renamed Strategic Policy Office. In 2009, the Centre for Strategic Futures (CSF) was established as a brain trust within the SPO. Since 2015, the CSF has become part of the Strategy Group in the Prime Minister's Office, partaking among others, work related to strategic foresight and horizon scanning.

innovations such as the Non-Constituency Member of Parliament (NCMP) and Nominated Member of Parliament (NMP) schemes have arguably undermined the importance of an elected opposition in parliament. Critics of these schemes have accused the PAP of creating them to placate the desires of the electorate to see more opposition in parliament. By introducing NCMPs and NMPs in parliament, the PAP is hoping to tame the electorate from casting votes for the Opposition during general elections. Similarly, the Elected President (EP) scheme is also a safeguard mechanism to ensure that the PAP has an 'insider' in the event the 'freak' Singaporean electorate decides to vote the Opposition into parliament. The GRCs also pose a great challenge to the opposition parties who are relatively small parties with limited resources. For the Opposition to contest in a GRC, they are forced to commit huge proportions of their limited resources for uncertain gains. The need to administer a town council has also made the voters cautious about voting in the Opposition as the voters know that they may be disadvantaged in terms of access to municipal services, lift upgrading, supermarkets, bank Automatic Teller Machines (ATMs), bus services, wet markets, etc. The trial of the key WP leaders who helm the Aljunied-Hougang Town Council in October 2018 on issues relating to the breach of "core fiduciary duties owed to residents and former constituents in their capacity as town councilors, in managing the money and assets entrusted to them" highlights part of the challenge facing any opposition running a town council and where the PAP has a clear advantage in these matters as it is the government.[5] In short, the PAP has been able to exploit state power to the maximum to remain in power, as has been argued by scholars such as Dan Slater.[6]

Thus, despite inheriting a Westminster parliamentary system, through its long-term control of government, the political system and structure have been drastically re-made, making it totally different from the one that the PAP inherited from the British colonisers. Through various political innovations, instead of a one-man-one-vote constituency as in the past, the Singapore's electoral system is essentially GRC-centric, with a many-men-many-votes-one-group constituency in operation. This, some have argued, has advantaged the ruling party at the expense of the

5. Wong Pei Ting, "Fiduciary duties of WP MPs under scrutiny in high-profile civil trial", *Today*, 10 October 2018.

6. Dan Slater, "Southeast Asia: Strong-State Democratization in Malaysia and Singapore", *Journal of Democracy*, April 2012, 23(2), pp. 19–33.

Table 11.3:   Number of GRC and SMC Seats Compared, 1988–2015

Year	No. of GRC Seats	No. of SMC Seats
1988	39	42
1991	60	21
1997	74	9
2001	75	9
2006	75	9
2011	75	12
2015	75	14

Source: Author.

Opposition. For instance, since the introduction of the GRC system in 1988, it was only in 1988 that there were more seats in parliament from the Single Member Constituencies (SMCs) compared to the GRCs (see Table 11.3). Since then, the trend has been for the GRCs to disproportionately outnumber the SMCs. The proportion of parliamentary GRC seats to SMC seats in the 1991, 1997, 2001, 2006, 2011 and 2015 general elections were 60 to 21, 74 to 9, 75 to 9, 75 to 9, 75 to 12 and 75 to 14, respectively, signaling clearly the unique first-past-the-post system in Singapore compared to other Westminster systems in the world.

PAP government policies are also responsible for the marginalisation of their political opponents. In the interest to protect the fragile fabric of society, certain issues have been made taboo in Singapore politics. Issues with regard to race and religion are clearly out-of-bounds and political parties are not allowed to exploit these traditional cleavages of politics for fear of igniting underlying tensions between the various ethnic communities in Singapore. Although this policy is respected and has helped to enhance social stability, it has advertently denied the Opposition a platform to contest against the PAP. Moreover, in all ethnic self-help groups such as the CDAC, MENDAKI, SINDA and the Eurasian Association, PAP ministers always serve as chairpersons and key advisers. For the Chinese Development Assistance Council (CDAC), the key PAP ministers and MPs involved include Ong Ye Kung, Baey Yam Keng, Chee Hong Tat, Sun Xueling, Sam Tan Chin Siong and Alex Yam Ziming. In the MENDAKI, the key PAP ministers and MPs include Masagos Zulkifli, Zaqy Mohamad, Rahayu Mahzam and Saktiandi Supaat. In the Singapore Indian Development Association

(SINDA), the key PAP ministers and MPs include Tharman Shanmugaratnam, Indranee Rajah, Vivian Balakrishnan, S. Iswaran, Vikram Nair and Murali Pillai. Finally, the Eurasian Association representative in cabinet is S. Iswaran. In this way, by 'capturing' these traditional cleavages of political bases and reducing them into apolitical organisations, the PAP has effectively denied the Opposition from capitalising on ethnic and religious issues. Paradoxically, the PAP is in a position to influence communal leaders, thereby commanding their loyalty and support, mainly through transactional politics of servicing various ethnic communities through educational and welfare programmes.

The current situation cannot be simply explained by the PAP's excellent organisation and political tactics alone. The opposition political parties themselves are largely to blame for the PAP's current domination of the political system. The weak Opposition's organisational capacity, its lack of an alternative and attractive ideology, and its incapacity as opposed to the lack of choice due to PAP's overwhelming dominance to recruit talent and amass resources to contest in elections have worked to the detriment of the Opposition. The opposition political parties in Singapore do not have a highly developed institutionalised organisation as that of the PAP. The opposition parties tend to be 'parties of personality' and where many of these parties are anchored on particular leaders. Such parties are personalised around key individuals and hence, are unable to institutionalise themselves into strong political parties as changes in leadership or the incapacitation of their leaders tend to render the political parties weak or worse, lead to their dissolution. The ease with which party leaders 'hop' from one party to another has also not helped the credibility of these leaders or the parties they represent. This weakness of the Opposition has been fully exploited by the PAP leadership when these leaders have fallen fault of the law in one way or another. PAP leaders such as Lee Kuan Yew and Goh Chok Tong have in the past used the long arm of the law against their political opponents. Key opposition leaders have been sued in court for defamation and often the liabilities and legal cost would bankrupt the targeted opposition leader. Examples of opposition leaders made bankrupt in suits by PAP leaders include J.B. Jeyaretnam and Chee Soon Juan of the WP and SDP, respectively.

Moreover, besides the banned Malayan Communist Party, no other opposition political party has a well-defined ideology that can be pitted against the PAP. Typically, the opposition parties justify their existence as a check and balance to the PAP instead of being an alternative to the PAP. This implicitly recognises the strengths of the PAP and the inability of the Opposition to replace the PAP as the government. Opposition parties, although being channels to articulate grievances against PAP rule, are unable to provide cohesive and credible alternatives to the PAP's policies and programmes. Often enough, the Opposition is only able to call for greater transparency in governance and can ask of little more than that. Many opposition parties have been wrecked by continuous internal dissension. Traditionally, opposition parties also had difficulties recruiting credible and talented Singaporeans to their ranks.

At the same time, the important role of political culture has also contributed to PAP's dominance. Singapore is a multi-racial state with a dominant Chinese majority population. Mainly of immigrant background, the population tends to be conservative, comfortable with the ruling party that has brought the Republic much sought-after stability and prosperity. A number of political cultural ethos have advantaged the ruling party. This includes the following: need to retain the PAP as the governing party; nature of national issues at any point in time; nature of local issues; and the need to signal to the ruling hegemonic party of what can and cannot be done. Hence, through a system of political bargaining, compacts and negotiations, a system of one-party dominance has been established and entrenched in Singapore since 1959, especially 1963.

To this can be added Singapore's political environment, especially its locale in Southeast Asia. As a small, urban-based city state, surrounded by large Malay neighbours, a sense of permanent uncertainty and insecurity has prevailed and pervaded over the future of Singapore, something appreciated by the populace. The sense of vulnerability is real and this has worked to the advantage of the ruling party. The PAP is seen as the only ruling party that has and can provide stability and security to the Republic and its people, and this, in part, has also ensured its entrenchment in political power.

The current one-party dominant system in Singapore has come about due to the initial success of the PAP to identify with the electorate and its eventual total consolidation of power in the parliament when the *Barisan Sosialis* boycotted the 1968 General Elections. Since then, the PAP has continued to better itself as an organisation and has used its privilege as the party in power to create an environment that perpetuates its hegemony. The opposition parties, on the other hand, have failed to further their influence in Singapore politics due to their own inherent weaknesses and also the barriers placed against them by the ruling PAP. Thus, in answering why the PAP is dominant, it is a case of both the PAP being excellent at what it does best as a political party and the inability of the other political parties to provide a credible challenge to the PAP and its rule. To that extent, the PAP can be expected to continue outdistancing the other political parties despite holding regular elections offering the electorate a choice of selecting amongst more than 20 functioning political parties in the system.

In this context, the key imperatives that have determined electoral behaviour in Singapore and hence, the one-party dominant state are the electoral demography and the inherent sharp fault lines, the politics of insecurity of a small state, the strong leadership of the PAP, especially under Lee Kuan Yew, the general weaknesses of the Opposition, the successful political socialisation and control exercised by the ruling party, and most importantly, the general population's satisfaction with the performance of the ruling party. Presently, even if some segment of the population may vote in some opposition parliamentarians, there is no sign of a tsunami against the PAP as it is still seen as a performing political machinery in Singapore that represents the interests of all Singaporeans.

This finally brings the discussion to the issue of hegemony as was propounded by Antonio Gramsci. What clearly exists in Singapore is PAP's electoral hegemony and this is a function of many factors, both PAP's hard policies of punishing and deterring its political adversaries as well as soft policies of delivering all-round political, economic and social goods that have attracted popular electoral support over the last six decades, leading to the institutionalisation of the PAP as the government and state. As was observed by Manuel Castells in 1988, "although clearly authoritarian, Singapore is not a dictatorship but a hegemonic state, in the Gramscian sense…it is based not simply on coercion but also on consensus."[7]

Gramsci argued that the capitalists entrenched themselves and maintained control, not through violence or coercion but through ideology. The capitalist state has the capacity to develop a hegemonic culture, whereby it propagates its values, mores and norms so much so that these become common sense values of the majority of the electorate. These values become identified with that of the

---

7. Manuel Castells, *The Developmental City-State in an Open World Economy: The Singapore Experiment*, Working Paper No. 31, The Berkeley Roundtable on the International Economy, February 1988, p. 78.

working class and electorate majority, and are viewed as being for the good of the society and nation. Hence, the convergence of the goals of the government and governed on the need to champion these values and the status quo, in the process, safeguarding the authority of those in power. This to Gramsci described a situation of what he called 'consented coercion'.

As was argued by a Singaporean scholar, "while significant impediments exist to prevent opposition parties from competing with the regime on an equal footing, it is undeniable that elections are not rigged, opposition parties are given space to participate in the political system and voters are not coerced into supporting the ruling party. The PAP's longevity is even more remarkable considering that Singapore is a developed country with one of the most highly-educated citizenries in the world, defying modernisation theories that predict democratisation would accompany development."[8] To explain the phenomenon of PAP's hegemony, one would need to understand the ideological underpinning of its rule and the hegemonic ideologies it has 'efficaciously promulgated' that include themes related to 'survival', 'meritocracy', 'multiracialism' and 'pragmatism'.[9] While 'armoured hegemony' exists through various legal measures that can be enforced, it is the ideological leadership that the PAP has instituted through consensual rule, persuasion and co-optation that has been more effective and successful in ensuring PAP's political dominance and hegemony all these years.[10]

Clearly, the PAP has remained in a dominant position since 1959 and there is no sign that its political durability is about to be challenged. In the final analysis, this is brought about by a convergence of a number of political factors but essentially the existence of a scalene triangle, with most of the power in the hands of the ruling PAP, and the rest unequally distributed between the voters and the Opposition. By whatever definition one refers to Singapore, politically, despite the trappings

---

8. Walid Jumblatt Abdullah, "Selective History and Hegemony-Making: The Case of Singapore", *International Political Science Review*, 2018, 39(4), p. 474.

9. Walid Jumblatt Abdullah, "Selective History and Hegemony-Making: The Case of Singapore", p. 475; Kenneth Paul Tan, "Meritocracy and Elitism in a Global City: Ideological Shifts in Singapore", *International Political Science Review*, 29(1), pp. 7–27.

10. Lisa Lim, *Hegemony and Political Dominance in Singapore*. Paper presented at the annual meeting of the American Sociological Association, Philadelphia, PA, USA, 12 August 2005.

of a democratic entity, it represents the existence of a competitive authoritarian system.[11] Such systems only exist with the support and endorsement of the voters. What is interesting about the Singapore system is the fact that even though many voters may be unhappy with the PAP, they have continued to vote and support the PAP during the regularly held general elections. Singapore voters have a litany of reasons to be unhappy with the PAP, be it over the lack of civil and political liberties, its many draconian laws, especially the ISA, the high cost but not standard of living, the manner the ruling party has flooded the country with foreigners over the last two decades and many more policies, but still, the PAP is voted into office election after election, with the ruling party receiving 70% of the votes in the 2015 General Elections.

In the end, the imbalance between the PAP, the Opposition and the voters' decision to support the PAP has accounted for the state of political affairs in Singapore and this will go a long way to answer the question, "is the PAP here to stay?" The continuous rule of the PAP has allowed it to implement policies with long-term consequences, one of which is to marginalise the Opposition and establish a compact with the voters. With the ability to both punish and co-opt dissenters, the PAP has remained at the apex of political power since 1959. With its excellent all-round performance, even though there is much to nag but still, there is overall, little to criticise. By being the incumbent since 1959, the PAP has engaged in rule-making that has established the rules of engagement and forced both the citizens and Opposition to operate within the PAP-created system that advantages the ruling party. This has not made it easy for the Opposition to operate and at times, even for the voters to support the Opposition. In fact, the Opposition has not totally rejected the political order established by the PAP except challenging marginally some of the policies. Most importantly, the PAP understands that the voters are primarily concerned with material benefits, something the ruling party is highly adept in. At the same time, despite criticising the PAP, most voters are not yet interested in more political goods and this has given the PAP a longer lead time compared to other similar systems and partly explains its longevity. While issues of redistributive justice are rising, as Singapore is dependent upon imported capital and investments, there is a limit to which this can be achieved, partly explaining the continued tolerance of the PAP despite rising inequalities in Singapore.

---

11. See Steven Levitsky and Lucan A. Way, *Competitive Authoritarianism: Hybrid Regimes after the Cold War* (Cambridge, UK: Cambridge University Press, 2010).

The long rule of the PAP has also helped the ruling party to create a Singapore in its image and thereby gaining control of the 'Singapore narrative', something that has assisted its political hegemony. By harping on concepts such as meritocracy and multi-racialism, the PAP has crafted a political system where only it appears as the provider and saviour of Singapore, its interests and hence, of Singaporeans. This is further strengthened by PAP's control of key institutions of the state, be it the civil service, trade unions, mass media, grassroots organisations and even the economy. Today, there are no competing elites outside the PAP's framework or any alternative elites to challenge the PAP's position of *primus inter pares* politically. Through deliverance of economic goods and a stable political and social order, the PAP has embedded and cemented its legitimacy and power bar none. To this has been added the concept of an exceptional Singapore that can only be ruled by exceptional leaders that the PAP is in a position to provide. In short, using a football analogy, the PAP is the Barcelona of the Spanish La Liga, the Juventus of the Italian Serie A and the Manchester City of the English Premier League.

This in turn has created a strange political situation of wanting and living with the status quo. There is an allergy to undertake political change for a whole host of reasons and this also explains the PAP's hegemony. Since 1965, there has been no major demand to replace the PAP as the ruling party and even key opposition parties such as the WP has articulated the view that it is not interested in replacing the PAP, yet. While the voters may have specific demands, such as lower cost of living and lesser foreigners in the country, it is never to replace the PAP as the government of Singapore. This is primarily because the PAP has been a successful government to the satisfaction of the majority of Singaporeans, the key impediment that stands in the way of the Opposition to displace the PAP in the short to medium term. The PAP has also created a system where the highly competitive Singaporean is more focussed on creating a good life for himself and his family rather than partaking in national politics of replacing the government. What is even more intriguing is the perception that one's well-being is directly linked to the continued rule of the PAP and hence, the compact between the PAP and the voters, with the Opposition on the receiving end of the triangle. As long the PAP continues to deliver the goods for the populace, the Singapore voter will adopt the attitude and posture of, 'leave politics to the PAP', and this advantages the PAP and its political dominance. Hence, from the perspective of a rational voter behaviour, the PAP has been successful in providing the 'goods' that the voters want and where the PAP is in a position to deliver, thereby entrenching even more deeply the PAP in the public's psyche as *the ruling party.*

The material well-being of Singaporeans, the PAP's ability to maintain domestic and external peace as well as Singapore's positive image internationally, best evident by being the host for the 2018 Trump–Kim Summit in the Republic, signposted the strong standing and credibility the PAP has among Singaporeans. While there may be fear of the ruling party's repressive measures, there is also the fear of losing the PAP that many Singaporeans believe would lead to the loss of a good, safe, secure and successful life. The continued existence of Singapore as an independent state has also been credited to the PAP. Hence, the PAP is seen as a successful guardian of Singapore and its interests, which no other political party can lay claim to. The voters' sense of disempowerment, as far as political issues are concerned and the unwillingness of major public interest groups to support an alternative political party to challenge the PAP have also created a situation of almost no real challenge to the PAP from the present set of opposition parties in Singapore. After nearly six decades, for all the faults of the PAP, the voters have also got used to the beast called the PAP and the love–hate relationship in a situation of a lack of alternative which has allowed the PAP to continue to rule Singapore with no sight of this being overturned in the short term. All of these have created an in-built, default position of bias towards the incumbent and status quo, immensely benefitting the PAP and disadvantaging any alternative discourse or political party that would endanger the PAP.

Conclusion

The attainment of PAP's effective political dominance in Singapore is evident on a number of fronts. First, is the parliamentary dominance of the PAP since 1959. In addition to the legislature domination, the imprimatur over the executive branch is also clearly evident with every prime minister and key office holder coming from the PAP, partly as a consequence of the Westminster parliamentary system. In addition to the decimation of the Opposition since 1963, the ruling party has also exercised control over the political and non-political organisations in Singapore. This includes the PAP's control over the grassroots organisations, mass media, civil service, trade unions, economy as well as being credited for the ethnic and inter-state peace and harmony. In short, there is a sense of pervasive control over the city-state despite exuding a political system of openness in various sectors. This also makes it clear that the PAP government has captured the non-government sectors of the society, thereby compelling the political, economic and socio-cultural organisations to work in tandem and not against the state that is controlled by the PAP.

If one harks to the various theories of political domination, it is clear that many of the explanations also apply to the PAP. First, the PAP is definitely, in line with Maurice Duverger, Singapore's 'epoch political party'. The PAP is identified as the party that helped to bring about the crucial political moments of Singapore, especially decolonisation from the British, merger with Malaysia and later, independence. The PAP also oversaw and successfully overcame key crises confronting Singapore, including the challenges posed by the communists and communalists, economic management following British withdrawal and the restructuring of the Republic's economy through various crises such as the 1973 oil crisis, the Asian Financial Crisis and the economic crises following the '9/11' attacks and SARS. More than that, Singapore has been created in PAP's image, be it national politics, economy, socio-cultural terrain, ethnic management, education policies, civil society, media, trade unions, grassroots organisations as well as the Republic's defence and foreign policy. Similarly, nation building and national identity have also been a function of PAP's policies and imagination. From this perspective, it is not surprising that the majority of Singaporeans have always supported the PAP and this is largely due to the populace's identification of Singapore's success as being primarily due to the PAP and its policies, from which the voters have benefitted immensely.

While the PAP has successfully projected and presented itself as a 'national movement' that transcends racial, religious and linguistic fault lines, the presence of charismatic leaders, especially Lee Kuan Yew, the party's political savvy in political mobilisation, its ability to recruit the 'best and brightest' and deliverance of political goods, especially economic and social stability, have also been its key source of legitimacy. While the successful engineering of the political system and rules of engagement have benefitted the PAP and disadvantaged the Opposition, had there been a lack of performance legitimacy, the PAP would not have been in the dominant position it has chalked up over the years or it is today, especially following the 2015 General Elections. There is no sign of the PAP collapsing as the *Barisan Nasional* (BN) did in Malaysia as PAP leaders are not seen as 'Najibs' and the PAP is not seen as the 'BN'.

Singapore's political culture of valuing and giving meritocracy a premium has also meant that a weak or sub-standard political organisation would not have won the support, endorsement and loyalty of its populace. Through effective policies, often a mixture of hard and soft policies, the PAP has succeeded in capturing the political centre of Singapore and the imagination of its voters. While the PAP is well-organised and funded, and has even loaded the political dice in its favour, still, it is the voters that have decided, at least for the time being, that the PAP's political dominance should be endorsed and maintained. To that extent, the society's political culture, partly created by the PAP, has helped to maintain the PAP in a position of political hegemony and pre-eminence. However, this is mainly due to the party's ability to successfully meet challenges with regard to the Republic's physical existence, economic growth and provision of the basic needs of its people.

In this regard, the party's ability to socialise succeeding generations of PAP's leaders and cadres of the party's epochal achievements, being responsive to public needs, especially in being corruption-free, and addressing and managing rising public disillusionment (cost of living with regard to housing, medical, education, transportation; income disparities; and influx of foreigners) have also been particularly critical in entrenching the PAP in Singapore's politics. While the 'people's' and 'action' aspects of the party have been continuously emphasised, the ability of the PAP ministers and MPs to identify with the ordinary Singaporeans and the high legitimacy and all-round skills of the party's leaders have also won the PAP much public empathy.

Finally, through various measures, the PAP has also succeeded in denying legitimacy to the Opposition and any alternative narrative that may surface with regard to Singapore's past, present and even near future. The marginalisation of the 'revisionist' narrative on 'Operation Coldstore' is a case in point. Through a combination of cultural and institutional factors, the primacy of successful economic policies and being able to alter the public's value system (such as downplaying the primacy of democracy and human rights but giving credence to political and social stability and economic growth), the Opposition has been made largely impotent with little public support and empathy. While the public may continue to demonstrate some support for the Opposition, largely as a protest against the PAP, when it comes to choosing a government for Singapore, since 1959, Singaporeans have continued to support the PAP, thereby explaining and demonstrating the resilience of the one-party dominant state in Singapore.

CONSEQUENCES OF SINGAPORE AS A ONE-PARTY DOMINANT STATE

Introduction

Clearly, a one-party dominant state is not only a Third World phenomenon. Research has shown that examples of this type of political and party system can also be found in developed countries such as Sweden, Israel, Japan and Italy.[1] Still, in the 1960s through to the 1980s, the party system in Asia and Africa was particularly prone to this type of political practice and remains resilient in many countries, including Singapore. Similarly, the Liberal Democratic Party (LDP) remains resilient in Japan, having won the last few elections on a continuous basis. Since 1954, when the Allied Powers granted total sovereignty to Japan after its defeat in the Second World War, out of 28 general elections, the LDP has on 23 occasions formed the government. In Singapore's case, the People's Action Party (PAP) has formed the government on 14 occasions continuously since 1959.

Implications of the one-party dominant state in Singapore

While many arguments have been made about the benefits of having a one-party dominant state, on the downside, there are also various negative consequences of such a political system. Analysing the positive spill-overs of the one-party dominant state, especially with reference to Israel, Myron J. Aronoff observed that "the stability and continuity of leadership and policy, which are characteristics of a dominant party system, may be particularly beneficial in the early stages of development of a new society and political system."[2] Aronoff also noted that "in conditions characterised by pervasive change and uncertainty, the predictability

---

1.   See Maurice Duverger, *Political Parties: Their Organization and Activity in the Modern State*, Second Edition, revised (London, UK: Methuen and Company, 1959).

2.   Myron J. Aronoff, "Israel under Labor and the Likud: The Role of Dominance Considered", in T.J. Pempel (ed.), *Uncommon Democracies: The One-Party Dominant Regimes* (Ithaca, New York: Cornell University Press, 1990), p. 279.

of a political regime that results when one party dominates a polity can make a significant difference in successfully meeting such challenges."[3] At the same time, "most relevant groups could be organised through the agency of the dominant party and its affiliated institutions, which simplified the tasks of national mobilisation and made it more efficient."[4]

Aronoff's arguments about the positive spill-overs of a one-party dominant state can also be applied to Singapore. From the perspective of the benefits stemming from the stability and continuity of the leadership, this was particularly true for Singapore from 1959 onwards. This was when the polity was confronted with serious challenges of meeting the population's needs regarding housing, jobs, education and basic physical security. The merger with Malaysia in 1963 and Singapore's exit from the Federation in 1965 required policies that were not only problem-solving but also needed a longer time frame to achieve results. This would largely represent the key benefit and advantage of PAP as the dominant party in Singapore in the period from 1960s to the 1980s. The continuity and stability of a regime in a condition of constant change and uncertainty, and where the various groups could be organised and co-opted was also helpful in organising a state for national unity and developmental purposes. In a state's drive for efficiency and being performance-oriented, a dominant party in control of government's resources would be able to bring all groups together for a single purpose for the benefit of the state and its people. This was very much true of Singapore, where the PAP government was able to control almost all political and non-political bodies such as the civil service, trade unions, media and even civil society for the single-minded goal of economic development and social stability.

In short, a one-party dominant state can advantage a polity. It can bring about stability through continuity of leadership and policies. This can enhance the predictability of government and its policies, thereby contributing to long-term goals. Such a state would be able to organise relevant groups through co-option and if this fails, through coercion. Such states can undertake effective mobilisation of its people and successfully maintain diversity. One-party dominant states are also adept in pursuing long-term based strategies, policies and objectives that can result in the development of strong economies as happened in Singapore, Taiwan and South Korea.

---

3. Ibid.

4. Ibid.

The issue, however, is, at what price is dominance to be achieved? What are the trade-offs or the advantages of such a state with regard to other goals and interests in the state? In analysing the negative consequences of one-party dominant states, Aronoff observed that:

> Prolonged dominance eventually had a debilitating effect on the party. It directly contributed to the strengthening of oligarchic tendencies, the degeneration of decision making in party institutions, and the breakdown of responsiveness of the leadership to the membership and to the public in general. Prolonged rule without serious challenge contributed to the arrogance of leadership, which in exceptional cases resulted in corruption. While cases of personal corruption were relatively isolated, the phenomena of disregarding practices that violated the party constitution and principles were widespread. Recruitment and advancement through patron–client relationships deprived the party and the nation of potential leaders who displayed initiative, independence and originality.[5]

Equally important and something often ignored or downplayed is Aronoff's observation about the impact one-party dominance can have on a state's opposition parties:

> Prolonged dominance by one party had a serious negative influence on the main opposition party. Perpetual opposition without likelihood of gaining a share in ruling encouraged irresponsible behavior. This was particularly the case when the party and its leaders were defined as pariahs without legitimacy by the dominant party and this charge was believed by significant sectors of the general public. Lack of access to public office deprived the party leaders of valuable experience in governing and the party of a potential pool of high-calibre public servants with administrative experience.[6]

The same point was emphasised by Maurice Duverger:

> The existence of a dominant party seems also to produce certain effects upon opposition. If dominance is prolonged the opposition is reduced to impotence; such a situation occurs chiefly under the two-party system, which it modifies considerably. It sometimes happens that the opposition, being kept long out of

---

5. Ibid, p. 280.

6. Ibid.

office, assumes a more violent and extravagant attitude. What particularly happens is that the country gradually loses interest in campaigns and elections because they are ineffective.[7]

What is even more significant is that "these negative influences can lead to problems of transition when eventually the dominant party loses its dominant position."[8]

In many ways, the minuses of a one-party dominant state, as observed by scholars such as Maurice Duverger and Myron J. Aronoff, are also applicable to Singapore. The unbroken protracted rule of the PAP since 1959 has created a PAP-centric and directed political system. *PAPism* can be seen and felt in almost every aspect of Singapore's political and non-political life. Using the office and power of the government, what has been described by Aronoff as the 'oligarchic tendencies' of the ruling party, are very much evident in the political life of Singapore, especially in terms of what can and cannot be undertaken in Singapore. The so-called 'OB Markers' culture, while justified in the name of the general public good, is also useful in denting challenges to the PAP and its policies. While many freedoms are in existence in Singapore, many others have been neutralised and suppressed in the name of racial and religious sensitivities as well as to ensure that nothing stalls the economic development of Singapore that has thus far benefitted the general public in the Republic.

In many ways, the PAP has also suffered from its long-term rule as many party leaders also believe in, not just the infallibility of the party, but also the strengths and power of the PAP's way of doing things. The often-heard mantra that 'what is good for the PAP is good for Singapore' is evidence of this arrogance and where much damage can result if this trend is not checked through an internal or external system of checks and balances. The dictum that 'absolute power corrupts absolutely' is definitely true and should be a reminder to PAP leaders that if no external checks and balances are in power due to the Leviathan position of the ruling party, then it would be extremely wise to establish internal checks and balances, lest what happened in Najib's Malaysia repeats itself in PAP's Singapore in future.

---

7. See Maurice Duverger, *Political Parties: Their Organization and Activity in the Modern State*, Second Edition, revised, p. 417.

8. Myron J. Aronoff, "Israel under Labor and the Likud: The Role of Dominance Considered", p. 280.

A key negative fallout of the PAP's long-term rule has been the effect it had on the opposition parties. For all intents and purposes, the Opposition operates in the second or third tier of politics in Singapore. The PAP has always been in the core first tier, controlling all aspects of politics, including ensuring how many opposition members can enter parliament through its various innovations such as the Non-Constituency Member of Parliament (NCMP) scheme. While the Singapore political system does not ban the opposition parties, many obstacles have been placed in their ways to make them largely impotent. While the Opposition has become part of the political landscape since 1981, it is largely marginalised, weak and not in a position to impact national policies and politics. The Opposition has never set the political agenda, even from the perspective of ideational superiority, what more, in terms of political power. Instead, it tends to gain traction mainly as a source of protest rather than support from the public. Today, the highest form of Opposition's access to office is being MPs and running a town council. This also means that the Opposition is largely inexperienced in running a government ministry and if ever the Opposition forms the government in the coming years, it will start from a serious deficit as far as experience in administration is concerned. With the Workers' Party (WP) leadership being charged in court for various oversights in the running of the Aljunied-Hougang Town Council, it only goes to show the manifold limitations the Opposition faces in Singapore against the overwhelming shadow of a one-party PAP dominant state in Singapore.

In view of the above discussion of the advantages and disadvantages of a one-party dominant system, Michael Shalev's discussion of the Mapai in Israel is very apt. The Mapai "clearly embraces, indeed epitomises, all of the functional hallmarks of one-party dominance: a routinized monopoly over the formation of governments, the ability to preempt or control non-party forms of political action and a high degree of legitimacy in the eyes of most of the mass public."[9] At the same time, political hegemony that arises as a result of a successful political machination by the dominant party, political culture and political economy would also result in the marginalisation and de-legitimisation of contending and opposing political parties in the state, as has largely transpired in Singapore.

---

9. Michael Shalev, "The Political Economy of Labor-Party Dominance and Decline in Israel", in T.J. Pempel (ed.), *Uncommon Democracies: The One-Party Dominant Regimes* (Ithaca, New York: Cornell University Press, 1990), p. 85.

CONCLUSION: WILL SINGAPORE'S ONE-PARTY DOMINANT SYSTEM ENDURE?

Introduction

By whatever yardsticks one measures, Singapore has confounded most predictions. As a Chinese-majority small state sandwiched between two large Malay neighbours, Malaysia to the north and Indonesia to the south, it was expected to be either 'Finlandised' or 'absorbed' by one or the other. None of these happened. Instead, Singapore strategically chose to merge with Malaysia in September 1963. Singapore's stint in Malaysia lasted 23 months and following the parting of ways from the Federation of Malaysia on 9 August 1965, few pundits believed that Singapore would survive. Doomsday scenarios abounded with the former British colonial territory, stricken with poverty, political instability, social divisions and military weakness, condemned to the backwaters of history. According to the late Michael Leifer, Singapore's racial composition, which was diametrically different from Malaysia and Indonesia "registered the alien regional identity of Singapore through an analogy with an embattled Israel standing alone in the Middle East against its adversary Muslim neighbours."[1] Here, Singapore's security planners could relate to the 416 BC Athenian invasion of Melos or the 1990 Saddam Hussein's invasion of Kuwait. Thucydides' narration of the 'Melian Dialogue' resonated well with the leadership believing that that "the strong do what they can and the weak suffer what they must."[2] This forced Singapore leaders to implement pragmatic but robust policies that ensured Singapore's survival and prosperity. While Singapore's all-round success went through a rite of passage that was coloured by turbulence and dangers, one major feature that continues to stand out politically is the sustenance

---

1. Cited in "Dilemmas and challenges for Singapore's security", in *Global Risk Insights* (2013), https://globalriskinsights.com/2013/04/dilemmas-and-challenges-for-singapores-security/

2. Thucydides, *The Peloponnesian War*. See Sam Seau, "The strong do what they can, and the weak suffer what they must", in *Return of Kings*, https://www.returnofkings.com/10535/the-strong-do-what-they-can-and-the-weak-suffer-what-they-must

and resilience of the one-party dominant system under the leadership of the People's Action Party (PAP). The PAP first came to power on 30 May 1959, winning the general elections in a landslide and on 12 September 2015, through an even more stunning landslide electoral victory, won the right to rule Singapore for another five years.

This study has briefly looked at the one-party dominant system as it is applied to the Singapore context. This was followed by a discussion of the PAP's ability to entrench itself in Singapore since 1959. The rules of engagement, as evident in the political system, was also analysed, especially the various political innovations that seem to load the dice in favour of the dominant PAP. The history of elections in Singapore and a case study of the 2011 and 2015 general elections was also undertaken. More important, how the 2015 General Elections reinforced the trend of one-party dominance system in Singapore and the factors behind it were elaborated. Why Singapore, despite its 'First World' status on most fronts, has continued to be politically conservative and in many ways, out of sync with other developed states, was also analysed. The consequence of PAP's political domination in Singapore since 1959 was also discussed. The impact of the May 2018 Malaysian General Elections on Singapore and where the one-party dominant system was terminated, was also examined. Finally, in view of the continued entrenchment of the ruling party, weak political opposition and general conservatism of the electorate, what type of politics can one look forward to in Singapore will be discussed in this chapter.

A useful way to enter into the foray of Singapore's political future would be to quote the man who oversaw the rise and maintenance of Singapore as a one-party dominant state, namely, Lee Kuan Yew. In a 2009 interview with Han Fook Kwang and his associates who were writing a book titled, *Lee Kuan Yew: Hard Truths to Keep Singapore Going*, Lee pondered the future of Singapore and the PAP in the following terms:

Q: *How confident are you that Singapore will survive you?*

Mr Lee: All I can say is I think Singapore is safe for 10 years. No trouble because there's a team in place that will handle it. Whether it will be 15, 20, 30 years depends on them getting a team of players very soon. Part of the team is in place but you need a leader man. You need somebody who can communicate, who can mobilise people, move people. It's not enough to have a good policy. You got to convince people.

Q: *What about beyond 10 years?*

Mr Lee: I think there will come a time when eventually the public will say, look, let's try the other side, either because the PAP has declined in quality or the opposition has put up a team which is equal to the PAP and they say, let's try the other side. It must come [emphasis added].

Q: *How will it happen?*

Mr Lee: It depends on when it happens and whether it happens all of a sudden or it happens gradually. If the decline in standards happens gradually, an opposition will emerge of quality. I mean, the public can sense it.

I think the more likely is a gradual evolution [emphasis added] because it is most unlikely the way we have evolved the party and the renewal of the party leadership that you will get such a clash of opinions that it will divide the whole leadership, the MPs and the party machinery into two, or into one major part, one minor part.

Q: *What will happen if it takes place suddenly?*

Mr Lee: If it is sudden, well, you're landed with an emergency. In that emergency I think the people will just take somebody like me and a few of those friends and say look, let's make a bid and stop this from going down the drain.

Q: *What could possibly make it happen suddenly?*

Mr Lee: You have a rumpus in the leadership. They disagree profoundly, either for reasons of principle or personality and suddenly it breaks up [emphasis added]...I cannot tell you what's going to be in maybe 20, 30, 40 years, not possible. We might have a genuine difference of perspective what the future should be, what kind of Singapore will survive and thrive in that future. We might have a clash. I don't know. I've lived long enough to know that nobody settles the future of his country beyond more than a decade or so of his life. Stalin grabbed the whole of eastern part of Europe, grabbed all the Asian republics right up to Siberia, took Outer Mongolia which belonged to China under his wing. That's 1945. He's dead. 1950s or something, Khrushchev came up. 1992, it dissolved — less than 40 years. They threw up a Gorbachev who never went through a revolution, who did not know that he was sitting on a boiling cauldron.

Q: *So there's nothing that can be done to prepare us for that eventuality?*

Mr Lee: Can anybody tell you how to prevent, from getting a stroke or an accident? That you will eventually die is a certainty, right? But how you will die, nobody can tell you.

Q: *What is your greatest fear for Singapore?*

Mr Lee: I think a leadership and a people that has forgotten, that has lost its bearings and do not understand the constraints that we face. Small base, highly, technically, organised, very competent people, complete international confidence, an ability to engage the big boys. You lose that, you're down. And you can go down very rapidly...

No system lasts forever, that's for sure. Ten years, I don't think it'll happen; 20 years, I can't say; 30 years, even more I cannot tell you. Will we always be able to get the most dedicated and the most capable, with integrity to devote their lives to this? I hope so but forever, I don't know.[3]

Clearly, Lee Kuan Yew, despite being the PAP's secretary-general for more than 30 years, and being at the helm of national politics in various capacities from 1959 to 2011, was quite agnostic about the PAP's future. This is best captured by his belief and it is worth repeating what the founder of modern Singapore stated:

There will come a time when eventually the public will say, look, let's try the other side, either because the PAP has declined in quality or the opposition has put up a team which is equal to the PAP and they say, let's try the other side. *That day will come* [emphasis added].[4]

In line with the crystal ball gazing into the future, both Ho Kwon Ping and Han Fook Kwang have talked about the future of the PAP and the one-party dominant state of Singapore. Ho, in his inaugural Institute of Policy Studies–S.R. Nathan Lecture Series, positioned the PAP's future in the following stark terms:

---

3. See Han Fook Kwang, "Singapore's future according to Lee Kuan Yew", *The Straits Times*, 27 March 2016; also see Han Fook Kwang, Zuraidah Ibrahim, Chua Mui Hoong, Lydia Lim, Ignatius Low, Rachel Lin and Robin Chan, *Lee Kuan Yew: Hard Truths to Keep Singapore Going* (Singapore: Straits Times Press, 2011), pp. 41–80.

4. Han Fook Kwang, Zuraidah Ibrahim, Chua Mui Hoong, Lydia Lim, Ignatius Low, Rachel Lin and Robin Chan, *Lee Kuan Yew: Hard Truths to Keep Singapore Going*, p. 68.

...there are only three basic scenarios for the PAP in the next 50 years:

1. The Status Quo Scenario. As it suggests, this scenario sees the PAP controlling, say, 85 per cent to 90 per cent of parliamentary seats, with the opposition controlling at most a dozen seats. This is regardless of the popular vote, where support for the PAP has dropped to a record low of 60 per cent, and may even decline further because control of Parliament is what really counts.
2. The Dominant Party Scenario. The PAP retains control of an important two-thirds majority or, at the very least, an absolute majority, of parliamentary seats. Assuming there are still around only 90 to 100 seats in Parliament, that means the opposition parties will control around 30 to 50 seats.
3. Two-Party Pendulum Scenario. A single opposition party or a coalition wins an election. Power then shifts between the PAP and the second major party in Singapore. This is pretty much the norm in all other developed, liberal democracies. A variant of this scenario is that the PAP splits and new coalitions form which alternate in winning elections.

These scenarios are quite obvious and commonsensical. It is the likelihood of the various scenarios occurring which may be controversial. Let me rate these probabilities into three categories: Unlikely, Possible and Likely.

And let me divide the next 50 years into three sets of 15 years, with each set roughly comprising three elections. We can therefore create a matrix for the scenarios:

*   Status Quo Scenario: first 15 years, possible; second 15 years, unlikely; third 15 years, unlikely.
*   Dominant Party Scenario: first 15 years, likely; second 15 years, possible; third 15 years, possible.
*   Two-Party Pendulum Scenario: first 15 years, unlikely; second 15 years, possible; third 15 years, likely.

Basically, all these scenarios foresee that the PAP will face a challenge to retain the same degree of control over Parliament as it has had in the past. So long as the very popular current Prime Minister Lee Hsien Loong remains in control — not only as PM but as Senior Minister or Minister Mentor, like his predecessors — the mantle of legitimacy can perhaps be extended to younger leaders. But even Mr Lee will be in his 80s by three more elections. The challenge will be considerable from then onwards.

This is not actually a radical conclusion — almost everyone I informally surveyed agreed with it broadly, but differed in their estimation as to how many years it would take before the PAP would lose an election, and how many terms it would stay out of power before bouncing back.

In fact, Mr Lee Kuan Yew himself has publicly pointed out that the PAP will eventually lose an election, but he did not foresee a date nor a cause.[5]

In response to Ho's diagnosis that the PAP would one day lose its dominant status in Singapore's politics, Han responded by asking the question, "under what circumstances can the PAP remain as dominant in the next 50 years as it has been in the past?" He responded in the following tone:

But, seriously, it's a question worth asking. And since we are into speculative scenarios, I can think of at least three where the ruling party might continue to reign supreme.

Scenario 1: All change at the party

Most commentators, including Ho [Kwon Ping], who doubt the PAP's long-term ability to continue in power, have rightly identified the many challenges it faces. One of the most difficult for the party is its loss of control of information because of the proliferation of social media. Singapore society is also much more diverse and fragmented today. Many divisions have grown — liberal versus conservative, gay versus straight, local versus foreign making it difficult for any party to represent the broad middle ground. On the economic front, the fruits of growth are not as evenly distributed as before, and even the growth itself isn't a given.

But, ultimately, it is the party's response to these challenges that will determine if it will be able to continue winning the mandate to govern. Its ability to meet these challenges is increasingly being questioned as it grapples with complex issues on many policy fronts. From the feedback I get, there is a sizeable group of Singaporeans who say they supported the PAP in the early years but now feel it isn't the party they knew. Their criticisms: It has become elitist, is no longer in touch with the lives of ordinary people, and its market-driven policies have departed too much from its socialist roots.

Which raises the intriguing question: Can the party change and win over these one-time supporters? Is it possible for it to again be the party it was in the 1960s and 1970s, trusted by the people to overcome the odds that must have seemed even

---

5. See "The next 50 years in Singapore's politics", in *Singapore Management University* (13 November 2014), https://www.smu.edu.sg/news/2014/11/13/next-50-years-singapore-politics; The excerpts were published in *The Straits Times*, 21 October 2014.

more insurmountable than today's challenges? If it is able to make the changes — whatever these might be — and transform itself who is to say it will not regain its past dominance? But can it?

More pertinently, can change come from within, or will it have to be from without? Political parties elsewhere have had to face this same question whenever their survival has been at stake…To be fair, the PAP has responded to many of the issues that caused it to lose ground in the 2011 General Election. But whether the changes have been far-reaching enough for it to retain its dominance remains to be seen.

Scenario 2: Out and back again

The second scenario starts with the PAP unable to make the changes needed to stem its decline. It loses a general election and perhaps the next one as well. But the opposition party in power lacks the experience and wherewithal to govern well, fumbles badly, and loses the support of the people. The PAP is voted back in. Another 50 years? That will require the PAP to be so chastened by its years in opposition it renews itself in heroic fashion to recapture the people's trust. This comeback scenario isn't unique and has been replayed elsewhere, most recently with the Liberal Democratic Party of Japan. Don't rule out it happening here.

Scenario 3: A near-death experience

Many people attribute the PAP's long hold on power to the trauma that Singaporeans experienced when the country was expelled from Malaysia in 1965. That separation was so life-threatening, the people rallied behind the Government to make a superhuman effort to succeed. Might another near-death experience for Singapore result in a similar outcome? A long, deep and paralysing global recession? Conflicts in the region? A war between the major powers in Asia? Faced with impending danger, Singaporeans are more likely to want to unite than divide, possibly behind the party they know. Without this external threat to their survival, it is likely the opposition tide of recent years will continue, and erode the PAP's dominance.[6]

Interestingly too, in April 2014, in Prime Minister Lee Hsien Loong's luncheon meeting with Gideon Rachman of *The Financial Times*, reportedly, there was a hint that the PAP may consider a coalition government as the way forward. According

---

6. See Han Fook Kwang, "Singapore's future according to Lee Kuan Yew".

to Rachman, he asked Prime Minister Lee the question, "So can he envisage a day when the PAP is not running Singapore?" "It could well happen," he replied mildly. "I don't know how it will work but it could happen." A little later, he hinted that the PAP is beginning to consider the possibility of one day forming a coalition government. "It may not be one team in, one team out, it may be more complicated — you're getting used to more complicated than that in Britain now."[7]

When news of the interview was made public by *The Financial Times* and reported widely by the Singapore media, Prime Minister Lee clarified his position in a Facebook post by stating that "the possibility of Singapore having a coalition government was not what he had in mind." What he said was that "he could imagine a situation in the future where the PAP is not dominant, but that he had no idea how that would work, or whether it could be made to work at all…To think that instead of PAP dominance we will have a stable two-party system is naïve. Just look at the UK today — even there the two-party system is no longer what it was. A coalition government for Singapore was not on my mind."[8]

Notwithstanding Prime Minister Lee's rejection of a coalition government option in the near future, this brings to the discussion of whether the existing political structure and system will survive in the coming years and what kind of PAP's dominance or lack of it will exist in future? Will the current political system survive the post-Lee Hsien Loong era? The incumbent prime minister is expected to step down for his successor to takeover after the next general elections (probably in 2020 or 2021, and earliest in September 2019), probably mid-way in the term of the next government — a practice the PAP has pursued since Lee Kuan Yew handed power over to Goh Chok Tong and Goh Chok Tong to Lee Hsien Loong. Also, what would trigger an earlier or later change in the political succession of Singapore and in turn how it can impact upon the politics of PAP's dominance in Singapore, are worth considering.

In the context of the discussion by Ho Kwon Ping and Han Fook Kwang, one can theoretically posit five scenarios about the future of the PAP and in turn, about

---

7.   See Gideon Rachman, "Lunch with the FT: Lee Hsien Loong", *The Financial Times*, 11 April 2014, https://www.ft.com/content/4511f092-bf2c-11e3-8683-00144feabdc0#ixzz2ycVjBh1M

8.   Robin Chan, "Coalition govt was not on my mind: PM Lee", *The Straits Times*, 15 April 2014.

the resilience of the one-party dominance political system in Singapore. In the first scenario, the PAP remains in a state of unchallenged dominance. The PAP's political dominance continues undisputed for the next decade or so and this is primarily due to its ability to deliver the political goods and the weaknesses of the Opposition. In short, this is the status quo scenario.

In the second scenario, the PAP's dominance remains but this takes place in an environment of rising Opposition's challenge. Even though there is a growing challenge to the PAP's dominance, the Opposition is still unable to mount a serious enough challenge to dislodge the PAP from power.

In the third scenario, the PAP loses its dominance but continues to rule Singapore in a simple majority. Hence, the concept of Singapore as a one-party dominant state ends and the PAP is unable to muster a two-thirds majority but remains as the government through a simple majority. The loss of the PAP's dominance can be caused by either the rise of a credible alternative, either from outside the PAP or even through a breakup of the PAP itself.

In the fourth scenario, the PAP's maintains its dominance but only through a coalition government. Even though the Opposition is able to mount a challenge to PAP's dominance, still through coalition politics and as the senior partner, the PAP remains in power in a coalition government. As the PAP would have achieved the status as the natural party of governance, it would be able to muster sufficient support to form a coalition government. Dominance through coalition politics has happened in many former one-party states such as in India, Indonesia, Japan and Israel.

In the final scenario, the PAP is defeated at the polls and becomes an opposition party, either as a united entity or breaks up into several new parties, or even its members joining other parties, be it in government or in opposition. As the PAP's dominance collapses in the face of Opposition's rise, as happened to the *Barisan Nasional* (BN) in Malaysia in May 2018, the PAP once again reverts to its position as an opposition party, which it first achieved following the 1955 General Elections. The PAP's dominance can collapse as a consequence of its internal decomposition, especially in the post-Lee Kuan Yew and post-Lee Hsien Loong eras, caused by sharp policy differences, inability to agree on a successor, corruption or being accused of gross nepotism and cronyism. Additionally, external factors such as conflict with neighbours, its inability to deal with various external crises and most important of all, its mismanagement of the economy, can doom the PAP.

Following the defeat of the BN in May 2018, a Facebook post by Calvin Cheng aptly captured how the status of Singapore as a one-party dominant state can change in future. He started by quoting Lee Kuan Yew who said "that day will come" when the PAP loses power:

> But Lee Kuan Yew himself said many times that if one day the PAP turns corrupt and/or incompetent, the people should and will vote them out. As President Halimah recently said [in her inaugural Presidential Address in Parliament in May 2018], the right to govern isn't inherited and the 4G [Fourth Generation] leaders have to win the trust of the electorate themselves.
>
> Do not also forget that the biggest factor in the Malaysian oppositions shock win was former PM Mahathir Mohammad's joining the Opposition as its leader. He was post-independent Malaysia's longest serving and arguably its most respected Prime Minister. Several former UMNO heavyweights also threw their support behind the Opposition.
>
> Many have said that the only way the PAP could ever lose power is if there were a split at the top of the PAP who then leads the opposition — I tend to agree. This also is unlikely to happen in the short run in Singapore.[9]

Hence, the notion that the end of the one-party dominant state in Singapore is unlikely to happen is a flawed one. It has happened elsewhere and can also happen in Singapore. Hence, the longevity of any ruling party cannot be taken for granted. Also, the changing scenarios about PAP's future, including the possible collapse of PAP's dominance can be best understood through Amitai Etzioni's analysis of the political changes in Israel, especially the rise of the Mapai. According to Etzioni:

> Mapai can be fruitfully compared to other state founding parties which have become highly institutionalized in young nations [like India and Ghana]…All seems to have in common a leader and a party with the charismatic role of gaining independence and establishing a state; left of center ideologies and control over the labour organizations; state-regulated economies; [and] a high degree of economic dependence on external sources.[10]

---

9. Calvin Cheng, "A new era in Malaysia, lessons for Singapore", in *Facebook* (9 May 2018).

10. Amitai Etzioni, "Alternative Ways to Democracy: The Example of Israel", *Political Science Quarterly*, 1959, 74, p. 214; Michael Shalev, "The Political Economy of Labor-Party Dominance and Decline in Israel", in T.J. Pempel (ed.), *Uncommon Democracies: The One-Party Dominant Regimes* (Ithaca, New York: Cornell University Press, 1990), p. 125.

However, with changing political culture brought about by transformations in the composition and orientation of the electorate such as demographic shifts with the new majority antagonistic towards right-oriented policies and shifting to the left-of-centre or even left-oriented policies, the PAP's dominance can be easily undermined. Probably the biggest challenge facing the PAP would be to maintain its unity in the post-Lee Hsien Loong era. The key reason behind the collapse of one-party dominant states worldwide, including Southeast Asia, has been splits and fragmentation among the elites in the ruling party. With a dominant party split along the 'status quo' and 'reform' group, it can lead to disagreements and defections, in turn, reducing the electoral appeal of the ruling party and eventually leading to its downfall. In Singapore's case, the possible causes of disagreements could be over leadership succession and renewal, pro-welfare policies, housing and medical costs, immigration and even possibly, defence and foreign policy. How these hot-button issues are managed in the next decade or so will determine how strong the PAP will remain in future and how long more will a PAP-dominated one-party state survive in Singapore.

Yet, it is not all doom and gloom. Political experience elsewhere has also shown that dominant parties can develop the stamina and resilience to overcome challenges and continue their politics of dominance. Hence, in contrast to Maurice Durveger's view that dominant parties become rigid and ossified, A. Arian and S.H. Barnes argued, that such parties can also become adaptative through 'dynamic conservatism': "That the dominant party, even after decades in power, is capable of pragmatic change to retain power — that dominant parties are perennially pragmatic, responsive, and with proper leadership, capable of political adaptation."[11] Hence, in the face of a weakening PAP, it can also become more adaptative and responsive to change with its pragmatic instincts driving it to change, reinvent and survive. This can be driven not only by ideological steadfastness but stemming more from strategic considerations to survive and remain dominant. Since 1990, on two occasions, after suffering a dip in the electoral performance, namely, in 1991 and 2011, the PAP was able to bounce back with vigour and retain its dominance without any doubt. Whether this political behaviour and response will remain innate in the PAP's DNA and body politics is yet to be seen and will determine

---

11. Ellis Krauss and Jon Pierre, "The Decline of Dominant Parties: Parliamentary Politics in Sweden and Japan in the 1970s", in T.J. Pempel (ed.), *Uncommon Democracies: The One-Party Dominant Regimes* (Ithaca, New York: Cornell University Press, 1990), p. 228.

how much longer will it beat the odds and remain the longest-serving one-party dominant state in the non-communist world.

Still, the PAP continues to enjoy a number of advantages over its political opponents on a systemic basis. It continues to benefit from the success the party had in overcoming major challenges to Singapore since the late 1950s and early 1960s, and succeeded in creating a Singapore in its image. The system of state capitalism that was introduced by a 'socialist PAP' continues to provide the ruling party with a very high dose of strong performance legitimacy. Incumbency has also been an added advantage with a predominant PAP able to craft whatever political rules it wants that would be passed by parliament with ease. The PAP has also created an electoral system through various innovations that are often justified for public good but which eventually benefits the party, such as the EP, GRC, NCMP and NMP. The recent laws dealing with fake news is another example of what incumbency permits the PAP. The PAP has also benefitted by tapping on the supporting role of para-political bodies such as the PA, NTUC, Civil Service and the national media. With the Elections Department under the Prime Minister's Office and its ability to control the Electoral Review Committee, the PAP has been at liberty to draw and redraw electoral boundaries to strengthen its advantages and diminish its weaknesses. Incumbency and a long period of political power have also given the PAP an unfair advantage to recruit and co-opt talented individuals from the public and private sectors through the largesse of power, money and public image. Finally, in addition to the existence of a generally weak opposition, the PAP has remained united, largely through a strong Leninist-esque and highly secretive cadre system that has been designed since the late 1950s to safeguard the party from a hostile takeover from within. For the plethora of these reasons, the advantage seems clearly with the PAP and this will, failing surprises, keep the PAP in power for another two to three elections cycles.

This, however, cannot deny that some headway has been made by the Opposition compared to the past. This, in part, is due to the rise of new issues such as poverty, social immobility and rising all-round costs. It is also due to the fact that the ruling party has lost some control of the new media and where views, including anti-PAP narratives and highlighting of PAP's mistakes, can no longer be stopped. The fact that Singaporeans have been gripped by 'Oxleygate' and the prime minister's quarrel with his siblings led to the parliament holding a session to answer questions regarding his conduct, something his siblings could not do, did not place the image and credibility of the prime minister on a pedestal. The situation of 'Lee Kuan Yew-less' Singapore and PAP, and where the family quarrel is in public view, has not helped the prime minister or the ruling party. This is all the more as Prime Minister Lee Hsien Loong's sister-in-law and nephew are now subject to legal proceedings and where the prime minister's brother is seen to be openly supporting Tan Cheng Bock and the Opposition in general, representing a new phenomenon that never existed in the past. How this will be played out politically remains to be seen especially in a situation where there is no strong and charismatic PAP leader and where many mistakes are being made by the PAP-controlled government. How the new generation of Singaporeans and millennials, who have no idea of the past and the only suffering they have experienced is at the hands of the PAP, will view these developments remain to be seen. While the odds of the David defeating the Goliath seems unlikely, the chase is certainly on.

This would mean that the PAP is likely to remain in an advantageous and asymmetrical position vis-à-vis the opposition political parties for at least the next 10 years or so. To reiterate, even Pritam Singh, the leader of the Workers' Party (WP), talked of capturing one-third of parliamentary seats and not overthrowing the party, on grounds that this was Singapore's political reality. Even K. Shanmugam talked of no political party in the non-communist world surviving a seven-decade stint of being power, which means that the PAP has another 10 years of 'political cruise'. The Opposition remains weak, divided and unable to win the popular imagination that would be sufficient to give confidence to the voters that dislodging the PAP would be in the public and national benefit. While all the good, bad and ugly can be blamed on the PAP that has been in power since 1959, clearly, to date, the good, by a wide margin, far outweighs the bad and ugly. From that perspective, the Goliath PAP is not in danger of being overthrown by the David Opposition, not at least, from K. Shanmugam's calculus of a PAP that would be in power till 2029. After that, it will depend on the PAP and the Opposition, and how the voters judge these two key competing political forces in Singapore.

Parting shot — should the dominant PAP facilitate the rise of a stronger opposition in Singapore?

Repeatedly, the PAP leadership has stressed that it is not its duty and obligation to nurture and facilitate the growth of a political opposition in Singapore. By any count and in any normal situation, this is a fair position to take as politics is a struggle for power and the winning party has no obligation and even no business in helping its defeated political opponents. For instance, Singapore's first foreign minister, S. Rajaratnam did not believe in the existence of an effective opposition, which he saw as nothing more than "non-communist subversion". He believed in a one-party dominant state and argued that "the capacity of such a government to act far more independently than if it were harassed by an opposition and by proxies, is obvious" as "in the game of competitive interference, pawns which can behave like bishops and castles and knights, can in certain circumstances be extremely inconvenient and very irritating."[12] By and large, this has been the position of the PAP.

Yet, in reality, the PAP has also instituted political reforms that have benefitted the Opposition. A major one is the introduction of the Non-Constituency Member of Parliament (NCMP) scheme in 1984. An NCMP is an individual who had contested in the general elections and is deemed to have been elected as an MP by virtue of being one of the best performing losers. Beginning with provisions for three NCMPs if the Opposition had not won any seats, by the next general elections there could be up to 12 NCMPs, provided the Opposition does not win any seat in the general elections. In short, even if the Opposition does not win a single seat in the next general elections, the Opposition is guaranteed of 12 parliamentary seats and hence, PAP's political reforms have facilitated the presence of Opposition in parliament since 1984. In 1984, the sole NCMP seat was not filled. In 1988, two seats were filled but one of them was disqualified. In 1991, as the Opposition won four seats, no NCMP seats were offered. In 1997, 2001 and 2006, one NCMP seat was filled respectively. In 2011 and 2015, following the increased in the numbers of NCMP seats offered, three seats were filled respectively. These reforms and policies had the effect of increasing the presence of the Opposition in parliament even though the Opposition has argued that the NCMP scheme was an attempt by the ruling party to ensure that the electorate would be tempted not to vote in more opposition as some opposition members would already be present in parliament by the grace of the ruling party.

Still, in view of a number of factors, one can still make a case for the ruling party in Singapore to be more accommodating and conciliatory towards the Opposition.

---

12. See S. Rajaratnam, "Non-Communist Subversion in Singapore", in Seah Chee Meow (ed.), *Trends in Singapore: Proceedings and Background Papers* (Singapore: Singapore University Press, 1975), p. 118.

What this accommodation entails can be debated and discussed but there are two key reasons for this. First, despite attempts at establishing an opposition coalition by Tan Cheng Bock, by and large, the Opposition in Singapore remains weak, largely marginalised, and largely party- and even individual-based and centric. The political, economic and even psychological, as well as structural and institutional obstacles facing the Opposition are insurmountable. Unless the ruling party commits serious and severe mistakes, the PAP will be difficult to dislodge from power. Hence, the Opposition continues to face an uphill challenge even though minor breakthroughs have been made since 1981. Even the WP's chief, Pritam Singh stated in January 2019 that the medium-term goal of the party is to win one-third seats in parliament and not to displace the ruling PAP yet.[13] Nevertheless, these breakthroughs are not serious enough to pose any serious challenge to PAP's dominance in Singapore's politics and the opposition presence has remained nothing more than tokenism since 1981.

Second, even if the PAP faces an internal crisis and splits due to whatever reason, or is suddenly defeated at the polls, say in the next two general elections in 2030, due to issues relating to personality, ideology or policy differences, or issues stemming from corruption, cronyism and nepotism, the PAP would have done Singapore and its people a serious disservice as the Opposition that stumbles into power would be largely inadequate and incompetent to administer Singapore. Clearly, "Singapore is not in a position to do a Malaysia" today or in the next five to 10 years as the Opposition is largely unprepared to shoulder the burden of administering Singapore's domestic and foreign policies.

This is very different from Malaysia which had opposition political parties such as the Democratic Action Party (DAP), *Parti Keadilan Rakyat* (PKR) and even PAS that had immense experience in administering states in Malaysia and what more, had the benefit of experienced politicians such as Mahathir Mohamad and Muhyiddin Yassin to handle the reins of government in the post-Najib Razak and post-BN era. Unquestionably, there is no Mahathir or Muhyiddin in Singapore and not even a DAP, PKR or PAS that can replace the PAP. While everything would tend to indicate that the PAP's staying power and stranglehold on power in Singapore is likely to stay, still it would be beneficial to plan and take measures to prepare the

---

13. Ng Huiwen, "WP chief Pritam Singh wants party to aim to win a third of Parliament seats", *The Straits Times*, 15 January 2019.

Opposition in case the unthinkable happens whereby an electorate fuelled by anger votes out the PAP and hands power to the Opposition that is largely inexperienced to administer a 'First World' Singapore.

This will pose a serious dilemma for the PAP; the more unprepared the Opposition is to administer Singapore, the more likely the PAP will remain in power. However, as one-party dominant states do not last for too long, and simply waiting for the PAP to fracture and for one faction to lead the Opposition to capture power, or worse still, what if the PAP is suddenly voted out of power, the harm to Singapore could be irreparable. Would it not be a duty and obligation for the one-party dominant state to also think of Singapore and its interests to prepare an alternative government that will continue administering the Republic in the best interest of its people? This is something worth thinking about for the long-term health of the Republic and its people, and moving beyond facilitating opposition presence through the NCMP scheme. Can some kind of power-sharing scheme be implemented and more opposition members placed in Government Parliamentary Committees, etc.? It will be good to think through this and even engage in a public discourse on the issue as the long-term goal is for the future of Singapore and its people. Party politics is important but even more important is Singapore and its future survival!

HISTORY OF GENERAL ELECTIONS IN SINGAPORE, 1948–2015

1948

Date: 20 March 1948

No. of Political Parties Contesting: 1

Progressive Party

Winner: Progressive Party won three of the six elected seats.

Table

Party	Seats Won	Total Votes	Percentage of Votes
Progressive Party	3	11,754	49.5
Independents	3	11,997	50.5

Key Personalities

The leader of the Progressive Party (PP) was **Tan Chye Cheng** (陈才清), who was a Singaporean lawyer and politician. He was a scholar and was educated at St Joseph's Academy in London where he became friends with the Malaysian judge Ong Hock Thye. During the World War II, he left Singapore with his wife and upon coming back after the war, he became involved in politics. In 1947, the PP was formed and Tan became its first president. It was said that he was not a good public speaker but has managed to come to lead the PP.

Christopher John Laycock was born in 1887 and was a British lawyer who founded one of Singapore's earliest law firm known as Laycock and Ong. Singapore's founding father Lee Kuan Yew started practising law upon graduation at the same law firm. Lee then acted as an election agent for Laycock and the PP in the 1951 General Elections. Laycock was also a founder of the Race Course Golf Club in Singapore, which was the first multi-racial club in 1924.

Sardon Jubir contested in the 1948 General Elections in Singapore as an independent candidate. He was a Malaysian politician and had served illustriously in

Malaysian politics. In Malaysia, he held the post of minister of health, became Malaysia's ambassador to the United Nations and later, the *Yang di-Pertuan Negri* of Penang.

Developments

This was the first time general elections was held in Singapore and six seats out of the 22 seats on the Legislative Council were directly elected. Electoral boundaries were divided into four districts: Municipal North-East, Municipal South-West, Rural East and Rural West.

By-Elections

A by-election was held in the Rural West constituency on 16 October 1948, which an Independent Balwant Singh Bajaj won against another PP candidate, Cheong Hock Chye and an independent candidate, Garangam Maganlal. Bajaj won 55% of the majority votes. The by-election was in view of Srish Chandra Goho's passing.

Source(s):

https://en.wikipedia.org/wiki/Singaporean_general_election,_1948

http://eresources.nlb.gov.sg/history/events/44e7b06b-05b0-4255-869f-1528a5ac35e7

https://en.wikipedia.org/wiki/Rural_West_by-election,_1948

1951

Date: 10 April 1951

No. of Political Parties Contesting: 2

Progressive Party

Labour Party

Winner: Progressive Party won six out of the nine elected seats.

Table

Party	Seats Won	Total Votes	Percentage of Votes
Progressive Party	6	11,202	45.4
Labour Party	2	7,335	29.7
Independents	1	6,156	24.9

Key Personalities

Christopher John Laycock came again into the picture of the general elections as the vice-chairman for Progressive Party (PP). He was a front-running contestant in the 1951 General Elections and was known to be pro-colonial. Laycock played an important role of bringing **Lee Kuan Yew**, who was then working in his law firm, into the election team. More significant was it has provided Lee greater insights on Singapore politics since he acted as the campaign manager for Laycock in the 1951 General Elections. After which, Lee started playing a prominent role in the Singapore polity.

Another notable personality was **Lim Yew Hock** who was a third-generation Straits Chinese, a legal clerk and a trade unionist. Lim had a strong support from the English-speaking workers.[1] In 1948, Lim was appointed by the governor to represent workers' interests in the Legislative Council. Lim used to be part of PP but later left and joined the Labour Party in 1949. In the 1951 General Elections, Lim was a candidate for Keppel (South) and won one out of the two seats filled by Labour Party. He was also the leader for Labour Party in the elections.[2]

Finally, **Tan Chye Cheng** led the PP and won six seats out of the nine seats. The English-educated lawyer was one of the candidates for Tanglin.[3] Tan together with Laycock founded the PP. The party dominated the general elections in 1948 and 1951.[4] Reason being, the multi-racial party was able to attract English-educated professionals; hence gathering a wide spectrum of support from the society.[5]

Developments

In this elections, the number of seats elected into the Legislative Council increased from six seats to nine seats out of 25 seats. There were a total of nine

---

1. http://eresources.nlb.gov.sg/infopedia/articles/SIP_2018-01-26_111726.html

2. https://en.wikipedia.org/wiki/Singaporean_general_election,_1951

3. https://en.wikipedia.org/wiki/Singaporean_general_election,_1951

4. http://eresources.nlb.gov.sg/infopedia/articles/SIP_1150_2008-11-30.html

5. http://eresources.nlb.gov.sg/infopedia/articles/SIP_1150_2008-11-30.html

constituencies according to municipal districts, as follows — Balestier, Bukit Timah, Changi, City, Katong, Keppel, Rochore, Seletar and Tanglin. Voting was not compulsory.

By-Elections

Nil.

Source(s):

https://en.wikipedia.org/wiki/Singaporean_general_election,_1951

http://eresources.nlb.gov.sg/infopedia/articles/SIP_2018-01-26_111726.html

1955

Date: 2 April 1955

No. of Political Parties Contesting: 8

Labour Front

Progressive Party

Democratic Party

People's Action Party

Malayan Chinese Association (Singapore Alliance Party)

United Malays National Organisation (Singapore Alliance Party)

Labour Party

Malay Union (Singapore Alliance Party)

Winner: Labour Front won 10 seats but was insufficient for a 13-seat majority. Therefore, Labour Front sought coalition with Singapore Alliance Party and where its three component parties each won a seat.

Table

Party	Seats Won	Total Votes	Percentage of Votes
Labour Front	10	42,300	27.1
Progressive Party	4	38,695	24.8
Democratic Party	2	32,115	20.5
People's Action Party	3	13,634	8.7
Malayan Chinese Association (Singapore Alliance Party)	1	6,203	4.0
United Malays National Organisation (Singapore Alliance Party)	1	5,721	3.7
Labour Party	0	1,325	0.8
Malay Union (Singapore Alliance Party)	1	1,233	0.8
Independents	3	15,098	9.7

Key Personalities

Carried forward from the previous elections, the top Chinese lawyer **Tan Chye Cheng** founded the Tan, Rajah & Cheah law firm in 1947. He embarked on his political journey in 1946 as a member of the Advisory Council and had since held several political designations. In the 1955 General Elections, he contested in Tanglin as the chairman of the Progressive Party (PP). However, he lost his seat to the Labour Front (LF) leader David Marshall, also a lawyer, who received 48% of the votes compared to Tan's 36%.[6] This was seen as a great setback for both Tan and the party. After the 1955 General Elections, PP had since been in decline.

In 1954, **Lee Kuan Yew** founded the People's Action Party (PAP) which would later take part in the 1955 General Elections. The contest at Cairnhill attracted attention as it was a fierce contest between David Marshall from the LF and Tan Chye Cheng from the PP. As Tan was preferred by the British colonialists to be Singapore's first chief minister, the PAP attacked PP to bolster support for Marshall, which eventually led to the loss of Tan and the party failed to retain power. In the elections, PAP won three out of the four seats.[7]

6.　http://www.singapore-elections.com/general-election/1955/cairnhill.html

7.　http://eresources.nlb.gov.sg/infopedia/articles/SIP_1150_2008-11-30.html

Lee had previously worked in Laycock and Ong law firm but went ahead to establish his own law firm known as Lee and Lee in 1955. One of the reasons for his departure from the law firm could have been because Lee advocated strongly for the trade unions and spent his time largely doing pro bono work at Laycock and Ong.[8] However, Laycock and Ong did not agree with Lee on such matters and had written a letter asking Lee to report information for cases to Laycock and Ong before the acceptance of any cases.[9] Thereafter, Lee decided to form his own law firm together with Lee Kim Yew and Kwa Geok Choo.[10] The founding of the law firm was imperative because it had served as a fertile ground to identify and recruit political talents. From which, several of the lawyers and legal clerks from the law firm emerged as ministers for Singapore in the later ruling years, such as Chua Sian Chin and S. Ramasamy. Lee and Lee continued to be of importance in identifying potential political leaders until today.[11]

David Marshall was the first elected chief minister from 1955 to 1956 and was a diplomat, a distinguished criminal lawyer, leader of the LF and one of the founding members of the Workers' Party.[12] For the 1955 General Elections, Marshall was one of the candidates for Cairnhill and fought against Tan Chye Cheng, also known as C.C. Tan, who was representing PP and Tan Khang Khoo representing the Democratic Party. LF called for self-government through unity with the Federation of Malaya. Some of the topics proposed were on welfare, affordable housing loans, medical services, unemployment and so forth. The party also called for the amendment of Trade Unions Ordinance to allow unions to associate with lesser restraints.[13] Marshall was previously from PP but left the party because of incompatible opinions with C.C. Tan. In 1954, he led Singapore Socialist Party to form alliance with the Singapore Labour Party to form LF, which contested in the 1955 General Elections. Lim Yew Hock and Thomas Francis were part of LF. Marshall led the 13-man LF into winning 10 seats out of the 25 seats and he became Singapore's first chief minister.[14]

---

8. https://www.straitstimes.com/opinion/the-law-firm-mr-lee-tapped-for-political-talent

9. https://www.straitstimes.com/opinion/the-law-firm-mr-lee-tapped-for-political-talent

10. https://www.leenlee.com.sg/our-people/the-firm/

11. https://www.straitstimes.com/opinion/the-law-firm-mr-lee-tapped-for-political-talent

12. http://eresources.nlb.gov.sg/infopedia/articles/SIP_283_2005-01-13.html

13. http://eresources.nlb.gov.sg/infopedia/articles/SIP_2014-07-07_134339.html

14. http://eresources.nlb.gov.sg/history/events/e4354a49-ada7-4710-a691-c696314bfd07

Marshall was an excellent speaker and has made impactful speeches throughout his political journey. However, his opinions had always clashed with that of the PAP's leader Lee Kuan Yew.[15] Prior to Marshall's political journey, he did not serve as a lawyer but instead went into politics. During the period that Marshall was the chief minister, there were numerous civil unrests including the Hock Lee Bus Riots.[16] After which in 1956, Marshall resigned as a chief minister due to failure to achieve internal self-government and embarked on his law career.[17] Marshall notable achievements included the creation of Meet-the-People Session and the passing of Labour Ordinance to end long work shifts and so forth.[18]

Lim Yew Hock was part of LF and was regarded as one of the strongest opposition together with the PAP in the Legislative Assembly. Lim was also a Legislative councilor and had previously been part of the PP. Upon winning the elections, Lim acted as the minister for labour and welfare in the new government.[19]

Lim was known for his representation of the workers and the trade unions. He formed the Singapore Trades Union Congress (STUC), was president for the Labour Party and later on one of the founding members of the LF.[20] He took over the position of chief minister upon Marshall's resignation.[21] He was especially known for his hard-handed ruling during the Chinese Middle Schools riots in 1956.[22] However, it was at the cost of losing the support of the Chinese electorate in subsequent elections.

Developments

Electoral boundaries underwent major changes as compared to previous elections in Singapore. Previously, the electoral map was only divided into four major boundaries. In the 1955 General Elections, it evolved into 19 electoral boundaries.

---

15. http://eresources.nlb.gov.sg/infopedia/articles/SIP_283_2005-01-13.html

16. http://eresources.nlb.gov.sg/infopedia/articles/SIP_283_2005-01-13.html

17. http://eresources.nlb.gov.sg/history/events/cd9853ff-acdc-40bf-8dfa-da17041418a8

18. http://eresources.nlb.gov.sg/infopedia/articles/SIP_2014-07-07_134339.html

19. http://eresources.nlb.gov.sg/infopedia/articles/SIP_2014-07-07_134339.html

20. http://eresources.nlb.gov.sg/infopedia/articles/SIP_2014-07-07_134339.html

21. http://www.nas.gov.sg/archivesonline/photographs/record-details/d08ec780-1161-11e3-83d5-0050568939ad

22. http://eresources.nlb.gov.sg/infopedia/articles/SIP_2014-07-07_134339.html

- Bukit Panjang: Absorbed part of Bukit Timah and Seletar
- Cairnhill: Absorbed part of Balestier, Rochore and Tanglin
- Farrer Park: Carved out of Balestier
- Geylang: Carved out of Katong
- Havelock: Absorbed part of City, Keppel and Tanglin
- Kampong Kapor: Carved out of Rochore
- Pasir Panjang: Absorbed part of Bukit Timah and Keppel
- Paya Lebar: Absorbed part of Changi and Katong
- Punggol-Tampines: Carved out of Changi
- Queenstown: Absorbed part of Bukit Timah, Keppel and Tanglin
- Sembawang: Absorbed part of Bukit Timah and Seletar
- Serangoon: Absorbed part of Balestier, Changi and Seletar
- Southern Islands: Absorbed part of Bukit Timah and Keppel
- Stamford: Absorbed part of City and Rochore
- Tanjong Pagar: Absorbed part of City and Keppel
- Telok Ayer: Carved out of City
- Tiong Bahru: Carved out of Keppel
- Ulu Bedok: Carved out of Changi
- Whampoa: Carved out of Balestier

By-Elections[23]

Upon David Marshall's resignation, a by-election took place in Cairnhill. He then also challenged PAP's leader Lee Kuan Yew to resign, which resulted in a by-election in Tanjong Pagar, which Lee had won in the previous elections. Candidate from LF eventually lost Cairnhill to the candidate from Liberal Socialist Party, Soh Ghee Soon. Lee managed to retain his seat in Tanjong Pagar against another candidate from the Liberal Socialist Party.

1959

Date: 30 May 1959

No. of Political Parties Contesting: 13

People's Action Party

Singapore People's Alliance

Liberal Socialist Party

---

23. https://en.wikipedia.org/wiki/Singaporean_by-elections,_1957

United Malays National Organisation (Singapore Alliance Party)

Malayan Chinese Association (Singapore Alliance Party)

Workers' Party

Labour Front

Citizens' Party

Singapore Malay Union (Singapore Alliance Party)

Malayan Indian Congress (Singapore Alliance Party)

Partai Rakyat

Katong United Residents' Association

Pan-Malayan Islamic Party

Winner: PAP won 43 out of 51 seats.

Table

Party	Seats Won	Total Votes	Percentage of Votes
People's Action Party	43	281,891	54.1
Singapore People's Alliance	4	107,755	20.7
Liberal Socialist Party	0	42,805	8.2
United Malays National Organisation (Singapore Alliance Party)	3	27,448	5.3
Malayan Chinese Association (Singapore Alliance Party)	0	5,593	1.1
Workers' Party	0	4,127	0.8
Labour Front	0	3,414	0.7
Citizens' Party	0	3,210	0.6
Singapore Malay Union (Singapore Alliance Party)	0	2,819	0.5
Malayan Indian Congress (Singapore Alliance Party)	0	2,092	0.4
Partai Rakyat	0	2,006	0.4
Katong United Residents' Association	0	1,759	0.3
Pan-Malayan Islamic Party	0	1,011	0.2
Independents	1	35,341	6.8

Key Personalities

Lim Yew Hock from the Labour Front had played a crucial role in helping Singapore to be out of control of the British colonial power. He had many talks with the British colonial power and finally agreed on the basis of complete internal self-government.[24] Hence, the 1959 General Elections was Singapore's first fully elected government.[25] However, the chief minister along with his other ministers eventually resigned upon PAP's winning of the 1959 General Elections.

Despite the People's Action Party being the opposition party then and facing accusations of recruiting Marxists and espousing communist ideals during the elections, its leader **Lee Kuan Yew** managed to push 51 candidates to run for the elections. The party had preached the idea of "stable, honest and just government", which had garnered huge support from the electorates and eventually won 43 out of the 51 seats.[26] Lim's resignation was an advantage for Lee who would later become Singapore's first prime minister.

Developments

Although the 1959 General Elections had seen Singapore's first fully elected government, internal security and defence remained under the control of the British colonial authorities.[27] It was not until 1965 that Singapore achieved full independence as a sovereign state. Singapore would continue to exercise control of its internal affairs even under its terms of engagement in Malaysia from September 1963 to August 1965 even though there were many issues that involved internal affairs between Singapore and the Federal Malaysian government during this period. It is also important to note that from 1959 onwards, voting was compulsory for all

---

24. http://eresources.nlb.gov.sg/history/events/bad3de1d-21ce-48de-99b6-6e717e47328e

25. http://eresources.nlb.gov.sg/history/events/bad3de1d-21ce-48de-99b6-6e717e47328e

26. http://eresources.nlb.gov.sg/history/events/bad3de1d-21ce-48de-99b6-6e717e47328e

27. http://eresources.nlb.gov.sg/history/events/bad3de1d-21ce-48de-99b6-6e717e47328e

Singaporean citizens.[28] This was to ensure that all Singaporeans were guaranteed the rights to vote for their government.

1963

Date: 21 September 1963

No. of Political Parties Contesting: 8

People's Action Party

Barisan Sosialis

Singapore Alliance

United People's Party

Partai Rakyat

Pan-Malayan Islamic Party

United Democratic Party

Workers' Party

Winner: PAP won 37 out of 51 seats.

Table

Party	Seats Won	Total Votes	Percentage of Votes
People's Action Party	37	272,924	46.9
Barisan Sosialis	13	193,301	33.2
Singapore Alliance	0	48,967	8.4
United People's Party	1	48,785	8.4
Partai Rakyat	0	8,259	1.4
Pan-Malayan Islamic Party	0	1,545	0.3
United Democratic Party	0	760	0.1
Workers' Party	0	286	0.1
Independents	0	6,788	1.2

28. http://www.nas.gov.sg/archivesonline/private_records/record-details/e5c9a2a0-115b-11e3-83d5-0050568939ad

Key Personalities

The 1963 General Elections was the third and final Legislative Assembly elections in Singapore. It was called on a 'short notice'[29] by **Lee Kuan Yew**, then prime minister, at an arguably well-calculated time. That is, just five days after Lee's People's Action Party (PAP) had successfully led Singapore to merge with the Federation of Malaya on 16 September, collectively forming the Federation of Malaysia.

One Eng Guan, previously part of the PAP in the 1959 General Elections, was expelled from the party in 1960. He and two others in the Assembly who had sided with him were dismissed on grounds of disavowing the "principles of collective leadership".[30] In 1961, Ong founded the United People's Party (UPP) after winning the Hong Lim by-election as an independent candidate against a member of the PAP.

Lee Siew Choh was a strong opposition leader who had opposed the merger with Malaya. The *Barisan Sosialis* member joined the PAP in 1958 after being persuaded by Goh Keng Swee.[31] However, in 1963, Lee Siew Choh was detained for being suspected of participating in the City Hall riot.[32] The Cantonese leader lost his seat in Rochore but *Barisan Sosialis* won 13 seats.[33]

Lim Chin Siong was one of the founders of PAP together with Lee Kuan Yew and Fong Swee Suan. Lim was an intelligent and charismatic speaker who had good ties with many trade unions and was popular among the Chinese workers.[34] He held his opinion strongly as a leftist in the PAP and was well-known for his fierce speeches in Hokkien, which appealed to the Chinese electorate. Lim often clashed with Lee due to his left-leaning opinions and eventually led to the expulsion of Lim

---

29. Stephanie Ho, "History of general elections in Singapore", in *Singapore Infopedia, National Library Board* (1 September 2014), http://eresources.nlb.gov.sg/infopedia/articles/SIP_549_2004-12-28.html

30. "Ong: The full story", *The Straits Times*, 21 June 1960, http://eresources.nlb.gov.sg/newspapers/Digitised/Article/straitstimes19600621-1.2.2

31. http://eresources.nlb.gov.sg/infopedia/articles/SIP_706_2005-01-12.html

32. http://eresources.nlb.gov.sg/infopedia/articles/SIP_706_2005-01-12.html

33. http://eresources.nlb.gov.sg/infopedia/articles/SIP_706_2005-01-12.html

34. http://eresources.nlb.gov.sg/infopedia/articles/SIP_1462_2009-02-18.html

and other left-leaning comrades from the PAP in 1961.[35] In 1963, Lim was arrested for links with the communist party and detained under the Preservation of Public Security Ordinance (now known as Internal Security Act).[36] He was imprisoned from 1963 to 1969.

Fong Swee Suan had very close ties with Lim Chin Siong and was also a left-leaning leader. The trio, Lee Kuan Yew, Lim Chin Siong and Fong Swee Suan, were the pioneers in the formation of PAP despite differing views on the Singapore polity. Like Lim, Fong was also an active advocator for the workers and worked with the trade unions. Fong was eventually expelled from the PAP together with Lim and other left-leaning members in the PAP. They then formed the *Barisan Sosialis*.[37] Despite being known to be close to the communists and leftists, Fong claimed that that he was a socialist rather than a pro-communist.[38]

Developments

The 1963 General Elections was deemed as a crucial period for the politics of Singapore. It was a period of discussions and negotiations between British colonial power, Singapore and Malaya. The talks covered, among others, the terms of decolonisation from the British and merger with Malaya. Another area that was of important concern was the spread of communism. Furthermore, it was an election in which all seats were contested by the opposition and independents.[39]

In 1963, the *Barisan Sosialis* alleged to have acted on behalf of the communists but disguised as a legitimate opposition party. Some of the known members were Lim Chin Siong, Fong Swee Suan and Hoe Puay Choo who left the PAP to join the *Barisan Sosialis*.[40] It was also said that *Barisan Sosialis* had ties with communist parties in Malaysia and Indonesia. The Operation Coldstore on 2 February 1963 led to the detention of left-wing opposition leaders. This resulted in the near obliteration

---

35. http://eresources.nlb.gov.sg/infopedia/articles/SIP_1462_2009-02-18.html

36. http://eresources.nlb.gov.sg/infopedia/articles/SIP_1462_2009-02-18.html

37. http://eresources.nlb.gov.sg/infopedia/articles/SIP_2013-07-29_173512.html

38. http://eresources.nlb.gov.sg/infopedia/articles/SIP_2013-07-29_173512.html

39. https://sg.news.yahoo.com/ge2015-9-key-figures-1963-060540771.html

40. http://www.singapore-elections.com/general-election/1963/

of the pro-communists and left-wing elements in Singapore, smoothening the way for Singapore's merger with Malaysia. After separation of Singapore from Malaysia in August 1965, the PAP emerged dominant in Singapore's politics with no apparent challenger.

Although in this elections, *Barisan Sosialis* managed to win 13 seats in the parliament, PAP won the majority of 37 seats, which strengthened its power base. The elections and politics of 1963 was characterised by the internal split within the PAP with Lim Chin Siong and Fong Swee Suan embracing diverging ideology from Lee Kuan Yew.

1968

Date: 19 April 1968

No. of Political Parties Contesting: 2

People's Action Party

Workers' Party

Winner: PAP won all 58 seats.

Table

Party	Seats Won	Total Votes	Percentage of Votes
People's Action Party	58	65,812	86.7
Workers' Party	0	3,049	4.0
Independents	0	7,033	9.3

Key Personalities

Lee Kuan Yew, Singapore's prime minister since 1959, led the People's Action Party in the first general elections of independent Singapore.

Prior to the 1968 General Elections, **Toh Chin Chye** was the vice chancellor of the University of Singapore (now National University of Singapore). He played a significant role in shaping Singapore's educational scene. Since winning the general elections in 1968, he had played multiple roles, managing his responsibilities in the cabinet as well as the educational sector. He saw education as one of the key aspects towards national development.[41] Upon winning one of the 58 seats in 1968, he served as the minister for science and technology. Toh was also the chairman of Singapore Polytechnic from 1959 to 1975.[42] As the 1960s was a period of industrialisation, Toh's efforts were remarkable as he pushed for tertiary education to focus more on engineering and architecture.[43]

S. Rajaratnam advised the Opposition to "think about their role in a democratic constitution". He was then acting in the capacity of Singapore's minister for foreign affairs.[44] As Singapore's first minister to hold the foreign affairs portfolio, he played a pivotal role of helping the young nation to build good relationships with Singapore's neighbours, establishing the Association of Southeast Asian Nations (ASEAN) and so forth.[45] Rajaratnam thus can be said to have been the key figure in setting out a solid foundation for the diplomatic ties between Singapore and other nations. Upon winning the 1968 General Elections, Rajaratnam also assumed the position of the minister for labour.[46]

Developments

The 1968 General Elections was the first poll that was held by Singapore after its independence.[47] Since new constituencies had been added, the PAP was said to have won in many constituencies even before the final results of the elections were out, as many of them were uncontested. Out of the 58 seats, only seven seats were contested.[48] The PAP was also the only party to have fielded candidates in all the

---

41. http://eresources.nlb.gov.sg/infopedia/articles/SIP_647_2005-01-11.html

42. http://eresources.nlb.gov.sg/infopedia/articles/SIP_644_2005-01-10.html

43. http://eresources.nlb.gov.sg/infopedia/articles/SIP_647_2005-01-11.html

44. http://www.nas.gov.sg/archivesonline/audiovisual_records/record-details/4d82598a-1164-11e3-83d5-0050568939ad

45. http://eresources.nlb.gov.sg/infopedia/articles/SIP_644_2005-01-10.html

46. http://eresources.nlb.gov.sg/infopedia/articles/SIP_644_2005-01-10.html

47. http://eresources.nlb.gov.sg/infopedia/articles/SIP_549_2004-12-28.html

48. http://eresources.nlb.gov.sg/infopedia/articles/SIP_549_2004-12-28.html

constituencies.[49] This eventually resulted in an absolute win for the PAP which has been the only ruling party governing Singapore since then. It is however important to note that *Barisan Sosialis* did not take part in the 1968 General Elections.[50] This could have contributed to the victory of the PAP in 1968.

1972

Date: 2 September 1972

No. of Political Parties Contesting: 6

People's Action Party

Workers' Party

United National Front

Barisan Sosialis

People's Front

Pertubuhan Kebangsaan Melayu Singapura

Winner: PAP won all 65 seats.

Table

Party	Seats Won	Total Votes	Percentage of Votes
People's Action Party	65	524,892	70.4
Workers' Party	0	90,885	12.2
United National Front	0	55,001	7.4
Barisan Sosialis	0	34,483	4.6
People's Front	0	22,462	3.0
Pertubuhan Kebangsaan Melayu Singapura	0	10,054	1.3
Independents	0	7,462	1.0

49. http://www.nas.gov.sg/archivesonline/audiovisual_records/record-details/4d82598a-1164-11e3-83d5-0050568939ad

50. http://eresources.nlb.gov.sg/history/events/be7d138c-56fc-4957-a949-3143d52d6220

Key Personalities

Lee Kuan Yew remained Singapore's prime minister, first from 1959 to 1965, when Singapore was a self-governing colony and later, as part of Malaysia. He also became Singapore's first prime minister following Singapore's separation from Malaysia in August 1965.

J.B. Jeyaretnam was the leader of the WP in the 1972 General Elections. He held leadership of the party from 1971 to 2001, and after participating in a number of electoral contests, he became the first opposition member to enter parliament in 1981 following the Anson by-election.

1976

Date: 23 December 1976

No. of Political Parties Contesting: 8

People's Action Party

Workers' Party

United Front

Barisan Sosialis

United People's Front

Pertubuhan Kebangsaan Melayu Singapura

Singapore Justice Party

People's Front

Winner: PAP won all 69 seats.

Table

Party	Seats Won	Total Votes	Percentage of Votes
People's Action Party	69	590,169	74.1
Workers' Party	0	91,966	11.5
United Front	0	53,373	6.5
Barisan Sosialis	0	25,411	3.2

(Continued)

(*Continued*)

Party	Seats Won	Total Votes	Percentage of Votes
United People's Front	0	14,233	1.8
Pertubuhan Kebangsaan Melayu Singapura	0	9,230	1.2
Singapore Justice Party	0	5,199	0.7
People's Front	0	2,818	0.3
Independents	0	4,173	0.5

Key Personalities

Chiam See Tong, who first contested in the 1976 General Elections, went on to become one of Singapore's longest-serving opposition member alongside the former WP leader, Low Thia Khiang. Chiam founded the SDP and later joined the SPP and helped found the SDA.

Tony Tan Keng Yam, who entered politics via a by-election in 1979, went on to become one of Singapore's leading politicians, helming key ministries, becoming the Republic's deputy prime minister and later, president.

1980

Date: 23 December 1980

No. of Political Parties Contesting: 8

People's Action Party

Workers' Party

United People's Front

Singapore United Front

Barisan Sosialis

Pertubuhan Kebangsaan Melayu Singapura

Singapore Democratic Party

Singapore Justice Party

Winner: PAP won all 75 seats.

Table

Party	Seats Won	Total Votes	Percentage of Votes
People's Action Party	75	494,268	77.7
Workers' Party	0	39,590	6.2
United People's Front	0	28,586	4.5
Singapore United Front	0	27,522	4.3
Barisan Sosialis	0	16,488	2.6
Pertubuhan Kebangsaan Melayu Singapura	0	13,435	2.1
Singapore Democratic Party	0	11,292	1.8
Singapore Justice Party	0	5,271	0.8

1984

Date: 23 December 1976

No. of Political Parties Contesting: 9

People's Action Party

Workers' Party

Singapore United Front

Singapore Democratic Party

United People's Front

Barisan Sosialis

Singapore Justice Party

Pertubuhan Kebangsaan Melayu Singapura

Angkatan Islam

Winner: PAP won 77 seats out of 79 seats. Workers' Party and Singapore Democratic Party each won a seat.

Table			
Party	Seats Won	Total Votes	Percentage of Votes
People's Action Party	77	568,310	64.8
Workers' Party	1	110,939	12.7
Singapore United Front	0	87,197	9.9
Singapore Democratic Party	1	32,102	3.7
United People's Front	0	27,217	3.1
Barisan Sosialis	0	24,212	2.8
Singapore Justice Party	0	10,906	1.2
Pertubuhan Kebangsaan Melayu Singapura	0	4,768	0.5
Angkatan Islam	0	359	0.0
Independents	0	10,586	1.2

1988

Date: 3 September 1988

No. of Political Parties Contesting: 8

People's Action Party

Workers' Party

Singapore Democratic Party

National Solidarity Party

United People's Front

Singapore Justice Party

Pertubuhan Kebangsaan Melayu Singapura

Angkatan Islam Singapura

Winner: PAP won 80 out of 81 seats. Singapore Democratic Party won one seat.

Table			
Party	Seats Won	Total Votes	Percentage of Votes
People's Action Party	80	848,029	63.2
Workers' Party	0	224,473	16.7
Singapore Democratic Party	1	158,341	11.8
National Solidarity Party	0	50,432	3.8
United People's Front	0	17,282	1.3
Singapore Justice Party	0	14,660	1.1
Pertubuhan Kebangsaan Melayu Singapura	0	13,526	1.0
Angkatan Islam Singapura	0	280	0.02
Independents	0	15,412	1.1

1991

Date: 31 August 1991

No. of Political Parties Contesting: 6

People's Action Party

Workers' Party

Singapore Democratic Party

National Solidarity Party

Singapore Justice Party

Pertubuhan Kebangsaan Melayu Singapura

Winner: PAP won 80 out of 81 seats. Singapore Democratic Party won one seat.

Table			
Party	Seats Won	Total Votes	Percentage of Votes
People's Action Party	77	477,760	61.0
Workers' Party	1	112,010	14.3
Singapore Democratic Party	3	93,856	12.0
National Solidarity Party	0	57,306	7.3
Singapore Justice Party	0	15,222	1.9
Pertubuhan Kebangsaan Melayu Singapura	0	12,862	1.6
Independents	0	14,596	1.9

1997

Date: 2 January 1997

No. of Political Parties Contesting: 6

People's Action Party

Singapore Democratic Party

Workers' Party

National Solidarity Party

Singapore People's Party

Democratic Progressive Party

Winner: PAP won 81 out of 83 seats. Workers' Party won one seat and Singapore Democratic Party won three seats.

Table			
Party	**Seats Won**	**Total Votes**	**Percentage of Votes**
People's Action Party	81	465,751	65.0
Workers' Party	1	101,544	14.2
Singapore Democratic Party	0	76,129	10.6
National Solidarity Party	0	48,322	6.7
Singapore People's Party	1	16,746	2.3
Democratic Progressive Party	0	5,043	0.4
Independents	0	3,210	0.4

2001

Date: 3 November 2001

No. of Political Parties Contesting: 5

People's Action Party

Singapore Democratic Alliance

Singapore Democratic Party

Workers' Party

Democratic Progressive Party

Winner: PAP won 82 out of 84 seats. Singapore Democratic Party and Workers' Party each won one.

Table

Party	Seats Won	Total Votes	Percentage of Votes
People's Action Party (PAP)	82	470,765	75.3
Singapore Democratic Alliance	1	75,248	12.0
Singapore Democratic Party	0	50,607	8.1
Workers' Party	1	19,060	3.0
Democratic Progressive Party	0	5,334	0.9
Independents	0	4,253	0.7

2006

Date: 6 May 2006

No. of Political Parties Contesting: 4

People's Action Party

Workers' Party

Singapore Democratic Alliance

Singapore Democratic Party

Winner: PAP won 82 out of 84 seats. Workers' Party and Singapore Democratic Alliance each won one.

Table

Party	Seats Won	Total Votes	Percentage of Votes
People's Action Party	82	748,130	66.6
Workers' Party	1	183,578	16.3
Singapore Democratic Alliance	1	145,628	13.0
Singapore Democratic Party	0	45,937	4.1

2011

Date: 7 May 2011

No. of Political Parties Contesting: 7

People's Action Party

Workers' Party

National Solidarity Party

Singapore Democratic Party

Reform Party

Singapore People's Party

Singapore Democratic Alliance

Winner: PAP won 81 (including the 5 uncontested seats) out of 87 seats. Workers' Party won six seats.

Table

Party	Seats Won	Total Votes	Percentage of Votes
People's Action Party	81 (including the 5 uncontested seats)	1,212,154	60.1
Workers' Party	6	258,510	12.8
National Solidarity Party	0	242,682	12.0
Singapore Democratic Party	0	97,369	4.8
Reform Party	0	86,294	4.3
Singapore People's Party	0	62,639	3.1
Singapore Democratic Alliance	0	55,988	2.8

Key Personalities

Prime Minister **Lee Hsien Loong** made a rare apology to Singaporeans, saying that the party is "sorry if [they] didn't get it right."[51]

---

51. https://sg.news.yahoo.com/blogs/singaporescene/pm-lee-didn-t-m-sorry-152850327.html

Chiam See Tong, secretary-general of the Singapore People's Party, left Potong Pasir Single Member Constituency (SMC) — in which his wife competed instead — to contest in the Bishan-Toa Payoh Group Representation Constituency (GRC). He and his team, however, lost to the People's Action Party (PAP). His wife was also defeated by PAP's Sitoh Yih Pin by a slim margin of 0.8%.

Previously contesting in Hougang SMC, Workers' Party chief **Low Thia Khiang** took the risk to compete in the Aljunied GRC with his other teammates, Chen Show Mao, Sylvia Lim, Pritam Singh, and Muhamad Faisal Manap. Low eventually led the Workers' Party to victory in that constituency for the first time.

Kenneth Jeyaretnam took over as the secretary-general of the Reform Party (RP) after his father's passing in 2008. The latter was also the founder of the party. The 2011 General Elections was the first of which the party had contested in, and it was also then that Kenneth Jeyaretnam had given his first election rally speech. According to its constitution, the RP aims to ensure that the parliament is "sovereign" and formed in accordance to the public's votes, to represent the people and hold the executive accountable "for every decision and policy"[52]; to ensure "an independently appointed Judiciary to uphold the Constitution and protect the citizens' rights from any interference by the Executive to deny the citizens fullest expression of their rights guaranteed to them by the Constitution"; "to secure to every member of the society his full political, social and economic rights"; and "to effect a fairer and just distribution of the wealth of the country and to eliminate poverty."[53]

Nicole Seah from the National Solidarity Party (NSP) "rose to fame"[54] as a notable member of the Opposition despite being one of the youngest in politics. She competed in the Marine Parade GRC and was often compared with the PAP's Tin Pei Ling — the latter not as well-liked on social media as Seah herself. A sense of the two's popularity can be gathered from, for instance, the number of 'likes' on Facebook that each had received: 98,493 for Seah, and only 7,396 for Tin.[55]

---

52. http://reform.sg/about-2/ourconstitution/

53. http://reform.sg/about-2/ourconstitution/

54. https://www.straitstimes.com/politics/former-nsp-star-nicole-seah-now-with-wp-in-east-coast-grc

55. http://lkyspp2.nus.edu.sg/ips/wp-content/uploads/sites/2/2013/08/Nikki_A-Personal-View-of-Social-Media-in-GE-2011_010911.pdf

Interestingly, however, Seah's online popularity did not translate into a victory for the NSP in the Marine Parade GRC.

Developments

The 2011 General Elections is commonly referred to as a watershed election given that the dominant party, PAP, had performed its worst since Singapore's independence in 1965. The five-seat Aljunied GRC went to the WP, making this the first time that the PAP had lost a GRC to the Opposition since "the system was introduced in the 1988 general election."[56] Following this was the retirement of the former anchor minister of the GRC, George Yeo, from politics. The WP also continued its hold in Hougang SMC and thus won a total of six seats in parliament — the most any opposition party had won since 1965.

By-Elections

A by-election was held in Hougang SMC in 2012, and it was the first of such in 20 years. This came after the dismissal of Yaw Shin Leong from the WP on grounds of him having "extramarital affairs"[57] shrouded in secrecy. This went against the WP's core principles of "transparency and accountability".[58] Nonetheless, the WP, this time represented by Png Eng Huat, saw victory once more in Hougang SMC against PAP's Desmond Choo.

Another by-election was held in Punggol East SMC in 2013. WP's Lee Li Lian won with 54.52% of valid votes, a 10.5% advantage over her closest opponent, PAP's Koh Poh Koon. The by-election was in place due to Michael Palmer's resignation from the PAP as a result of an extramarital affair.[59]

---

56. http://eresources.nlb.gov.sg/history/events/fc853af7-5476-439c-83b2-7ff9469d6037

57. https://www.channelnewsasia.com/news/singapore/yaw-shin-leong-not-appealing-against-expulsion-8439846

58. https://www.channelnewsasia.com/news/singapore/yaw-shin-leong-not-appealing-against-expulsion-8439846

59. https://www.straitstimes.com/singapore/commentary-punggol-east-by-election-was-a-tipping-point

2015

Date: 11 September 2015

No. of Political Parties Contesting: 9

People's Action Party

Workers' Party

Singapore Democratic Party

National Solidarity Party

Reform Party

Singaporeans First

Singapore People's Party

Singapore Democratic Alliance

People's Power Party

Winner: PAP won 83 out of 89 seats. Workers' Party won six seats.

Table

Party	Seats Won	Total Votes	Percentage of Votes
People's Action Party	83	1,579,183	69.9
Workers' Party	6	282,143	12.5
Singapore Democratic Party	0	84,931	3.8
National Solidarity Party	0	79,826	3.5
Reform Party	0	59,517	2.6
Singaporeans First	0	50,867	2.3
Singapore People's Party	0	49,107	2.2
Singapore Democratic Alliance	0	46,550	2.1
People's Power Party	0	25,475	1.1
Independents	0	2,780	0.1

Key Personalities

Prime Minister **Lee Hsien Loong** led his party to a comeback in the 2015 General Elections, although many had thought that the People's Action Party (PAP) would fare poorly, after the watershed election of 2011. Some argued that it was due to the passing of Lee Kuan Yew, Lee Hsien Loong's father, who was also the first prime minister of Singapore and secretary-general of the PAP.

Chee Soon Juan, chief of the Singapore Democratic Party (SDP), gave his first "election rally speech"[60] in 15 years at the 2015 General Elections. His last electoral contest was in 2001, before he was sued by previous prime ministers, Goh Chok Tong and Lee Kuan Yew, in the same year. A case was made against him on grounds of defamation because of his claim that the PAP government had lost S$18 billion in a loan to Indonesia's president, Suharto. Unable to pay, Chee was then declared bankrupt and barred from competing in elections. He was discharged from his bankruptcy in 2012 after paying a reduced sum of S$30,000 — of which both Goh and Lee were willing to accept. In 2015, Chee then led his team to compete in the Holland-Bukit Timah Group Representation Constituency (GRC). He also commented that the SDP's rally speeches were centred around the theme of Singaporeans coping with the "cost of living and sustaining their livelihood."[61]

At the age of 80, **Chiam See Tong**, secretary-general of the Singapore People's Party, did not compete in the election for the first time since 1976.[62] Nonetheless, he was still present at rallies and at Kong Hwa School, one of the vote-counting sites, to support his wife. Despite his health problems, he still remains involved in the country's political scene. In fact, 2015 marked "an almost 30-year career in parliament, where Chiam became Singapore's longest-serving opposition MP."[63]

---

60. Idayu Supart, "GE2015: SDP's Chee Soon Juan says 'crowd kept him going' at first rally speech in 15 years", *The Straits Times*, 4 September 2015, https://www.straitstimes.com/politics/ge2015-sdps-chee-soon-juan-says-crowd-kept-him-going-at-first-rally-speech-in-15-years

61. https://www.straitstimes.com/politics/ge2015-sdps-chee-soon-juan-says-crowd-kept-him-going-at-first-rally-speech-in-15-years

62. https://sg.news.yahoo.com/ge2015--chiam-see-tong--the-people-s-politician-062433261.html

63. https://sg.news.yahoo.com/ge2015--chiam-see-tong--the-people-s-politician-062433261.html

COMMENTS BY PAP LEADERS ON A ONE-PARTY DOMINANT STATE IN SINGAPORE

1. Lee Hsien Loong, Prime Minister, April 2011

Speech by Prime Minister Lee Hsien Loong at Kent Ridge Ministerial Forum 2011, 5 April 2011 at the University Cultural Centre

"Leadership Renewal: The 4th Generation & Beyond"

1. The theme you have chosen for me this evening, "Leadership Renewal: The 4th Generation & Beyond" is a timely one for two reasons.
2. Firstly, it is a vital question which concerns your future. Secondly, it is going to be an important issue in the forthcoming general elections. But important as it is for us in Singapore, by the standards of other countries, to talk about future leadership, and then the future, future leadership, is a luxury.
3. Today, my colleagues and I are doing our duties. They call us the 3rd generation leadership. And I think we can serve Singapore for another decade before we grow too old. So when we talk about the 4th generation leadership, we are planning, not for the next ten years, but for the ten years after that, beyond 2020.
4. Very few countries worry about leadership so far into the future. Either the leaders on all sides are preoccupied with immediate problems or they are completely busy, taken up with staying in power, and winning the next elections. Singapore is different. Why do we in Singapore have this luxury, and indeed this necessity, to worry about this long term future?
5. We have been stable for the last five decades. The PAP has been in power for all of that time. We have had two leadership renewals. We are bringing in and grooming a 4th generation leadership in this election. We are thinking beyond that to continue to find good people to come and serve Singapore.
6. Tonight, I would like to discuss two aspects of this issue. First, how did it come about that we are sitting pretty like this? When I say we are sitting pretty like this, I mean Singapore is sitting pretty like this. And secondly, how can Singapore continue to do well for many years to come?
7. Today, the PAP is politically dominant and people take it for granted. But we did not start like that. It happened partly because of historical accident. In the

early years, before independence, there were ferocious battles, both among the political parties and even within the PAP. Within the PAP, the communists and their sympathisers on one side, and the non-communists on the other side, battled over the future of Singapore and over political control of the country, or at that time, of a self-governing state.

8. Eventually in 1961, the leftists split off from the PAP and they formed the Barisan Sosialis, went into the opposition and for a time, the PAP and the opposition were almost evenly matched in Parliament. In fact, there was a period when the PAP was a minority government with less than half the seats in the legislative assembly.

9. Then in 1966, after Independence, the Barisan Sosialis made a strategic mistake. Lee Siew Choh, who was their leader, took the party out of Parliament and onto the streets and ceded the political ground to the PAP. So in the general elections after that, in 1968, the PAP made a clean sweep, and it has remained dominant ever since.

10. But long ago, events in the 1960s are not the only reason why we are here today. The actions that the PAP has taken over the last 50 years have been crucial. Firstly, the inclusive policies which were pursued. Secondly, the consensus politics we have fostered. Thirdly, the political system which we have built to work for Singapore, and fourthly, the leadership we have built, and the leadership renewal which we have implemented, which has made this whole system work.

11. But firstly, it works because the PAP pursued policies which gave all citizens a stake in the country. We brought all citizens, whether you are rich, whether you are poor, whether you are Chinese or Malay, whether you are blue-collar or white-collar, to have a stake in Singapore and brought their interests close together so that the interests align with the interest of the country. We promoted growth, we created jobs and we raised incomes for everybody. We invested in education to give every child a bright future. We promoted home ownership for all, and gave every household a substantial nest-egg to protect. We created an egalitarian and meritocratic society, where everybody is comfortable to mingle with one another — you go to the same hawker centres, you jog in the same parks, whether you are rich or poor, and even the poorest families in the land can aspire to have their children — if they work hard, and are talented and do well — rise to the top.

12. Having given everybody an interest in the progress of the country, the PAP then sought to represent a broad mass of Singaporeans and not just a segment of Singaporeans. Again, whether you are rich or poor, white collar or blue, whatever

your race, whatever your religion, the PAP stood for you. This is your party. Into the party we co-opted all those who are committed to serve the country and to make the country better in order to form a broad national movement. Therefore, we made the PAP a national government that drew support from all segments of society. So, we got the policies right, people align their interests, we got the politics right, the PAP sought to represent the broad mass of Singaporeans, then we got the system right by adapting it to work for Singapore.

13. We introduced Non-Constituency MPs (NCMPs) to ensure a minimum representation of opposition voices in Parliament. We introduced Group Representation Constituencies (GRCs) to guarantee a minimum representation of minorities in Parliament and also to push politics toward multiracial and inclusive politics instead of racial partisan extremist politics. Then we created Nominated MPs (NMPs) to widen the range of non-partisan views and to enrich the public debate in Parliament. We created the elected President to protect our reserves, to make sure that key appointments are not corrupted, and honest people are appointed in the critical jobs in the land, and to promote responsible politics because if the President is holding the key to the goodie jar, no politician can say, "Come, I am distributing goodies now, vote for me and you will get more." Because you have to get the President's permission and the President can say no. So if you want to spend, you have to show how you are going to fund your spending. I think that promotes responsible politics. Because of all these adaptations of our political system, we have been able to avoid destructive politics in Singapore, and the Government has been able to pursue constructive long-term policies that work for Singapore. We have continued to refine our systems as we have gone ahead. In the last few years since the last elections, we have increased the number of non-constituency MPs from 3 to 9. We have created more single constituencies, smaller GRCs, and therefore we have opened up more space for alternative views to be expressed and debated in Parliament.

14. But the system is as good as the people who work it, and to make it work you must have good leadership. Good leadership is a leadership that is in sync with the times, in tune with the population, is renewed and does not get older and older year by year. So we have talent spotted, groomed new people, inducted them — both backbenchers and office holders. Every time we have an election, the most important thing for us is to find one-third to one-quarter of new MPs who can come in to replace the old ones, or those not yet so old, but to replace the existing MPs so that we bring in fresh blood, fresh ideas, fresh energy and stay in step with the population, despite many years in power.

15. This way, we have got a system which has delivered honest, high quality, efficient government. It is capable, competent, it works for Singaporeans and it is cheap because we actually spend very little money running the government. It is not perfect, there are many areas where we have to improve, and from time to time we do make mistakes and we have to learn from them and try not to make the same mistake twice. But overall, I think I can honestly say, without blowing our own trumpet, that it is a good system that has served Singapore well.

16. We have gone through crises, like the JI terrorist group, like SARS, like the global economic crisis, and each time we have not just come through, but emerged intact and strengthened. We compare well with any other government in the world, in any other country, whether it is a single-party government or a multi-party government, whether it is a democracy or whatever.

17. This system that works well for Singapore is an important and enduring competitive advantage for us that makes up for our smallness and vulnerability. It is something that is special and something that has taken us many years to build up. It is something which others can see and study but not so easy to replicate. And it is something that is getting more widely recognised in the world. The Economist magazine recently published a special report in the late March issue. The cover story has to do with something else, something to do with Japan's problems but inside there is a special article on the *Future of the State: Taming Leviathan*. It is written by the editor of The Economist. He came to Singapore and he met me and he met MM. He interviewed a lot of people, the government and I think also the opposition, and he wrote us up in this special article, one piece on Singapore as a model of a state which is working. And the title is *Go East, Young Bureaucrat*. If you want to be a good civil servant — where can you see good civil servants? Go to Singapore. He puts us as a positive example as a government that works. How does it work? Well he says we are authoritarian but accountable to the people — he would have said authoritarian anyway but you would not have expected him to say "accountable to the people". Able to think long term with a high-quality public service, and he says that if you go sit in the Civil Service College, sitting around 30-something mandarins is more like meeting junior partners at Goldman Sachs or McKinsey than the cast of "Yes, Minister". I do not know if you have heard of "Yes, Minister" but I hope you do not meet either of such Ministers or civil servants here. He says the person on your left is on secondment at some big oil company, and on your right sits a woman, who between spells at the finance and defence ministries, has picked up degrees from the London School of Economics, Cambridge and Stanford. High-fliers pop in and out

of the Civil Service College for more training; the Prime Minister has written case studies for them.

18. They have a high opinion of us and particularly of our education system, and he did not write up the NUS, but he wrote up the ITE because there are good universities in many countries in the world, but there is hardly any other country in the world with a first class institution like the ITE, providing outstanding, valuable, effective technical training for people who did not go to university or polytechnic and enabling them to get good jobs. So that is just one example. I could cite you half a dozen others just from the last few months.

19. You may have seen one more in the newspapers recently. I do not know whether you read the newspapers, I hope so, but you should have heard of the International Monetary Fund (IMF), and the IMF has one key committee in the organisation called the International Monetary and Financial Committee (IMFC). This is the policy steering committee of the IMF. It is really the heart of the organisation where the key countries come together to debate issues concerning the global financial systems, concerning global imbalances, monetary reforms, banking, and so on. The new chairman of the IMFC, I am not sure how many of you can name him, but he is Tharman Shanmugaratnam — our Finance Minister. He was elected last month to chair the IMFC. It is not because we campaigned for the position. We did not campaign for the position but Tharman was elected because Singapore had a high reputation as a state which worked, and a successful economy, and Tharman himself personally is held in very high regard internationally. They know the quality of the person, they know the contributions he can make, they did not do this just out of politeness to us.

20. Our reputation and the realities of our good government are of great value to Singapore. It gives us influence in the world, it gives you good standing in the world, it opens doors for our businesses and it creates many opportunities for Singaporeans. If we did not have this — if we were just an ordinary city with a few million people in Asia — there are dozens, if not hundreds of cities in Asia, with a few million people — you would not stand out and we would be just one of many.

21. So this is the happy situation in which we are discussing 4th generation leadership and if we are looking forward and asking how we carry this forward into the next decade, then the issue is not just "Can we spot the next PM?", "What does he look like?", but rather "How can we keep this virtuous circle going — political stability, good government, economic and social success, good leadership feeding back again and moving forward."

22. We are in a stronger position today than we used to be — much stronger — but we will continue to face challenges, internally as well as externally and just because you are flying higher does not mean you can switch to auto-pilot because you never know when you will run into rough weather. If you are on auto-pilot, and it malfunctions, you will crash. So to fly the plane higher and faster, you need to find the best crew, chart carefully the most promising path forward, and work hard together to make it happen.

23. The basic factors will not change — I think our policies will still have to be right, we have still to give all Singaporeans a stake in the country's future. The issues may be the same but the challenges are different, the opportunities we have also changed. We need to ensure that all Singaporeans will benefit from growth. But it is more of a challenge than before because with globalisation, there is pressure on the wages of the lower end, of unskilled workers — everywhere, not just in Singapore — and even middle-income jobs are under pressure in developed countries as more work is sent to India, more work is outsourced to China, and as robots and computers and software become smarter and take over jobs which used to require human beings and human intelligence. That is a challenge.

24. But on the other side, we have a lot of resources, we can do a lot more for ourselves. We have got our education system sorted out. We can make every school a good school. We can provide every child maximum opportunity to develop his or her full potential. Every time I come to NUS I not only look at the buildings on this side of the road, I look at the buildings coming up on the other side of Ayer Rajah Expressway, and this evening I could see how they are up, ten storeys, almost complete, and I think some of you would be young enough to make it to get into the University Town before you graduate. The next institution — the liberal arts college, Yale-NUS, will also be there. And what we are doing in NUS, we are doing in NTU, SMU, with the polytechnics, the ITEs — many paths forward and therefore many opportunities for Singaporeans to do well for themselves and take advantage of globalisation rather than lose out because of it. We also have to keep social mobility high, because we must have the ability to allow talent to rise up from whatever his background. Your parents may be poor — but if you are hardworking and able you can make life better for yourself and for your parents. Your parents may be well-off — but if you do not have the ability to look after yourself, you will not inherit positions and responsibilities just because of your name. Therefore we must have a society where we can keep on having this free flow of talent moving up all the time, and all the talent in the country can be garnered and given maximum opportunity to flower.

25. We have to strengthen racial and religious harmony. It is something which you have heard year in and year out and I hope that it is something you will remember, if you have been in school in Singapore, from your National Education classes. But it is also something which is more urgent now because of extremist terrorism, which threatens many countries in the world, Malaysia, Indonesia. We are in this region and we may be targets too. With the right policies, I think in the next two decades we can solidify our sense of Singapore identity. Having done that we also must have the PAP continue to represent all Singaporeans — always be open to new ideas, new talents to accommodate a broad range of views and approaches in tackling issues, and seeing our opportunities and problems, and to attract even those who disagree with us on specific things and policies, to join us and make common cause and argue with us within the party, and try and persuade us and benefit from the exchange of different views, so that we can get the best solution for Singapore. We will not reject critics. In fact the party should seek them out to discover fresh ideas, fresh views. That is the way to stay open and not to become closed-up and fossilise or ossify.

26. Thirdly, we have got to preserve the strengths of our political system while continuing to adapt it to changing conditions. In Parliament, we must encourage a serious debate focusing on important issues which concern the country and including all significant views. The NMPs and NCMPs have made useful contributions. They have participated fully, and therefore we have entrenched the Nominated MP scheme so it is now part of the system and we have expanded the Non-Constituency MP scheme so that now there will be up to nine Non-Constituency MPs, so that whatever happens in the General Elections, there will be at least nine Opposition voices in Parliament. But of course, quality is as important as numbers. You have three now in Parliament. There is nothing to stop them from holding the Government to account, from propounding ideas and strategies, from challenging the Government's assumptions, and forcing the Government to justify why it is thinking, what it is doing. After all, the PAP started off small. In 1955 when the PAP first got into the Legislative Assembly, there were only three PAP members in the Opposition — one was MM Lee, one was Lim Chin Siong, one was an old man, Mr Goh Chew Chua — and with the three of them there, the PAP established itself so effectively that when the next General Election came within four years, it was able to win a landslide and come into power. More representation in Parliament, through the NCMP scheme, is helpful, but really quality — a responsible, sensible Opposition — is more important than numbers. We also

have to keep our system open and contestable. The political system must be such that it is easy for people to come in to contest, form a party and participate. To win cannot be so easy because if you win, that is a big thing, and your voice will count so you must achieve a high standard to win. But to contest it cannot be difficult. You cannot require a lot of money.

27. In America, it costs a lot of money. If you want to run for President, you should start thinking how you will find US$500 million because that is about what it costs to run for President. Even to be a Congressman, of whom there are about five hundred, it costs you a few million dollars a shot and you spend all your time in Congress making sure you do not offend people who might contribute to your next election campaign. But in Singapore, we set a limit of $3.50 spending per party per voter during Parliamentary Elections — and in fact, most parties spend a lot less than that. It is cheap to contest but the hurdle to get elected should be high because you want to maintain the quality of the MPs and the quality of the political leadership and the political debate. The way to make the hurdle high is for voters to vote for the party and the leaders who will serve them best. The system encourages that because once an MP is elected, he looks after your constituency, he is responsible for your Town Council, he does not just make speeches in Parliament. The voters therefore have a direct stake in electing good MPs. But whatever the election outcome, there would be eighteen of them who are non-Government in Parliament and they will question the Government and hold it to account.

28. So you want a system which is not biased for any particular party, but a system which is biased towards producing an effective government for Singapore, while at the same time allowing adequate expression of opposition, alternative non-partisan views in the political system, because there will be 25 to 30 per cent of voters who will vote opposition. There will be other people who are not politically partisan and they have a voice and they ought to be heard.

29. Finally, we have to continue renewing our political leadership. You look at me and ask what I am going to do and I look back at you, the students particularly, and I would say it also depends on you, the Singaporeans amongst you. Because each generation has to produce people who have the ability, the passion and the commitment, who will contribute to the community, who will become leaders in their own right, who will help build the Singapore which you want to see in your lives and in your future. Do not wait for a tea party invitation. We are looking for people who will come forward, who have ability and integrity, regardless of family background. If you have ideas, if you have energy, if you care about it, come forward, serve and make a mark. It is not

just your grade point average which counts or even your IQ. Yes, they mean something, but character and values are as important as intellect and ability.

30. You have to be committed, you have to care about the country, you have to be able to connect with people, and you must have a contribution to make. It could be looking after constituents at the grassroots or in welfare homes. It could be thinking out national policies, or it could be mobilizing a segment of the population. You have leadership, people follow you, what you say counts and will be taken into account of very carefully.

31. Because leadership is so important, for this general election, we have met more than 200 people for tea, and finally we are fielding just 20 plus new candidates. We decided not to field many who had outstanding qualifications. On the other hand we are fielding quite a number who did not necessarily excel academically. In fact, one of them said he took his O' levels twice, but they possess other important qualities. I am proud of our new candidates, individually and collectively. We will give them responsibilities to test their mettle and their ability to solve problems for the people. Over the next 20 plus years, some of them will be playing key roles in Singapore. The search goes on. We will continue to look for new talent to reinforce the leadership in the next general elections. If the general elections are this year, five years from now will be 2016, and beyond in each elections. But within two terms from now, the new MPs will have to choose from among themselves the new leadership team and a new leader — the new PM. They will have to start assembling the next leadership team after to succeed them, to take Singapore forward.

32. But no system lasts forever, as even MM himself acknowledges in his latest book called *Hard Truths to Keep Singapore Going*. So we do not assume that the PAP will remain dominant indefinitely. We have to ask ourselves a question — what is the alternative? It could be another party, just as dominant, or it could be some other configuration. Now what other configuration could that be? A lot of people say, "Can we have a two party system?" That is the ideal that is many developed countries work, that is what you should aim for, a change of government from the first party to the second, and from the second to come back, and then you are considered to have matriculated.

33. But how could this happen in Singapore that we have two parties? I can imagine several scenarios. First, the society splits based on race or religion. You have one party representing one race or religion, another party representing another race or religion. That is the worst possible scenario for Singapore and we have done our best to make sure that it never comes about. Because if we

are split on race or religion, you are not just going to have political quarrels, you are going to divide the society and that is the end for Singapore.

34. The second possibility is that you divide on class lines. We do not get our economic policies right or maybe it is just that the world trends are such, the rich get richer, the poor do not make progress. After a while the poor lose hope in the system, the rich lose interest in the rest of society. So one side says, "Tax me less, let me keep my wealth". The other side says, "Give me more transfers, more welfare, more goodies, more benefits". And you have two parties forming, one representing one group, the other one representing the other group, rich and poor. And that is how, I mean highly oversimplified, but that is how things roughly work in many countries. Like Britain, where you have the Conservatives and the Labour Party, and now the Lib Dems (Liberal Democrats) somewhere in the middle. Or in the US, where you have the Democrats who are representing more of the working class, and the Republicans who represent more of the well-off people. But I do not think that is a good outcome either. We are working hard to prevent this because I think we should try and to the maximum extent that we can align all the interest of the Singaporeans and make sure that one party can represent you, whether you are the CEO or the taxi driver.

35. The third possibility is that we split on policy grounds, you argue that this set of policies will be best for Singapore to grow, promoting MNCs. They argue that no I do not want MNCs; sending them all away and depending on Singaporeans and Singapore companies is the way to grow. And we cannot reconcile and we split and we argue over the policies and fight it out at the polls. I think that could happen but it is not so likely because the PAP is a pragmatic party and we are ready to take in good ideas. If you look at it at a higher level, frankly, the range of feasible options of Singapore is not that wide. So it is possible it could happen, but it would mean that something has gone wrong too.

36. But the most important reason, why a two party system is not workable is because we do not have enough talent in Singapore to form two A-teams, to form two really first class teams to govern Singapore really well. More than any country, Singapore needs exceptionally able leadership to tackle challenges and to minimise the risks for our countries. We are small, we are vulnerable. With a mediocre government, other countries may muddle through, and have to muddle through, but Singapore will fail. The most effective way to get a two party system, if you really want to do it, is to split the PAP in two. Because the talent is there, gathered. We will have two persons, I choose one, you choose one. Now we have two teams, now we play, we toss the coin.

37. We seriously considered making the PAP two parties, not that way, but in principle. But we did not do it because we could not solve one problem: how can you make two teams, each one as good as the original one team which we had, which took, really, what would have been the best players from both teams? Or, to put it in very hard, direct and tangible terms, where can you find two Finance Ministers and two Defence Ministers? I have one Finance Minister and one Defence Minister. If you have a spare one somewhere, please let me know. Why do I choose these two? Because these are two of the most difficult jobs in the Cabinet to fill. In Finance, you have to make judgments on taxes affecting all Singaporeans and on expenditures affecting all ministries. On the Budget — you are talking about 50 billion dollars of expenditure every year, as well as our reserves — GIC, Temasek, MAS and others adding up to more than 100 billion US dollars. To find one of them is not easy. To find two of them, you must really *tiok beh pio* (strike the lottery).

38. It is the same with Defence in a curiously opposite way. Because Finance is about money and it is very difficult, and Defence is very difficult because it is not about money, because the bottom line is intangible — security, risks, threats, judgment. What is worth spending on, what is worth investing on, which is the right aeroplane to buy, how many ships do you need, which colonels to make general, how to shape the SAF. Which threats are getting serious? When do I recommend to mobilise the SAF? When do I decide I must deploy and defend? Can you easily find anybody off the street to do that sort of job? It's very, very difficult.

39. Therefore, have one team, get the best people together, fill each job with the best man. If we split it into two teams, then whichever one is in charge, the government is going to be weaker, and the chances of something going wrong will go up. Even if things do not go wrong, standards will go down. That is why my predecessors and I have gone out of our way to scour the land for talent to join the team. At every election, we have 20-odd candidates become new MPs, and out of these, on average — I did a count over the last 5 or 6 elections — about 3 make it to become Minister. But we have 14 Ministries to fill, and then on top of that, you need some supervising Ministers, some DPMs, Senior Ministers, because you need some additional experience and oversight of the system. Just say 14 Ministries to fill, and I can get 3 Ministers each term, you do the math — 14 divided by 3 means, on average, each Minister has to serve at least 4 terms. So, over the weekend, SM Goh expressed his personal view that perhaps in future, Ministers should serve only 2 terms. But I think that is not possible, simply because of the numbers. We are not able to generate the

talent in order to produce those numbers of people who are able to do the job competently, to the satisfaction of Singaporeans at that rate.

40. The opposition parties pitch themselves as offering Singapore a fallback should the PAP fail. It sounds plausible, but if you think about it, what does it depend on? Most critically, it comes back to talent again. If the PAP cannot assemble a second team, I do not think the Opposition will find it easier to do that. You look at it from the micro view. Consider a capable person weighing his options. He wants to serve the nation, he is trying to decide how to do it, which way he should go. And he has two choices: first choice, join the Opposition, oversee the PAP, but really spend his life — and it can be quite a long time — waiting and watching, just in case the PAP screws up, then he will be ready to take over. The other alternative is, join the Government, help it to make better decisions, implement good policies, and avoid making mistakes and screwing up. Now, which makes more sense for him and for Singapore?

41. For all these reasons, I think the best thing for us to do is to concentrate our resources and form one really strong Singapore team. Some people will want to join the Opposition. Yes, they want to propound alternative policies, or they want to be a check on the Government, that is valid. By all means, join the Opposition, especially if the Government is wrong or incompetent. But so long as the Government is competent and doing a good job for Singaporeans, I hope you will make common cause with it, and help us to ensure that things stay right. What we can do and must do to assure Singapore's future is to develop the strongest possible 'A' team with depth and resilience. Competent Ministers, people with expertise in different Ministries, plus depth — younger ones learning the job, so that as the situation changes, as we have new needs, we can always find the right person for the right job. If one person does not work out, I can do a replacement, I can call a time out, change my team member, and the game goes on.

42. Actually, that is how soccer is played. If you watch World Cup soccer, every country only has one team. No country fields two teams for the World Cup. You have one national soccer team, you have reserve players, you have coaches, you can change players, and if need be, you can even change the coach. But you concentrate all your talent, make one team, and give it your best shot whether it is Johannesburg or Rio de Janeiro. I think that is what we should do. We are not so successful in soccer but we are not doing badly in government and I think that we should keep up our winning streak and stay in the championship league in the international contest of nations.

43. We are now putting together the next 'A' team for Singapore. The PAP candidates in this round will form key members of this team and in the next

couple of rounds. They need the voters' full support, not just to get elected but to deliver results for you, because this is the way to safeguard our common future, not to weaken the 'A' team in the hope of buying insurance, but to strengthen the 'A' team to give it the best chance of succeeding.

44. This General Election matters to you. I imagine most of you will be voting, especially the men, because you are a bit older, you have done NS. You will be graduating soon, and over the next 40, 50 years, you will be building your careers and your families. For you to do this in a secure, stable and prosperous Singapore, we have to maintain the same high quality of government we have enjoyed, that you have enjoyed, and that has enabled you to come thus far. That is why leadership succession is a major issue in this election. We have to press hard on leadership renewal now, so that in ten years' time in 2020, we will have a younger team ready not just to maintain our present high standards, but to take this as our foundation to fly even higher and do even better.

45. Ten years is not a long time. It is not a long time to build a new team for Singapore. It is not a long time in your life. Take my word for it — in ten years' time, you will still be young people. Early thirties, young adults, about to enter your prime years, making progress in your careers, hopefully making progress starting your families. You need this leadership renewal to succeed, and this leadership renewal needs your help to succeed. If we can succeed in doing this, then we will have good policies that will bring prosperity and progress to Singapore, and then we can maintain the virtuous cycle. In another 20 years' time, you can invite somebody else to come here, update this title, and we can talk about the 6th generation leadership.

2. Tharman Shanmugaratnam, Deputy Prime Minister, April 2013

Robin Chan, "PAP: To remain dominant without being dominating", *The Straits Times*, 19 April 2013.

THE People's Action Party (PAP) wants to remain a dominant party anchored in society — without dominating in all areas, said Deputy Prime Minister Tharman Shanmugaratnam.

It can do this as an open political party, he said, that galvanises a diversity of views and ideas, including critical opinions.

"I believe we can play a dominant role, retain a dominant position without wanting to completely dominate," DPM Tharman said in an interview with The Straits Times.

"It's in Singapore's interest that you do have a dominant party, but it's got to be one that's open to diversity, welcoming of a responsible opposition."

But Mr Tharman also took pains to stress that economic policy must remain important for the kind of society Singaporeans want, even as the politics may be changing.

He urged them to preserve what has allowed the average Singaporean to raise his standard of living over time, amid a debate on the continued importance of economic growth.

Mr Tharman was answering questions related to politics chosen by readers in an online poll conducted by *The Straits Times*' Singapolitics website. The questions came in fourth, eighth and 10th out of 20 questions.

Mr Tharman said he was optimistic about the future role of the PAP because the party has changed significantly over the last five years, and continues to change with a younger generation of ministers leading the charge.

"If we can continue to involve people and to help them to take responsibility collectively for making a better Singapore, I think we can retain our anchor role in Singapore society," he added.

Mr Tharman, who is second assistant secretary-general of the PAP, admitted that the party is, however, facing challenges on two fronts.

One challenge is that it is a natural part of human psychology to "want a check on the PAP", which has been in power with a large majority in Parliament since Independence.

A second challenge: it is becoming more difficult to raise the quality of life for Singaporeans at the same rate as in the past.

But this is the case in other Asian economies such as Hong Kong, Taiwan and South Korea, as well as in the United States and Europe, he added.

Singapore, however, has managed to help the average person continue to improve his life, he said. Any young person can find a job quickly, "in fact faster than anywhere else in Asia", and that must be preserved.

"So economic policy is not irrelevant to the type of society we want because we are a society that still has aspirations to move up.

"People do want to move up, basically. Families want to move up. They want their children to do better than the parents."

Since the 2011 General Election, which saw the PAP lose its first GRC and record its lowest margin of victory, Singapore has become better off, he said.

People are much more engaged and civil society is more active.

"Part of a healthy political system is one with a decent opposition presence in Parliament and outside, and a responsible opposition," he said.

Outlining how Singapore can get its politics right, he said it is with a government that does not "just go with the whims of the day" but focuses on the long term.

It must also communicate policies well and have MPs who serve with a heart on the ground.

"In deciding on our basic policy objectives and our preferences for the long term...when you involve people in the thinking process, they become very aware of the trade-offs."

3. Tharman Shanmugaratnam, Deputy Prime Minister, July 2015

Wong Siew Ying, "Having a dominant party in politics is beneficial: Tharman", *The Straits Times*, 4 July 2015.

One-party states with no political competition face a disadvantage, but having a dominant player in politics is an edge, said Deputy Prime Minister Tharman Shanmugaratnam at a dialogue.

He did not, however, elaborate on the advantage.

Mr Tharman also said Singapore is not a one-party state and that the ruling party had to be subjected to serious competition, as it was.

His remarks prompted dialogue moderator Fareed Zakaria, a Washington Post columnist, to ask if the competition was serious as the People's Action Party (PAP) occupied most of the seats in Parliament. "That's an outcome, that's not a design," Mr Tharman said.

The PAP holds 79 out of 87 elected seats in Parliament, with the Workers' Party holding seven, and one seat is vacant after the death of Tanjong Pagar GRC MP and former Prime Minister Lee Kuan Yew in March.

As he acknowledges that competition is useful, Mr Tharman was asked if there was some inherent virtue in having different political parties lead the country.

While such rotation makes for a meaningful debate in theory, he said, in practice, "do you put your citizenry at risk by saying, 'Look, let's try this out, and see how it works'?".

Mr Tharman said he would rather let others try it out, and that Singapore preserves its current system.

He also said the dominant party has to be accountable to the people, both through a vote that comes through an election once every five years, as well as in between. "People see results…Singaporeans are not fools at all. They know what's what, they know whether things are working and whether they are not. And they will have to judge."

He added: "So it only works if you're subjected to contest, and you're held accountable."

Mr Tharman said he spends about one-third of his week on the ground interacting with people by attending community events and visiting residents in their homes.

"It's not what you see in typical one-party states, not even what you see in a multi-party state," he said.

A version of this article appeared in the print edition of The Straits Times on July 04, 2015, with the headline 'Having a dominant party in politics is beneficial: Tharman'.

4. Ng Eng Hen, Defence Minister, January 2017

Sau Ming En, "Don't measure progress by number of political parties, say Defence Minister", *Today*, 13 January 2017.

SINGAPORE — The extent of progress in a country should not be measured by its number of political parties, said Defence Minister Ng Eng Hen on Friday (Jan 13) at a dialogue with Yale-NUS students, in response to a question on whether having one or multiple parties is better for governing a country.

"If the country's progress is measured by the number of political parties in it, I think you will have an interesting result. That's not been shown to be the determinant to how a country progresses," said Dr Ng, who spoke after delivering his keynote address at the Yale-NUS College Asia Pacific Model United Nations Conference.

Turning to China as an example, he noted that despite being led by a state party, no one has questioned the economic progress the country has made in the last few decades.

On the other hand, countries with multiple parties can draw on the good ideas from each party, but they could also face political gridlock, such as in the case of Australia and the United Kingdom, noted Dr Ng.

"I asked the question, why there was this trend globally, as we've seen in the last decade, towards even more authoritarian leaders and systems?"

"It is the fact that that model hasn't delivered as well. And the reason is political gridlock, there is a price to pay for accommodation, in other words you have a coalition party," he added.

A wide range of questions was posed to Dr Ng during the 45-minute dialogue, ranging from his views on the Israeli settlements on Palestinian-occupied lands, to what the Government's plans were for women to play a larger role in defending the country.

In response to the last question, Dr Ng noted that the number of countries with such military conscription have dwindled, and Singapore is one of the few countries that are able to continue with it.

"The reason why it's been very difficult for other countries (to do so)…is that you can only maintain the commitment to national service if you are fair to everybody," he said.

As such, it would be hard for Singapore to do what others have suggested: Enlist men for the army and bring women in to make them nurses or teachers.

"I find it very hard to tell people or (for) any government to say to its population, I want you to subsume your individual needs for a need other than military defence," he said.

5. Ong Ye Kung, Second Minister for Education, January 2017

Martha Soezean, "Ong Ye Kung: Singapore's one-party system, a result of free and fair election", *The Online Citizen*, 24 January 2017.

Singapore is a small country, so it has to stay agile, a one-party system may give Singapore its best shot at success, said Education Minister (Higher Education and Skills) Ong Ye Kung at the annual Institute of Policy Studies' Singapore Perspectives conference on 23 January.

Opinions were shared by a panel discussing whether rule by a single political party is best for Singapore. The panel also conversed on the possibility of Singapore having a two or multi-party system.

Pointing out the long-term risks for Singapore if Singapore has a multi-party system, Mr Ong who is a Member of Parliament from People's Action Party (PAP) said, "50 years from now, if we have a multi-party system, what will define the key political difference between parties? What is the partisan line? Is it over the extent to which we should subsidise public services, healthcare and social assistance? If that is so, it may well be something we can manage."

"What if it is over something more sinister that divide Singapore by race, language or religion? As we all know politics, race and religion is a toxic mix," he said.

Mr Ong gave a justification on a one-party system by saying, "Our equilibrium as a small country may well be a single party system. The party can be PAP today, but another party in the future — so long it is the most capable at that time."

"The reason is geographic. Because between Singaporeans living in Changi and Jurong, their concerns and views on national issues may be somewhat different, but nothing like people living in Alaska or New York City, Jakarta or the westernmost of Indonesia. For big countries, geographical separation translates into different lifestyles, outlook, values and political affinities…"

"The single party in the case of Singapore, therefore, is not a prescription, but the most likely outcome of choice — a result of free and fair elections. It is not different from Massachusetts being dominated by Democrats for long periods, or Scotland dominated by Labour and until recently Scottish National Party (SNP). Smallness and concentration often come together."

Mr Ong also said that complacency, elitism and corruption are not inevitable outcomes of single-party rule, and these traits have shown up across all political systems.

Executive chairman of Banyan Tree, Ho Kwon Ping, spoke on the same topic and warned that one-party systems may cause its political elites becoming slow to change, resulting in a culture of entitlement and corruption as he did in prior talks that he held.

He noted that the most desirable scenario for Singapore might be a system of robust internal competition within the PAP.

But Mr Ho said history shows that a ruling political party which faces no competition tends to turn complacent.

Pointing to the declines of India's Indian National Congress and the Kuomintang in Taiwan, Mr Ho said a founding party's political values can be passed down only over three or four generations of leaders. Beyond that, complacency will overwhelm the self-discipline instilled by the party's pioneers and its political culture will erode, he said.

However, Mr Ho thought the PAP, because of its 'ability to self-correct and obsessively talk about problems' and find solutions to them, had the best chance of any long-term party to set a new record for staying in power.

He suggested that the party should introduce a formal way for competing policies to be aired internally.

Mr Ong seemed to have agreed, saying that the PAP needed to be as pluralistic a party as possible and must take in people with different views.

"This will lead to internal competition which will be a good thing. Today it exists, there are diverse views, the public doesn't see them, but perhaps we ought to formalise this over time," he said.

But Mr Ho responded that internal party competition by itself cannot ensure political elites remain relevant.

"Civil society should also be nurtured and information should be shared more freely, so that the public can have robust discussions on policies," he said.

Professor Tommy Koh, Ambassador-at-Large at the Ministry of Foreign Affairs, who was in the audience, asked if the PAP could buck the trend of history, or if it might falter within the next 10 years.

Mr Ho said, "I thought the party was unlikely to decline with Prime Minister Lee Hsien Loong around, even if he is no longer Prime Minister but is Minister Mentor or Emeritus Senior Minister."

"So long as he is around, the party's adherence to its core values will remain," said Mr Ho.

Mr Ong said the new leadership team will face a severe test in the next few years, "How do we then ensure we have the bond with the rest of the party members to continue to hold everything together, while ensuring the PAP is as pluralistic and diverse as possible?"

Prof Koh called Mr Ong a 'credible and leading candidate to be our next prime minister'. Mr Ong was recently made an organising secretary of the PAP and has been touted as the possible future prime minister succeeding.

Mr Ong had earlier contested in the General Election 2011 at Aljunied GRC but was defeated by the "A-team" of Workers' Party led by its Secretary-General, Low Thia Khiang. After his defeat in 2011, Mr Ong was given the position of NTUC's Deputy Secretary-General and eventually entered Parliament through Sembawang GRC before being appointed a Minister.

Charissa Yong, "One-party rule 'may be way for Singapore to succeed': Ong Ye Kung", *The Straits Times*, 24 January 2017.

A one-party system may give Singapore its best shot at success, because it is a small country that needs to stay nimble, said Education Minister (Higher Education and Skills) Ong Ye Kung yesterday at the Institute of Policy Studies' annual Singapore Perspectives conference.

But Banyan Tree executive chairman Ho Kwon Ping, who spoke on the same topic, warned that one-party systems face the danger of its political elites becoming slow to change, resulting in a culture of entitlement and corruption.

He added that the most desirable scenario for Singapore would be a system of robust internal competition within the People's Action Party (PAP).

Likewise, Mr Ong stressed that the PAP must stay open-minded and grounded in reality, and have integrity beyond reproach.

Both men were on a panel discussing whether rule by a single political party is best for Singapore.

The panel also addressed the possibility of Singapore having a two- or multi-party system.

In his speech, Mr Ong made the case that single-party rule is the best way for a small country like Singapore to succeed.

He said the party need not be the PAP, but whichever party is the most capable.

For a multi-party system to form, said Mr Ong, there must first be at least two sufficiently different paths for Singapore to take, and political views distinct enough for different parties to uphold.

But Singapore is not big enough to have geographically separate towns which evolve drastically different views on national issues, he said.

Another reason he cited is that Singapore needs to stay nimble and move fast in a changing global environment. Mr Ong questioned whether it could do so with a multi-party system.

He said: "A country's success is always idiosyncratic and can never be replicated wholesale by another."

"The formula for success is based on different political processes and ours happens to be a one-party system," said Mr Ong, who was recently made an organising secretary of the PAP and has been touted as a possible future prime minister.

He added that complacency, elitism and corruption are not inevitable outcomes of single-party rule, and these traits have shown up across all political systems.

However, Mr Ho said history shows that a ruling political party which faces no competition tends to turn complacent.

Citing the declines of India's Indian National Congress and the Kuomintang in Taiwan, Mr Ho said a founding party's political values can be passed down over three or four generations of leaders.

Beyond that, complacency will overwhelm the self-discipline instilled by the party's pioneers and its political culture will erode, he told the 960 policymakers, businessmen and students in the audience.

Nevertheless, Mr Ho thought the PAP had the best chance of any long-term party to set a new record for staying in power, because of its "ability to self-correct and obsessively talk about problems" and find solutions to them.

He suggested that the party introduce a formal way for competing policies to be aired internally.

To this suggestion, Mr Ong said the PAP needed to be as pluralistic a party as possible and must take in people with different views.

"This will lead to internal competition which will be a good thing."

"Today it exists, there are diverse views, the public doesn't see them, but perhaps we ought to formalise this over time," he said.

But Mr Ho said internal party competition by itself cannot ensure political elites remain relevant.

Civil society should also be nurtured and information should be shared more freely, so that the public can have robust discussions on policies, he said.

Ambassador-at-large Tommy Koh, who was in the audience, asked if the PAP could buck the trend of history, or whether it might falter within the next 10 years.

Mr Ho thought the party was unlikely to decline with Prime Minister Lee Hsien Loong around, even if he is no longer Prime Minister but is Minister Mentor or Emeritus Senior Minister.

"So long as he is around, the party's adherence to its core values will remain," said Mr Ho.

Mr Ong — whom Prof Koh called a "credible and leading candidate to be our next prime minister" while asking his question — also said the new leadership team will face a severe test in the next few years.

Describing their challenge, Mr Ong said: "How do we then ensure we have the bond with the rest of the party members to continue to hold everything together, while ensuring the PAP is as pluralistic and diverse as possible?"

What if Singapore becomes a two or multi-party system?

Minister for Education (Higher Education and Skills) Ong Ye Kung addressed the Institute of Policy Studies' Singapore Perspectives Conference on Monday, where he spoke on the issue of 'What if Singapore becomes a two or multi-party system?' Below is an edited excerpt of his speech.

Let's talk about the elephant in the room — which is the PAP. The scenario painted to us is that by 2065, it is replaced by several smaller elephants that will take turns to govern after each election or rule through coalitions. It's a drastic departure from the status quo, which we cannot rule out half a century from now. Question is: What happens then?

I would like to present my remarks in three parts. First, while life will change in many ways, we will adapt and in many ways, life goes on. Second, I will explain why this can give rise to a couple of serious long-term risks for Singapore. Third, which is what many Singaporeans will ask: 'What is the Government going to do about it?'

First, what will change and how will life go on?

A major change in a multi-party system will be the shifting of the political ground. Expect intense ground jostling — different parties reaching out to various groups to garner support. The Unions may not be as cohesive as they are today, working with the PAP in a symbiotic relationship. They may be split into two or more groupings, or there will be a competing federation, like the days when we had SATU and NTUC. Likewise, there will be split affiliations amongst associations, clans, societies, even recreational clubs, civil societies, socio-political sites, sports and arts bodies, etc. Media houses can be split too.

It's not a new phenomenon. It has been the case in more hotly contested constituencies. After GE2011, when the Worker's Party won Aljunied, I found myself becoming the opposition party in the GRC. Then, there are groups which will invite me as guest-of-honour for their functions, and others that will invite the Workers' Party MP. Most will invite both, and I got the feeling the guests enjoyed watching the jostling. In a multi-party system, the scale of that happening will be larger, nationwide, at events, and behind the scenes.

I believe the institution that will be most tested will be the civil service. The holy grail of the civil service is to be politically neutral and serve whichever party forms the Government, regardless of their differences in governance philosophy. Offer the policy options, state the pros and cons, let the political leaders with the mandate decide, and civil service will support regardless. It is a professional ideal, but in practice, easier said than done. You can work on one set of policies for five years and someone new comes along and ask you to undo everything you have done and move to a new direction. We see that now happening — the Affordable Healthcare Act in the US is being unwound, Trans Pacific Partnership being put to a stop. That can be very frustrating and disheartening.

It is useful to see how other countries deal with it. America ended up politicizing the top echelons of the civil service. The top few layers of bureaucrats are political appointees, and whenever there is a change in Administration, they are all replaced. That is why the new Trump Administration has to make 4,000 appointments.

The alternative is the Australian or UK system, where all civil servants in the Ministries stay intact, but the Minister's office is packed with his own staffers — presumably more aligned to his thinking. In Australia, the Ministers spend most of their time with these staffers in Parliament, and not with the civil servants in the Ministries — because Parliament is where the political contest is.

We will have to adapt to all these, which also means status quo as we know it will change. But adapt we will.

Real risks

Second, I will touch on the real long-term risks for Singapore in a multi-party system that be beyond adapting and getting used to. The risk is not so much being in a multi-party system per se, but what are the forces and processes that will lead us there.

For a two or multi-party system to take shape, there must first have been at least two paths sufficiently different for our country to take. But these paths can be a narrow fork in the road that can even merge further down, or a T-junction pointing in opposite directions and will never meet.

Take the UK for example. From the mid-1990s to early 2010s, the Conservatives and New Labour in UK both believed in a pro-business, market economy that upholds equality of opportunities instead of equality in outcomes. Both eschew labour unrest and strikes — which was a major shift for New Labour. The key divergence in policy was probably in their attitudes towards the European Union. Today, that has widened into a gulf between those who believed in Brexit and Remain. That difference has split the society between the young and old, urban and rural residents, the more and less educated.

In the US, the key historical divergence between the Republicans and Democrats was slavery. The situation has evolved. Slavery is no more, and today, the two parties hold distinct views on the size of Government, taxation, abortion, and gun control. But in the recent Presidential elections, those positions widened, pitting nationalism against globalisation, whites verses other races. It was a bitter, divisive election which both candidates openly acknowledged.

Political parties are essential in representing the diverse views of people, and elections a necessary and peaceful discourse in finding compromises and seeking a way forward for the country. This is the essence of democracy. But that same essence can take a nasty twist, sow discord and divide societies. Hence Winston Churchill said "...democracy is the worst form of Government except all those other forms that have been tried from time to time."

Fifty years from now, if we have a multi-party system, what will define the key political difference between parties? What is the partisan line? Is it over the extent to which we should subsidize public services, healthcare and social assistance? If that is so it may well be something we can manage. What if it is over something more sinister that divides Singapore by race, language or religion? As we all know politics, race and religion is a toxic mix. If that happens, we will be broken as a country and society.

Another major risk is whether a multi-party system will slow down decision making, and our nimbleness in navigating an ever-changing external environment. If we have a multi-party system back in 1965, would we have come this far so quickly?

Back then, we could move to attract FDI (foreign direct investments) from multi-national companies when it was not politically correct to do so in a post-colonial era. We forged omnidirectional, bilateral free trade agreements while others pledge allegiance to the WTO multilateral system. We must move fast in embracing new digital technologies, even though it can be uncomfortable and disruptive.

If we envisage a future of tough challenges — a shifting geopolitical landscape, more intense economic competition, challenging demographic trends, rising sea levels — unity, common purpose and the ability to move faster than others will be central and vital for us. While other countries are either slow but big, or small but fast, will we end up suffering the worse of both worlds — small and slow?

The current system has worked well for the majority of Singaporeans so far. It still gets my vote as the best system for Singapore.

Ensure current system works

So, given these risks, what can Government do about it?

To answer this question, let me rewind to 2011 when I was first introduced as a PAP candidate. I was asked by a journalist what I thought of a single party system in Singapore. I said that our equilibrium as a small country may well be a single party rule. The party can be PAP today, but another in the future — so long it is the most capable at that time.

Because between Singaporeans living in Changi and Jurong, their concerns and views on national issues may be somewhat different, but nothing like people living in Alaska or New York City, Jakarta or the Eastern and Westernmost places in the Indonesian archipelago. For big countries, geographical separation translates into different lifestyles, outlook, values and political affinities, which then lends itself to multi-party politics.

The single party in the case of Singapore, is not a prescription, but the most likely outcome of choice — a result of free and fair elections. It is not different from Massachusetts being dominated by Democrats for long periods, or Scotland dominated by Labour and now SNP. Smallness and concentration do often come together.

So the answer to the question what are we going to do about it, is to make sure the current system continues to work for Singaporeans!

To do so, we must understand what factors made it work so far. Complacency, elitism, and corruption are not inevitable outcomes of dominant party rule. These ills have shown up across all political systems.

The PAP knows that our integrity must be unquestionable. If something goes wrong, it will be rectified and the perpetrators must face the consequences and action has to be swift.

We must be a party that is open minded and keeps up with the changing expectations of the population — so that we can be at the forefront of new ideas, and policies can adapt to the needs of the society and our people. Never think that today's solutions are the best they can be. Keep our eyes and ears open to changes in our surroundings, consult widely, improve our co-creation skills, and work together with the citizenry in creating solutions. We must attract talent from as diverse a background as possible to serve. That is why every term, we replace a quarter to a third of our candidates.

The PAP must constantly self-reflect, on areas that it has not done well, and why the Singapore Dream did not work out for some Singaporeans. Our policies must be rooted in the ground. A sizeable proportion of our work must be on the ground. And in this age of inequality, ours cannot just be a system which rewards the best and brightest, it must also be a system that compensates for poor family circumstance and the role of luck.

Every country in the world is different. A country's success is idiosyncratic and can never be replicated wholesale by another. The formula for success is based on different political processes. Singapore's formula may well be a single party system.

Ultimately, the political future of a country will be determined by the will of the people. If the people wish for a change to a multi-party system, it will be so. The job of the opposition parties is to highlight to people the risks of the current system. Likewise, it is the job of the PAP to do our best to make sure Singapore flourishes, point out the risks of a multi-party system for a small country like Singapore, and keep out the ills of complacency, elitism and corruption.

Whatever the 'what ifs' — single or multi-party — among all parties and all Singaporeans, we need a singularity of purpose and a wide agreement on means of implementing this purpose. This is not mere politics, but it is about our collective journey, as a people, as a country, to improve the lives of yours and mine.

POTENTIAL OF COALITION BUILDING AMONG OPPOSITION POLITICAL PARTIES IN SINGAPORE

1. Dr Tan Cheng Bock's Facebook Post, 29 July 2018

Singapore's interest must always come first

Yesterday I had a meeting with 7 opposition parties (Singapore Democratic Party, the People's Power Party, the Democratic Progressive Party, the Reform Party, the National Solidarity Party, the Singaporeans First Party and a new, as yet, unregistered People's Voice Party). These parties have something in common: they are all political veterans without a single seat in parliament for the last decade. They had a frank discussion on their shortcomings and aspirations. I was invited as an Observer.

The 7 parties proposed an opposition coalition and asked me to lead them. They know they have fallen short at the last GE. Wanting to do better, they sought my thoughts. I told them that to do better, Singapore's interest MUST ALWAYS come first — ahead of self and even their own party's interest. To be fair, many from the 7 parties stood in past elections because they believed they acted in Singapore's best interests. But I think some may also need to stand down and serve from the backroom if it is for the good of the country.

One commentator recently said these 7 parties are 3rd, 4th and 5th rate politicians, and that if I mix with them, my reputation will be tarnished. I'm curious what yardstick the commentator has used to measure these men. I know men like Paul Tambayah is a 1st rate human being and doctor who cares for the country. I find it hard to label him otherwise. I believe that the men and women I met yesterday, were more than willing to make way for better men and women who would stand in their place. They have guts. They have put themselves out there. That is sufficient for the moment.

Right now, the 7 parties have asked for my help. They are not the only ones who have spoken to me. I think I must help but in what capacity, I have not decided.

I am now 78 years old. I may only have a short time to mentor a team to work for the good of the nation. This is a small window of opportunity, a moment for ubah (change in Malay). I want to put my last years to good use. I want to pass all that I have acquired and learned in the political arena to the next generation.

I would regret it if I had the chance to make a difference, but did nothing.

2. Lim Tean's Facebook Post, 28 July 2018

My Statement at the meeting of Opposition Parties

This afternoon, at the premises of the SDP, various Opposition parties came together to explore how we can co-operate for the greater interests of serving the People of Singapore.

This is the Statement I delivered at the meeting...

Statement by Lim Tean

On behalf of the Party that I am forming — Peoples Voice, I pledge our total commitment to the greater cooperation of the Opposition parties in Singapore and to our common cause of displacing the PAP, which has been the government for 59 years.

It is our hope that in the very near future, all the relevant Opposition parties in Singapore will be able to join together in a real partnership and alliance. This would be in line with the fervent wishes of a great many Singaporeans.

As Politicians, we have the solemn duty to listen to the people whom we ask for the chance to serve.

On our own, each of our parties may not have the numbers to dislodge the PAP from its present position but if we are joined in a great and common venture, we will have the ability to do so.

However, we must be real partners and not in name only. We must realise that in such an alliance and partnership, the problems of my alliance members are also my party's problems and that our future are inextricably tied to one another.

Our Alliance must strive to form the next Government in the upcoming General Elections. We must offer real change to better the lives of Singaporeans. We must be a real alternative. We have a convincing message to Singaporeans that this is the worst government in our Nation's history and that it must be removed.

The message that the Opposition should be voted into Parliament to be a check and balance on the government is no longer relevant or enough.

Unfortunately, this was always the message by the Opposition in the past and that relegated the Opposition to be second best. Voters have no desire to vote for second best. We have no time for futile concepts such as not contesting all seats and have the PAP returned to power on nomination day, the so-called by-election effect.

If we continue to allow such self-defeatist concepts to fester, we will always be vulnerable to the fear mongering of the PAP, warning voters that they may lose power.

Such fear mongering was highly effective in GE 15 and was a major factor in the big win for the PAP.

The winds of change are here and they have buffeted the World for the past 2 years. It is a global wind as seen in the phenomena of Brexit, Bernie Sanders, Trump, Corbyn and now Pakatan Harapan.

Those who try to suggest that what happened in the West and now Malaysia cannot possibly happen in Singapore are myopic and in denial, because they refuse to recognise that the winds of change originate from peoples' weariness with the Neo-liberal economic order which has been dominant for the last 40 years. It was a reckless experiment where making the rich richer did not have the desired trickle-down effect and led instead to the impoverishment of a great many in our society. The PAP were already practising Neo-liberalism even before it became the trend.

We, in the Opposition must set our sails to catch this wind of change and bring hope and a better life to our Citizens.

Lim Tean

Party Leader of Peoples Voice (pending approval)

3. Opposition parties express desire to cooperate; invite Tan Cheng Bock to lead effort

2018 July 28

Singapore democrats

At a working lunch hosted by the SDP this afternoon, several opposition parties came together to explore the possibility of working closer together to present a unified front at the next elections.

The SDP also took the opportunity to propose that presidential candidate Dr Tan Cheng Bock help lead the effort in building such a coalition. Those present welcomed the move.

"With his experience and leadership," Dr Chee Soon Juan said, "the SDP is confident that Dr Tan will be able to lead the effort."

The former PAP MP, who attended the meeting as an observer, said: "If you want me to lead, then we must think of country first. If we go in, we must go in as a team."

The luncheon saw leaders and representatives of various opposition parties express their enthusiasm in greater cooperation with one another.

Mr Lim Tean, leader of the People's Voice said that while the exact form of such cooperation remains to be worked out, it is important that there be a more centralised form of leadership.

This sentiment was echoed by People's Power Party's Secretary-General Mr Goh Meng Seng who added that without discipline, such a coalition equals trouble.

Mr Ben Pwee, Democratic Progressive Party pointed out that whatever differences parties had in the past must be submerged. "There must not be ego politics within such a framework," he said.

Other parties present were the Reform Party, National Solidarity Party, and Singaporeans First Party.

For the SDP, Dr Chee said that the party "was excited about the prospect of making a historic advancement in Singapore's politics by forging a competent and credible oppositional force" with like-minded parties.

But he sounded a word of caution. He told participants that the cooperation cannot just be in form and not substance. "If it is merely the former, then it will be a matter of time before the electorate finds us wanting and repudiates the effort."

Dr Chee also warned that there will be powerful forces that will do their utmost to ensure that our effort fails and that the opposition remains divided and dysfunctional. "We must ensure that they do not succeed," he said.

As to SDP's contribution, he assured those present of the party's cooperation in making the endeavour a success. However, the Singapore Democrats do not seek to spearhead the effort.

"Rather, we see our role as a facilitator, of doing our part to contribute towards a common and greater good," he said.

He then took the opportunity to propose that Dr Tan Cheng Bock undertake the task of leading the effort and called on him to initiate future steps.

Dr Chee concluded: "On the eve of our 53rd National Day, we are presented with the an opportunity to take Singapore forward into a promising future. May we all have the wisdom to seize it and act with moral clarity and good sense."

The SDP also proposed a joint resolution to be signed by all opposition parties and invited everyone to consider endorsing it.

4. Newspaper reports on opposition coalition building

Small window to effect political change and mentor team 'for nation's good': 78-year-old Tan Cheng Bock on opposition coalition

Dr Tan Cheng Bock said in a Facebook post that he "may only have a short time to mentor a team to work for the good of the nation".

Seow Bei Yi

29 July 2018

SINGAPORE — Former veteran People's Action Party MP Tan Cheng Bock says that at the age of 78, he has just a "small window of opportunity" to effect change in Singapore politics.

Speaking on plans for a proposed opposition coalition which he has been invited to lead, he said: "I think I must help but in what capacity, I have not decided."

In a Facebook post on Sunday, Dr Tan — an MP of 26 years who lost the 2011 Presidential Election by 0.35 per cent to Dr Tony Tan — said that he "may only have a short time to mentor a team to work for the good of the nation".

"This is a small window of opportunity, a moment for ubah (change in Malay). I want to put my last years to good use. I want to pass all that I have acquired and learned in the political arena to the next generation.

"I would regret it if I had the chance to make a difference, but did nothing."

On Saturday, seven opposition parties met to discuss the possibility of forming a coalition to contest the next general election due to be held by 2021. Dr Tan attended as an observer.

They are: the Singapore Democratic Party (SDP), the People's Power Party (PPP), the Democratic Progressive Party, the Reform Party, the National Solidarity Party (NSP), the Singaporeans First Party, and former NSP chief Lim Tean, who has applied to form a new party — the People's Voice Party.

The Workers' Party (WP) and the Singapore People's Party, which is led by opposition veteran Chiam See Tong, were also invited to the meeting. But they did not attend it.

In its first public comments on the matter, the country's biggest opposition party WP remained non-committal about the prospects of joining the coalition.

Instead, WP said its priority is to build up the party's organisation given its leadership change. In April, Mr Pritam Singh took the helm as secretary-general, succeeding Mr Low Thia Khiang who was party chief for 17 years.

Responding to media queries, its spokesman said on Sunday: "WP is going through a leadership transition and is focused on organisation building to better serve Singaporeans." He declined to elaborate further on why it decided not to attend the meeting although it was invited.

At the meeting held at SDP's headquarters, SDP secretary-general Chee Soon Juan proposed that Dr Tan lead the coalition, given his experience and leadership. According to those present, there was no objection to this proposal.

When approached by The Straits Times at his home on Sunday, Dr Tan declined further comment on the matter.

However, in his Facebook post later that day, he noted that the seven parties all involve political veterans who have not landed a single seat in Parliament for the past decade, adding that he has advised them to put Singapore's interest ahead of their own, or even their party's interest in order to do better.

"To be fair, many from the seven parties stood in past elections because they believed they acted in Singapore's best interests. But I think some may also need to stand down and serve from the backroom if it is for the good of the country."

In his post, he also responded to observers' comments on the proposed coalition, and the invitation to have him lead it.

Political observer Derek da Cunha had earlier wrote on social media that "mixing with this particular crowd — which in the pecking order of non-PAP parties rank as third, fourth and fifth raters, will not do anything for (Dr Tan's) reputation. He will simply be tarnishing his reputation".

In response, Dr Tan said he was curious to know what yardstick was used for this measurement: "I believe that the men and women I met yesterday, were more than willing to make way for better men and women who would stand in their place. They have guts. They have put themselves out there. That is sufficient for the moment."

On Sunday, PPP secretary-general Goh Meng Seng noted on Facebook as well that it is "premature to say that this coalition will definitely be formed as there will be a lot of issues to be discussed and sorted out".

On why WP was not represented at the meeting, he added: "As a serious attempt to form the biggest coalition challenge to PAP ever, we of course would be all inclusive and wanted WP to be part of the coalition.

"I believe at this current stage, we will still continue to put in effort to persuade and convince WP to take part in this coalition building."

As for questions on why Dr Tan — a former PAP MP — was invited to lead the coalition if formed, Mr Goh said it is not about which party one used to be from, "but where your heart lies".

"Dr Tan has convinced us that he is pro-country and his fundamental motivation is to serve the country, in another way," he said. "Dr Tan has a proven record of being more of a critic of PAP's policies even when he was a PAP back bencher."

"We have to see things beyond partisan baggage and interests before we could serve the country wholeheartedly."

SDP Secretary-General Chee Soon Juan proposed Dr Tan Cheng Bock lead the coalition, given his experience and leadership.

Published

Jul 28, 2018

Yuen Sin

SINGAPORE — Seven Singapore opposition parties have come together to discuss the possibility of forming a coalition to contest the next general election, led by former People's Action Party MP and presidential candidate Tan Cheng Bock.

In a news release, the Singapore Democratic Party (SDP) said that six other opposition parties were present at a meeting hosted at the SDP headquarters on Saturday (July 28).

These were: the People's Power Party (PPP), the Democratic Progressive Party, the Reform Party, the National Solidarity Party, the Singaporeans First Party, and former NSP chief Lim Tean, who has applied to form a new party — the People's Voice Party.

At the meeting, SDP Secretary-General Chee Soon Juan proposed that Dr Tan lead the coalition, given his experience and leadership. According to those present, there was no objection to this proposal.

Dr Chee also called for a joint resolution to be signed by all opposition parties in the future, although it is not clear what the resolution would say.

Dr Tan, 78, who attended the meeting as an observer, said: "If you want me to lead, then we must think of (the) country first. If we go in, we must go in as a team."

Dr Tan, a PAP MP of 26 years, lost the 2011 Presidential Election by 7,382 votes or 0.35 per cent. The four-corner election was won by Dr Tony Tan.

The largest opposition party, the Workers' Party, was not at the meeting. When contacted, WP did not comment on its plans for the proposed coalition, or whether it was invited to the meeting.

A spokesman for Dr Tan said that he is currently not a member of a political party. When contacted, PPP Secretary-General Goh Meng Seng said that it is too early to comment on whether he needs to join one of the parties in order to run in the next General Election, due by April 2021.

He added that discussions on an opposition coalition have been going on "for a long time" — since 2015 at least.

In the press statement, Dr Chee said that the SDP has no intention to lead the coalition effort. "Rather, we see our role as a facilitator, of doing our part to contribute towards a common and greater good," he said.

In a Facebook post, Mr Lim said: "Our alliance must strive to form the next Government in the upcoming general election. We must offer real change to better the lives of Singaporeans."

Asked if the move was inspired by Malaysia's Dr Mahathir Mohamad, the former prime minister who had led a coalition of opposition parties to secure a shock election victory in May, Mr Lim said: "The Malaysian election is a continuation of the global trend of the last two years, which shows that people want change. I don't believe that phenomenon is confined only to the West or to Malaysia."

The Straits Times understands that the Singapore People's Party, led by opposition veteran Chiam See Tong, was invited to the meeting on Saturday but did not send a representative.

The last opposition coalition was the Singapore Democratic Alliance, in the lead up to the 2001 general election. It has since faded away, after NSP and Mr Chiam left the coalition.

Political observer Eugene Tan said a coalition led by Dr Tan, who has popular support from the ground, can be a catalyst for the opposition at the next general election, and can help reduce fragmentation within the opposition.

Whether this could be a game changer for the opposition remains to be seen, he added, pointing out that the minimum number of opposition MPs, including Non-constituency MPs, will go up from nine to 12 after the Constitution was amended in 2016.

"Candidates will be vying for seats in constituencies where they think the PAP is not as strong, and three-cornered fights may occur."

WILL THE OUTCOME OF MALAYSIA'S 2018 GENERAL ELECTIONS HAVE AN IMPACT ON SINGAPORE?

a. YES, it will

Bridget Welsh, "'New Malaysia' makes Singapore look outdated", *Nikkei Asian Review*, 10 July 2018.

Over two months after Mahathir Mohamad's election in Malaysia, the political reverberations for Singapore show no signs of fading.

The new Malaysian prime minister's reviews of the key water-supply deal with Singapore and of the planned costly high-speed rail link from Kuala Lumpur to the city-state are only visible signs of a different — and more charged — Singapore-Malaysia relationship.

The key problem for Lee Hsien Loong's People's Action Party (PAP) is that developments north of the Johor-Singapore Causeway have exposed vulnerabilities at home. The PAP has become the longest-governing incumbent party in Southeast Asia, and it no longer has undemocratic immediate neighbors. Mahathir's Pakatan victory mirrors the PAP's worst fear: its own possible defeat.

Worse yet, some of the factors that contributed to the loss of Barisan Nasional (National Front) are also present in Singapore. The first is the challenge of leadership renewal. Over the past three years, the PAP has been locked in a battle over who should succeed Lee, 66, as prime minister, with the fourth generation (4G) leaders on display.

Among the leading contenders are Chan Chun Sing, the minister for trade and industry and former army chief, Finance Minister Heng Swee Keat, former managing director of the Monetary Authority of Singapore and Ong Ye Kung, the minister of education and second defense minister.

The problem is that these leaders are 4G without the connectivity. They are in a highly elitist party, largely unable to relate to ordinary Singaporeans. 4G leaders also suffer from the same issue that haunted the National Front, namely they are embedded in the system. Emerging from within the party and government, particularly the military, they are from the system and are seen to be for the system. The intertwining of the PAP and the bureaucratic state has created singular agendas and resulted in a distancing from the electorate and its needs.

For the first two decades of Singapore's existence after independence in 1959, PAP secured all the seats in the legislative assembly. Since 1984, opposition politicians have won seats despite what the government's critics describe as the sustained political harassment of opponents and the repression of public protests, combined with the alleged manipulation of electoral boundaries.

In the last election in 2015, PAP secured 83 out of 89 seats with 70% of the vote. Since that resounding victory, more conservative forces within the party have gained ground. Despite their popularity, reform-minded leaders such as Tharman Shanmugaratnam and Tan Chuan-Jin have been pushed aside in favor of conservative alternatives. At the same time, Singapore's system has moved in a more authoritarian direction, with curbs on social media and attacks on civil society activists.

Prime Minister Lee, the son of Singapore's founding father Lee Kuan Yew, is making the same mistake Najib did after the 2013 polls. He is depriving the system of a necessary valve for dissent, and moving the country away from needed reforms. He has failed to recognize that greater openness and policy reforms were integral parts of the PAP's 2015 victory. The dominant mode has been to attack the Worker's Party, its leaders and other opposition figures. These moves do not show confidence in a more open and mature political system — or even in the PAP itself.

At the same time, rather than being an asset to his party, Lee is becoming more of a liability. This is the same trajectory that occurred for Najib. Questions have been raised about Lee's leadership from the very public "Oxleygate" row with his siblings over their father's home to the managing of Temasek, the republic's sovereign wealth fund, by his wife Ho Ching.

Singapore's handling of scandal over 1 Malaysia Development Berhad (1MDB), the Malaysian state-run investment fund which saw millions of dollars siphoned out on Najib's watch, will be in the more immediate bilateral spotlight; assessments will be made as to whether Singapore responded effectively to the alleged malfeasance and whether in fact Singapore's purchase of 1MDB bonds strengthened the fund.

Meanwhile, in Malaysia, Mahathir's readiness to deal with 1MDB signals a willingness not only to clean up the system but to begin much-needed economic reform. Singaporeans will see obvious parallels with their own country's economic policies.

Singapore's gross domestic product growth is expected to reach 3% this year, which is a significant drop from a decade ago. Importantly, much of this growth is being driven by public spending (as occurred in Malaysia under Najib), notably on infrastructure. New jobs are not being created in Singapore at the same high rate as in the past. Even more constraining, PAP continues to rely on immigration as a driver of growth, failing to move on from using a combination of low-cost labor and imported foreign talent to expand the economy. Population pressures remain real for ordinary Singaporeans, who continue to feel displaced. They are disappointed with the PAP's tenacious grasp on old and unpopular models for growth.

The pendulum of discontent has swung against the PAP. The government opted to increase water prices by 30% in 2017, and this year indicated it will raise the goods and services tax (GST) from 7% to 9%. The electricity tariff has risen by 16.8% to date this year alone. The cost of living remains high; Singapore has topped the Economist Intelligence Unit's list of most expensive cities to live in for five years running. High costs are compounded by persistent inequalities that are increasingly entrenched. The Gini coefficient is at 0.46, but income gaps are deeply felt. Many locals feel they are being impoverished on account of foreigners. The social reform measures introduced for the "pioneer generation" (people born before 1950), and increased handouts before the 2015 polls, are being seen as inadequate to address the current social needs of disadvantaged communities.

By comparison, Malaysia has removed the unpopular GST, and reform pressures for addressing contracting social mobility and inequality are substantial. Malaysia is now seen as a potential role model in areas of governance. For example, greater transparency and attention to inclusivity are evident in the multi-ethnicity of new government appointees. Singapore's 2017 Malay-only presidency contest in contrast sent a signal of exclusion and an embrace of race-based politics. This is being compounded by the fact that Malaysia is being seen as bucking regional authoritarian trends, promising substantive political reforms and the removal of many of the draconian laws that Singapore has on its books.

Changes in Malaysia have reduced Singapore's regional comparative advantage. It is not just about greater democracy and changes in governance next door but also the attention "New Malaysia" draws to how Singapore has remained locked in the past, moving away from embracing an alternative future.

b. NO, it will not

Karim Raslan, "Why Singapore won't be repeating Malaysia's political dramas any time soon", *The South China Morning Post*, 25 July 2018.

As a political underdog, new Prime Minister Mahathir Mohamad had a legacy, a cause and a corrupt adversary to fight against. Aside from higher costs of living, the Lion City has little to inspire a change at the top.

Malaysian Prime Minister Mahathir Mohamad is Asia's most quotable leader.

In May, soon after the surprise victory of his Pakatan Harapan (PH) alliance in elections, he quipped that Singaporeans "must be tired of having the same government, the same party since independence", a clear reference to the republic's ruling People's Action Party's (PAP) almost six-decade monopoly on power.

Mahathir, as history will tell us, is no fan of Singapore.

Understandably, the 93-year-old's pronouncements on the city state since returning to power have drawn a lot of attention.

Intrigued by the possibility of change in Singapore, Team Ceritalah travelled across the causeway to see what local residents thought of Malaysia's historic election and how — if at all — it would impact them.

Try Foo, a 25-year-old Southeast Asian Studies student at the National University of Singapore, thinks Singaporeans will stick with the political status quo.

"It was exciting that PH won. But I think that Singaporeans will still vote for some semblance of the status quo," says Try Foo, a 25-year-old Southeast Asian Studies student at the National University of Singapore.

"There's a lack of factors for an opposition win — like the 1MDB [financial scandal] and Najib [Razak]," explains Martino Tan, co-founder of independent media platform mothership.sg.

Indeed, former prime minister Najib Razak and the Barisan Nasional (BN) coalition faced three critical obstacles.

First, it was dogged by a strong sense that Malaysia's economy, under the BN's watch, was failing to deliver equal opportunities against the backdrop of rising food prices and costs of living.

Second, a much-hated and little-understood sales tax (better known as the GST) seemed to have accelerated inflationary pressures on many everyday staples. Its introduction back in 2015 shocked and angered millions of Malaysians, who for the first time felt the brunt of consumption taxes, prompting, in turn, calls for greater scrutiny of government spending.

GST's introduction in 2015 happened just as the 1Malaysia Development Berhad (1MDB) financial scandal — which implicated the then-premier — exploded into the public arena. The revelations served to erode the government's already shaky credibility and further spurred popular disaffection.

Enter Mahathir. Having never lost an election since 1969, the nonagenarian wove together a simple narrative uniting the failure of trickle-down economics, the introduction of GST and Najib's alleged corruption into a powerful electoral message.

Could the same happen in Singapore?

Certainly, it's true that the economy is beginning to make life tough for ordinary Singaporeans.

Many like 34-year-old Melissa Teoh (not her real name), a mother of one and an Operations Associate, have had to grapple with the rising costs of living.

"I buy my 4-year-old's milk powder from Malaysia. One tin there is 64 Malaysian ringgit (HK$124), versus S$64 (HK$368) here. Our cost of living is so high…we worry for our children."

In March 2018, The Economist Intelligence Unit ranked Singapore as the most expensive city in the world out of 133 for the fifth consecutive year, outpacing Hong

Kong, Tokyo and Paris. Singapore's own GST is already 7 per cent — higher than Malaysia's former 6 per cent.

But Prime Minister Lee Hsien Loong's political travails pale in comparison to Najib's.

Lee's worst "scandal" to date — if one can even call it that — was a mid-2017 spat with his siblings, Lee Hsien Yang and Lee Wei Ling over the fate of 38 Oxley Road, the former residence of their late father and Singapore's founder, Lee Kuan Yew.

"I was really worried when the siblings made the argument public — we had just lost Lee Kuan Yew. I was worried the government was going to fall through," Melissa recalls.

Martino Tan, left, co-founder of mothership.sg, discusses the lack of opposition strength with Karim Raslan.

Yet, as Martino observes, "It's still not enough. There's no popular figure among the opposition who is well-known across the young and old, who can rally and mobilise Singaporeans to consider the possibility of a change in government".

Some Singaporeans are pinning their hopes on Pritam Singh, secretary general of the Workers' Party (WP) and leader of the opposition.

He was part of the WP team that seized the Aljunied Group Representation Constituency (GRC) in the unprecedented 2011 general elections. However, the 41-year-old has yet to attain Mahathir's stature or accomplishments; the WP retained Aljunied in 2015 by a margin of less than 2 per cent.

Moreover, Singaporean politics arguably lacks an issue — besides the rising costs of living — to rally voters to effect change.

Like it or not, Singapore is not Malaysia, despite the many things that bind them together.

Malaysia's highly emotional moment of democratic change is certainly something Malaysians and Southeast Asians can be proud of.

Nonetheless, with neither the headline controversies or opponents with gravitas, Singapore's PAP looks like it won't be going anywhere any time soon.

At least for now.

SELECT BIBLIOGRAPHY

Books

Bellows, T.J., *The People's Action Party of Singapore* (New Haven, Connecticut: Yale University Southeast Asian Studies, 1970).

Chan, H.C., *Singapore: The Politics of Survival, 1965–1967* (Singapore: Oxford University Press, 1971).

Chan, H.C., *The Dynamics of One-Party Dominance: The PAP at the Grassroots* (Singapore: Singapore University Press, 1976).

Duverger, M., *Political Parties* (London, UK: Methuen, 1954).

Giliomee, H. and Simkins, C., (eds.), *The Awkward Embrace: One Party Dominance and Democracy* (Cape Town, South Africa: Tafelberg, 1999).

Han, F.K., Ibrahim, Z., Chua, M.H., Lim, L., Low, I., Lin, R. and Chan, R., *Lee Kuan Yew: Hard Truths to Keep Singapore Going* (Singapore: Straits Times Press, 2011).

Huntington, S.P., *The Third Wave: Democratization in the Late 20th Century* (Norman, Oklahoma: University of Oklahoma Press, 1991).

Institute of Policy Studies, *Insights on Singapore's Politics and Governance from Leading Thinkers* (Singapore: World Scientific, 2019).

Josey, A., *The Crucial Years Ahead: Republic of Singapore General Elections 1968* (Singapore: Donald Moore Press, 1968).

Pang, C.L., *Singapore's People's Action Party: Its History, Organization and Leadership* (Singapore: Oxford University Press, 1971).

Pempel, T.J., *Uncommon Democracies: The One-Party Dominant Regimes* (Ithaca, New York: Cornell University Press, 1990).

Sartori, G., *Parties and Party Systems* (Cambridge, England: Cambridge University Press, 1976).

Shee, P.K., "The People's Action Party of Singapore, 1954–1970: A Study of Survivalism of a Single-Dominant Party" (PhD Dissertation, Indiana University, 1971).

Spiess, C., *Democracy and Party System in Developing Countries: A Comparative Study of India and South Africa* (Routledge Advances in South Asian Studies), 1st Edition (London, UK: Routledge, 2009).

Thucydides, *The Peloponnesian War*. See Sam Seau, "The strong do what they can, and the weak suffer what they must", in *Return of Kings*, https://www.returnofkings.com/10535/the-strong-do-what-they-can-and-the-weak-suffer-what-they-must

Yeo, K.W., *Political Developments in Singapore 1945–1955* (Singapore: Singapore University Press, 1973).

Chapters in books

Doorenspleet, R. and Nijzink, L., "One-Party Dominance in African Democracies: A Framework for Analysis", in Renske Doorenspleet and Lia Nijzink (eds.), *One-Party Dominance in African Democracies* (Boulder, Colorado: Lynne Rienner Publishers, 2013).

Krauss, E.S. and Pierre, J., "The Decline of Dominant Parties: Parliamentary Politics in Sweden and Japan in the 1970s", T.J. Pempel (ed.), *Uncommon Democracies: The One-Party Dominant Regimes* (Ithaca, New York: Cornell University Press, 1990).

Pontusson, J., "Conditions of Labor-Party Dominance: Sweden and Britain Compared", in T.J. Pempel (ed.), *Uncommon Democracies: The One-Party Dominant Regimes* (Ithaca, New York: Cornell University Press, 1990).

Quah, J.S.T., "Political Science in Singapore", in Basant K. Kapur (ed.), *Singapore Studies: Critical Surveys of the Humanities and Social Sciences* (Singapore: Singapore University Press, 1986).

Shalev, M., "The Political Economy of Labor-Party Dominance and Decline in Israel", in T.J. Pempel (ed.), *Uncommon Democracies: The One-Party Dominant Regimes* (Ithaca, New York: Cornell University Press, 1990).

Starner, F.L., "The Singapore Elections of 1963", in K.J. Ratnam and Robert Stephen Milne (eds.), *The Malayan Parliamentary Elections of 1964* (Singapore: University of Malaya Press, 1967).

Turnbull, C.M., "Constitutional Developments 1819–1968", in Ooi Jin Bee and Chiang Hai Ding (eds.), *Modern Singapore* (Singapore: Singapore University Press, 1969).

Journal articles

Asher, A. and Barnes, S., "The Dominant Party System: A Neglected Model of Democratic Stability", *Journal of Politics*, Vol. 36, 1974.

Lusztig, M., James, P., and Moon, J., "Falling from Grace", *Publius*, Vol. 27 , No. 1, 1997.

Ong, C.C., "The 1959 Singapore General Election", *Journal of Southeast Asian Studies*, Vol. 6, No. 1, March 1975.

Reports

Abedi, A. and Schneider, S., *Big Fish in Small Ponds*, ECPR Workshops 24 paper, 2005.

Citizens and the Nation: National Orientations of Singapore Survey (Singapore: Institute of Policy Studies, 2010).

Dhamani, I., *Income Inequality in Singapore: Causes, Consequences and Policy Options*, National University of Singapore, May 2008, http://www.scribd.com/doc/3661870/Income-Inequality-in-Singapore

Federalism, Parliamentary Government, and Single-Party Dominance, APSA paper, 2006.

Human Development Reports (HDR), United Nations Development Programme, 2009, hdrstats.org/ en/indicators/161.html; also see "Singapore ranked 2nd highest on Gini Coefficient Score in UN report", singaporenewsalternative.blogspot.com/2009/10/spore-ranked-2

Shaw, B.J. and Ismail, R., *Good Fences Make Good Neighbours? Geographies of Marginalisation: Housing Singapore's Foreign Workers*, Paper presented for Southeast Asian Geography Association (SEAGA), 23–26 November 2010, Hanoi, Vietnam, http://www.seaga.xtreemhost.com/seaga2010/ CS2A-ShawIsmail.pdf?i=2

Singapore Parliamentary Debates, Official Report (24 July 1984), Vol. 44, cols. 1724–1726.

Newspaper articles

"8 promises that Lim Tean made as leader of People's Voice", *The Must Share News Team*, 30 October 2018.

Abdullah, Z., "No reason why ending streaming won't remove stigma if society plays its part: Ong Ye Kung", *The Straits Times*, 10 March 2019.

Ahmad, M.L., "Sarawak BN not joining Pakartan Harapan: Abang Johari", *New Straits Times*, 14 May 2018.

"An Opposition alliance under Tan Cheng Bock", *Under the Angsana Tree*, 1 August 2018, https:// undertheangsanatree.blogspot.com/2018/08/an-opposition-alliance-under-tan-cheng.html

"Analysts and the AHPETC and the voters", *The New Paper*, 1 September 2015.

Ananthalakshmi, A., "Malaysia's first lady linked to $30 mln worth of jewelry bought with IMDB funds", *Reuters*, 16 June 2017.

Ang, M., "Tan Cheng Bock announces return to politics with new Progress Singapore Party (PSP)", *Mothership*, 18 January 2019, https://mothership.sg/2019/01/tan-cheng-bock-returns-new-political- party/

Ann, D., "Rosmah vs Imelda Marcos? Who is the true Southeast Asian First Lady of seized luxury?", *Alvinology.com*, 24 May 2018, https://alvinology.com/2018/05/24/rosmah-vs-imelda-who-is-the- true-southeast-asian-first-lady-of-seized-luxury/

Au-Yong, J. and Tham, Y.-C., "8 reasons for surge of support", *The Straits Times*, 13 September 2015.

Au-Yong, R., "Leaders will do what it takes to put things right: Heng Swee Keat", *The Straits Times*, 9 February 2019.

Baharudin, H., "Digital Defence to be sixth Total Defence pillar, signalling importance of cyber security", *The Straits Times*, 14 February 2019.

Balji, P.N., "Aljunied-Hougang Town Council saga: What is the end game?", *Yahoo News Singapore*, 31 July 2017, https://sg.news.yahoo.com/comment-aljunied-hougang-town-council-saga-end- game-101158627.html

Balji, P.N., "Comment: How Heng Swee Keat can return the favour to PAP cadres", *Yahoo News Singapore*, 25 November 2018.

"Blood donor data leak: HSA's vendor says information that went online was accessed illegally and possibly extracted", *Channel NewsAsia*, 30 March 2019, https://www.channelnewsasia.com/news/singapore/personal-data-of-800-000-blood-donors-accessed-illegally-hsa-ssg-11395364

Board, J., "Mahathir brings together old brigade, doubles down on Najib in Melaka", *Channel NewsAsia*, 5 May 2018, https://www.channelnewsasia.com/news/asia/mahathir-melaka-malaysia-ge14-najib-10204378

Brown, C.R., "Bustari The Bag Man? How Najib bought the Sarawak election", *The Sarawak Report*, 29 May 2017.

Business Day (South Africa), 31 May 1999.

Capri, A., "Why Malaysia's surprise election result should be a wake-up call for global leaders", *Forbes*, 10 May 2018, http://www.globaladvisors.biz/blog/2018/05/11/why-malaysias-surprise-election-result-should-be-a-wake-up-call-for-global-leaders/

Chan, F. and Chan, R., "Housing not a 'make-or-break' election issue", *The Straits Times*, 25 April 2011.

Chan, V., "Does Singapore's Ministry of Health deserve immunity for data breach?", *The Independent*, 17 February 2019.

"Changes to electoral system to encourage wider range of views in Parliament", *Channel NewsAsia*, 27 May 2009.

Cheng, K. and Choo, C., "The Big Read: Opposition parties banding together — a grand plan or a last throw of the disc?", *Today*, 4 August 2018.

Cheng, K. and Wong, P.T., "With no Tan Cheng Bock-led alliance in sight, opposition parties turn to plan Bs", *Today*, 8 April 2019.

Chia, L., "Current approach to streaming in secondary schools to be phased out by 2024", *Channel NewsAsia*, 5 March 2019, https://www.channelnewsasia.com/news/singapore/streaming-secondary-schools-o-n-levels-ong-ye-kung-11312252

Chia, R.G., "People donated over S$1 million in 4 days to the Workers' Party MPs embroiled in a multi-million dollar lawsuit", *Business Insider*, 29 October 2018, https://www.businessinsider.sg/workers-party-mps-embroiled-in-multi-million-dollar-lawsuits-raise-more-than-s1-million-in-4-days/

"Chiam pulls party out of alliance", *Today*, 3 March 2011, www.todayonline.com/Singapore/EDC110303-0000259/Chiam-pulls-partyout-of-alliance

Chow, J. and Lim, J., "SAF armoured vehicles seized in Hong Kong port, Mindef expects shipment to return to Singapore 'expeditiously'", *The Straits Times*, 24 November 2016.

Chua, C.H., "24 hours to cool off before Polling Day", *The Straits Times*, 1 December 2009.

Chua, L.H., "Commentary: Few surprises despite the many changes", *The Straits Times*, 25 February 2011.

Chua, L.H., "Cost of living: We are doing what we can", *The Straits Times*, 22 April 2011.

Chua, M.H., "Has trust in the government been eroded? It's time to talk frankly", *The Straits Times*, 1 February 2018.

Chua, M.H., "Malaysian General Elections: 5 takeaways for Singapore", *The Straits Times*, 13 May 2018.

"Conference Celebrating Democracy in Malaysia", Inaugural Conference of FORSEA, 16–17 February 2019, Kuala Lumpur. See https://forsea.co/human-rights-for-all/

"Departure of Sarawak parties from Barisan Nasional is Pakatan Harapan's gain, analysts say", *The Straits Times*, 13 June 2018.

Dzulkifly, D., "May 9 polls prove change is possible for Singapore too, says exile", *The Malay Mail*, 30 August 2018.

"Former PM Najib arrested", *The Business Times*, 3 July 2018.

"GE: SDA says Chiam pulling SPP out of alliance", 2 March 2011, *ChannelNewsAsia.com*, http://channelnewsasia.com/stories/Singaporelocalnews/view/1113966/1html

Goh, M., "Mahathir launches new party; promises to abolish GST if opposition wins", *Channel NewsAsia*, 15 January 2017, https://www.channelnewsasia.com/news/asia/mahathir-launches-new-party-promises-to-abolish-gst-if-oppositio-7579242

Goh, T., "800,000 blood donors' personal data accessed illegally and possibly stolen; police investigating", *The Straits Times*, 30 March 2019.

"Good for 4G ministers not to be constrained by 'artificial deadline' to select leader: Ong Ye Kung", *The Straits Times*, 29 January 2018.

Han, F.K., "Singapore's future according to Lee Kuan Yew", *The Straits Times*, 27 March 2016.

Heng, J., "Budget 2019 could be generous — election or not: Analysts", *Business Times*, 21 January 2019.

Henson, B., "And the winner of that KL meeting is…Dr M", *Today*, 2 September 2018.

"Housing remains a hot election issue, says Mah", *The Straits Times*, 31 January 2011.

Hussain, Z., "PAP unveils new leadership: Key challenge will be keeping party cohesive and united", *The Straits Times*, 24 November 2018.

Inderjit Singh, *Facebook*, 16 September 2015.

Koh, T., "10 reflections on GE 2015", *The Straits Times*, 17 September 2015.

Kwang, K., "Singapore health system hit by 'most serious breach of personal data' in cyberattack; PM Lee's data targeted", *Channel NewsAsia*, 18 October 2018, https://www.channelnewsasia.com/news/singapore/singhealth-health-system-hit-serious-cyberattack-pm-lee-target-10548318

Kwok, F., "Mahathir: Singaporeans must be tired of having the same government since independence", 29 May 2018, *The Online Citizen*, https://www.theonlinecitizen.com/2018/05/29/mahathir-singaporeans-must-be-tired-of-having-the-same-government-since-independence/

Lee, A., "Dr M birthday message to UMNO — 'Go back to your roots'", *Malaysiakini*, 11 May 2018, https://www.malaysiakini.com/news/424240

Lee, K.Y., "Voters should look at the fundamentals", *Today*, 26 April 2011.

Leong, G., "More than 100 Hyflux investors protest at Hong Lim Park", *The Straits Times*, 31 March 2019.

Leong, W.K., "We have made mistakes: PM Lee", *Today*, 4 May 2011.

Leong, W.K., "Many remain hurt by MM's Lee's remarks", *Today*, 13 May 2011.

Lim, A., "IT error led to wrong Chas subsidies for 7,700", *The Straits Times*, 17 February 2019.

Lim, A. and Au-Yong, R., "AHTC wrap-up: What are the 2 lawsuits about?", *The Straits Times*, 4 November 2018.

Lim, A.L. and Teoh, S., "Malaysia election: Mahathir calls for change at Reformasi rally site", *The Straits Times*, 7 May 2018.

Lim, J., "Singaporeans are tired of the same government too, says Tun M", 31 May 2018, http://says.com/my/news/tun-m-like-malaysians-singaporeans-are-tired-of-the-same-government-too

Loh, A., "Opinion: Opposition alliance 'on the cards': Are Cheng Bock and WP the key to unity?", *The Independent*, 15 July 2018, theindependent.sg/opinion-opposition-alliance-on-the-cards-are-tan-cheng-bock-wp-the-key-to-unity/

Loh, A., "Spore exile Tan Wah Piow meets Mahathir; says M'sia is a beacon for democracy", *The Independent*, 31 August 2018, http://theindependent.sg/spore-exile-tan-wah-piow-meets-mahathir-says-msia-is-a-beacon-for-democracy/

Loh, C.K. and Paulo, D.A., "Seeking 'room to manoeuvre', NSP leaves SDA", *Today*, 19 January 2007.

Loh, V. and Mokhtar, F., "The leaders of at least five opposition parties told TODAY that they are open to an alliance with Dr Tan", *Today*, 19 January 2019.

Low, A., "What does it say when Singaporeans look to Mahathir to bring change in Singapore?", *The Online Citizen*, 31 August 2018, https://www.theonlinecitizen.com/2018/08/31/what-does-it-say-when-singaporeans-look-to-mahathir-to-bring-change-to-singapore/

Low, A., "For the PAP, Mahathir is the elephant in the room", *The Online Citizen*, 3 September 2018, https://www.theonlinecitizen.com/2018/09/03/for-the-pap-mahathir-is-the-elephant-in-the-room/

"Low: GRC win a boost for opposition", *The Straits Times*, 14 March 2011.

"Low Thia Khiang: Opposition renewal an important issue for voters", *The Online Citizen*, 13 March 2011, http://www.theonlinecitizen.com/2011/03/low-thia-khiang-opposition-renewal-an-important-issue-for-voters/

"Malaysia PM Mahathir Mohamad wants to raise price of raw water sold to Singapore by more than 10 times", *The Straits Times*, 14 August 2018.

Malaysians Must Know the Truth, 23 May 2018, http://malaysiansmustknowthetruth.blogspot.com/2018/05/as-macc-chief-exposes-king-of-cash-mp.html

"MHA responds to activists' letter of complaint to PM Lee Hsien Loong", *The Straits Times*, 6 September 2018.

"Minister Ong Ye Kung: Democracy would ruin Singapore, success formula is PAP", *ST Review*, 24 January 2017.

Mohan, M., "PDPC fines IHiS, SingHealth combined S$1 million for data breach following cyberattack", *Channel NewsAsia*, 15 January 2019, https://www.channelnewsasia.com/news/singapore/ihis-singhealth-fined-1-million-data-breach-cyberattack-11124156

Mokhtar, F., "MM Lee on PAP losing power: That day will come", *Singapore Scene*, 15 March 2011, sg.news.yahoo.com/blogs/singaporescene/mm-lee-pap-losing-p

Mokhtar, F., "'Foolish mistake' to think PAP will suffer the same fate as Malaysia's former government: Ho Kwon Ping", *Today*, 12 July 2017.

Mokhtar, F., "Exclusive: Revealed — the people behind Tan Cheng Bock's proposed new party and its election plans", *Today*, 8 February 2019.

Mokhtar, F., "Ho Ching to step down as chairman of Temasek's subsidiary", *Today*, 19 March 2019.

"Mr Ong quits the Assembly", *The Straits Times*, 17 June 1965.

Naidu, S., "Malaysia PM Mahathir invited to speak at democracy conference by political activists", *Channel NewsAsia*, 31 August 2018, https://www.channelnewsasia.com/news/singapore/mahathir-tan-wah-piow-thum-ping-tjin-democracy-conference-10668618

"Najib-BN's 'blatant corruption' led to gov't change, 'won't happen to Singapore'", *Malaysiakini*, 13 July 2018.

"Najib's circle of family, friends and cronies", *Reddit*, https://www.reddit.com/r/malaysia/comments/8lkzxm/najibs_circle_of_family_friends_and_cronies/?st=jllsagxc&sh=16504bc6

Neo, C.C., "PAP: Will Wijeysingha pursue gay agenda? SDP: No, we will not", *Today*, 27 April 2011.

"New party now registered", *The Straits Times*, 22 July 1961.

Ng, H., "Chas subsidies for about 7,700 people miscalculated due to IT error: MOH", *The Straits Times*, 16 February 2019.

"'Nobody wanted to acknowledge we have a problem': UMNO youth chief Khairy on BN's defeat", *Channel NewsAsia*, 15 May 2018, https://www.channelnewsasia.com/news/asia/khairy-umno-ge14-defeat-barisan-nasional-malaysia-10234396

"Nur Jazlan: Najib should have foreseen BN's collapse", *The Sun Daily*, 21 May 2018, http://www.thesundaily.my/news/2018/05/21/nur-jazlan-najib-should-have-foreseen-bn%E2%80%99s-collapse

Ong, T., "Chee Soon Juan debunks as 'not true' text message with details of opposition coalition manifesto", *Mothership*, 7 August 2018, https://mothership.sg/2018/08/chee-soon-juan-opposition-coalition-manifesto-fake/

"PAP banks on the future with new line-up", *The Straits Times*, 18 April 2011.

"PAP New CEC", *People's Action Party*, 23 November 2018, https://www.pap.org.sg/pap-new-cec

"Parliament approves increase in President's salary, expenditure", *Today*, 11 March 2011.

"Personal data of 808,000 blood donors compromised for nine weeks; HSA lodges police report", *Today*, 15 March 2019.

"PM Lee calls on PAP to unite Singaporeans, continue with pragmatic and centrist approach", *The Straits Times*, 11 November 2018.

Rahim, N.A., "A little sad, a bit regretful: Shanmugam on activists' move to engage Mahathir", *Channel NewsAsia*, 2 September 2018, https://www.channelnewsasia.com/news/singapore/shanmugam-on-tan-wah-piow-thum-ping-tjin-meeting-mahathir-10676820

Rakin, E., "Dr Chee Soon Juan discredits the contents of an election manifesto allegedly written by a coalition made up of opposition parties in Singapore", *Business Insider*, 8 August 2018, https://www.businessinsider.sg/chee-soon-juan-discredits-the-contents-of-an-election-manifesto-apparently-written-by-a-coalition-made-up-of-opposition-parties-in-singapore/

Ramesh, R., "1MDB: The inside story of the world's biggest financial scandal", *The Guardian*, 28 July 2016, https://www.theguardian.com/world/2016/jul/28/1mdb-inside-story-worlds-biggest-financial-scandal-malaysia

Romero, A.M., "Lim Tean debuts new political party — People's Voice", *The Independent*, 31 October 2018.

Romero, A.M., "#SGBudget2019 an election budget?", *The Independent*, 19 February 2019.

Sagar, "Singapore Ministry of Health reveals details of another serious medical data breach", *Opengov*, 30 January 2019, https://www.opengovasia.com/singapore-ministry-of-health-reveals-details-of-another-serious-medical-data-breach/

Salma, K., "Ground less sweet, says Khaw but he's confident", *The Straits Times*, 25 April 2011.

"Seah Kian Peng — retract your Facebook post and issue an apology", *The Online Citizen*, 3 September 2018.

Seow, B.Y., "Tan Cheng Bock yet to decide on role in opposition coalition, says small window to effect political change", *The Straits Times*, 29 July 2018.

"Show-cause letter widens rift in SDA", *The Straits Times*, 11 February 2011.

Sim, R., "MP Seah Kin Peng urges netizens not to get 'personal or abusive' in debate over Thum Ping Tjin's comments", *The Straits Times*, 3 September 2018.

Sim, R., "Ex-diplomat Bilahari Kausikan asks historian Thum Ping Tjin to make clear his loyalties", *The Straits Times*, 4 September 2018.

Sim, R., "Thum refutes notion he is a traitor: MP calls for calm online", *The New Paper*, 4 September 2018.

"Singapore has been clear and consistent that Malaysia lost its right to review water price in 1987: MFA", *The Straits Times*, 31 July 2018.

"Singapore's younger office holders will settle on a potential leader 'in good time'", *Channel NewsAsia*, 4 January 2018, https://www.channelnewsasia.com/news/singapore/singapore-s-younger-office-holders-will-settle-on-a-potential-9832326

Siow, M., "GE: Ground 'not so sweet' for elections, says SM Goh", *Channel NewsAsia*, 18 April 2011, http://www.channelnewsasia.com/stories/singaporelocalnews/view/

Soezean, M., "Ong Ye Kung: Singapore's one-party system, a result of free and fair election", *The Online Citizen*, 24 January 2017.

Stolarchuk, J., "Mahathir boldly states: 'The people of Singapore must be tired of having the same government since independence'", *The Independent*, 30 May 2018, http://theindependent.sg/mahathirs-boldly-states-the-people-of-singapore-must-be-tired-of-having-the-same-government-since-independence/

"Tan Cheng Bock's application to form political party approved 'in principle'", *Channel NewsAsia*, 16 March 2019, https://www.channelnewsasia.com/news/singapore/tan-cheng-bock-s-application-to-form-political-party-approved-in-11351438/

"Tan Cheng Bock's Progress Singapore Party officially registered", *Channel NewsAsia*, 1 April 2019, https://www.channelnewsasia.com/news/singapore/tan-cheng-bock-s-progress-singapore-party-officially-registered-11398996

Tan, M., "Minister Ong Ye Kung asked at IPS conference: 'What if S'pore becomes a 2 or multi-party system?'", *Mothership*, 23 January 2017.

Tan, M., "WP & SDP respond to Ong Ye Kung's speech about risks of two- or multi-party system S'pore", *Mothership*, 26 January 2017.

Tan, M., "S'pore's Budget 2019 is definitely not an election budget. The one coming next year will be", *Mothership*, 21 February 2019.

Tan, N.A., "Inside the lavish world of Malaysia's Rosmah Mansor", *Arab News*, 9 June 2018.

Tan, R., "Abdul Azeez: I'm a victim of name dropping", *The Star*, 3 March 2018.

Tan, S.K., "Higher salary threshold for local workers from July under rules for hiring foreigners", *Channel NewsAsia*, 5 March 2019, https://www.channelnewsasia.com/news/singapore/higher-salary-threshold-local-workers-foreigners-11313012

Tan, W., "Multi-party political system in which parties align along sinister lines could ruin S'pore: Ye Kung", *Today*, 24 January 2017.

Tay, S., "Malaysia votes: What the General Election means for Malaysia's stability and Singapore–Malaysia ties", *Singapore Institute of International Affairs*, 20 April 2018, http://www.siiaonline.org/malaysia-votes-what-the-general-election-means-for-malaysias-stability-and-singapore-malaysia-ties/

Teh, S.N., "At least 5 potential ministers in new slate", *Business Times*, 18 April 2011.

"Temasek, GIC made gains over long term: Indranee", *The Straits Times*, 11 July 2018.

Teng, A., and Kaur, K., "WP not being upfront on issue: Shanmugam", *The Straits Times*, 4 September 2015.

Teng, Y.P., "Tan Cheng Bock open to leading proposed opposition coalition", *Yahoo News Singapore*, 28 July 2018, https://sg.news.yahoo.com/tan-cheng-bock-expresses-interest-leading-opposition-coalition-113957990.html

Teoh, S., "Najib sacks DPM, four ministers and A-G", *The Straits Times*, 29 July 2015.

Teoh, S., "Malaysia will honour water deal with Singapore, says Foreign Minister", *The Straits Times*, 25 July 2018.

Tham, I., "Singapore's privacy watchdog fines IHiS $750,000 and SingHealth $250,000 for data breach", *The Straits Times*, 15 January 2019.

Tham, S.Y., "Chinese investments in Malaysia: Five years into the BRI", *ISEAS Perspectives*, 11, 27 February 2018.

"The AHTC lawsuits against Workers' Party MPs explained in 5 minutes", *The Must Share News Team*, 2 October 2018, https://mustsharenews.com/ahtc-lawsuits/

Then, S., "Sarawak Pakatan Harapan will fight new GPS coalition of former BN parties in the next state polls", *The Star*, 12 June 2018.

Toh, E., "ESM Goh Chok Tong says settling 4G leadership an urgent challenge, hopes next PM can be designated 'before 2018 ends'", *The Straits Times*, 31 December 2017.

Toh, E. and Tham, Y.C., "Singapore opposition take lessons from Malaysian election result", *The New Paper*, 31 July 2018, https://www.tnp.sg/news/singapore/singapore-opposition-take-lessons-malaysian-election-result

Toh, Y.C. and Lim, J., "SDA scores worse result in post-independence history", *The Straits Times*, 27 January 2013, http://www.asiaone.com/News/Latest+News/Singapore/Story/A1Story20130127-398101.html

"Tun Mahathir: 'When Najib became a thief, everyone under him became a thief'" — your days are numbered", *The Coverage*, 30 August 2018, https://thecoverage.my/news/tun-mahathir-najib-became-thief-everyone-became-thief-days-numbered/

Uihua, "Is Muhyiddin's new party a rebranded UMNO? Or could it be a stroke of genius?", *Cilisos. my*, 17 August 2016, https://cilisos.my/is-muhyiddins-new-party-a-rebranded-umno-or-could-it-be-a-stroke-of-genius/

"Under Najib, many became thieves, says Dr Mahathir", *Today*, 26 August 2018.

Wong, C.H., "Why Malaysia's opposition picked an old foe as its leader", *The New York Times*, 11 January 2018.

Wong, K., "'Foolish' to think PAP will suffer the same fate as Barisan Nasional: Ho Kwon Ping", *Nikkei Asian Review*, 20 July 2018.

Wong, P.T., "The Big Read: No easy answers to HDB lease decay issue, but public mindset has to change first", *Today*, 5 June 2018.

Wong, P.T., "Former political dissident, Singapore civil activists meet Dr Mahathir", *Today*, 30 August 2018.

Woon, W., "Punishing corporate corruption", *The Straits Times*, 30 April 2018.

Xu, T., "K Shanmugam masterfully links photo and comment of Thum Ping Tjin as him inviting foreign politician to intervene in Singapore politics", *The Online Citizen*, 2 September 2018, https://www.theonlinecitizen.com/2018/09/02/k-shanmugam-masterfully-links-photo-and-comment-of-thum-ping-tjin-as-inviting-foreign-politician-to-intervene-in-singapore-politics/

Yahya, Y., "Parliament: S'pore will honour 1962 Water Agreement and expects Malaysia to do the same, says Vivian Balakrishnan", *The Straits Times*, 9 July 2018.

Yahya, Y., "No harm in asking foreigners to influence local politics: Activist Jolovan Wham", *The Straits Times*, 5 September 2018.

Yong, C., "WP MPs 'have not shown integrity'", *The Straits Times*, 24 July 2016.

Yong, C., "One-party rule 'may be way for Singapore to succeed': Ong Ye Kung", *The Straits Times*, 24 January 2017.

Yong, C., "G-20 finance ministers concerned about preparing for risks, strengthening global system: Heng Swee Keat", *The Straits Times*, 2 December 2018.

Yong, C., "Cabinet reshuffle to take place sometime after Budget 2019: PM Lee Hsien Loong", *The Straits Times*, 4 December 2018.

"Yoursay: Harapan win a 20-year effort, not just due to Dr M", *Malaysiakini*, 20 July 2018.

Yuen-C, T., Yi, S.B. and Ng, J.S., "Trump-Kim summit: The making of a last-minute meeting in Singapore", *The Straits Times*, 17 June 2018.

Yuen-C, T., Yi, S.B. and Toh, E., "4G ministers say they will settle on a leader 'in good time'; Ong Ye Kung says he has someone in mind", *The Straits Times*, 4 January 2018.

"Zaobao: Recent major lapses involving public services may be result of a 'muddling along' culture taking root", *Mothership*, 2 February 2019, https://mothership.sg/2019/02/zaobao-editorial-major-public-service-lapses/

INDEX